# SOCIAL CHANGE AND CULTURAL CONTINUITY AMONG NATIVE NATIONS

CONTEMPORARY NATIVE AMERICAN COMMUNITIES
Stepping Stones to the Seventh Generation

Acknowledging the strength and vibrancy of Native American people and nations today, this series examines life in contemporary Native American communities from the point of view of Native concerns and values. Books in the series cover topics that are of cultural and political importance to tribal peoples and that affect their possibilities for survival, in both urban and rural communities.

**SERIES EDITORS:**

Troy Johnson, American Indian Studies, California State University, Long Beach, Long Beach, CA 90840, trj@csulb.edu

Duane Champagne, Native Nations Law and Policy Center, 292 Haines Hall, Box 951551, University of California, Los Angeles, Los Angeles, CA 90095-1551, champagn@ucla.edu

*BOOKS IN THE SERIES*

1. *Inuit, Whaling, and Sustainability*, Milton M. R. Freeman, Ingmar Egede, Lyudmila Bogoslovskaya, Igor G. Krupnik, Richard A. Caulfield and Marc G. Stevenson (1999)
2. *Contemporary Native American Political Issues*, edited by Troy Johnson (1999)
3. *Contemporary Native American Cultural Issues*, edited by Duane Champagne (1999)
4. *Modern Tribal Development: Paths to Self Sufficiency and Cultural Integrity in Indian Country*, Dean Howard Smith (2000)
5. *American Indians and the Urban Experience*, edited by Susan Lobo and Kurt Peters (2001)
6. *Medicine Ways: Disease, Health, and Survival among Native Americans*, edited by Clifford Trafzer and Diane Weiner (2001)
7. *Native American Studies in Higher Education: Models for Collaboration between Universities and Indigenous Nations*, edited by Duane Champagne and Jay Stauss (2002)
8. *Spider Woman Walks This Land: Traditional Cultural Properties and the Navajo Nation*, by Kelli Carmean (2002)
9. *Alaska Native Political Leadership and Higher Education: One University, Two Universes*, by Michael Jennings (2004)
10. *Indigenous Intellectual Property Rights: Legal Obstacles and Innovative Solutions,* edited by Mary Riley (2004)
11. *Healing and Mental Health for Native American: Speaking in Red* edited by Ethan Nebelkopf and Mary Phillips (2004)
12. *Rachel's Children*, by Lois Beardslee (2004)
13. *A Broken Flute: The Native Experience in Books for Children*, edited by Doris Seale and Beverly Slapin (2005)
14. *Indigenous Peoples & the Modern State*, edited by Duane Champagne, Karen Torjesen & Susan Steiner (2005)
15. *Reading Native American Women: Critical/Creative Representations*, edited by Inés Hernández-Ávila (2005)
16. *Native Americans in the School System: Family, Community, and Academic Achievement,* by Carol Ward (2005)
17. *Indigenous Education and Empowerment: International Perspectives,* edited by Ismael Abu-Saad and Duane Champagne (2005)
18. *Cultural Representation in Native America*, edited by Andrew Jolivétte (2006)
19. *Social Change and Cultural Continuity among Native Nations*, by Duane Champagne (2007)

**EDITORIAL BOARD**

# SOCIAL CHANGE AND CULTURAL CONTINUITY AMONG NATIVE NATIONS

DUANE CHAMPAGNE

ALTAMIRA PRESS
*A Division of Rowman & Littlefield Publishers, Inc.*
Lanham • New York • Toronto • Plymouth, UK

ALTAMIRA PRESS
A Division of Rowman & Littlefield Publishers, Inc.
A wholly owned subsidiary of The Rowman & Littlefield Publishing Group, Inc.
4501 Forbes Boulevard, Suite 200
Lanham, MD 20706
www.altamirapress.com

Estover Road, Plymouth PL6 7PY, United Kingdom

British Library Cataloguing in Publication Information Available

**Library of Congress Cataloging-in-Publication Data**

Champagne, Duane.
    Social change and cultural continuity among Native Nations / Duane Champagne.
        p. cm. — (Contemporary Native American communities)
    Includes bibliographical references and index.
    ISBN-13: 978-0-7591-1000-7 (cloth : alk. paper)
    ISBN-10: 0-7591-1000-X (cloth : alk. paper)
    ISBN-13: 978-0-7591-1001-4 (pbk. : alk. paper)
    ISBN-10: 0-7591-1001-8 (pbk. : alk. paper)
    1. Indians of North America—Social conditions. 2. Indians of North America—Government relations. 3. Social change—North America. 4. North America—Ethnic relations. 5. North America—Social conditions. I. Title.
    E98.S67C43 2007
    305.897—dc22
                                                2006022476

Printed in the United States of America

∞™ The paper used in this publication meets the minimum requirements of American National Standard for Information Sciences—Permanence of Paper for Printed Library Materials, ANSI/NISO Z39.48-1992.

# CONTENTS

# Introduction

T HIS BOOK BRINGS TOGETHER previously published articles on culture
and social change in American Indian nations. The common premise
is that indigenous nations are seeking to preserve institutional order,
political autonomy and community, land, and identity and culture within
changing national and global environments. The emphasis on social change,
instead of assimilation, race, or ethnicity, is not an accident or ideology.
American Indian communities and indigenous nations around the world are
increasingly gaining self-consciousness about their histories, colonial relations,
and future prospects. They are choosing a path to the future that is grounded
in their own traditions, religions, institutions, and communities. Theories of
individual and group assimilation or ethnicity do not capture the diversity or
the focus on self-determination in economy, politics, and culture. Having
been independent nations in the sense of managing land and having autonomous political, cultural, and economic institutions from time immemorial, indigenous nations strive to maintain (and often in contemporary and
historical colonial experience), recover, and restore powers and institutions of
government and society. Indigenous peoples pursue these national goals not
because they don't want to cooperate with nation-states, but because their religions and founding institutional teachings inform them that they have a sacred purpose to accomplish in the world. Native nations struggle to maintain
their collective political and cultural autonomy despite powerful political,
economic, and cultural forces toward individual and collective assimilation
into surrounding nation-states. The Native self-determination movement is a
marker of determination and motivation to restore and maintain tribal cultures and ways of life. The indigenous struggle for political and cultural autonomy, if we can read back into history, has been consistent. While Native

voices were often marginalized and silenced by emerging non-Native nation-states, the struggle for cultural and political autonomy are enduring and will continue into the future.

The story of American Indian self-determination has not been a primary focus of social scientists. The theories and conceptualizations that have been used to account for the place of American Indians in American society have been largely based on ethnic marginalization and racial conceptualizations that are recognized as not good fits. Since Indians are a small group with little impact in American mainstream life, they are residualized statistically, conceptually, and analytically. Theory and policy do not account well for the American Indian experience, but this is not a reason to argue they are not significant. Rather, there is an opportunity to extend existing theory and policy to give a more complete accounting of the role of indigenous peoples in contemporary nation-states. A clearer understanding of the contentions between nation-states and indigenous nations promises better understanding, analysis, and policy than current positions. Indigenous nations contend with nation-states over fundamental political, cultural, and philosophical issues such as ownership and use of land, institutional order, political process, cultural understandings and goals, as well as the meaning and purpose of government and institutions of justice. Since indigenous peoples were not party to the consensus that created the contract of the nation-state, indigenous nations contend for the autonomy to live their lives and manage their governments and communities according to their own teachings and understandings. Indigenous communities believe they have not given up, and cannot give up, their sacred mandates to carry out individual and collective goals and tasks, and live according to their own moral, religious, and community understandings.

The indigenous self-determination movement is about maintaining land, culture, institutional relations, government, and self-sufficiency under terms compatible with indigenous cultures and beliefs. They do not seek these goals as a political party, as a collection of individuals, or as a race or ethnic group. Self-determination is sought within the context of whole cultural communities; it is a collective and nationalistic enterprise. Consequently, any analysis of the processes of change and cultural continuity for indigenous communities must start at the collective social, cultural, and religious community, and must take seriously the goals and values of indigenous communities or nations. The primary unit of analysis used in this book is nation, society, cultural community, or peoples. This is a collective unit of analysis reflecting the collective goals and institutional foundations of indigenous peoples. This approach—that indigenous peoples are continuing societies with culture, economy, government, and community, and are struggling collectively in colonial and nation-state contexts—uncovers a variety of analytical tools. Societies are composed of institutions that are sustained by the goals and values of groups and individuals. We can study change and continuity through the study of process, change, and continuity in political, cultural, economic, and community institutions.

Since indigenous societies have different cultures, governments, and community organization, we have a basis of analyzing and conceptualizing change and continuity among diverse indigenous communities throughout the world. In the United States there are some 560 federally recognized Indian nations, and perhaps another 400 that are not recognized. Most Indian nations have distinct language, ceremonies, traditions, religion, and other institutional relations. Since we can identify and conceptualize significant differences in institutional and cultural order among many Native communities, we understand and give empirical reference to their diversity. In addition, we can use the diversity of institutional and cultural orders to understand how communities respond to differing conditions of colonial and nation-state incorporation.

We have to be careful, though, and adopt an open and critical mind-set toward the tools we use for analysis. The terms "society" and "nation" are helpful, but they do not reflect the conceptualizations that indigenous peoples have about their own communities. While "nation" is a term often used nowadays to emphasis the government-to-government relation between indigenous peoples and nation-states, the term implies that the political community is composed of loyal and supportive citizens. Indigenous community members are loyal and committed to their governments, but the term "nation" often includes relations with forces in nature that are not part of the worldview among communities of secularized nation-states. The expression *oyate* in Lakota means the community of people, but also implies relations to the spirit powers and forces within nature. The universe is a community of beings, and the community or nation in indigenous cultures requires respect, understanding, and appropriate moral and ritual action toward the powerful forces within the universe. Consequently, it is difficult to conceptualize the terms "nation" or "community" from an indigenous perspective and use them for analytical purposes. For example, the terms "society" or "nation" are borrowed directly from American society and academic thought and are designed for analysis of American social relations. At the same time, I am not advocating the abandonment of terms such as "society" or "nation," since they are good places to start. We need to see how far those terms and conceptions take us, but use them critically so that if they fail as certain points, we must look for alternatives or ways to extend concepts and theory so that the indigenous nation-building and self-determination movement fits well and fruitfully. Again I see this enterprise not as critique of existing conceptualizations, but as an opportunity to critically evaluate them and see ways to expand their analytical power or (if necessary) suggest other conceptualizations or methods that will allow accurate, insightful, and theoretically informed analysis that will enable greater analytical explanatory power. No theory of society or social change will be complete unless the indigenous national experience can be explained and accounted for.

The terms "society" and "nation" tend to imply analytical isolation. Indigenous communities do not conceptualize themselves as an isolated and centered human group, but rather as one power within a universe of powers. This conceptualization is more compatible with current, although generally materialist, conceptions of globalization. The colonial experience over the past several hundred years has been a primary relation for most indigenous communities. The forces of colonialism have been powerful and account for much of the change and disruption within Native communities. In many ways, a definition of contemporary indigenous relations invites conceptualization of contended relations with a surrounding nation-state. Since the beginning of the colonial experience, the powers and effects of political, cultural, and economic colonialism have been deepening, with increasingly powerful and externally controlled impacts on indigenous cultures. Indigenous societies and nations have not struggled for change and continuity inside a vacuum. Left alone, most indigenous nations would not have followed the paths of change they are now traveling. Choices for change are made with the limiting constraints of colonial forces, which are often powerful enough to push indigenous peoples and individuals in directions they do not control and in fact deem undesirable. Colonial relations form significant constraints on the choices and patterns of change available to indigenous peoples and therefore must be given analytical attention in any analysis of change.

The colonial experience presents many constraints and patterns of forced change. The patterns of forced change are not the primary focus of the present book and analytical project. Coerced change is sustained by power and/or resources, but is inherently unstable when power and resources cannot be sustained. The patterns of change that are the focus of the present study are self-directed change that finds its support within the consensual processes of the indigenous community. Without significant consensual support for an innovation, there is little likelihood that the proposed change will be implemented and sustained without significant outside force or resources. The patterns of change we are looking for are those that express the values and interests and gain the consensual support of the indigenous communities. Such innovations will have a chance to become part of the everyday institutional life of the communities and endure for long periods.

Patterns of self-directed significant institutional change are the main focus of this book. What are the change processes found in indigenous communities? What are the colonial contexts and causes of coerced and consensual change? How do individual communities change, while others go in different ways? What are the main factors that help us understand the patterns of self-directed change within indigenous communities? These are some of the questions investigated in the chapters of this volume. The chapters cover a range of early to recent writings, but the focus is generally consistent. I use theories, analytical concepts, and methods in pragmatic and eclectic ways. I propose to search for theories, conceptualizations, and methods that will give the most accurate understanding of the processes of social change and cultural continuity in indigenous nations. The theories and methods are useful to the extent they help conceptualize and explain patterns of change. There is some good effort in analytical terms in this collection, but there is still considerable room for critique and rethinking of theories, methods, and explanations.

Direct relations and fieldwork in Native communities have been fruitful to me in developing the case studies and analysis. Communities are struggling with contemporary issues of self-sufficiency, education, and self-determination, and are finding culturally informed ways to achieve their ends. Contemporary theory does not explain or predict patterns of change within indigenous communities. The actual experiences and strategies of indigenous nations are often grounded in Native culture and institutions in ways that are not conceptualized or anticipated by social science theory. The richness and commitments of tribal communities, groups, and leaders are inspiring as they seek culturally informed solutions to restore and maintain whole communities according to their values and interests. Case studies are an important way to gain in-depth understanding. Since each Native nation is culturally and institutionally distinct, the processes and patterns of change may take on unique features and outcomes. Detailed ethnographic case studies of change, culture, and self-determination will greatly extend our understanding of the Native experience, and may be necessary for a detailed empirical body of knowledge and may enable a more complete theoretical and policy discussion.

In these chapters, Native peoples and communities take center stage. Institutions, groups, cultures, religions, and colonial relations are marshaled to contextualize the processes of self-directed change. Native people are seen as active participants and creators of their own patterns of institutional change within the constraints of their own cultural and institutional orders and colonial contexts. Native people have models of cultural order they want to preserve and which inform their patterns of choice when confronting issues with nation-states and globalization. Often Native communities want to preserve holistic institutional relations, where kinship, government, courts, and economic institutions significantly overlap or, more technically, are not differentiated. For example, highly profitable casinos in Southern California are managed by tribal governments where a general council or tribal council is organized by families or clans. Any enduring continuity for such institutionally nondifferentiated political, community, and economic relations is not predicted and considered unlikely by present-day development theory. The practice of indigenous communities in their efforts to construct culturally informed and institutionally nondifferentiated nations in the contemporary globalized world and under the dominion of alien nation-states is not well understood or predicted by present-day theory and therefore begs for empirical case studies, comparative studies, and theoretical reconceptualizations.

The chapters in this volume are divided into three topical areas, although content is not mutually exclusive. The first four chapters form Part I, "Culture, Institutional Order, and Worldview," and invite the reader to explore analytical and detailed analysis of Native culture. Chapter 1, "Renewing American Indian Nations: Cosmic Communities and Spiritual Autonomy," discusses how community in Native societies extends beyond relations with human groups. All power beings form a cosmic community and therefore social action by individuals and nations must give respect and act as a member of a balanced and potentially dangerous cosmic order and community. Chapter 2, "The Cultural and Institutional Foundations of Native American Conservatism," provides arguments for the Native cultural emphasis on preserving institutional order and cultural orientations. Why do indigenous peoples favor and sustain traditional institutions and cultures? Several mutually supporting arguments based on religious understandings, as well as institutional and cultural differentiation, suggest that Native communities will emphasize preservation of culture and community. Chapter 3, "Tribal Capitalism and Native Capitalists: Multiple Pathways of Native Economy," investigates the recent rise of Native individual entrepreneurship, mainly in urban areas, and a different pattern of predominantly collective tribal capitalism in reservation communities. Cultural and institutional relations are used to explain the differing patterns of approach to market economy. Chapter 4, "Renewing Tribal Governments: Uniting Political Theory and Sacred Communities," investigates the cultural foundations and difficulties of forming constitutional tribal governments. Many tribal communities are seeking to strengthen tribal governments as part of their goal of enhanced self-determination. Clashing assumptions about institutional relations and culture inhibit sustained tribal government development. Greater understanding of the assumptions surrounding U.S. constitutional government and Native political forms are suggested as ways to discuss and seek construction of Native constitutional governments that are informed by community values, yet are capable of protecting and managing community interests and goals.

Part II, "Economic, Political, and Cultural Relations with Colonizing Nations," focuses on relations of colonial domination and patterns of self-directed change within colonial contexts. Chapter 5, "Self-Government from Time Immemorial," lays out the indigenous argument for self-determination. Some of the cultural imperatives given in creation stories are discussed and applied during the colonial period. Chapter 6, "A Multidimensional Theory of Colonialism: The Native North American Experience," presents an analytical outline for a multidimensional theory of colonialism. Colonial relations are conceptualized as three autonomous forces of economic, political, and cultural relations. Each can have a relatively autonomous effect and one is not analytically mutually reducible to another, although in any empirical setting they all can have mutually reinforcing effects. Chapter 7, "Native-Directed Social Change in Canada and the United States," presents a more detailed and empirical comparative overview of colonial relations and nation-state policies in Canada and the United States. The emphasis is on defining colonial periods, such as competitive colonialism or the self-determination period, and analyzing and observing their constraint or support of self-directed social change or nation-building in Native nations. Chapter 8, "Border Towns," presents an autobiographical analysis of border towns from the point of view of a member of the Turtle Mountain Band of Chippewa and a scholar interested in nation-building in Native communities. Border towns are generally seen as places that extract resources from reservations, but they can also be places where resources and networks are found to pursue nation-building projects in Indian country. Chapter 9, "Ramona Redeemed? The Rise of Tribal Political Power in California," describes the struggles of California Native nations to secure gaming compacts. An unexpected consequence of California Indian gaming revenues is political access and influence. California Indian communities, destitute only twenty years ago, have greater self-sufficiency and command attention from California officials, legislature, and political interest groups.

Part III, "Change and Continuity," presents methods, case studies, and possible future trends and directions for Native nations. Chapter 10, "Toward a Multidimensional Historical-Comparative Methodology: Context, Process, and Causality," presents arguments and methodology for historical and ethnographic analysis of patterns of change in Native nations. A case study of how the Chickasaw formed a constitutional government in the 1850s is presented and an explanation provided. Chapter 11, "The Delaware Revitalization Movement of the Early 1760s: A Suggested Reinterpretation," analyzes and provides historical evidence and arguments for why the Delaware religious reorganization took place in the early 1760s. The movement fostered the relatively well-known militant Delaware Prophet, who aided Pontiac's Rebellion. Less well known, however, are religious and political change within the Delaware nation, and these changes are described and analyzed. Chapter 12, "Colonial and Contemporary Religious Movements," discusses coalition-building and religious revitalization movements in colonial and contemporary indigenous North America. An overview of the religious movements is given, and they are analyzed as fundamentalist, using traditional cultural orientations to achieve their ends, and reform movements that guided adherents to change moral and institutional relations. Chapter 13, "Culture, Differentiation, and Environment: Social Change in Tlingit Society," analyzes the emergence of Sealaska Corporation, a bureaucratic-electoral government, and the political activism of the Alaska Native Brotherhood among the Tlingit and Haida of southeast Alaska. At the same time, the southeast Alaska Natives retained matrilineal clans and moieties that were integrated by regular potlatch and related ceremonies. The Tlingit and Haida made political, cultural, and economic changes that accommodated the contemporary world, but at the same time retained identity, community, ceremonies, and culture that preserve their social and community solidarity. Chapter 14, "Economic Incorporation, Political Change, and Cultural Preservation among the Northern Cheyenne," describes Northern Cheyenne community and culture, which are strongly oriented to support collective community and cultural preservation. The Northern Cheyenne engaged in activist community and tribal government actions to protect clean air and prevent reservation strip mining that threatened the Cheyenne control over reservation land and threatened community disruption. Chapter 15, "Indigenous Strategies for Engaging Globalism," discusses current issues, policies, and Native strategies for meeting the challenges of nation-states and increasing globalization of information, culture, and economy. Chapter 16, "Native Issues in the Twenty-first Century," argues that effects of globalization pose significant challenges to indigenous cultural integrity and economic self-sufficiency and self-determination. Even more so than the policies of nation-states, globalization brings economic market competition and easy access of culture and information. Native nations engaging in the project of self-determination will meet the challenges of globalization within the frame of their cultural and institutional orders.

# Renewing American Indian Nations: Cosmic Communities and Spiritual Autonomy

⊞

I N WESTERN PHILOSOPHY and social science, indigenous communities are often characterized as primitive, preindustrial, small-scale, acephalous, or precapitalist. Such characterizations provide little detail into the structure and organization of indigenous communities and present an inherently evolutionary model in which indigenous communities are allocated to the lowest rungs. Except for some anthropologists and environmentalists, indigenous communities are often considered doomed to destruction at worst, or submerged within nation-states at best. Current theories of globalization and world systems suggest that indigenous communities will be drawn into dependent, exploited relations with core economies and remain backwaters of economic and social organization. Melting pot theories and multicultural views leave little room for indigenous rights, claims to territory, and political and cultural autonomy.[1] The image of the vanishing Indian continues to find subtle sway in intellectual as well as popular circles.[2]

During the 1980s and 1990s, many indigenous groups around the world increasingly found their voice in national and international forums. Land rights and political recognition in New Zealand, Australia, and Canada have taken major positive turns in favor of indigenous groups when compared to conditions that existed several decades ago. Native communities weathered by the colonial experience seek renewal, demand rights to self-government and cultural autonomy, and increasingly negotiate relations with nation-states. Many Native communities and identities have not disappeared or assimilated, contrary to the predictions of evolutionary, integrative, and multicultural theories.[3] Native communities promise to be enduring participants in international and national affairs in coming centuries.

Indigenous communities generally are characterized in terms of the views and interests of nation-states. However, understanding Native communities from their own perspective provides insight into the construction and continuity of Native community life. Much of this continuity derives from commitments to fundamental worldviews and associated understandings of community and community relations.[4] While there are hundreds, perhaps thousands, of indigenous communities in North America alone, Native people offer unique ways to understand social and community relations. Despite five hundred years of colonialism, many Native people are loath to give up the primary aspects of Native life and community. Native communities offer a spiritual holism and philosophy of life that emphasizes balance in social and natural relations, as well as social and individual autonomy. Even among relatively assimilated individuals and communities, the norms of balance and social and individual autonomy often persist, though the religious and ceremonial roots of these relations may no longer be explicitly acknowledged or practiced.

Native communities start with powerful views of community and human relations. These views have persisted into the present, even though strong influences from colonial relations have moved Native communities into directions and changes they may not have taken if left to their own devices. I propose to characterize fundamental aspects of Native communities in terms of the conception of community and emphasis on social and individual autonomy. I will then characterize colonial relations and discuss their influence on Native communities. Finally I will characterize the complexity of contemporary American Indian community relations in terms of identity by descent, pan-Indian and urban communities, and the continuity of Native views of social and individual autonomy and holistic community.

American Indian communities comprise social and sacred understandings that create rules and norms of social action and relations with the nonhuman world. Consequently, understanding the viewpoints of social and worldly relations is necessary for comprehending the dynamics of Native communities. Although this discussion is restricted to communities in the United States, many of the views presented here, in varying degrees, also apply to indigenous groups in other parts of the world.

## The Cosmic Community

There is no one "Native community." On the contrary, there are hundreds of Native communities in North America alone. Each community is organized along unique lines according to its history and creation teachings. To investigate even one Native community from an ethnohistoric perspective is a daunting task; community members often take years to understand the complex aspects of their own traditions. Significant social relations in many Native communities are based in the creation and cultural teachings. Often a trickster figure, prophet, or central intermediary (e.g., Sky Woman among many woodland cultures) provides the people with gifts of teachings and the origins of major social groupings such as families, clans, moieties, or villages.[5] Among the Tlingit, Raven is a central trickster figure. He gave the people their moiety and clan relations as well as the potlatch ceremony, and he is generally considered to have brought civilization to the Tlingit.[6] Similarly among the Creek Indians of the Southeast, the most sacred and important villages were ordained in the creation teachings. The Creek had a polity made up of village coalitions that met at the sacred central towns for purposes of managing national affairs in both war and peace.[7] Similar interpretations can be given to the Delaware, who in the 1760s were organized by three groups, or phratries, consisting of twelve clans. Each group of clans (thirty-six clans altogether) participated in the Big House religion, which annually reenacted the Delaware creation in a twelve-day ceremony. Each day the community was raised to a higher level of heaven, with unity with heaven being achieved on the twelfth and final day.[8] Again, among the Iroquois, the demigod Deganawidah offers the gift of the Iroquois confederacy to the Seneca, Cayuga, Onondaga, Oneida, and Mohawk. Deganawidah's message of peace and formation of the Iroquois Confederacy according to clans and the five nations is considered a message from the Great Spirit. Among the Iroquois, and many other American Indian communities, the social relations of community are often given to the people from the sacred realm through spiritual intermediaries.[9]

Because social relations are constructed through the sacred realm, the organization and relations of the community itself are considered sacred, gifts from the Great Spirit—the principal organizing force of the universe. In most Native cultures, the Great Spirit or ultimate force of the universe is a benevolent gift giver. Ceremonies and social relations such as clans, moieties, sacred villages, or other institutions are viewed as sacred gifts. The central force of the universe is not known to humans; it is neither male nor female, and its purpose or ultimate goal cannot be ascertained by humans. The Great Spirit is too busy to interfere in human affairs, and consequently their relations with the sacred are conducted through intermediaries such as trickster figures, seers, and powerful spirit beings that reside in nature.

The relation between social institutions and the sacred dimension is not unique when compared with other communities around the world. Institutional arrangements are considered sacred in many different cultures. In American

Indian communities the sacredness of institutional arrangements is embedded in a broader sacred and moral community. The Great Spirit is the organizer of the universe, and, in American Indian views, human relations are not central to the direction and forces of the universe. Humans are one among many spirit beings in the universe, and many forces (e.g., the sun, moon, wind, lakes, lightning) are considered more powerful beings than humans. The Great Spirit created or formed the universe with its many spirit beings, including the plants, animals, earth and heavens, birds—all the animate and inanimate elements that make up the universe. Humans, as spirit beings in the universe, must have relations not only among themselves but also with other spirit beings. The Native view of community extends to every spirit being in the universe, as well as to fellow humans and institutional relations.

Humans must have relations with the plants, animals, lakes, and other powerful forces of the universe in order to live. Humans must eat food and consequently must appease the spirits of animals and plants that are taken for human use and consumption. If a plant is taken for medicine, then tobacco or some other appropriate gift such as food is offered to the plant. If animals or fish are taken for food, then ceremonies must be performed in order to appease the spirits of the animals so that the people are not retaliated against for disturbing other, often more powerful, spirit beings. Humans must observe the sacred order and must maintain friendly and respectful relations with other spirit beings who, if disturbed, will retaliate by causing harm in the form of disease and will withdraw their willingness to give themselves to humans for food. In many creation teachings, animals volunteer to give themselves up for food, as long as people treat them with respect and perform specific rituals to honor the spirits of the animals. If people honor this agreement, animals will freely give themselves for their needs. Through the appropriate ceremonies the spirits of the animals will be preserved and will be reborn, and therefore the game and fish will be replenished and plentiful for the people. Humans in return perform respectful ceremonies and take only what is necessary for their survival.[10]

These covenants with the spirit beings of the universe form a cosmic community in which relations of respect and balance ideally are to prevail in order to promote harmony and order in the universe. Then the spirit beings, including human communities, will enjoy peace, prosperity, health, and harmonious social and worldly relations. Of course in any community people do not live up to the ideal, and transgressions and strife occur. Those individuals invite harm upon themselves from angry spirit beings, including disease, death, hunger, bad luck, and disrupted social relations. Dispute resolution mechanisms and ceremonies are used to correct the consequences of breaking sacred relations with the spirit world.

The universe as a gift from the Great Spirit and the rules and ceremonies for maintaining harmony and order are an essential part of Native views of a cosmic community. Human community and relations cannot be understood or carried out without understanding the sacred relations and obligations that humans have toward other spirit beings. While social relations and institutions are sacred and require mutual obligations and responsibilities, Native communities are not set apart from the "natural" environment, and social relations and institutions are part of a set of rules, relations, and community with all beings of the universe. Harmony and order in social relations cannot be obtained without respectful and harmonious relations with the nonhuman spirit beings. While creation traditions vary and the specific institutional relations among clans, villages, individuals, and political relations differ considerably among Native groups, the embeddedness of human community within a cosmic community of spirit beings in found widely among Native peoples. Here there is no radical separation between human and natural realms as there is in Western philosophy and Christian religious views; in Native communities human relations are embedded within the entire community and relationships with spirit powers. The Native view of cosmic community is one important way to understand the Native community and its internal relations.[11]

## Social and Individual Autonomy

Every animate or power being in the universe must be respected; otherwise, it will retaliate against the transgressor. Harmony and order are preserved through respectful relations with the animate beings of the universe. Human relations are included in the principle that every action is countered by reaction. A harmful action against a spirit being will result in retaliation unless the spirit being is appeased through ceremonies and offerings. Human relations operate under the same rule. Humans cannot be treated disrespectfully or they will retaliate. Each human is a spirit being and is part of the cosmic and social community. Each individual has a role to play in the cosmic order; that role often is not apparent to people since the direction and purpose of the universe in not knowable to humans.

An individual's life role in the cosmic and social community is sought through a variety of ceremonial means. Visions, puberty ceremonies, and dreams are all ways in which men and women seek knowledge of their role and purpose within the social and cosmic order. Visions and life tasks are often revealed gradually, and people may seek their calling through much of their life. Often the sacred task for an individual, as it is revealed by ceremonies, visions, or the advice of spiritual leaders or elders, is kept secret. Because every individual is a power or spirit being with a calling in the cosmic order, challenging the motivations or actions of individuals who are seeking to fulfill their sacred life tasks is considered unruly. One cannot know what task an individual might have, and therefore considerable leeway is given to individuals who appear to be legitimately seeking to fulfill their revealed life tasks. Since others cannot vouch for the wisdom of such tasks, individuals are given considerable individual autonomy within the rules of the cosmic and social community. Actions that do not challenge the sacred rules of the cosmic order and social order and are believed to be part of a person's life mission are generally not questioned by others. Individuals have a sacred right as an autonomous power being to fulfill their sacred life tasks as long as their actions conform to the rules of social and cosmic order, which if violated would bring retribution from angry power beings upon the social community and the transgressor.[12]

The principle of autonomy of spirit beings entails specific types of community relations and decision-making processes. Each individual in the social community must be respected as an autonomous power being, and therefore each individual has the right to provide input into any decision-making process. In every community, though, while everyone has the right to participate the decision-making process, some individuals may have more influence than others because they are believed to have particularly strong spirit helpers which make the person a relatively stronger power being. Power, however, is an elusive entity; sometimes the spirit helpers are strong and other times they are not useful. So spiritual power and influence is fluid in most Indian communities.

A social community of autonomous power beings makes its decisions through discussion and consensus. The word "caucus" is an Algonkian expression that has become part of the English language, but it describes the process of decision making used in many Native communities. Individuals are invited to participate through discussion of families, bands, clans, and village councils, according to the group's usual practice. Women often have their own councils, and they often have considerable influence within their lineages or clans. The exemplar of female political power for the feminist movement has long been the Iroquois clan matrons who have the power to appoint and impeach lineage and clan leaders.[13]

The political processes of Native communities preserve the view of individuals as autonomous power beings, and decision making is often a process of negotiation and consensus formation among community members. There is often considerable disagreement in these meetings, and if no consensus is obtained there is no binding decision on the community.[14]

Clans, lineages, and villages often have autonomous rights too. Depending on how an Indian community is organized, local groups (villages, clans, lineages) often discuss issues and form positions through consensus. If there is disagreement, a majority or powerful group is not allowed to force its decision on others. Local groups retain their autonomy, and national or regional decisions must also be made through the social construction of agreement and consensus. Local groups and individuals retain considerable power. They do not delegate their rights to appointed representatives or chiefs. Among the Iroquois the clan and lineage "chief" is a spokesperson for the consensus of the group and no more. If he takes on more than his assigned task, which is to report the consensus of the lineage or clan to others, he will be dismissed from office. Political relations in Indian communities often amount to a process of gathering agreements from local groups and lineages who do not grant their autonomy to any central authority or to any other community.[15]

The emphasis on individual political process and political community through consensus formation intrigued early colonial observers, who reported these processes back to Europe. The decentralized, egalitarian, and processual decision-making procedures sharply contrasted with the hierarchical and centralized authoritarian states of Europe. Many critiques of the old regimes in Europe used North American community examples to argue that mankind in nature is free and that Natives possess natural forms of freedom and political rights that were lost in the centralized state systems of Europe. The French philosophes developed critiques of the French state and offered views of freedom and democracy that were based in part on information about Native political freedoms and political processes. The philosophy of natural human rights helped frame U.S. political theory and became a unique feature of American democracy.[16]

Native social and political forms of decentralized process, however, derived not from the theory that man has natural or God-given rights but from the imperative to preserve harmony and order within the cosmic community. In this view social groups and individuals exercised considerable autonomy as part of the plan of the Great Spirit. Cosmic harmony and order were preserved by maintaining respectful relations with all spirit beings, including human groups and individuals. Native communities reflected this philosophy in decentralized social and political organization, often with no centralized leader or delegation of power beyond local groupings. Decentralization and individual rights to social and political participation characterize many Indian communities and were often puzzling to colonial officials who were expecting centralized authorities. When Native communities did not arrive at a decision, colonial authorities became frustrated and described the process as fractionated. Even now many Native communities exercise their local autonomy and rights to individual participation in ways that are not well understood by outside observers who are looking for centralized decision-making powers.

The two significant characteristics of Native communities—cosmic community order and individual autonomy—help explain the dynamics and uniqueness of Native community relations, which remain important to the present day.

## The World Out of Balance

The colonial era introduced a series of rapid changes. Native communities were in a state of change before significant colonial contact, but colonial relations initiated a sequence of greater economic incorporation, cultural interchange, and political competition. Economic relations had a lasting impact on many Indian communities, especially those incorporated into trade relations for furs and skins. The fur trade started in the middle 1500s, was active during the 1600s, and lasted until the 1840s, when beaver were depleted in the eastern Rocky Mountain region. Buffalo was hunted until the early 1880s on the Plains. Many American Indian communities in the midwestern and eastern United States were brought into the fur trade. American Indians became dependent on the trade and started exchanging furs and skins for a variety of European manufactured goods, such as iron tools, guns, cloth, and beads. The fur trade threatened the covenant relations with animals as the Indians began to supply furs to traders who wanted to work on the basis of market relations rather than through Native beliefs and obligations to maintain respectful relations with the animal nations. Most American Indians, however, accepted their dependency on trade for European goods and hunted only enough animals to supply their trade and social needs. American Indians did not become capitalists by engaging in the fur trade; rather, they were responding to need rather than seeking to accumulate individual wealth. Nevertheless, the fur trade by the middle 1600s was depleting game, and traders moved farther into the interior, followed generally by land sales and colonists. The fur trade meant the American Indians specialized by spending more time hunting and curing furs, and harvested more furs than they would have otherwise.[17] Few if any Natives became entrepreneurs in the fur trade and the Native worldview remained intact, although Natives were now incorporated into European markets. When the fur trade and buffalo trades collapsed in the midwestern and eastern United States, the American Indian communities were generally impoverished and were forced to sell land and take up life on reservations.

Social contact with colonists had considerable impact on Native communities. Colonial officials did not recognize women in political councils and preferred to conduct economic trade relations with young, economically productive men. Women and elders were often pushed to the side as young men captured the economic and political attention of colonial officials. With the fur trade and diplomatic relations in their hands, the young men wielded more economic and political power than they had previously. Women and elders struggled for their usual respect, but the new economic and political relations favored younger males.[18] Reservation life, however, greatly attenuated the economic and political influence of productive men.

Relations with colonists ultimately led to the introduction of the Christian religion and new worldviews within many American Indian communities. Many communities became multicultural with the appearance of Christian members as well as slave-owning cotton market entrepreneurial members among, for example, the Choctaw, Chickasaw, Creek, and Cherokee during the 1800s. Among the Iroquois, the introduction of Protestant Christianity led to deep cultural cleavages in the community between Christians and non-Christians. These cleavages continue to the present day on many Iroquois reservations.[19] Other groups, including the Cherokee and Choctaw, adopted Christianity and allowed community members to make independent choices.[20] Some groups such as the Northern Cheyenne accept Christianity, the Native American Church, while maintaining many key aspects of the Northern Cheyenne tradition.[21]

Colonial relations had deep and significant impacts on Native communities. New religions and ideas challenged traditional worldviews. Many individuals who adopted Christianity or were educated in boarding schools away from their family and community took on American worldviews and did not participate in the cosmic community. The old worldviews were severely challenged by economic collapse, political subjugation, and religious-cultural alternatives introduced by American assimilation programs. Nevertheless, many aspects of the ceremonies and the Native understanding of cosmic spiritual relations remained, although sometimes forced underground and practiced by small but dedicated groups. A whole series of religious movements preserved important aspects of Native worldviews while adopting elements of Christianity. Such movements were the Ghost Dances, the Native American Church, the Indian Shaker movement, the Handsome Lake movement, and others. Many Christian Indians, such as among the Choctaws and Creeks, created their own churches where they sang songs and heard sermons in their own languages.[22] Theological understandings often reflect Native understandings of sacred relations. Some Christian groups joined mainstream churches but mixed Native religious understandings and norms with Christian doctrine. The concept of cosmic spiritual relations and community remain among many people and are often directly and indirectly represented in Christian Indian communities, especially those led by Native ministers.

Decentralization and the autonomy of individuals and social groups has remained a general characteristic of most Native communities through the colonial period to the present day. Families, clans, and villages generally retain considerable autonomy in their own right or within newly constructed constitutional governments created on reservations, to a large extent by U.S. officials.[23] Native political processes tend to focus on consensus building, and conflict may arise when leaders neglect consensual protocols. Much of the present-day literature about factionalism and political conflict within Native communities underestimates the deeply embedded cultural orientation toward individual and local spiritual autonomy. What outsiders interpret as conflict or factionalism is often individuals and groups asserting their autonomy under Native rules and cultural orientations. American officials, scholars, and even many Native leaders try to assert more centralization of political authority in Native communities than is culturally supported, given their worldview of balance among the power beings of a cosmic community. On many reservations, community members may not have a direct understanding of spiritual relations but reside in social environments where individual and local autonomy is an implicit cultural norm.

## Multiple Communities, Multiple Identities

Contemporary Native life abounds with multiple communities and situational identities. Traces of the cosmic community are found in both reservation communities and urban Indian communities. Native social and political relations remain decentralized, and individual autonomy is recognized implicitly. Some of the political difficulties on reservations (e.g., among the Hopi and Lakota) are caused in part by overly centralized tribal governments that run contrary to decentralized Native forms of social organization and political process. Many Native communities continue to find constitutional political forms introduced by Bureau of Indian Affairs officials too rigid and contrary to Native political traditions, where political power is consensual and not concentrated in elected delegates. Opposition to tribal government actions is often raised in Native communities and is often the result of fundamental conflicts between American and Native political processes and views of social and individual rights and obligations. Many Natives believe that while the American Indian Civil Rights Act introduced some protections of the bill of rights, such as right to a speedy trial, privilege of habeas corpus, freedom from double jeopardy, and others, this act infringed on Native political sovereignty by imposing a form of individual rights alien to tribal communities. Although many Native tribal governments are based on U.S. constitutional models, Native consensual-based rules and individual and group autonomy are ignored because decisions are made by majority rule—leaders elected by majority vote—and leaders are delegated concentrated and centralized political power. Furthermore, most constitutionally based tribal governments are secular, whereas many Natives feel that separating the cosmic community from political relations is dangerous and may lead to inappropriate guidance among secular Native leaders. In recent years, the Navajo tribal government exemplified Native retrenchment from centralized authority. Since 1985 the Navajo court system has increasingly incorporated traditional culture and methods in Navajo Peacemaker courts and common law. Navajo local political groups have passed legislation to decentralize the government and distribute more decision-making authority to local chapters, which generally represent local and traditional family and kinship groups.[24]

Conflict within tribal governments is generated by the mismatch among political governments imposed by the U.S. government and Native views of community and individual and local political processes. Such situations generate strong conflicts over procedures and processes and often leave Native individuals and groups alienated if their normative means of handling process are overruled by the American political process. Many scholars and other observers call such conflicts factionalism and blame the Natives for their alleged incapacity to find workable solutions. Many Native reservation communities need to rethink their political constitutions and make them more compatible with Native political processes and the sense of cosmic community. Political procedures and legal orders that to a large extent represent U.S. forms on reservations do not provide Natives with culturally compatible institutions. Native groups will increasingly renegotiate their political and legal institutions, as the Navajo are now doing, in order to make them more culturally compatible. Nevertheless, most Native communities will not strive to reestablish "traditional" cultural and political orders, and many tribal members have multiple cultural orientations. Contemporary political and economic challenges require institutional arrangements that can manage market relations and competition from states and federal agencies. As reservation communities realize self-determination, however, they will increasingly find ways to adapt modifications to tribal government and legal arrangements that reflect their own philosophies of social and cultural order.

While Native communities struggle over forms of political organization and process, new forms of community and identity have emerged on the national scene and in urban areas. Pan-Indian identities emerged during the activism of the 1970s.[25] Such identities have not replaced tribal identities but have added another layer of identity for most Native people. A pan-Indian identity as a supratribal identity has not emerged. Many people will say they are American Indian, but often this identification is driven by the context of the situation. Most Americans recognize American Indians but are not familiar with tribal or clan names. Consequently Natives use those identifications only with people who have knowledge of them, usually other tribal members. American Indian is a concept that is used widely in U.S. society, and it functions as an ethnic group label. Nevertheless, the term is used by American society as a homogeneous ethnic group label that abstracts past specific tribal identities.[26]

Most reservation Natives do not agree that there is an American Indian ethnic group. Most Natives who are associated with a community primarily identify with their community group. Nevertheless, about 6 million individuals in the 1990 census claimed an American Indian ancestor, about half claiming a Cherokee ancestor. The Native descent group probably does not form an ethnic group or community. Rather, it is a population of individuals who acknowledge some tie to Indian ancestry and have an interest in American Indian issues. The American Indian ancestry group far outnumbers the Native population identified by race—1.96 million in the 1990 census. The number of people who live on or near a reservation totals a half million. The ancestry group is by far the largest but lacks social or political organization, and many have primary identities that are not American Indian.[27]

Major national American Indian organizations reflect tribal identities more than pan-Indian identities. For example, the National Congress of American Indians (NCAI) is organized by tribal representations. Each tribe, regardless of its population size, is granted one vote in the NCAI conventions. Consequently large tribes such as the Navajo, with a reservation population over 200,000, have the same vote as a small California tribe of fewer than forty members. For this reason, some larger tribes do not participate in the NCAI. The principle of representation within NCAI preserves the autonomy rules of Native cultures. Each tribe is given the right to represent its position and vote, even if it has only a few members. Local cultural and political autonomy is preserved in this manner. The NCAI forms a loose coalition of tribal groups, each preserving its local cultural and political autonomy. Any effort to impose an ethnic or supratribal identity would likely generate considerable opposition and even dissolution of the organization, as each tribal group would preserve its autonomy by leaving the organization.

## Renewing the Cosmic Community

The colonial period did much to dislocate Native institutions and relations. While Native norms of political process appear deeply embedded in Native communities and national organizations, the holistic views of cosmic community have been disassociated from many tribal governments and institutions. Since the 1970s many tribal spiritual leaders have shown greater confidence in reclaiming the philosophies and covenants of the cosmic community through ceremonies. The revival of ceremonies that went underground during the cultural and religious repression of the late nineteenth and early twentieth centuries, as well as the current self-conscious emphasis on preserving Native language and renewing knowledge about religion and religious practice, will help maintain the philosophy and understanding of cosmic community in many Native groups.[28] Ceremonies that renew covenant relations with the power beings of the cosmic community are quite common among Native nations, helping to restore confidence in Native institutions and to revitalize Native reservation communities. Native community and institutions that are based on specific ceremonies and cultural philosophies will do much to recreate and reinvigorate life on reservations. The philosophies of cosmic community were not designed to manage bureaucracies and make market decisions; nevertheless, the principles of the cosmic community can inform values and orient decision making within reservation communities. A major challenge for Native communities in the next century is to reclaim and renew cultural and institutional relations while at the same time meeting the challenges of multicultural reservation communities, competitive market globalization, and preservation of tribal political autonomy. True self-determination in Native communities will come through forming institutional relations that are broadly informed by Native values, such as the principles of cosmic community, and at the same time provide capability to engage in the global market while preservation of tribal political integrity. In many Native communities, however, the combined goals of maintaining cultural philosophies with institutions capable of political and economic competition may be considered contradictory. Each Native community faces this challenge but has the right to meet the challenge in it own way based on its own history, community relations, and specific Native philosophies and institutional arrangements. Each Native community will assert its own solution in its own way, thus exercising the autonomy inherent in the Native worldview.

# Notes

An earlier version of this chapter appeared as Duane Champagne, "Renewing American Indian Nations: Cosmic Communities and Spiritual Autonomy," in *Diversity and Community: A Critical Reader,* ed. Philip Alperson (Oxford: Blackwell, 2003), pp. 167–81.

1. For a critique of multicultural and postcolonial views, see Arif Dirlik, "The Past as Legacy and Project: Postcolonial Criticism in the Perspective of Indigenous Historicism," in *Contemporary Native American Political Issues,* ed. Troy Johnson (Walnut Creek, CA: AltaMira, 1999), pp. 73–92; Duane Champagne, "Multiculturalism: New Understanding or Oversimplification?" in *Controversial Issues in Multiculturalism,* ed. Diana de Anda (Boston: Allyn & Bacon, 1997), pp. 27–35, 39–40.

2. Brian Dippie, *The Vanishing American: White Attitudes and U.S. Indian Policy* (Middleton, CT: Wesleyan University Press, 1982); Katarine Ramirez Kenya, "Healing through Grief: Urban Indians Reimagining Culture and Community in San Jose, California," *American Indian Culture and Research Journal* 22, no. 4 (1998): 311–15.

3. Fae L. Korsmo, "Claiming Memory in British Columbia: Aboriginal Rights and the State," in *Contemporary Native American Political Issues,* ed. Troy Johnson (Walnut Creek, CA: AltaMira, 1999), pp. 129–30; Stephen Quesenberry, "Recent United Nations Initiatives Concerning the Rights of Indigenous Peoples," in *Contemporary Native American Political Issues,* ed. Troy Johnson (Walnut Creek, CA: AltaMira, 1999), p. 104.

4. Duane Champagne, "The Cultural and Institutional Foundations of Native American Conservatism," special issue on North American Indians: Cultures in Motion, ed. Elvira Stefania Tiberini, *L'Uomo: Societa, tradizione, sviluppo* 8, no. 1 (1995): 17–43.

5. Barbara Mann and Jerry Fields, "A Sign in the Sky: Dating the League of the Haudenosaunee," *American Indian Culture and Research Journal* 21, no. 2 (1997): 130–34.

6. Catherine McClellan, "The Interrelations of Social Structure with Northern Tlingit Ceremonialism," *Southwest Journal of Anthropology* 10 (1954): 75–96; Duane Champagne, "Culture, Differentiation, and Environment: Social Change in Tlingit Society," in *Differentiation Theory and Social Change,* ed. Jeffrey C. Alexander and Paul Colomy (New York: Columbia University Press, 1990), pp. 58–65.

7. Duane Champagne, *Social Order and Political Change: Constitutional Governments among the Cherokee, the Choctaw, the Chickasaw, and the Creek* (Stanford, CA: Stanford University Press, 1992), pp. 33–38.

8. Frank Speck, *A Study of the Delaware Indian Big House Ceremony* (Harrisburg, PA: Pennsylvania Historical Commission, 1931), p. 75; William Newcomb Jr., "The Culture and Acculturation of the Delaware Indians," *Anthropology Papers* (Ann Arbor: Museum of Anthropology of Michigan, 1956), pp. 125–75; David Zeisberger, *David Zeisberger's History of the North American Indians,* ed. Archer Hulbert and William Schwarze (Columbus: Ohio State Archeological and Historical Society, 1910), pp. 92–97; Duane Champagne, "The Delaware Revitalization Movement of the Early 1760s: A Suggested Reinterpretation," *American Indian Quarterly* 12, no. 2 (1988): 107–26.

9. Arthur C. Parker, *Parker on the Iroquois* (Syracuse, NY: Syracuse University Press, 1968), pp. 65–126.

10. Luana Ross, *Inventing the Savage: The Social Construction of Native American Criminality* (Austin: University of Texas Press, 1999), pp. 30–31; Ron Trosper, "Traditional American Indian Economic Policy," *Contemporary Native American Political Issues,* ed. Troy Johnson (Walnut Creek, CA: AltaMira, 1999), pp. 140–42; Huston Smith and Reuben Snake, eds., *One Nation*

*under God: The Triumph of the Native American Church* (Santa Fe, NM: Clear Light, 1996), pp. 16–20; Reuben Snake, *Reuben Snake, Your Humble Serpent: Indian Visionary and Activist* (Santa Fe, NM: Clear Light, 1996), pp. 36–39, 225–32.

11.  Kenneth Morrison, "Native American Religions: Creating through the Cosmic Give-and-Take," in *The Native North American Almanac,* ed. Duane Champagne (Detroit: Gale Research, 1994), pp. 633–41; Carol Miller, "Telling the Indian Urban: Representations in American Indian Fiction," *American Indian Culture and Research Journal* 22, no. 4 (1998): 49–51, 54–56; Robert A. Williams, *Linking Arms Together: American Indian Treaty Visions of Law and Peace, 1600–1800* (New York: Oxford University Press, 1997), pp. 98–123.

12.  Morrison, "Native American Religions," pp. 633–41; Smith, *One Nation,* pp. 16–20.

13.  Judith Brown, "Economic Organization and the Position of Women among the Iroquois," *Ethnohistory* 17 (1970): 151.

14.  Bernhard Stern, ed., "The Letters of Asher Wright to Lewis Morgan," *American Anthropologist* 35 (1933): 144; John Noon, *Law and Government of the Grand River Iroquois* (New York: Viking Fund Publications in Anthropology, 1949), p. 28.

15.  Anthony C. Wallace, *The Death and Rebirth of the Seneca* (New York: Vintage, 1972), pp. 44–50; Edmund Wilson, *Apologies to the Iroquois* (New York: Farrar, Straus & Cudahy, 1959), p. 174; William Fenton, "Cultural Stability and Change in American Indian Societies," *Journal of the Royal Anthropological Institute of Great Britain and Ireland* 83 (1953): 172; Fred Gearing, "Priests and Warriors: Social Structures for Cherokee Politics in the 18th Century," *American Anthropologist Memoir* 93, no. 64 (1962): 31–39; James Adair, *Adair's History of the American Indians* (Johnson City, TN: Watauga, 1930), p. 406; John Swanton, "Source Material for the Social and Ceremonial Life of the Choctaw Indians," *Bureau of American Ethnology Bulletin* 103 (1932): 91.

16.  Donald A. Grinde and Bruce E. Johansen, *Exemplar of Liberty: Native America and the Evolution of Democracy* (Los Angeles: UCLA American Indian Studies Center, 1991), pp. 61–72; Jeffrey Alexander, "The Paradoxes of Civil Society," *International Sociology* 12, no. 2 (1997): 118–20.

17.  E. E. Rich, "Trade Habits and Economic Motivation Among the Indians of North America," *Canadian Journal of Economics and Political Sciences* 26 (1960): 53; Arthur Ray, *Indians and the Fur Trade* (Toronto, ON: University of Toronto Press, 1974), p. 68.

18.  Edmond Atkins, *Indians of the Southern Colonial Frontier,* ed. Wilbur Jacobs (Columbia: University of South Carolina Press, 1954), p. 10; William Steele, *The Cherokee Crown of Tannasy* (Winston-Salem, SC: Blair, 1977), p. 43; Nancy Bonvillain, "Gender Relations in Native North America," *American Indian Culture and Research Journal* 13, no. 2 (1989): 18–20.

19.  Robert B. Porter, "Building a New Longhouse: The Case for Government Reform within the Six Nations of the Haudenosaunee," *Buffalo Law Review* 46, no. 3 (1998): 805–945; Bruce Johansen, *Life and Death in Mohawk Country* (Golden, CO: North American Press, 1993).

20.  Champagne, *Social Order,* pp. 140, 179–240; Albert Wahrhaftig, "Institution Building among Oklahoma's Traditional Cherokees," *Four Centuries of Southern Indians,* ed. Charles Hudson (Athens: University of Georgia Press, 1975), pp. 132–47.

21.  Personal communication, various informants, 1983; also see Reuben Snake's comments about the compatibility of Ho Chunk and Christian teachings in Snake, *Your Humble Serpent,* pp. 109–213.

22.  James May, personal communication, 1999, Joan Weibel-Orlando, *Indian Country, L.A.: Maintaining Ethnic Community in Complex Society* (Chicago: University of Illinois Press, 1991), pp. 153–77.

23. Thomas Biolsi, *Organizing the Lakota* (Tucson: University of Arizona Press, 1992), pp. 126–50.

24. Office of Navajo Government Development, *Navajo Nation Government Book* (Window Rock, AZ: Navajo Nation, 1998), pp. 33–40.

25. Stephen Cornell, *The Return of the Native: American Indian Political Resurgence* (New York: Oxford University Press, 1988); Joan Nagel, *American Indian Ethnic Renewal: Red Power and the Resurgence of Identity and Culture* (New York: Oxford University Press, 1996), pp. 187–205.

26. James Fenelon, "Discrimination and Indigenous Identity in Chicago's Native Community," *American Indian Culture and Research Journal* 22, no. 4 (1998): 285–88.

27. Angela Gonzalez, "The (Re)Articulation of American Indian Identity: Maintaining Boundaries and Regulating Access to Ethnically Tied Resources," *American Indian Culture and Research Journal* 22, no. 4 (1998): 200–203.

28. Ross, *Inventing the Savage*, 38–41.

# The Cultural and
# Institutional Foundations of
# Native American Conservatism

**2**

⊞

I F ONE GENERALIZATION CAN BE MADE about Native North American
peoples over the past five hundred years, it may be that they have survived
as communities and cultures. Contemporary Native American communities, however, are different from those existing before Columbus arrived in
1492. After significant North American colonization, Indian life was exposed
to new forms of political competition, markets, and cultural and religious
ideas that had great effect. Nevertheless, even to the present, Native American groups place great emphasis on community survival and cultural maintenance. They may not always be successful, and their cultures and communities
may not survive quite in the ways that they prefer, for the forces arrayed
against them for change and assimilation are extremely strong. The conservative emphasis on cultural and community survival helped preserve Indian
identity and a sense of nationality; however, it also constrained the ways in
which Indian groups adapted to Western contact.

Native Americans adapted to the changes of the past five hundred years in
many ways, such as revitalization movements among the Paiute, Iroquois,
Delaware, Kickapoo, Shawnee, Creek, and others; state formation among the
Cherokee, Choctaw, Chickasaw, and Creek; conservative resistance as among
some Apache, Sioux, Navajo; or conservative integration as among the Ojibway Drummer movement, and the Crow and Wind River Ute.[1] Whether it is
the Cherokee, who tried to preserve their nationality by building a state government in the 1820s, or the San Carlos Apache, who willfully resisted reservation life and assimilation, the emphasis on community preservation and
cultural survive is central to the strategies and concerns of Indian people. The
wide range of differences in Indian responses to colonial conditions is due to
regional and local ecological variations and differences in political, economic,

and cultural relations with colonizing societies. Finally, each Indian nation defends a different cultural and institutional order from the others. For example, the Iroquois, with their clans and confederacy, defend a different cultural and institutional order than Tlingit, with their potlatches and moieties. A combination of Indian cultural and colonial conditions helps explain the diversity of change patterns among Native American cultures over the past five hundred years.

Nevertheless, throughout the history of Indian and colonial relations, Indians have emphasized maintenance of their institutions and cultural orders. Despite major efforts by the United States, Canada, and other colonial powers, Indians generally prefer to live in their own societies and usually decline to assimilate. The persistence of reservations and reserves within the United States and Canada is a testament of the Indian quest for cultural and political survival. Continuing legal and political struggles, land claims cases, and emphasis on tribal sovereignty and national or tribal rights in both the United States and Canada attest to the desire by Indian communities to retain self-government and cultural heritage. The history of most Indian nations over the past five hundred years can be viewed as a struggle to retain institutional and cultural integrity. Many groups changed aspects of their culture, but they did so reluctantly and often under extreme conditions of political competition or economic necessity, or by means of new cultural forms and ideas introduced by agents of the colonizing society. Indian groups changed because their economic, political, and cultural relations and environment were drastically modified by colonizing nations.

The emphasis on retaining cultural integrity, whether worldview, ceremonies, religion, art, dress, identity, or kinship groups, is not an antiquarian or ad hoc interest or merely created in defiance of colonial assimilation efforts, but is deeply seated in the values and orientations of Indian cultures and in the organization of Indian social orders. There are cultural and institutional reasons for the pervasiveness of Indian conservatism, which can be examined and analyzed through ethnographic and historical means.

# Theories of Change and Traditionalism

In comparison with modern or Western societies, Indian groups before 1492 and since do not emphasize the accumulation of wealth with the intention to reinvest wealth in the means of production according to the demands of the marketplace. Hence Indian societies did not emphasize economic innovation or use wage labor or capitalism entrepreneurship as engines of economic accumulation and material progress. For Karl Marx, the constant demands for technological innovation and profit making characterize capitalist society.[2] Indian societies such as the Iroquois represent an earlier form of primitive communism, primarily because for Marx and Engels, Iroquois society did not have the technological or productive capacity to free people from the demands nature made on them.[3] For Marx and Engels, true communism will arise only after society gains productive and technological capacity to relieve people from most basic material needs. Weber agrees generally with Marx's analysis but emphasizes that while Marx explains the formation of the English working class through the historical process of enclosure of the English commons, he does not fully explain the rise of the capitalist spirit among entrepreneurs. In general, Weber's work focuses on the question of why capitalism or modern society rose in Europe and not in other parts of the world. He investigated the history, politics, economic organization, and cultures of the major civilizations of the world, including India, China, and Judaism, and he was working on a study of the history of Christianity.[4] Through his comparative historical and cultural studies, Weber searched for the conditions that led to the rise of rational capitalism: the strong emphasis on market-oriented economic accumulation and production. While looking at multiple arguments, for Weber, worldview and religion are primary elements in his explanation.

In particular, Weber argues that Calvinist doctrines are critically important in understanding the motivations for the rise of an entrepreneurial capitalist class. For Weber, Marx explained how the working class came about in England, but did not explain why capitalists were ready and waiting to exploit the labor of workers who had been separated from the means of production and had little but their labor power to sell for a living. Marx assumed that simple self-interest explains capitalist motivations to exploit workers' labor. Weber argues, however, that rational capitalism, the productive organization of labor and factors of production according to the demands of the marketplace, is not an inherent feature of human nature for truck and barter, but rather a constructed and particular form of social, political, and cultural order. Some prerequisites to markets are stable economic laws and courts, a formally free labor force, rational accounting systems, money as a *medium* of exchange, as well as values fostering the accumulation and economic reinvestment of wealth.[5]

People have been economically interested, and for that matter self-interested, throughout human history, and in every society and culture. But the willingness to exchange or barter or to engage in self-interested activity is not enough for Weber to explain the rise of rational capitalism in the West. For Weber, there are a variety of economic ethics and cultures. A traditional worker or trader does not act according to the demands of the marketplace. A traditional worker, given the opportunity to earn more money at a higher rate, will work only enough to gain a customary level of pay or subsistence and will not work more in order to accumulate wealth or to reinvest in business. Rather than work to accumulate wealth, the traditional worker will prefer to spend time in leisure after securing a customary subsistence level.[6] This type of labor ethic is observed in many societies. Weber also characterizes adventure capitalism, where great risks are taken in hopes of high reward, as a form of accumulation that is not congruent with the relative low risk taking of rational capitalism and accumulation. Merchant capitalism, where the entrepreneur buys cheap at one location and sells dear at another, also does not characterize rational capitalism, since there is no direct management of the means of production. Weber further distinguishes traditional capitalism, where entrepreneurs engage in business but are satisfied with customary levels of profit and do not exert themselves to outperform their fellow businessmen; after achieving their usual profit share, they prefer to engage in leisure. Weber characterizes much of the economic ethic in Europe before the 1500s, and elsewhere in the other major civilizations, as having various forms of merchant and traditional capitalism, and the workers having traditional labor ethics.[7]

For Weber, an explanation for the rise of capitalism needs to explain the spirit of capitalism or the rise of rational capitalism; since market-oriented rational capitalism is not inherent in the nature of people, the motivation for capitalists to exploit labor and organize the means of production according to the demands of the marketplace must be a specific social and cultural form.

While Weber recognizes that a variety of legal, political, and monetary conditions were necessary for the rise of capital markets and production, he argues that these features are not enough to explain the rise of capitalism without explaining the motivation of the capitalists to break the norms of traditional capitalism in favor of the competitive and innovative action of rational capitalism. Weber finds an explanation for the breakdown of European traditional capitalism in Calvinist doctrine. He argues that the specific features of Calvinist doctrine motivated Protestant Calvinists to cast aside the customary norms of traditional capitalism in favor of competitive rational capitalism. Calvinist doctrine proclaimed that God's will was predetermined for all time, only the elect received salvation, and all had a specific calling. Weber interpreted Calvinism as an otherworldly religion, where people sought to achieve salvation in the next world, not in this world, which was considered evil, corrupt, and full of sin. Although otherworldly salvation is the primary goal, Calvinists needed to show that they belonged to the elect, those chosen to go to heaven. Although the elect were predetermined, none knew if they belonged to the chosen, and each person was enjoined by the Calvinist community to act like one of the elect and do the work of God on earth. Calvinists were not allowed to enjoy worldly comforts but were enjoined to be moral, work hard, and accumulate wealth as signs of their labor and moral fortitude. Wealth was a sign of the fruits of constant labor but could not be used to satisfy personal pleasures; therefore, it was reinvested in order to make more wealth and provide more work for others. Hence Calvinist entrepreneurs broke the norms of traditional capitalism by working longer hours, accumulating wealth as an end in itself, and reinvesting wealth as a means of generating more economic wealth. Once Calvinist entrepreneurs started innovating and producing cheaper goods, they attracted more customers. The traditional capitalists were now forced to either follow the acquisitive and innovating path of the Calvinists or go out of business.[8] This is what Weber called the Iron Cage; once the initial breakthrough is made to rational capitalism, all entrepreneurs are forced to follow the path of constant innovation, change, and capitalist accumulation, which Marx and Weber both characterize as the core of capitalism or modern society.

Marx and Weber, as well as most observers, characterize Indian societies not as capitalist or modern but rather traditional. According to Engels, one reason American Indian societies did not take up agriculture (as opposed to horticulture, which employs handheld instruments while agriculture requires a plow and draft animal) is that there were no domesticated animals in North America. Consequently, without the rise of agriculture, Indians could not move toward capitalist society on the evolutionary scale. Weber makes few comments on Native American societies within his comparative studies, mainly because he believes that the religious orientations of indigenous groups, which depend largely on magical beliefs, excludes them from consideration for a likely place where capitalism and/or significant internally generated change may occur. That Indian societies are conservative or traditional is widely observed.

Nevertheless, the conservatism of Indian societies demands more attention and deserves more exacting explanation. The reason for this is not so much that such an explanation will change the assessment of anthropologists and theoreticians like Weber and Marx that Indian societies are conservative, but rather the classification of Indian societies as traditional does not do justice to their complexity and their individual cultural and institutional variations. Although both the Apache and Hopi can be characterized as conservative, they vary considerably in terms of religion, kinship structure, economy, political structure, and other features. The classification of traditional is not an adequate characterization for indigenous societies. In many theories of the rise of modernity or capitalism, Indian societies play no significant theoretical or empirical comparative role, hence their bunching into the traditional category. Theories of social change and the organization of human societies that are not so centered on the models of change found in Europe or on modernity or capitalism will need more explicit understandings of Indian cultures and institutional orders with respect to their inherent possibilities of change. The specific features of Indian societies are of interest to a theory that explains patterns of change and adaptation of indigenous societies to colonialism or the expansion of the world economic system.

It is beyond the scope of this chapter to set out a theory of change for Indian societies over the past five hundred years of colonial contact. A prerequisite to such a theory, however, is a systematic assessment of the possibilities of change inherent within Indian cultures and societies. Despite the variations of colonial contact, the conservatism of precontact Indian societies carries over to the processes of adaptation during the colonial period. The pervasive conservative orientation in American Indian societies deserves explanation, since it is one of the most general and notable features about Indian communities over the past five centuries.

## Culture and Societal Differentiation

Weber's theory for the rise of the spirit of capitalism points to a major place to look for the genesis of conservative orientations in the specific doctrines of religion or more broadly cultural worldview. Weber's analysis of Calvinist doctrine provides clues to analyzing culture with respect to social change. For example, his analysis of Calvinism emphasizes several features of religion, such as the relation of radical dualism of this world and other world, the emphasis on domination of the earth, the emphasis on this world as evil and changeable, and the view of an omniscient but unapproachable God. The latter features of Calvinism and Christianity can be compared with the cultural norms and beliefs within Indian societies in order to investigate worldview, orientation toward change, and economic ethic.

A second and complementary argument, indirectly given to us from Marx and Weber through Parsons, is the theory of societal differentiation, which provides means for conceptualizing relations among major societal institutions such as culture, polity, economy, and community.[9] This argument of institutional differentiation differs from arguments of role differentiation, where specialized roles emerge such as shaman, head warrior, or chief. There may be specialized roles in a society, although major institutional relations are not distinguished or specialized. While all major societal institutions are interrelated to some degree in all societies, the theory of societal differentiation suggests that some specific configurations of institutional relations may be more predisposed for change than others. The theory argues that more highly differentiated institutional orders, those where culture, polity, economy, and community are relatively more specialized and insulated from the activities of the others, will have greater general capacity for change and adaptation than less differentiated societies, where the major institutions are overlapping, less specialized, and less autonomous from one another.[10]

It is possible to create a complex scheme of relations among specialized activities within major institutions, such as polity or economy. For example, an internally differentiated polity is often characterized as a democratic state with political parties, separation of political powers among executive, judiciary, and legislature powers, and special rules of political decision making. A specialized economy is a market economy with many businesses, factories, financial exchanges, banks, and mass consumers. This degree of theoretical description is not necessary for the argument presented in this chapter, so we will consider primarily the relations among major institutions: economy, polity, community, and culture.

Much of differentiation theory is based on systems relations, but this is an abstract formulation; it is more pragmatic and empirically useful to work with concrete ethnographic case studies. Relations among culture, polity, economy, and community can be studied from the ethnographic and historical literature available on any particular society. For example, among the Iroquois it is well-known that matrilineal clans elect leaders within the Iroquois; clans and family lineages are primary political decision-making groups. This tells us that the families and clans that make up the Iroquois community define and manage Iroquois political relations. Matrilineal clans and families legitimately control the leadership within the Iroquois Confederacy. Clan rights supersede confederacy prerogatives, unless the clans grant unanimous consent to the confederacy. Furthermore, in Iroquois society most economic activity is undertaken and organized by families and clans. Women cultivate the fields and control the horticultural output, and males deliver the results of their hunting to their wives or mothers. Thus in Iroquois society, economy and polity are closely interrelated through family and clan relations. The rules and norms of Iroquois economy, polity, and community or kinship relations were understood by most Iroquois.[11] This kind of knowledge was not hidden and was accessible to most interested adult members of the society, if not understood from childhood. Ethnographic descriptions of a society, or the ways in which economy, polity, culture, or community activities are carried out in specific historical instances, provide clues to understanding how major societal institutions are related and how they operate in historical and normative situations.

One advantage to an ethnographic and historical approach to understanding relations of societal differentiation is that it avoids theoretical abstractness and ahistoricity. The theory of differentiation was formulated to understand broad evolutionary trends of change, but is relatively less helpful for understanding the process of how societies moved from one arrangement among culture, polity, economy, and community relations to another arrangement. The theory also classified indigenous societies as relatively undifferentiated, which overlooks considerable variation in institutional relations among them. For example, the major institutions in Iroquois society are undifferentiated, but so are those of the Creek. However, the Creek do not have the same clan, economy, and polity relations as the Iroquois. An ethnographic approach to understanding relations of societal differentiations allows the researcher to avoid a too Western and evolutionary bias in the abstract formulation of the theory, where highly differentiated societies always look like industrialized Western democracies such as the United States. An empirical and ethnographic approach to understanding relations of societal differentiation helps underscore the systemic ways in which societal organization varies. Differentiation theory assumes that institutional relations and interchanges are fundamentally similar across societies, but empirically relations among polity, economy, community, and culture are unique to each society, and their patterns of interrelations deserve considerable empirical and theoretical attention. An empirical and ethnographic understanding of institutional differentiation can account for the unique and holistic relations of polity, economy, community, and culture found in all societies. Only after having gained such knowledge will we be in a better position to survey the many permutations of institutional orders found in human societies, and be in a better position to study their empirical patterns of change through history.

The theory of societal differentiation suggests that undifferentiated societies will be less capable of generating change. Change is defined as a process of increased societal differentiation, such as the increased insulation of polity from religion, as, for example, in the U.S. constitution with its policy of separation of church and state. Undifferentiated institutional orders are more difficult to change because institutional relations are overlapping, and any group seeking to present an innovation or change in institutional relations (e.g., increased separation of political and religious relations) must legitimate and gain the affirmation of the new relations from most members of the community. Force is often used to impose change, but we are considering consensual change and institutionalization of more differentiated institutional relations, such as increased separation of kinship and polity or religion and polity. Change created by force is often unstable and fails to become institutionalized.[12]

One reason that undifferentiated institutional relations are not easily changed is that an innovation toward increased institutional differentiation requires major reorganization of fundamental institutions such as kinship, religious worldview, political relations, or economic organization. Most peoples are reluctant to change kinship organization or religion without good reason. For example, in the Iroquois case, where economy and polity are closely interrelated with family-clan relations, Iroquois and missionaries who introduced innovations (e.g., democratic government modeled after the U.S. government) encountered considerable opposition from many Iroquois who preferred to live by the traditional patterns of clan-elected political leadership and organization.[13] In such cases, clans, kinship groups, and religious leaders will have vested interests in resisting the formation of a government that formally excludes their historical interests and cultural prerogatives from political organization and decision making. Such groups will consider their traditional rights and interests threatened and will not accept a new, more differentiated arrangement as proper or legitimate. Consequently, unless there are extenuating conditions or situations, such groups will strongly resist change. Whether they are successful in resisting change may depend on their political power and social-cultural influence for upholding and maintaining the traditional institutional order.[14]

Both differentiation theory and Weber's cultural theory of change provide tools for understanding institutional and cultural conservatism among American Indian societies. Both theories, however, pay relatively little attention to indigenous societies and their cultural and institutional uniqueness and variation. Nevertheless, it is possible to borrow concepts and ideas from both theories that help improve understanding of the institutional and cultural patterns of Native American conservatism.

## Native American Worldview and Conservatism

There are hundreds of Native American religions with their own creation stories, rituals, sacred objects, and particular relations with the sacred. For each of the hundreds of Indian cultures there are associated beliefs, cultural norms, and understandings. For example, the Hopi creation stories of people rising from the earth through three underworlds provide for a very different moral order than the Tlingit creation stories based on the culture hero,

Raven. Although the specific content of Native American cultures varies considerably, there are many fundamental similarities when compared to world religions, especially Weber's view of Protestant Calvinism.[15] Weber argues that Calvinist doctrines provided cultural motivation for the rise of the capitalist spirit and, more generally, modernity, with its emphasis on change and progress. Consequently the features of Calvinism that motivated orientations toward change should be absent or differently ordered as to have an opposite effect in a traditionalistic culture. Some features of Weber's argument that might be compared with Native American cultures are the radical dualism of this-worldliness and otherworldliness, emphasis on otherworldliness, denigration of this-worldliness, emphasis on domination of the earth, predestination of God's will, individual salvation, and guilt and sin. If American Indian cultures foster orientations toward preservation of the social and cultural order, then we can expect to find those doctrines and differences expressed when compared with Weber's analysis of Calvinist doctrines.

Many interesting comparisons can be made between American Indian religions and Christianity, but here we are interested only in those aspects of cultural orientation that motivate change and innovation, or orientations that motive strong commitment and maintenance of a cultural order. One aspect of Christianity, and more specifically Calvinism, that fosters orientations toward accepting change in political and economic institutions is the radical dualism of sacred and profane. While most cultures emphasize sacred and profane situations or places, in Calvinism the entire earthly existence is profane. The world is full of sin, death, hunger, disease, and suffering. This world is a place of trial, and the real world is heaven, the sacred place where individual salvation is obtained. The view that this world is an evil and corrupt place, and that heaven is the real world, has implications of understanding possibilities for accepting change. If this world is evil, then there are no injunctions against changing and transforming it; also, man-made institutions are temporary and therefore inherently imperfect and subject to improvement. The Christian God commands the faithful to populate the world, subdue its raw materials, and make the world Christian. Even though people are to work according to God's divine plan while on earth, the perfect world is in heaven, and it is God's will that people work to make a more perfect world, a world that more completely reflects the sacred world of heaven. This idea of a corrupt world implies that the world is and must be changed for the better. The idea of utopian societies is derived from the belief that the good society is possible. No good Calvinist can accept the current moral and institutional condition of the world, but must strive to make it better.

Native American worldviews do not exhibit Christianity's radical dualism or its denigration of this world. For most Native Americans, this world is the primary world, and it is a gift of the Creator, a benevolent gift giver. While there is pain and suffering in this world, earthly existence is not seen as a corrupt and evil travail. Rather Native American religions view the world as a great gift, full of great power and sacredness.[16] Since this world is a gift and sacred, ordained place, Native American religions do not condone orientations that threaten to change fundamental characteristics of the world order. To change the order of the given world would challenge the wisdom of the Creator and upset the sacred balance and order of the universe. A people who renounced the sacred ceremonies that gave thanks to the creator for health, harmony, victory in war, good harvests, or good hunting would forfeit the favor of the Creator and lose divine protection and aid. Such an immoral people would find divine retribution in misfortune such as death, disease, sickness, bad hunting and bad harvests, losses in battle, and other injuries. The Creator universe is composed of beings who have will and are capable of retaliation against any abuse perpetrated on them by people. If people live in ritual harmony with the other beings of the universe, as the Creator decrees, then the Creator will favor and reward the people. Ceremonies underscore the thankfulness and respect of the Indian people toward the Creator and many other beings who are significant in their environment. While people must kill animals and collect plants to live, they show their sorrow and respect for the spirits of the plants and animals through ceremony.[17] Ritual balance and harmony are preserved through the ceremonies that honor the beings who are killed so that people may live. Only those animals and plants that are necessary for the subsistence of the people are harvested, for to take more would show disrespect for the animal spirits and invite their retaliation through poor hunts, poor harvests, or disease. The universe is composed of powerful beings that can harm or favor people.[18] Respecting and honoring the beings of the universe is the surest means of maintaining harmony, order, and well-being among people. Similarly, in social group relations, respect and honor of traditional rules, values, and institutions are the means to ensure harmonious social relations.[19]Consequently, there are strong incentives to uphold traditional law, sacred law, and community norms, because upsetting existing social arrangements jeopardizes the group harmony and invites divine retribution on the entire community for failure to maintain sacred law and proper ceremonies. Upholding the traditions and ceremonies leads to harmony and order in the community and with the beings of the universe, while breaking tradition and disrespecting nonhuman beings invites individual and collective disaster.

Pain and suffering are experienced in this world; in comparison to Christianity, there is much less emphasis on rewards in the otherworld.[20] Indians do not have a view of guilt and sin but emphasize relative states of ritual purity. A person who has broken a sacred rule is ritually impure and therefore potentially dangerous, and must be restored to purity and harmony through ceremony.

In many Indian societies, the institutions of society are seen as given by the Creator or one of his intermediaries. For example, among the Tlingit, the clan-moiety system and the potlatch ceremonies are believed to have been given by Raven, a being who manifests the Creator's will. Consequently Tlingit clan and ceremonial order is considered divine and therefore not changeable under normal circumstances.[21] Similarly, among the Iroquois, the demigod Deganawidah, as the spokesperson for the Creator, decreed the sacred law of the Iroquois Confederacy and gave the Iroquois the organization of the confederacy through families and clans. Hence the ceremonies, organization, constitution, and law of the confederacy are considered sacred and therefore not subject to change.[22] Any significant change in the organization of the confederacy, without divine approval expressed in some way, was a transgression of sacred law and bound to lead to misfortune, such as social disharmony, sickness, death, poor crops, or losses in war. Analogous examples are readily found among the Creek, Hopi, and Cheyenne.[23]

Since in many Indian societies institutional orders are sacred and many aspects of nature are sacred and therefore must be respected, Indians are not motivated to dominate, control, or change this-worldly ceremonies, institutions, or the organization of nature.[24] To do so would challenge the divine will and lead to this-worldly misfortune.[25] Hopi conservatives believe that the ceremonies must be performed each year and according to exact tradition, otherwise the Hopi fourth world will be destroyed by flooding caused by a water monster.[26] Many Indian conservatives believe that the Indians have covenant relation with the Creator, who sustains and gives the order of the universe, while people are to respect the world and perform ceremonies of respect and thanksgiving. Failure to perform the ceremonies may cause the Creator to destroy the world.[27]

The Indian view of accepting the world as a sacred gift and therefore not transformable was reflected in their attitude toward managing and preserving the ecological resources in their environment. Most Indian peoples did not kill more animals or take more plants than was needed for their traditional needs. Animals were to be treated respectfully after they had been killed in the hunt and thanked for their contribution to preserving the lives of the people.[28] By such ceremonies and signs of respect Indians ensured a ritual balance of relations with their food, and within their worldview ensured that the animals were reborn and would continue to offer themselves for people's sustenance.[29]

During the colonial period, European traders were baffled over the economic ways of the Indians who did not conform to their expectations. When the Indians were induced by traders to bring in more furs by lowering the price of trader goods relative to furs (the traders gave more goods for the same number of furs), the Indians brought in fewer furs. The Indians needed only a limited bundle of trade goods, and they stopped hunting furs to trade after they secured the required goods. If the needed trade goods could be gained with fewer furs, then the Indians needed to hunt less.[30] This is the same traditional labor ethic that Weber describes.[31] Indians did not exhibit capitalist or materially acquisitive economic orientations even during the colonial period, and in the few cases where Indian entrepreneurs emerged, as among the Cherokee, Choctaw, Chickasaw, and Creek, the economic values were borrowed from European traders and were not derived from Indian cultures.[32]

Some anthropologists argue that the potlatches of the Northwest Coast peoples, where large quantities of wealth are accumulated for giveaways in exchange for future gifts and acknowledgment of rank, are similar to capitalist accumulation. The goods exchanged in the Northwest coast potlatches are not reinvested into means of production according to the demands of the marketplace, and therefore do not fit the definition of rational capitalism. There is no formally free labor or exchange value markets among the Northwest Coast peoples, and hence they are not economic capitalists. Among the Tlingit, the potlatch is a ceremony of material exchange as well as (and perhaps more important) a ceremony for honoring and remembering the clan ancestors. In many ways the Tlingit potlatch is an ancestor cult in which honor and prestige are gained through giving away goods as a sign of love and respect for the clan ancestors. The material object is given to the living recipient from another clan and moiety, but the spirit of the object honors the departed clan ancestors. The more a Tlingit clan house gives away in the potlatch, the more respect and prestige it earns for dutifully honoring the clan ancestors.[33]

In general, Indian cultures view the world as holistic, this-worldly, benevolent, and sacred, with a Creator who can be approached through ceremony and respectfulness, and a place where harmony must be preserved through ritual and ceremonial action. Primary human action in this Indian worldview is aimed at upholding the sacred social and universal order and working to maintain or restore ritual balance with human and nonhuman beings. Preserving social order, social and cultural institutions, and ceremonies leads to harmony and well-being, while changing social, cultural, or religious norms and ceremonies invites disorder, harm, and, in some cases, world destruction. There are strong religious and cultural reasons for Indian conservatism, since Indian religions and worldviews emphasize preserving traditional ceremonies and institutions and maintaining harmonious relations with the spirit beings of the universe. Indians do not see the world as needing change, since it is the sacred gift of a benevolent Creator. The sacred order cannot be changed without risk to the individual or community. Since social and religious ceremonies and traditions are sacred, they must be preserved as a sign of respect and honor. Efforts to dominate and transform the world will cause retaliation and harm from powerful beings. Indians see themselves not as having a mandate to control, dominate, or transform the world or their own social-cultural institutions, but rather as powerless beings who can best assure their well-being through learning to live harmoniously and respectfully with the other beings of the universe. Humans are not central to the purpose of the universe, and people cannot know the Creator's purpose or plan. Humans must accept their ordained role in the universe, and learn to accept and play out their part in the Creator's divine plan.

## Conservatism and Undifferentiated Cultural Elements

An additional method for analyzing cultural conservatism is drawn from differentiation theory, and refers to the relative autonomy among major cultural features such as religion, morality, causality, art, and ceremony. In societies where there is a relatively high degree of differentiation among major cultural elements—religion, causality, art, morality, and ceremony—each forms a relatively independent activity insulated from the influence of the others. For example, in the West since after the Renaissance, secular culture emerged and religion became increasingly separate from ceremony, artistic expression, and science. For many people in Western societies, science provides an explanation for causality within the empirical world, and most people do not believe religious interpretations of the origin of the universe or history. In a culture where religion, morality, art, causality, and ceremony are fused together, most cultural activity such as artistic expression, ceremonies, moral actions, and even causal interpretations of events or the order of the universe are given religious meaning and interpretation. For example, whenever a Navajo is sick, he or she seeks out a shaman who can perform ceremonies that will restore the patient's health by reestablishing relations of harmony with the sacred universe.[34] The cause of many illnesses in Navajo culture is the breaking of moral rules. This view is different from the Western germ theory, which is a scientific theory distinguished from a religious or moral cause. In Navajo culture, ceremonies must be performed to reestablish the patient's moral relation to the sacred world order. To restore health, the shaman creates a sandpainting—a representation of sacred beings and the order of the universe—and performs ceremonies to restore order, balance, and health to the patient. After the ceremony the sandpainting is destroyed, since it is not an object of beauty as in Western culture, but rather a sacred object with spiritual power capable of helping restore sick people to health. When the ceremony ends, the painting has served its purpose. The Navajo healing ceremony illustrates the close interrelation of religious belief, morality, the causes of illness and health, the religious context for the performance ceremonies, and the religious and causal purpose of art. The nondifferentiation of cultural elements such as religion, morality, art, ceremony, and causality fosters conservative orientations because such cultural relations inhibit change owing to the necessity to change multiple relations among cultural elements. For example, during the 1940s and 1950s some Navajos started selling sandpaintings to tourists, who regarded them as art objects in the secular Western sense. Other Navajos argued that it was not proper to sell sandpaintings, since their purpose was religious. The sellers of the sandpaintings replied that they purposely made mistakes in the marketed sandpaintings and consequently the paintings did not possess sacred power; therefore, there was nothing wrong with selling them. Nevertheless, selling sandpaintings was highly controversial among the Navajo because sandpaintings were seen by many as sacred helpers in ritual healing, not secular art objects for market. Shamanistic practices, which are universal among the indigenous peoples of North America, testify to the general presence of undifferentiated cultural elements within Indian cultures. As in the Navajo sandpainting example, inherent within shamanistic beliefs is the understanding that ritual ceremony has causal effect and breaking sacred rules is a cause of illness and misfortune.

In comparison, Weber describes Calvinist predestination as ruling out the possibility that ceremony, prayer, and confession of sins could change or influence history or one's prospects for salvation.[35] In the Calvinist view, religion, causality, ceremony, and morality were relatively independent, and therefore Calvinists had a relatively secular view of everyday mundane life and of the causes of history and worldly activity. Such a secular worldview was a precursor to the ubiquitous secularism of contemporary modernity.

The argument that undifferentiated cultural elements foster conservatism relies primarily on the structural relations of the cultural elements: in Indian cultures they are interrelated and they interpenetrate one another. Cultural change is more difficult in undifferentiated than more differentiated structures because several elements of culture must be changed simultaneously, whereas in a more differentiated arrangement of cultural elements groups might be willing to change fewer features of cultural organization than change all elements of a tightly undifferentiated cultural complex. As in the Navajo sandpainting case, there was resistance to selling sacred objects and redefining them as secular art. Indian communities will be reluctant to deconstruct and secularize religious ceremonies or put aside belief in the causal effects of ceremonies for healing, as well as belief in the religious or sacred underpinnings of art and morality.

The argument of undifferentiated cultural elements appeals only to the structural relations among cultural elements, not to the content and meaning of cultural worldviews. If we combine the earlier arguments—the conservative emphasis in Indian worldviews with the undifferentiated relations of Indian cultural elements—which reinforce each other, we find a plausible explanation for conservative orientations within Indian cultures. The conservative worldview expressed in Indian religions is included within the undifferentiated culture elements and serves to reinforce the undifferentiated relations among art, morality, ceremony, religion, and causality. The content (or the purpose and meaning found in Indian cultures) and the undifferentiated structural relations among cultural elements combine and interpenetrate to foster conservative orientations among Indian peoples.

## Conservatism and Societal Differentiation

Most hunting and gathering societies in North America are characterized by decentralized local band organization with little centralized political or ceremonial organization. Many of the subarctic hunters and gatherers such as the Athapascans, and many Algonkian-speaking nations such as the Cree, Montagnais, and Ojibway, are generally characterized as being decentralized and having undifferentiated or segmentary cultural, political, economic, and community relations. The Paiute and Ute of the Great Basin are similarly organized, as were the migrant Athapascan, such as the Navajo and Apache. The hunters and gatherers usually live in small kin-based bands or villages with local political and religious leadership. The hunting and gathering nations of the Northwest Coast are materially and culturally rich, but their social, economic, and cultural orders are based largely on family and clan relations, with little political centralization beyond villages.[36] The horticultural societies of the east, southeast, and southwest are organized differently and have more role differentiation, but relations among cultural, economic, community, and political institutions are relatively undifferentiated. For example, clans and families within villages organize Hopi religious, ceremonial, and political leadership. Although the particular way in which Hopi institutions are constructed is unique to them, a pattern of undifferentiation is observed among them because religious, political, economic, and kinship structures are tightly interrelated and interpenetrating. Because of this pattern of undifferentiated institutional relations, the Hopi will be reluctant to consider institutional innovations such as change in political relations if such change requires major reorientations in creation stories, religious ceremonies, and kinship relations. When multiple institutional relations are required for accepting an institutional innovation, then there is great likelihood of resistance to change, since people are generally reluctant to change fundamental features of social organization without extreme cause. The conservatism of the Hopi and their resistance to political change such as an Indian reorganization government is apparent in their history.[37] The Hopi case behaves according to the predictions of theory. The Indian nations of North America show considerable ethnographic diversity when comparing relations among economic, political, cultural, and community institutions. In each nation or tribe, the specific ways in which economy, polity, culture, and community are interrelated is unique and form a holistic entity. These variations are essential to understanding each culture on its own terms and will provide clues, causes, and insight into the ways in which particular Native American societies changed, adapted, and persisted during the colonial period. Since there are so many unique religions, cultures, and institutional orders among American Indian nations, it is an oversimplification to categorize them all as one particular type of society, such as undifferentiated. On this occasion, however, it is possible only to note Native American cultural and institutional diversity and point out that they have predominately decentralized and/or relatively undifferentiated institutional relations of one or another degree. Societies with undifferentiated institutional relations tend to have conservative orientations toward change, since any particular innovation for increased institutional specialization requires change in multiple fundamental institutional arrangements, which often engenders more resistance than when fewer institutional arrangements require change.

## Native American Conservatism

Native North American conservatism is a product of worldview, culturally undifferentiated cultural elements, and relatively undifferentiated institutional orders. The combination of conservatism in worldview and relatively undifferentiated societal orders accentuates and complements orientations toward preserving traditional institutions and ceremonies, and ways of resisting assimilation and institutional change imposed by colonizing nations. Since many American Indian groups retain much of their culture, worldview, and social order, they will continue to emphasize community and cultural preservation. This argument is based on cultural and normative views and implies not that Indians are culturally or racially incapable of change, but rather that their social and cultural views place great and explicit emphasis on cultural preservation. All cultures are changeable and must be maintained through continuous compliance and commitments from their adherents. Culture is learned, and changing circumstances, new generations, and variations in socialization all contribute to small changes in differing interpretations of culture. Indian cultures are not different in this regard from other peoples. During the past five hundred years Indians were exposed to extensive changes in economic, political, and cultural conditions, and many adapted and changed according to circumstances. Some individual Indians culturally assimilated into U.S. or Canadian society, but many have not fully assimilated, and many others prefer to retain as much of their traditional cultures and institutions as present conditions permit. The continued and persistent Indian emphasis on cultural retention and preservation is inherent within Indian worldviews and is complemented and accentuated by conservative orientations generated by relatively undifferentiated cultural and institutional relations.

## Conclusion

Native American peoples are often considered to be conservative or traditionalistic. Over the past five hundred years they have strongly emphasized retention of cultural identity, community organization, and social-cultural institutions. The conservative orientations found in Native American communities are inherent in their cultural worldviews, their cultural organization, and sociocultural institutional orders. Weberian and contemporary sociological theory suggests three mutually complementary and supporting explanations for American Indian conservatism. American Indian worldviews are interpreted as emphasizing preservation of the sacred social and natural order. The relations among Native American cultural elements—religion, art, ceremony, causality, and morality—are undifferentiated and inhibit cultural change. The relations among cultural, political, economic, and community institutions in American Indian societies, while varying greatly, tends toward undifferentiation and also inhibits change in social and cultural relations. All three arguments are mutually supportive and point toward inherently and powerfully conservative orientations for Native American community members and culture bearers. The combined arguments help explain the persistence of Native American communities and identities after five hundred years of colonialism. Studies of change or cultural traditionalism among Native Americans must take into account their inherently conservative cultural orientations and cultural and institutional relations in order to arrive at more holistic and complete understandings of Indian life, change, and preservation.

## Notes

I gratefully acknowledge research support from the UCLA American Indian Studies Center and the National Science Foundation. An earlier version of this paper appeared as Duane Champagne, "The Cultural and Institutional Foundations of Native American Conservatism," special issue on North American Indians: Cultures in Motion, ed. Elvira Stefania Tiberini, *L'Uomo: Società, tradizione, sviluppo* 8, no. 1 (1995): 17–43.

1. J. Jorgensen, *The Sun Dance Religion* (Chicago: University of Chicago Press, 1972); T. Vennum, *The Ojibway Dance Drum: Its History and Construction* (Washington, D.C.: Smithsonian Institution Press, 1982); D. Champagne, *American Indian Societies: Strategies of Cultural and Political Survival* (Cambridge, MA: Cultural Survival, 1989).

2. Karl Marx, *Capital* (New York: International, 1967).

3. F. Engels, *The Origin of the Family, Private Property, and the State* (New York: International, 1972), pp. 96, 160.

4. Max Weber, *The Sociology of Religion* (Boston: Beacon, 1963); Weber, *The Religion of India* (New York: Free Press, 1967); Weber, *The Religion of Judaism* (New York: Free Press, 1967); Weber, *The Religion of China* (New York: Free Press, 1968).

5. Max Weber, *General Economic History* (New Brunswick, NJ: Transaction, 1981), pp. 275–78.

6. Max Weber, *The Protestant Ethic and the Spirit of Capitalism* (New York: Scribner's, 1958), pp. 59–65.

7. Weber, *Economic History*, pp. 352–69.

8. Weber, *Protestant Ethic*, pp. 180–83.

9. T. Parsons, *The Evolution of Societies* (Englewood Cliffs, NJ: Prentice-Hall, 1977).

10. Engels, *Origin of the Family*, pp. 96, 160; Parsons, *Evolution*.

11. L. Morgan, *The League of the Iroquois* (New York: Burt Franklin, 1901), p. 221; A. Parker, *Parker on the Iroquois* (Syracuse, NY: Syracuse Press, 1968), pp. 100–108; A. Wallace, *The Death and Rebirth of the Seneca* (New York: Vintage, 1972), pp. 44–50.

12. Parsons, *Evolution*, p. 25; E. Durkheim, *The Division of Labor in Society* (New York: Free Press, 1984), pp. 310–22.

13. T. Donaldson, ed., *Extra Census Bulletin: Indians. The Six Nations of New York* (Washington, D.C.: U.S. Census Printing Office, 1892), pp. 2, 34–44; W. Fenton, "Toward the Gradual Civilization of the Indian Natives: The Missionary and Linguistic Work of Asher Wright," *Proceedings of the American Philosophical Society* 100 (1956): 567–81; L. Hauptman, *The Iroquois and the New Deal* (Syracuse, NY: Syracuse University Press, 1981), pp. 9, 179.

14. S. Eisenstadt, "Transformation of Social, Political, and Cultural Orders in Modernization," in *Comparative Political Systems,* ed. R. Cohen and J. Middleton (Austin: University of Texas Press, 1967), p. 444; Eisenstadt, *Revolution and the Transformation of Societies* (New York: Free Press, 1978), pp. 32–34, 66; J. Alexander and P. Colomy, "Toward Neofunctionalism," *Sociological Theory* 3 (1985): 13–16; P. Colomy and G. Rhoades, "Toward a Micro Corrective of Structural Differentiation Theory," *Sociological Perspectives* 37, no. 4 (1994): 547–83.

15. Weber, *Protestant Ethic.*

16. A. Hultkrantz, *The Religions of the American Indians* (Berkeley: University of California Press,1979), p. 10; P. Beck, A. Walters, and N. Francisco, *The Sacred Ways of Knowledge, Sources of Life* (Tsaile, AZ: Navajo Community College Press, 1992), pp. 3–44.

17. J. Loftin, "Traditional Religious Practices Among Contemporary American Indians," in *The Native North American Almanac,* ed. D. Champagne (Detroit: Gale Research, 1994), pp. 648–58.

18. Ken Morrison, "Native American Religions: Creating through Cosmic Give-and-Take," in *The Native North American Almanac,* ed. D. Champagne (Detroit: Gale Research, 1994), pp. 633–48.

19. J. Loftin, *Religion and Hopi Life in the Twentieth Century* (Bloomington: Indiana University Press, 1991), pp. 76–77.

20. Hultkrantz, *Religions,* p. 136.

21. C. McClellan, "The Interrelations of Social Structure with Northern Tlingit Ceremonialism," *Southwest Journal of Anthropology* 10 (1954): 86, 96.

22. E. Wilson, *Apologies to the Iroquois* (New York: Farrar, Straus & Cudahy, 1959).

23. P. Powell, *The Cheyenne, Maheo's People: A Critical Bibliography* (Bloomington: Indiana University Press, 1980); Powell, *People of the Sacred Mountain: A History of the Northern Cheyenne Chiefs and Warrior Societies, 1830–1879, with an Epilogue, 1969–1974* (San Francisco: Harper & Row, 1981); Loftin, *Hopi Life,* pp. 3–61; Duane Champagne, *Social Order and Political Change: Constitutional Governments among the Cherokee, Choctaw, Chickasaw, and Creek* (Stanford, CA: Stanford University Press, 1992).

24. Weber, *Sociology of Religion,* p. 269; J. Campbell, *Occidental Mythology* (New York: Penguin, 1976), pp. 5–6, 106, 190–92, 449.

25. S. Stanley, "American Indian Power and Powerlessness," in *The Anthropology of Power,* ed. R. Fogelson and R. Adams (London: Academic Press, 1977), pp. 237–42.

26. Loftin, *Hopi Life,* p. 78.

27. Stanley, "American Indian Power," pp. 237–42.

28. Loftin, "Traditional Religious Practices," pp. 648–58.

29. J. Campbell, *Mythologies of the Great Hunt* (New York: Harper & Row, 1988), p. 234.

30. E. Rich, "Trade Habits and Economic Motivation among the Indians of North America," *Canadian Journal of Economics and Political Science* 26 (1960): 53; A. Ray, *Indians and the Fur Trade* (Toronto, ON: University of Toronto Press,1974), p. 68.

31. Weber, *Protestant Ethic,* pp. 59–65.

32. Champagne, *Social Order.*

33. J. Swanton, "Social Conditions, Beliefs, and Linguistic Relationships of the Tlingit Indians," *Twenty-Sixth Annual Report of the US. Bureau of American Ethnology, 1904–05* (Washington, D.C.: U.S. Government Printing Office, 1908), pp. 343, 462–63; F. de Laguna, "Some Dynamic Forces in Tlingit Society," *Southwestern Journal of Anthropology* 10 (1954): 185–91; McClellan, "Tlingit Ceremonialism," p. 80.

34. Campbell, *Mythologies,* pp. 244–48; Beck, *Sacred Ways,* pp. 267–89.

35. Weber, *Protestant Ethic,* pp. 103–6, 168–69.

36. P. Drucker, *Cultures of the Pacific Northwest* (San Francisco: Chandler, 1965).

37. Loftin, *Hopi Life;* R. Clemmer, "The Hopi Traditionalist Movement," *American Indian Culture and Research Journal* 18, no. 3 (1994): 125–66.

# Tribal Capitalism and Native Capitalists: Multiple Pathways of Native Economy

**3**

⊞

T HE TWENTY-FIRST CENTURY PROMISES to extend the world capitalist market economy deeper into the lives of individuals and communities. Its origins have been traced variously to Europe as early as the eleventh century or to multiple local and regional "world economies" from various locations and historical eras. The emerging world market promises to be more inclusive and far-reaching than any observed heretofore. Since 1990, the major socialist nations have struggled with the transition to capitalism and market production. As the case of Russia shows, such transitions are difficult, especially when a nation's culture and institutions are not compatible with capitalist market ethics, norms, and values. Many non-Western cultures have values and institutions that are incompatible with capitalist enterprise. To preserve their cultural autonomy, these communities will engage in an internal dialog that, within limits, reinterprets capitalist market activity to suit local cultures and institutions.

The Japanese have developed a large-scale capitalist society, and yet their social and political institutions remain recognizable as Japanese. Similarly, China has experienced colonialism and socialism during its long history and now is moving toward capitalist enterprise and production. The changes are significant and are not without political and cultural costs. Socialist and third world societies are struggling with gaining profitable access to markets. Like those societies, indigenous peoples are confronted with deeper penetration of markets into their communities.

U.S. Natives, or American Indians, are facing the same dilemmas within the largest national economy in the world. Will Native communities survive incorporation into the world capitalist market system? Will Native communities and individuals accept change? Will they still be Indians if they are capitalists?

According to Max Weber, and for that matter, Karl Marx, the emergence of capitalism forms an "Iron Cage." Once its forces are unleashed, other economic actors must follow suit or be forced out of business.[1] Capitalism threatens to envelop the world and transform all the cultures of the world into capitalist communities. This argument assumes that individuals and communities will readily choose more income and productivity associated with capitalist market incorporation. Individuals and communities will cast off their "traditional fetishes" and join the relatively secular, modern, and production-oriented market system. Anyone who fails to meet the challenges of capitalist competition will be marginalized. The conditions predicted by Marx and Weber appear to be unfolding in the contemporary world, assuming that it proceeds in the same manner in the next century or so.

Echoing Marx and Weber, many contemporary economists continue to argue that modernization (or capitalist culture) will sweep the globe and transform its social and cultural institutions. Since the fall of the major socialist economies in the 1990s, conditions for realization of the Iron Cage argument have never seemed more favorable. Will the nations of the world converge toward a relatively similar capitalist culture based on a world market? Or will the nations and communities of the world retain identifiable social, political, and cultural institutions and values within a world capitalist system?[2]

Ultimately, I do not believe that all nations and communities will converge toward a common market-based institutional order. The rationalist and materialist Iron Cage argument leaves little room for cultural values or institutional relations, since they are assumed predetermined by economic relations. An alternative view suggests that institutional relations and cultures are autonomous and not determined entirely by broader economic conditions. Communities can take on capitalist elements and participate in capitalist markets and still retain core aspects of identity, tradition, institutional relations— the close interconnectedness of polity, culture, economy, and community —and cultural values. Perhaps the distinct cultures of Japan and China exemplify this line of reasoning, even as proponents of the Iron Cage viewpoint might argue that since the world capitalist market has only recently extended to those nations, time will prove them correct.

## Economic Orientations in Indian Country

U.S. Native communities are facing the same expanding world capitalist market and are confronted with issues of retaining and enhancing political economy and cultural heritage. Can Native groups retain their community, institutional relations, and cultural values while participating in the world economic market? These issues confront many contemporary Native communities. Some Native leaders argue that the only way to uphold cultural and political sovereignty is through capitalist economic development. The rapid movement toward gaming enterprises since 1990 illustrates this point. Gaming enterprises have become a means for some Native communities to accumulate economic capital quickly. This wealth often is used to rebuild tribal social and economic enterprises and preserve tribal cultures and institutions. Many tribes are helping members obtain an education, developing cultural centers, promoting large cultural events such as powwows, and providing jobs and social service support to elders and other members.[3] Yet relatively few Native communities realize sufficient revenue from gaming to develop sustaining economies, and most cannot rely on it for economic support. Gaming, however, has introduced more capital into Indian country than any other economic enterprise and has greatly enhanced the economic, and sometimes political, opportunities of Native communities.

For most Native communities, economic development is a means to an end. Even the most strongly market-oriented tribal economic planners see economic development as a way to support the reservation community, retain tribal members on the reservation, and promote viable, self-supporting Native communities. The gaming agreements under the IGRA (Indian Gaming Regulation Act) require using at least 70 percent of the profits for tribal community benefit.[4] This measure ensures that Native communities will reinvest their profits in social, economic, and cultural infrastructure. These provisions are generally compatible with Native values and inclinations.

If we apply the Iron Cage argument directly to Native American communities, past and present, it still does not work very well. Most Native individuals and communities have not been strongly attracted to capitalist enterprise. Native Americans have not been quick to accept capitalist enterprise, either at present or historically. Both cultural and institutional reasons account for the relative absence of interest in capitalist enterprise. To illustrate, it helps to follow Max Weber who defined capitalism as the entrepreneurial allocation of labor and capital for production of goods according to the demands of the marketplace.[5] By Weber's definition capitalism did not exist in North America before Columbus. Certainly Native communities traded. There is evidence of extensive trading networks throughout the Mississippi Valley during the period between A.D. 800 and 1600. Pipestone found mainly in present-day Minnesota evidently was widely traded. During the same period, there was an extensive network of trade and cultural exchange linking the present-day Southwest with the Indian nations and empires of Mexico and Latin America. While Indians exchanged skins, as well as corn and other foods, much of the trade was in goods used for crafts manufacture, often for sacred purposes. Furthermore, giveaways, gift giving, and gambling were common forms of exchange and material redistribution throughout the Northwest Coast and beyond. However, none of these extensive ceremonial and economic exchanges constituted capitalism as it is defined previously. No one lived by organizing the factors of production, maximizing technological innovation and wage labor, to meet the demands of a market. Few Native persons worked for others as wage laborers because most had access to land and sustenance. Redistribution was not for profit, but according to ceremonial needs and to maintain social-political relations. Even the well-known giveaways of the Northwest Coast cultures were mostly oriented toward redistribution, ceremonial purposes, and accumulation (and confirmation) of status. Tlingits of southeast Alaska redistributed goods in potlatches, but believed they were honoring and feeding their clan ancestors and fulfilling their moral obligations to clan and ancestors.[6]

The values of Native communities also mitigated against capitalist activity. Generosity and redistribution of gifts to kin and strategic allies were the rule. Those who were materially well-off through trade, farming, hunting, or warfare were expected to share their assets. Those who did not were bitterly criticized as stingy. Wealth was a means to consolidate social and political relations through redistribution, not the means to create more wealth by investment in greater production.[7]

The overlapping of economic, political, kinship, community, and ceremonial relations in most Native communities created multiple demands and patterns of distribution over material goods.[8] Objects occupied a place in the cosmos through their relationship to the community as a whole, and they assumed social and sacred meaning and value. Most Native nations believe in maintaining respectful relations among humans and other entities of the universe such as places, water, air, fire, earth, animals, birds, heavenly bodies, and the rest of the cosmos.[9] Humans are only one of many spirit beings on earth, and they do not have any exceptional role to play in the cosmic community. All beings should be respected and their roles within the cosmos comprehended. Since many beings have power and are to be respected, humans must show them respect or be subject to supernatural retribution. If animals that give themselves to humans for food are not properly prayed to and shown ceremonial respect, then they will no longer sacrifice themselves to the humans for their needs and nutrition.[10]

In Western and capitalist worldviews, the cosmos lacks particular spiritual powers, and only humans have souls. The earth is spiritually inert and is a place and resource for the comfort and needs of humans, who are obligated to scatter about the earth and use its resources to transform the world. The earth is not seen as a spiritual and sacred part of the cosmos, as among many Native religions, but rather as a place of suffering and travail, where the resources of the earth are needed for human comfort and needs. There is little need to respect the animals, plants, and other beings of the universe since they are spiritually inert, created to serve human needs. Capitalist philosophies see the earth as a natural resource, where exploitation of raw materials through labor transforms raw materials into useful objects for further economic production or consumption and the creation of additional wealth.[11]

In Native worldviews, disrupting the powerful spirits of the cosmos will cause disorder and harmful retaliation. Only by respecting and honoring the beings of the cosmos will humans sustain harmony and well-being. To many Native communities, the earth and the cosmos are a gift from the Creator, or Great Spirit. The Great Spirit is the central force and direction of the cosmos and all the beings in it, including humans. Humans do not know the direction or purpose of the universe, but they play a part in the sacred cosmic plan. Individuals may seek visions or develop life tasks or sacred duties to perform within the grand sacred path of the Great Spirit. The resulting economic ethic is one where plants and animals must be honored for their life-giving powers. This kind of labor ethic leads to a subsistence economic orientation, where only limited goods are taken from the environments, and only those that are necessary for life and spiritual purposes.

## Indians and Markets

The introduction of European markets did not change the basic worldviews and economic orientations of many Native communities. Natives accepted various trade goods: metal hatchets, traps, knives, guns, ball, textiles, beads, jewelry, and other commodities. Natives, generally in the eastern half of North America, soon became dependent on European trade goods and were producing less of their own goods.[12] This resulted in economically dependent relations for European goods, and Natives could be forced to hunt and bring in furs for goods that had became necessities.

There are arguments that Native worldview broke down as the Indians began to hunt animal skins for the fur trade. Some scholars say that the Natives' worldview changed to one of more exploitation of animals and their skins or furs for market sale to Europeans. Nevertheless, most Indians did not abandon their worldviews about respect for the beings of the cosmos. European traders went to great lengths to ensure that Native hunters brought in enough furs to satisfy demand. The Native hunters generally needed only a limited collection of goods and hunted only enough for the supplies needed. If the European trader gave more goods per fur to induce more trade, then the Indian hunters generally brought in fewer goods. They were not looking to make a profit, but were trading only to obtain necessities. This orientation fit into their worldview.[13]

Many Native individuals and communities hold traditional non-Western economic values to the present day. When many Native communities and individuals were engaged in the fur trade from about 1600 to 1840, no Native capitalists or entrepreneurs emerged in the fur trade. Natives usually hunted and trapped, often in roles akin to labor.[14] Some became middlemen in the trade, but even here Natives accumulated only enough furs to purchase annual or semiannual requirements at the trading post. An Indian middleman trader often traveled into the interior to trade, since the value of European goods was higher in the interior. Native middlemen engaged in a form of barter but did not organize production for a capitalist market. Exposure to the fur trade did not develop capitalism among Natives, but rather encapsulated Native nonmarket economic orientations within fur trade market relations.[15]

## Early Native Capitalists

Native capitalists emerged during the nineteenth century under very special conditions. In the American South during the early 1800s, there arose a class of plantation and slave owners among the Cherokee, Choctaw, Chickasaw, and Creek. These plantation owners fit our definition of capitalists since they organized black slave labor, land, and management to produce cotton, corn, cattle, and other agricultural products for export to markets. The southern Indian entrepreneurs were generally mixed bloods of Native and Scottish, English, or Irish descent. During the seventeenth century many European traders traveled into the southern interior. They often found companionship among Native women of important clans. Most southern Indian nations had matrilineal clans, where the child's heritage was reckoned through the kin of the mother. The traders cohabited with Indian women, sometimes married them, and often had children. A European trader thus had a ready set of kinship ties for trading partners, since often the female conducted much of the business of trade with her female kin. Since the children were born into matrilineal clans, their social and kinship status gave them automatic membership in their tribe. Consequently many mixed-blood children were born into prominent clans with considerable political support and strong social and economic ties.

Sometimes a European trader would bring his male children into the fur trade business. In this way the values of trade, business, and market participation were taught to some mixed-blood children. Trader families composed only a small portion of the families among the Cherokee, Choctaw, Chickasaw, and Creek. A few full-blood families also took up capitalist farming and other business activities (e.g., managing inns). Following the decline of the fur trade in the South by the first decades of the 1800s, mixed-blood Indian families of the South turned to cotton production. Cotton demand was spurred by the Industrial Revolution in Britain during the early nineteenth century, and with the resumption of trade following the War of 1812, mixed-blood trading families turned their few slaves and land into the cultivation of cotton. Soon many mixed-blood families owned several plantations on tribal lands. Many became relatively wealthy, built mansions, and lived in the style of the American southern plantation class.[16]

Yet most mixed bloods could not easily move into southern society. The government awarded some of them small "reservations" of land, but when they tried to live on them near American settler communities, most were harassed into moving. Around 1819, John Ross, the future principal chief of the Cherokee and a successful merchant and plantation owner, tried to move onto a 640-acre plot of land set aside for him by U.S. government agents, only to be forced to return to the Cherokee nation. Many Native entrepreneurs then cast their lots with their tribal communities, where they were welcomed even with their unusual market orientations. At least 95 percent of the southern Indian families in the 1820s continued to live within their traditional economic orientations and lifestyles. When the fur trade declined in the 1820s, many conservatives among the southern tribes turned to small-scale cotton farming and raising cattle and hogs for trade. The conservatives continued to work their own crops and raised cattle for their own use, while trading limited agricultural products and cattle in exchange for the manufactured goods to which they had become accustomed.[17]

During much of the nineteenth century, the southern Indian planters and conservatives combined to struggle against American intrusions to their land and political sovereignty. The major southern Native nations formed constitutional governments in an effort to increase their ability to resist U.S. legal and political demands. But following removal, differences in worldview and ultimately political orientation increasingly divided communities. While Indian planters adopted the values of the American South, most conservatives were reluctant to take up capitalist or entrepreneurial activities, but remained on small farms and worked a subsistence economic strategy of limited production for consumption and trade. The planters among the Cherokee, Choctaw, Chickasaw, and Creek generally sided with the South during the American Civil War. Cherokee and Creek conservatives sided with the

North, believing it would preserve their treaty agreements. On the other hand, Choctaw and Chickasaw conservatives sided with the South and their planter compatriots. The Choctaw and Chickasaw nations were located close to the southern Confederate states of Arkansas and Texas and had fewer options to side with the Union than did the Cherokee and Creek conservatives.

After the Civil War, the planters lost their slaves and started to employ U.S. citizen tenant farmers to work their land. Many planters turned to cattle raising on a large scale after 1870, when railroads made markets more accessible. Conservatives opposed the introduction of tenant farmers, fearing the increased presence of non-Indians on their lands. The railroads brought new markets into Indian Territory, and with them a deluge of U.S. settlers and workers. Soon the settlers overwhelmed Indian Territory, and the U.S. government moved to abolish the Cherokee, Choctaw, Chickasaw, Creek, and Seminole governments. Generally by the 1890s, many of the more entrepreneurial Native leaders reconciled themselves to the abolition of Native governments and took allotted land that opened surplus Indian land to U.S. settlers. The more assimilated entrepreneurs were willing pursue their economic interests within the American national market. Most conservatives, among the Five Civilized Tribes, were reluctant to join the United States and protested the abolition of their governments. While Indian entrepreneurs generally had the economic advantage of easy access to land within their nations, many Native farmers and cattlemen saw that their future economic interests lay with the United States, instead of preserving their Indian governments. The U.S. government did not provide many alternatives, and many probably tried to make the best of a bad situation. In 1906 the Indian Territory governments of the Cherokee, Choctaw, Chickasaw, Creek, and Seminole were abolished. Thereafter, many Native entrepreneurs entered the Oklahoma power structure and, for the most part, did not return to participate in tribal politics.

The southern Indian agrarian capitalists were unusual in American Indian history. The formation of Native entrepreneurship in the American South resulted from a combination of cotton market opportunities and the emergence of mixed-blood tribal members who internalized entrepreneurial values and skills from their fur trader fathers. Since for much of the nineteenth century the mixed-blood social and economic interests lay with their particular Indian nations, most retained Native identities and were active in tribal political and economic life. But, by the end of the nineteenth century many accepted the offer to economically and politically assimilate into Oklahoma society and politics.[18] Many continued to identify as Native, and many individuals were successful in business and professional life. The Indian conservatives resisted allotment and the abolition of their governments through protest organizations, and legal and legislative lobbying, but in the end they were not successful. One has to wait until the end of the twentieth century to find another significant group of Native capitalist entrepreneurs.[19]

## Contemporary Individual Native Capitalist Entrepreneurship

Through the twentieth century there was little Native American capitalist entrepreneurship in Indian country. Some individuals moved to cities early and became businesspeople or worked as wage laborers. At the beginning of the twentieth century, most American Indians lived on reservations or in Native communities where capitalism was culturally and socially discouraged. During the economic boom of the 1920s, a wave of Indian migrants moved to cities. Most were seeking work, as reservations conditions were very poor economically. Reservations were almost totally controlled by Indian Department officials, who were instructed to help Indians become economically self-sufficient. Irrigation, cattle raising, and farming enjoyed some success on reservations during the 1920s, but most of these efforts fell victim to the Great Depression and climatic dust bowl conditions of the 1930s, which made small-scale farming and cattle raising difficult. Indian Department policies focused on assimilating young Native Americans and providing them with workman-like skills. Basic education skills and training were emphasized and few were trained for college or capitalist entrepreneurship.[20] While many Native individuals became successful businesspeople, as a group, few Natives were engaged in capitalist entrepreneurship.

Two major patterns of contemporary Native entrepreneurship emerged by the middle of the twentieth century: tribal enterprise and individual capitalist entrepreneurship. Individual Indian entrepreneurship was developed largely by Natives who migrated to urban areas and worked for the most part within the mainstream U.S. economy. After the first major wave during the 1920s, migration to cities resumed during World War II and accelerated from the 1950s through to the end of the century. Most migrants sought employment opportunities not available on Indian reservations. Many Indian migrants preferred to stay home if economic opportunities were available. Some visited their home reservations frequently and maintained ties with their relatives, tribal ceremonies, and communities. Others arrived in the cities and never went back. They married non-Indians and often prospered over the years. They found that a tribal identity in the city was possible and developed many pan-Indian organizations and powwows. Christian Indians who migrated to urban areas might not have attended powwows, but preserved an Indian identity through faith and gatherings like picnics and church. As Indians began to attend college in significant numbers in the 1960s and 1970s, many graduated and found employment in urban areas. The brain drain of trained and professional Indians toward urban areas was a reflection of continued weak economic conditions on Indian reservations, where unemployment rates remained high throughout the century.[21]

The 2000 census indicates over 70 percent of Indians are living in urban areas. While many Indians who first migrated to urban areas found the transition difficult, others were comfortable with it. Now there are second-, third-, or sometimes fourth-generation Indian people living in urban areas. Many long-term urban Indians did not maintain strong ties to a Native community but retain some sense of Indian identity.

During the 1970s and 1980s, economic development plans for Indian reservations and within Indian communities greatly increased. Individual Indian capitalist entrepreneurs appeared in significant numbers during the 1970s and 1980s, but few invested their assets on Indian reservations, preferring to start businesses in urban areas that are conducive to business entrepreneurship and economic opportunities. As Indian people became more familiar with the urban setting, they increasingly moved into small businesses. Many learned from their work experience, and then developed small businesses, mostly mom-and-pop family enterprises. At first, many Indian-owned businesses were small grocery stores, gas stations, mechanical repair stations, arts and crafts stores, and similar small operations. As time went on, urban Indians began to look into increasingly larger and more innovative businesses. National organizations for promoting Indian capitalist entrepreneurship started to emerge, such as the National Center for American Indian Enterprise Development. Indian chambers of commerce were formed in large cities like Los Angeles. Indians started businesses on the Internet, producing and delivering computer supplies and support, as well as providing graphic design.[22]

In the 1980s and 1990s individual Indian entrepreneurship increased at very high rates. The number of U.S. businesses owned by American Indians, Eskimos, and Aleuts increased 93 percent between 1987 and 1992, from 52,980 to 102,271. By contrast, the rate of increase for all U.S. firms was 26 percent from 13.7 million in 1987 to 17.3 million in 1992.[23] In 1992, the United States had 95,040 American Indian–owned, 2,738 Aleut-owned, and 4,493 Eskimo-owned firms.[24] The total estimated receipts for the nation's American Indian, Eskimo, and Aleut businesses increased 115 percent from 1987 to 1992, from $3.7 billion to $8.1 billion, while receipts for all U.S. firms during the same period grew by 67 percent, from $2 trillion to $3.3 trillion.[25]

More recent Census Bureau information indicates that the number of Native businesses continues to expand at a fast pace. In 1997 there were 197,300 Native-owned firms, of which 4,982 (2 percent) had more than $1 million in receipts, while 26 percent, or 50,433, had receipts of less than $5,000. The number of Native businesses grew 84 percent from 1992 to 1997 while the number of all U.S. firms grew 7 percent. The receipts for Native businesses grew 179 percent, while the receipts of all U.S. firms grew 40 percent during the same period. Total receipts for Native businesses in 1997 were over $34 billion. Native business in 1997 were concentrated in industries not classified (45 percent), services (17 percent), construction (14 percent), retail trade (8 percent), agricultural services (5 percent), manufacturing (3 percent), transportation (3 percent), finance, insurance, and real estate (2 percent), and wholesale trade (2 percent). Compared with all U.S. businesses, Native businesses are overrepresented in industries not classified, construction, and agricultural services. Native businesses are underrepresented in services, finance, retail trade, wholesale trade, transportation, while Native businesses are equally represented in manufacturing. Except for industries not classified, Native businesses average less receipts than the average for all U.S. firms in the same industry. In the category of industries not classified, Native firms averaged receipts of $109,000 while all U.S. firms averaged $42,000. The five states with the largest number of Native firms are California (26,603), Texas (15, 668), Oklahoma (15,066), Florida (10,546), and North Carolina (7,148). The five metropolitan areas with the most Native-owned businesses are Los Angeles-Long Beach (8,541), Tulsa (3,822), Oklahoma City (3,295), Houston (3,128), and New York (2,801).[26]

Consequently the numbers of Native businesses are growing at a rate more than three times as fast and receipts are increasing at more than double the rate of the U.S. business community as a whole. Census data over the past two decades indicate continued growth and diversification of Native business enterprises. This suggests that Native capitalism and businesses will become an increasingly active part of the U.S. economy and will in the future play a stronger and more visible roles in Native social and political issues.

The Native business community has arisen largely within the urban environment where entrepreneurial values and opportunities are relatively unaffected by the poverty, culture, and social community of Indian reservations. Exposed to business values and opportunities within the cities, over 197,000 individual Natives have formed businesses and continue to create enterprises at a high rate. Many Natives business leaders continue to maintain ties to urban and reservation Indian communities, though often their businesses have little to do with reservation cultures or community life. Business ownership has not obliterated Native identity, but most Native businesses are not located on reservations, and this reflects the relative poor business opportunities present on Indian reservations. It also reflects the continuity of Native cultural values, political relations, and values, which tend to remain less than conducive to capitalist market values.

## Tribal Capitalism

Most government economic development plans focus on reservation economies. Yet they ignore a central problem: the general absence of individual capitalist entrepreneurs on Indian reservations. While tribal members own many small businesses such as bars, gas stations, and grocery stores, most are owned by non-Indians. Most reservation communities have not fostered individual business entrepreneurship. Most Indian entrepreneurs have moved off the reservation into the urban markets, where opportunities are greater and businesses are supported and encouraged by law, government, and culture.

On most reservations, the presence of multiple worldviews, many the products of assimilation through government education programs, individual experiences, and the introduction of Christian religion, influences the business climate. Most Native communities include groups and individuals with considerable experience and knowledge about American culture, values, and institutions, and many who have internalized such views. Most Native reservation communities, however, explicitly honor Native traditions and philosophies about the cosmos. Even well-educated Christian tribal members who have lived many years in the community continue to uphold the values and normative rules of the reservation community. This is to argue not that decision making and community action in a reservation reflect traditional orientations but that traditional values tend to prevail throughout the community's social and political relations.

The general absence of a significant private entrepreneurial section in most reservation communities is not by accident. Most Native reservation communities do not support individual capitalist activity, accumulation of wealth, and a central life focus on production and market enterprise. Values of generosity, redistribution, and egalitarianism continue to prevail among many community members. Tribal governments, which are often alien forms of representative democracy, also discourage private capitalism. Few tribal governments actively support individual business enterprise with legal and political protections. Private businesses need predictable legal and political environments, and few reservations have expended their efforts to create the legal, economic, or political infrastructure to foster a stable capitalist business climate. Many Native entrepreneurs find reservation business environments are not supportive and prefer to move off the reservation to establish their companies. Most tribal communities do not see private enterprise as a primary value or goal. Native culture and worldviews do not support the values of capitalist accumulation and market participation.

Tribal governments continue to operate within the holistic orientations of Native community life. Unlike U.S. society, institutional relations among economy, community, kinship, and politics are not separated. Consequently many tribal leaders are reluctant to promote a private capitalist sector that is outside the political guidance and control of the tribal community. Most Native communities and their political leadership see an autonomous private sector as a possible social and political threat to the community. They feel more comfortable with community and political guidance and control over economic enterprise. The Indian Reorganization Act of 1934 (IRA) allows tribal governments to create relatively independent economic corporations to foster economic development on Indian reservations. However, while more than one hundred tribes eventually adopted a representative form of government, only one tribe adopted the corporate model as originally proposed by the IRA. In this early IRA corporate model, an economic development corporation would be created for the tribal community, and each tribal member would have a share and voting rights. A board of directors would be elected to manage and guide the corporation. The tribal government would not manage or control the economic corporation. Except for the Seminole of Florida, Indian communities rejected the IRA's reservation corporate plan. Many tribal communities have adopted a revised version of the IRA's economic corporate plan, placing the corporation under the control of the elected tribal government. Even with the prodding of the U.S. government, increasing demands of market globalization, and more diverse values within the reservation communities, most reservation communities prefer relatively holistic institutional relations among economy, community, polity, and culture.[27] Some private Native businesses operate on many reservations, but they are not strongly supported culturally or politically and, as a result, have limited opportunities.

Tribal governments and communities, however, are cognizant of the demands and needs of economic development. Tribal leadership often argues that sovereignty is not possible without freedom from economic dependence on government programs and funding. High rates of poverty and unemployment on reservations, with their attendant problems and issues, are a major stimulus for tribal governments to promote economic development. Tribal governments, however, still prefer to manage reservation economic development and enterprise. The mode of capitalism that has emerged in reservation communities makes the tribal government the main owner and manager of major economic development projects. Tribal leaders make important decisions about investment and management. This overlapping management of political and economic leadership is discouraged within mainstream American political and economic life, but it is the preferred mode of economic development on Indian reservations. A preference for political control over economic development and an aversion toward significant private capitalist enterprise is rooted in the Native cultural affinity for interrelated institutional relations. Natives are opting for a form of collective capitalism rather than individual capitalism. Some, like the Winnebago of Nebraska, are experimenting with American-style corporate models where economic decisions are insulated from the politics of tribal government. In Alaska, thirteen Native for-profit corporations are mandated by congressional act and are separate institutions from tribal governments. But throughout Indian country, the preferred way of proceeding with economic development is to apply political, community, and cultural values to economic decision making and institutions.[28] Native communities are greatly concerned about economic issues, but they do not wish to sacrifice culture, preferred institutional relations, and their internal social relations in favor of economic development. Native communities want economic development, but on their own terms and, to the largest extent possible, within their cultural and institutional arrangements. If there is a choice between economic gain and the sacrifice of central cultural and institutional relations, many Native communities prefer to refrain from economic development projects they believe will endanger or change their communities in unwanted ways.[29]

Native capitalism has taken a different path from U.S. or Western capitalism. Tribal governments are expected to preserve the political sovereignty of the Native community, as well as protect and promote cultural values and community survival. Economic development is seen as a means to enhancing tribal sovereignty, empowering the community with independent resources, and mitigating the hard effects of poverty.[30] Economic development and enterprise is not seen as an end in itself, and not necessarily as a response to market demands or comparative advantages. Many tribal communities will accept a comparatively lower standard of living, since material interests and values are less central to their lives, while community relations and cultural activity and preservation are more highly valued.[31] Tribal leaders must manage the trade-offs between community culture and the needs for economic development. A private sector with its main interest in capitalist accumulation may potentially threaten and disrupt the social and cultural relations of the community.[32]

The Mississippi Choctaw, where the tribal government makes the investment decisions and executive personnel decisions, offer an example of Native capitalism at work. Highly successful in creating manufacturing plants, sustaining their economic initiatives, and hiring many tribal members as workers and managers, Mississippi Choctaw enterprises are market oriented and profitable concerns, but with a tribal or collective purpose. The tribal government accumulates profits not for private purposes, but for the good and future investment of the tribal community. Individual workers can be motivated to take pride in their work because the tribal enterprises represent and support the entire community.[33] This model of tribal capitalism enshrines the tribal government as manager of economic enterprises for the well-being of the tribal community. Jobs and wealth are managed for the collective well-being, at least in theory, and individuals participate wholeheartedly because they are contributing to the collective and future economic well-being of the community. Since the tribal government controls economic enterprises, the goals and values of the community are protected; accumulated wealth from capitalist enterprises is reinvested or redistributed with the well-being of the community in mind.

Other successful examples of tribal capitalism are found in the rapid growth of gaming enterprises on Indian reservations. Gaming emerged because of the need for economic development on Indian reservations and because tribal sovereignty provided a legal opening to take advantage of gaming. After several legal cases and the Indian Gaming Regulatory Act of 1988 (IGRA), Indian gaming has become established. Some tribes make considerable money from their gaming, while most make small profits. The more isolated tribes have less success than those located nearer to large populations. With the exception of the Florida Seminoles, gaming operations are managed by tribal government, with most of the gaming profits being redistributed for community benefit according the IGRA. This provision fits well with collective or community-oriented Native values and helps justify gaming enterprises by promoting development and alleviating poverty. In the late 1990s, the Proposition 5 and Proposition 1A campaigns to gain gaming compacts for California Indian tribes relied heavily on themes of self-reliance, payment of taxes, and alleviation of poverty and government dependence.[34] The campaigns resonated with the California electorate, which approved both propositions with over 60 percent of the vote. They also underscored Native values and goals for gaming and redistributive economic development.[35]

Tribal capitalism does not put accumulation of wealth as its central goal. Community and cultural protection and enhancement of tribal sovereignty are major values. Tribal capitalism discourages individual capitalism because it introduces new values and new power centers, as well as unwanted concentrations of wealth within the community. Historically, Native communities are not class-based societies, and tribal culture and holistic institutional order mitigate against the formation of a capitalist class as an explicit feature of Native reservation communities. Because of government employment, farming, cattle raising, and other reservation occupations and businesses, economic class differences do emerge within Indian reservation communities. Class formation and interests are often explicitly noted by tribal community members and leaders and opposed within tribal communities as nontraditional viewpoints and social formations[36] Nevertheless, most tribal communities currently contain mixed class and cultural orientations, with many members adhering to multiple worldviews and situational identities.

Tribal governments are seen as protectors of the long-term cultural and political interests of the Native reservation communities. Economic development is desirable as long as it supports the goals of preserving and enhancing community culture and prospects. Tribal governments, when they work properly, are the stewards of the tribal community estate and must preserve community, culture, and reservation environment. Economic development is desirable when it serves community values and interests, and is threatening when market or capitalist institutions threaten to disrupt community organization.[37]

The model of tribal capitalism is widely distributed in various forms throughout Indian country. It embodies the values and interests of the Native reservation communities. Efforts by economic planners to impose Western capitalist models on Native communities generally meet opposition and have great difficulty establishing enduring economic innovations. Although the specific features, ceremonies, and stories of Native religions and worldviews vary, Native communities tend to share similar holistic understandings of the cosmos. Consequently tribal capitalism, rather than individual entrepreneurship, embodies Native cultural understandings and preferences.[38] The continued cultural and institutional foundations of contemporary Native reservation communities support the tribal capitalist model and discourage individual entrepreneurship. However, these issues continued to be discussed and even challenged by various groups, classes, and individuals. Many Native communities vigorously debate the role of tradition and institutional order—the tight interrelations of culture, community, polity, and economy—within the contemporary world. These political, cultural, and economic debates will continue and will ultimately form the basis of developing consensus on what types of change the community will accept.

Tribal capitalism faces great challenges in the twenty-first century and beyond. Global markets mean that gaining a foothold within the capitalist system is more important than it was in the past. The penalty for not participating is economic and political marginalization of Native reservation communities. Some degree of economic viability will be necessary to ensure tribal sovereignty and provide resources to preserve and extend Native cultures and traditions. Tribal governments also face continuing challenges to tribal sovereignty from local, state, and federal governments, as well as their constituent group interests. Most tribal governments do not have the resources or the organization to defend their sovereignty from local, state, and federal encroachment. Economic success will need stronger tribal governments to meet the globalized economic, political, and cultural challenges of the future. Tribal governments and tribal communities will need to negotiate and decide for themselves how to preserve their cultural and holistic institutional relations and worldviews, and at the same time promote the innovations that will allow them to meet the economic, political, and cultural challenges of the future.

## The Iron Cage in Indian Country

If we return to Marx and to Weber's Iron Cage argument as manifested in Indian country, we see Native participation in the globalized market system as moving in two major directions. Some American Indians have embraced capitalism. Over 197,000 Natives currently own businesses in the United States. Natives are relatively new to business entrepreneurship and ownership. In the last decades of the twentieth century, Native individual capitalism made significant strides and outpaced growth rates of the U.S. economy as a whole. Native individual capitalist entrepreneurship will continue to be largely urban and entrepreneurs will gain greater influence on Native issues and national policies. Since more than 197,000 business owners retain Native identities and many have strong tribal identifications, they may influence economic development and policy in Indian country.

Reservation economic development has not followed the Iron Cage model entirely. Tribal capitalism is the result of market competition, which forces Native people to engage in the market for economic sufficiency. Nevertheless, the motivations for tribal capitalism are not based solely on maximization of profits on the market but rather preservation of community, culture, and tribal sovereignty. Market competition forces the Indian communities to consider and engage in market enterprise, but they wish to do so under their own terms, which means subordinating capitalist accumulation to collective goals of community and cultural and political enhancement and preservation. Tribal capitalism makes concessions to market competition, but only as a means to further its noneconomic goals of collective community values. The struggle between the powerful forces of market competition and preservation of Native communities will play out in the next century, and will lead to many interesting social and cultural innovations as Native communities accommodate themselves to the globalized cultural, economic, and political environment.

The effects of the capitalist Iron Cage in Indian country is mixed. Nevertheless, Native community and identity has survived and will most likely will continue to meet the challenges of the globalized economy in diverse ways.

# Notes

An earlier version of this chapter appeared in Duane Champagne, "Tribal Capitalism and Native Capitalists: Multiple Pathways of Native Economy," in *Native Pathways: American Indian Economic Development and Culture in the Twentieth Century,* ed. Brian Hosmer and Colleen O'Neill (Boulder: University Press of Colorado, 2004), pp. 308–29.

1. Max Weber, *The Protestant Ethic and the Spirit of Capitalism* (New York: Scribner's, 1958), p. 182; Karl Marx, *Capital,* vol. 1. (New York: International, 1967). See also the articles on India in Karl Marx, *Surveys from Exile,* ed. David Fernbach (New York: Random House, 1973); Max Weber, *General Economic History* (New Brunswick, NJ: Transaction, 1981), pp. 275–78.

2. For an opposing view, see S. N. Eisenstadt, "Convergence and Divergence of Modern and Modernizing Societies: Indications from the Analysis of the Structuring of Social Hierarchies in Middle Eastern Societies," *International Journal of Middle Eastern Studies* (1977); Eisenstadt, "Transformation of Social, Political, and Cultural Orders in Modernization," in *Comparative Political Systems,* ed. Ronald Cohen and John Middleton (Austin: University of Texas Press, 1967); Eisenstadt, *Revolution and the Transformation of Societies* (New York: Free Press, 1978).

3. Mary Ann Andreas, "Perspective of Mary Ann Andreas, Morongo Tribal Chairperson," in *Indian Gaming: Who Wins?* ed. Angela Mullis and David Kamper (Los Angeles: UCLA American Indian Studies Center, 2000), pp. 166–68; Priscilla Hunter, "Perspective of Priscilla Hunter, Chairwoman, Coyote Band of Pomo Mission Indians," in *Indian Gaming: Who Wins?* ed. Angela Mullis and David Kamper (Los Angeles: UCLA American Indian Studies Center, 2000), pp. 169–71.

4. Indian Gaming Regulatory Act of 1988 (25 USC SS2701-2721).

5. Max Weber, *Economy and Society*, ed. Guenther Roth and Claus Wittich (Berkeley: University of California Press, 1978), 1: pp. 160–66; Weber, *General Economic History* (New Brunswick, NJ: Transaction, 1981), pp. 275–78, 352–69; Weber, *Max Weber on Capitalism, Bureaucracy, and Religion,* ed. Stanislav Andreski (London: George Allen & Unwin, 1983), pp. 21–29.

6. Duane Champagne, "Culture, Differentiation, and Environment: Social Change in Tlingit Society," *Differentiation Theory and Social Change: Comparative and Historical Perspectives,* ed. Jeffrey C. Alexander and Paul Colomy (New York: Columbia University Press, 1990), pp. 77–84.

7. See Frank Speck, *The Iroquois: A Study in Cultural Evolution,* Cranbook Institute of Science Bulletin no. 23, 1945, p. 33; Hope Isaacs, "Orenda and the Concept of Power among the Tonawanda Seneca," in *The Anthropology of Power,* ed. Raymond Fogelson and Richard Adams (New York: Academic, 1977), pp. 168–82; Raymond Fogelson, "Cherokee Notions of Power," in *The Anthropology of Power,* ed. Raymond Fogelson and Richard Adams (New York: Academic, 1977), pp. 186–88; James Adair, *History of the North American Indians,* ed. Samuel Williams (Johnson City, TN: Watauga, 1930), pp. 7, 406, 465; Emile Durkheim, *The Elementary Forms of the Religious Life* (New York: Free Press, 1965), p. 222, chaps. 6–7; Theda Perdue, *Slavery and the Evolution of Cherokee Society, 1540–1866* (Knoxville: University of Tennessee Press, 1979), pp. 13–15.

8. On the theory of differentiation, see S.N. Eisenstadt, "Social Change, Differentiation, and Evolution," *American Sociological Review* 29 (1964): 375–86; Talcott Parsons, *Societies* (Englewood Cliffs, NJ: Prentice-Hall, 1966); Duane Champagne, *Social Order and Political Change: Constitutional Governments among the Cherokee, Choctaw, Chickasaw, and Creek* (Stanford, CA: Stanford University Press, 1992), chaps. 1–3.

9. Jean Chaudhuri and Joyotpaul Chaudurı, *A Sacred Path: The Way of the Muscogee Creeks* (Los Angeles: UCLA American Indian Studies Center, 2001), pp. 5–14, 95–115.

10. Duane Champagne, "Renewing American Indian Nations: Cosmic Communities and Spiritual Autonomy" in *Diversity and Community: A Critical Reader,* ed. Philip Alperson (Oxford: Blackwell, 2003), pp. 167–81.

11. Duane Champagne, "The Cultural and Institutional Foundations of Native American Conservatism," special issue on North American Indians: Cultures in Motion, ed. Elvira Stefania Tiberini, *L'Uomo: Societa, tradizione, sviluppo* 8, no. 1 (1995): 17–43.

12. William Steele, *The Cherokee Crown of Tanassy* (Winston Salem, NC: Blair, 1977), p. xii; James Adair, *Adair's History of the American Indians,* ed. Samuel Williams (Johnson City, TN: Watauga, 1930), p. 456; C. A. Weslager, *The Delaware Indians* (New Brunswick, NJ: Rutgers University Press, 1972), p. 216; Werner Crane, *The Southern Frontier, 1670–1732* (Philadelphia: University of Pennsylvania Press, 1929), p. 177; George Hunt, *The Wars of the Iroquois: A Study in Intertribal Relations* (Madison: University of Wisconsin Press, 1940), p. 19; Rennard Strickland, "Christian Gotelieb Priber: Utopian Precursor of the Cherokee Government," *Chronicles of Oklahoma* 48 (1970), p. 270.

13. Max Weber, *The Protestant Ethic and the Spirit of Capitalism* (New York: Scribner's, 1958), pp. 59–60; E. E. Rich, "Trade Habits and Economic Motivation among the Indians of North America," *Canadian Journal of Economics and Political Science* 26 (1960), p. 53; Arthur Ray, *Indians and the Fur Trade* (Toronto: University of Toronto Press, 1974), p. 68; Adair, *Adair's History,* pp. 394–96, 444; Thomas Norton, *The Fur Trade in Colonial New York, 1686–1776* (Madison: University of Wisconsin Press, 1974 ), p. 70; Roul Narrall, "The Causes of the Fourth Iroquois War," *Ethnohistory* 16 (1969), pp. 58–59.

14. Paul Phillips, *The Fur Trade* (Norman: University of Oklahoma Press, 1961), 2: p. 524; Sherman Uhler, *Pennsylvania Indian Relations to 1754* (Allentown, PA: Donecker, 1951), p. 61.

15. Dean Howard Smith, *Modern Tribal Development: Paths to Self-Sufficiency and Cultural Integrity in Indian Country* (Walnut Creek, CA: AltaMira, 2000), pp. 80–82; Phillips, *Fur Trade,* 2:524; Uhler, *Indian Relations,* p. 61.

16. Champagne, *Social Order,* pp. 90–91; see notes 4–8.

17. Champagne, *Social Order,* pp. 90–91.

18. Champagne, *Social Order,* pp. 208–40.

19. Many Native communities have attempted to cope with changing economies and markets set upon them in reservations and urban areas. Some of these pathways of innovative

community and individual economic changes are presented in this volume. In this chapter, I am concerned primarily with the Native forms of capitalism, a term I am using in the Western sense. Capitalist entrepreneurship must be distinguished from more general forms of economic entrepreneurship or even non-Western or Native forms of economic organization. I believe it is crucial to understand the patterns and processes of capitalist entrepreneurship and change in Native communities, and so I am focusing on these issues.

The evidence for Native-owned businesses between 1900 and 1950 is very thin. The U.S. government survey for minority-owned businesses was not developed until 1972. Here are some references that indicate the general dearth of Native business ownership during much of the twentieth century. The fifteenth census of the United States in 1930, *The Indian Population of the United States and Alaska* (Washington, D.C.: U.S. Government Printing Office, 1937), p. 202, indicates that in the 1910 census, 1,116 Natives were classified as proprietors or managers of nonfarm business. Also in 1910, 21,947 Natives were classified as owners or tenants of farming businesses. In the 1920 census, 643 Natives managed retail, wholesale, or other business establishments, while 22,181 Natives were engaged in farming businesses as owners or tenants. In 1930, 1,242 Natives managed nonfarm businesses, and 28,038 Natives were owners or tenants of farming businesses.

The trends into the 1940s and later show declining numbers of Natives engaged in farming and farm management. In 1940, 1.4 percent of the Native working population was engaged in nonfarm management or proprietorship. The percentage of working Native proprietors or managers increased to 2.8 percent in 1960, and 5.0 percent in 1970. Farmers and (farm) managers represented 46.7 percent of the Native workforce in 1940, but those figures declined to 9.5 percent in 1960 and 2.3 percent in 1970. See J. Milton Yinger and George Eaton Simpson, eds., "American Indians Today," *Annals of the American Academy of Political and Social Science*, March 1978, p. 3. See also Alan L. Sorkin, *American Indians and Federal Aid* (Washington, D.C.: Brookings Institution, 1971), pp. 18–19; *American Indian Policy Review Commission: Final Report* (U. S. Government Printing Office, 1977), 2: pp. 349–50; Robert Bennett, "Economic Development as a Means of Overcoming Indian Poverty," *Toward Economic Development for Native American Communities,* vol. 1, pt. 1, Congress of the United States, Joint Economic Committee, *Development Prospects and Problems* (Washington, D.C.: U.S. Government Printing Office, 1969), p. 108; "Forward: Economic Development in the American Indian Community; Role of the Small Business Administration," in *Toward Economic Development for Native American Communities,* vol. 1, pt. 1 of *Development Prospects and Problems* (Washington, D.C.: U.S. Government Printing Office, 1969), pp. 400–402; Lewis Meriam, ed., *The Problem of Indian Administration* (New York: Johnson, 1971), pp. 431, 469, 526, 652; Robert C. Cauthorn, "Programming for Entrepreneurship among American Indians," *Arizona Review,* May 1968, pp. 11–15.

20. Alice Littlefield, "Indian Education in and the World of Work in Michigan, 1893–1933," in *Native Americans and Wage Labor* (Norman: University of Oklahoma, 1996), pp. 100–120.

21. Smith, *Tribal Development*, pp. 135–44.

22. The National Center for American Indian Entrepreneurship, which is funded by the Small Business Administration as part of its minority program, has a website at http://government .about.com/gi/dynamic/offsite.htm?site=http percent3A percent2F percent2Fwww.ncaied.org percent2F.

23. www.census.gov/Press-Release/cb96-127.html

24. www.census.gov/Press-Release/cb96-127.html

25. www.census.gov/Press-Release/cb96-127.html

26. www.census.gov/csd/mwb/AIAN/sld

27. Joseph S. Anderson and Dean Howard Smith, "Managing Tribal Assets: Developing Long-Term Strategic Plans," *American Indian Culture and Research Journal,* Summer 1998, pp. 139–49.

28. The thirteen corporations created by the Alaska Native Claims Settlement Act of 1970 (ANCSA) may appear to be exceptions to this rule, but they follow a similar pattern. In Alaska, the Native communities, villages, and regional associations have long demanded that the corporations focus on more than economic profit and also emphasize protection of land, culture, and community. See Thomas R. Berger, *Village Journey: The Report of the Alaska Native Review Commission* (New York: Hill & Wang, 1985); and Duane Champagne, "Culture, Differentiation, and Environment: Social Change in Tlingit Society," *Differentiation Theory and Social Change: Comparative and Historical Perspectives,* ed. Jeffrey C. Alexander and Paul Colomy (New York: Columbia University Press, 1990), pp. 77–84.

29. Duane Champagne, "Socio-Cultural Responses to Coal Development: A Comparison of the Crow and Northern Cheyenne," in *Research in Capital and Development: Native American Economic Development,* ed. Carol Ward and Matthew Snipp (Greenwich, CT: JAI Press, 1996), 10: pp. 131–46.

30. Stephen Cornell and Joseph P. Kalt, "Sovereignty and Nation Building: The Development Challenge in Indian Country Today," *American Indian Culture and Research Journal,* Summer 1998, pp. 187–214.

31. Champagne, "Socio-Cultural Responses," pp. 131–46.

32. Smith, *Tribal Development,* pp. 71–90.

33. Peter Ferrera, *The Choctaw Revolution: Lessons for Federal Indian Policy* (Washington, D.C.: Americans for Tax Reform Foundation, 1998).

34. Angela Mullis and David Kamper, eds., *Indian Gaming: Who Wins?* (Los Angeles: UCLA American Indian Studies Center, 2000).

35. Mary Ann Andreas, "Perspective of Mary Ann Andreas, Morongo Tribal Chairperson," in *Indian Gaming: Who Wins?* ed. Angela Mullis and David Kamper (Los Angeles: UCLA American Indian Studies Center, 2000), pp. 166–68; Priscilla Hunter, "Perspective of Priscilla Hunter, Chairwoman, Coyote Band of Pomo Mission Indians," in *Indian Gaming: Who Wins?* ed. Angela Mullis and David Kamper (Los Angeles: UCLA American Indian Studies Center, 2000), pp. 169–71; Ernie L. Stevens Jr., "Perspective of Ernie L. Stevens Jr., Tribal Councilman, Oneida Nation," in *Indian Gaming: Who Wins?* ed. Angela Mullis and David Kamper (Los Angeles: UCLA American Indian Studies Center, 2000), pp. 172–75.

36. See Castle Mclaughlin and Tracy J. Andrews, "Introduction," *American Indian Culture and Research Journal,* Summer 1998, pp. 1–12; Tracy J. Andrews and Castle McLaughlin, eds., special issue on Farming and Ranching in Reservation Economies, *American Indian Culture and Research Journal,* Summer 1998, pp. 13–138.

37. Ronald Trosper, "Mind Sets and Economic Development on Indian Reservations," in *What Can Tribes Do? Strategies and Institutions in American Indian Economic Development,* ed. Stephen Cornell and Joseph P. Kalt (Los Angeles: UCLA American Indian Studies Center, 1992), pp. 303–33.

38. Kathleen Pickering and David Mushinski, "Making the Case for Culture in Economic Development: A Cross-Section Analysis of Western Tribes," *American Indian Culture and Research Journal,* Winter 2001, pp. 46, 58–59.

# Renewing Tribal Governments: Uniting Political Theory and Sacred Communities

## 4

COLONIZERS OFTEN INTRODUCED POLITICAL CHANGE into Indian country that reflected their own political interests and understandings. The Spanish appointed captains and caciques, while the British introduced or acknowledged kings and emperors in an effort to centralize Native political relations. The early New England settlers gave the name and the title of King Philip to the Wampanoag leader. Similarly in the southeast the British recognized emperors among the Cherokee, Choctaw, and Creek, and a king among the Chickasaw. Often colonial officials understood that the Native political institutions and relations did not correspond directly to European political models, but they had few other examples to apply at the time.

Some European observers, however, discerned contrasting political and social relations among the Native nations in the newly discovered Americas. For example, many Native communities were not centralized politically or socially, and each individual had considerable freedom to express his views. The observation that Native peoples often had considerable individual freedom, in contrast to the lower classes of Europe, influenced the philosophy of natural rights and became models for how to construct community-based polities. Early portrayals of Native political relations as egalitarian and negotiated, again not necessarily accurate, were used as critiques of European social and political relations, and they heavily influenced the French philosophes such as Rousseau and Voltaire. Undoubtedly their ideas helped frame the French Revolution and contributed to the discussion of contemporary democracy.[1]

The contemporary tradition of tribal constitutional governments, however, only indirectly derives from the ideas that led to Western democracies. While Native cultures may have influenced the debates and movements of democracy and constitutionalism in the West, Native peoples and governments have not been major players in the construction of Western forms of democracy. Instead the constitutional movement in Indian country, by and large, was introduced by the U.S. government through its agents and policies and, in some cases, by missionaries.

Soon after the U.S. constitution was ratified, U.S. policymakers began an active plan of civilizing the American Indians. Already in 1790 during the first Congress, funds were allocated to promote farming and American living patterns among the Indians. As missionaries were among the first government agents to promote civilization in Indian country, Christian religion and associated forms of social-political organization were also promoted among the Indians. Many Protestant missionaries promoted wholesale adoption of the Protestant worldview, including Protestant-U.S. forms of social and political organization.[2] Government agents in treaties and day-to-day policies increasingly advocated change in Native life, abolishing blood revenge and adopting U.S. political and social forms. The Cherokee gradually adopted a constitutional government between 1810 and 1828. During the rest of the 1800s, the Choctaw, Cherokee, Chickasaw, Creek, and Seminole, all removed to Indian Territory, adopted constitutional governments under the guidance and encouragement of U.S. agents and policies. Many remnant Native communities in New England adopted Protestant teachings and formed into town hall political communities often lead by Native ministers.

As power relations between Indian nations and the United States turned in favor of the Americans, U.S. policy increasingly sought to extend civilization, education, agriculture, and constitutional institutions to Indian nations. American policy adopted the stance of radical reconstruction of Native peoples. As the tribes were isolated onto reservations, Indian people were slated for assimilated into U.S. society. The plans for change within Native communities usually were administered without consent or general discussion with Native leaders and community members. While many Native people adopted Christianity and embraced the new forms of social and political organization, others resisted U.S. assimilation policies and managed to retain many cultural and political aspects of their community practices.

The most direct introduction of U.S. government forms came from the assimilationist policies pursued between 1880 and 1934 and followed the introduction of representative forms of government made available by the Indian Reorganization Act of 1934 (IRA). Many reservation communities were asked to adopt IRA constitutions, which were often introduced in boilerplate fashion by Indian service officials. Many tribes who did not adopt the IRA constitutions were convinced by government officials to adopt constitutional governments or bylaws. By the 1940s most reservation communities were governed by a constitutional form of government of one kind or another.[3]

Even though most reservation communities adopted constitutional governments, there was much controversy. Some communities (e.g., Iroquois and Pueblo communities) rejected the IRA constitutions because the new governments were radically different from their own political arrangements. Some IRA governments were adopted under controversial actions, as among the Hopi, as conservative and traditionally oriented villages and segments of the Hopi community vigorously challenged the new government.[4] Lakota communities such as Pine Ridge and some Iroquois communities had sustained discussions about the forms of government and the legitimate rights of constitutional governments. Many other communities sustained similar debates but less controversy, while a few communities are said to have benefited significantly from the centralization brought on by an IRA government.[5]

The struggle within Native communities over the appropriateness of U.S. constitutionalism or Native forms of political community is not the only issue facing contemporary tribal governments. Tribal governments since the middle 1960s have gained increasing control over program resources and land, and have sought to extend tribal sovereignty and self-government. With the U.S. and global economy becoming increasingly competitive and widespread, many tribal communities are pursuing economic development through market-driven economic activities. The increasingly competitive marketplace and the struggle of tribes to assert greater degrees of political sovereignty and self-government have led many tribal leaders and communities to doubt the soundness of their constitutional governments. These doubts arise from their long-standing incompatibility with tribal cultures and political relations, and many question whether the governments are capable of serving the long-term economic and political interests of the tribal community. Can present-day tribal governments effectively manage political and bureaucratic competition with the U.S. government, states, and counties? Are tribal governments able to provide an infrastructure that will enable tribal communities to participate in the market economy and provide an economic base for sustaining tribal goals of cultural and political autonomy?

Many tribes are looking for constitutional and political change that will enhance cultural compatibility as well as economic and political viability. The widespread community dissatisfaction with tribal governments is likely to continue and thereby induce many communities to revise their political and constitutional arrangements.[6] These efforts will be conducted under the supervision and authority of the Department of Interior. The old tribal constitutions need serious revision, and the future well-being of the reservations will depend on how successfully tribal communities craft new constitutional relations that not only incorporate tribal culture and social relations, but also establish leadership and political institutions that promote cultural preservation, economic viability, and political sovereignty. The future of tribal communities is at stake. Without constructing more culturally compatible and energetic tribal governments, Native communities may be relegated to long-term economic and political marginalization that will threaten tribal cultural survival.

## Constitution Building

In some ways, the situation in Indian country is analogous to the crisis related to the U.S. Articles of Confederation during the 1780s. The colonies were experiencing political disunity and were unable to wield international and sustained military power, and the Continental Congress was unable to command consistent resources and commitment from the individual colonies. There were international diplomatic crises, international trade and domestic economic crises, and the absence of national political authority and power to manage the international and domestic situation.[7] A convention was called to revise the Articles of Confederation, but the members of the convention decided to write an entirely new constitution. The Founding Fathers used the Constitution to solve several significant issues: how to concentrate power in order that the government be effective in international diplomacy and treaty making, how to create the institutional framework for the organization and facilitation of a domestic national economy, how to delegate power to the center but with the consent and participation of the states, and how to prevent the center from arbitrary exercise of political power. Through discussions and compromise during the constitutional convention, the Founders arrived at several solutions to the disintegrating Articles of Confederation. Within the framework of the U.S. constitution, a national market was given national support; the executive was given considerable power but was checked by the legislature, judiciary, and electorate; the nationally unified administration of international and Indian affairs was established; and a direct relation was created between the new federal government and the individual.

The Founding Fathers did not believe they had proposed the perfect government. Many were displeased with the arrangement but signed on largely because they believed it was the best arrangement that could be had at the time.[8] A unified national community, however, did not support the Constitution; rather, the body politic was composed of a coalition of autonomous and self-interested states and localities. The Founders were troubled by the absence of a unified national commitment to the federal government; in the 1780s political allegiances and identities were more strongly tied to states and localities than they were to the national government. The Founding Fathers feared that regional and economic interests would threaten the unity of the United States and result in conflict.[9] These fears were ultimately realized in the conflicts that lead to the Civil War. After the Civil War, the North imposed its values and political culture over the South and the United States made significant strides toward a national community in which citizens' allegiance is stronger to the federal government than to states and localities. The federal government was recognized as the paramount government in the United States. The Seventeenth Amendment (1870) gave individuals the right to elect senators, further weakening the state governments in favor of the federal government. Thereafter, senators were no longer elected by state legislatures.

The Founding Fathers rejected a religious confederacy as an enduring form of government. James Madison argued that throughout history religious-political confederacies proved unstable and were prone to breakup and factionalism.[10] This observation was appropriate for the time, since in the late 1700s market systems were becoming increasingly global. Throughout history many religious-normative confederacies and many tribal groups had endured and prospered under less competitive political and economic environments. In the 1780s, however, intensifying world international economic and political competition ensured that the colonies could not endure under the Articles of Confederation. The Founding Fathers suggested that the colonies needed to concentrate resources and political power in order to accommodate both international and domestic market interests, as well as international diplomatic and military competition, all of which required centralized authority and power to take appropriate actions.[11] At the same time, the centralized authority must not degenerate into absolutist power. The U.S. constitution's checks and balances on concentrated central powers of Congress, the judiciary, and the executive were part of the proposal to solve the problems of government capable of vigorous action but constrained to avoid tyranny.[12] The Founding Fathers rejected a religious confederacy because they believed that religious and normative allegiances would not withstand the processes of division created by market competition, unequal distribution of wealth, and international political competition. In this sense the Founding Fathers rejected the normative-religious frameworks through which most Indian governments and confederacies were organized.

Many of the Founding Fathers feared that international competition from rival state powers would form alliances with states and turn their allegiance away from the Union. The Founding Fathers feared that the U.S. Confederacy was unstable and that international diplomacy and intrigue would stimulate segments of the Union to defect and seek economic and political alliances with foreign powers. Hence their argument for a relatively strong federal government with the concentration of military and political power greater than the individual states. One reason that the Founding Fathers rejected the confederate form of government was this tendency for defection when states or regional segments became dissatisfied with the rule of the majority of the confederacy. The Founding Fathers developed their views based on the military and diplomatic intrigue of European history for the most part and to some extent drawing on world history.[13]

It is difficult not to argue that the rules of many Indian confederacies and sociopolitical relations conformed to the view that socioreligious and political confederacies were unstable during periods of intense economic, military, and political competition, which characterized European history after the fall of the Roman Empire. Often in Indian political relations, local groups such as villages, lineages, clans, or bands had considerable autonomy over economic and political decisions. If one group went to war against an enemy, the entire community was not obligated to give support. Many raids and counterraids were based on revenge motives organized through kinship or clan relations and obligations. In the villages of Creek Confederacy, a group might argue for war in a particular case, but if unanimity was not achieved, those who chose to fight did so and those who wished to remain at home were free to do so.[14] Similarly in the Iroquois Confederacy, if a village or nation was attacked, the other members of the confederacy were not obligated to go to their defense. Families and villages determined questions of alliance to the French, British, or Americans during times of diplomatic negotiation or war. Only when unanimity could be obtained did the Iroquois act as an entirely unified diplomatic or military force. During the turmoil of the American Revolutionary War, the Iroquois were divided among neutrality or alliance with the British or Americans. Since there was no consensus, villages, families, and nations chose their own paths in the war and Iroquois fought on both sides.[15] In many ways the military and diplomatic choices of the Iroquois nations, clans, and villages illustrate the argument made by the Founding Fathers concerning the political instability of confederate political unions during times of intense political and diplomatic competition.

This is not to say the tribal confederacies were inherently unstable. Tribal confederate forms served Native nations for many thousands of years and were very compatible with their spiritual interpretation of the universe as composed of numerous autonomous powers within a unified cosmic purpose. Nations, clans, villages, families, and individuals formed autonomous groupings within a worldview that honored them as independent forces and powers, not only within the political arena but also within the spiritual and cosmic arena. The local autonomy of tribal social-political groups is ordained within the cosmic understanding of most Native spiritual beliefs and serves to uphold the spiritual powers and rights of autonomy of individuals, villages, families, clans, or nations. The exact relations and spiritual hierarchies between autonomous groups within a tribe is often determined by tribal creation beliefs, and so each tribe has unique arrangements of spiritually integrated sociopolitical organization. Nevertheless, through most of the history of Native confederacies, such organizations served the Native people well and conformed to their worldviews. They thrived during the precontact period of economic exchange and relatively small-scale military and diplomatic intrigue and power relations.

European colonialism brought to North America the economic, diplomatic, and military competition that characterized the militarily competitive states of Europe. In many ways, the early colonial experience of North America is unique because of the multiple rivalries and competition of the early European colonies such as New France, the British colonies, and Spanish colonies, as well as the Dutch and Swedish colonies. Major economic and political competitions emerged among the rival colonies that were only settled sometime after the emergence of the United States. No similar competitive situations are found in Central and South America or New Zealand and Australia. There is only one treaty recognized in New Zealand, while the indigenous peoples in most of the rest of the world do not have treaties with their colonial governments and, until recently, had less claim to territory and self-government than most tribes in the United States and Canada. When such competitions emerged among the political relations of the colonists and Native nations, many tribes established trade, political, and military alliances with one or more of the colonial powers.[16] Throughout the period of colonial economic, diplomatic, and military competition Native tribes made treaties of friendship, as well as diplomatic, trade, and military agreements with the colonial powers. Since the tribes were an economic and military force in the region, colonial officials courted the tribes who used their leverage to gain economic, diplomatic, and military concessions from the colonial powers. During the period of colonial competition, many Native confederacies held their political interests and territories but had to adapt to the new conditions. During this period there was little pressure to revise Native forms of political organizations, although colonial officials often tried to centralize Native confederacies by appointing a chief or an emperor in order to conduct diplomatic relations with a few leaders rather than the leaders of numerous decentralized villages or kinship groups.

While the Native confederacies and related forms of sociopolitical organ-ization had endured from time immemorial before the colonial period, the Europeans brought with them new forms of military, economic, and diplo-matic competition. The colonials introduced trade that was tied to distant markets in Europe. Many eastern tribes began to produce furs and skins for the European markets and quickly became dependent on European manufac-tured goods, especially traps, guns, ammunition, and metal tools. By the mid-dle 1700s many tribal groups were tied to market relations with the Europeans for critical goods. The economic dependency was exacerbated by increased military competition. The period from 1640 to 1815 was characterized by nearly constant warfare. There were many European-declared wars, and even when wars were not openly declared, diplomatic, trade, and backcountry conflicts were constant. The Europeans introduced an intensified economic, diplomatic, and military environment than was the custom for the long-standing Native confederacies. The wars were larger and involved more men, heavier equipment, and greater casualties. Indians moved from relatively au-tonomous subsistence economies to regular trade and market relations with the Europeans. The Native confederacies and governments had never experi-enced such intense market, diplomatic, and military competition.

How well did the Native confederate organization fare during the colonial period? The Native confederacies behaved generally as the Founding Fathers expected. The Native confederacies and governments resisted colonial en-croachments but were ultimately not successful in their economic and politi-cal struggles with the colonies and the United States. The tribal confederacies and governments could not muster resources from subgroups for long periods of time. Native warriors often contributed to military efforts for a limited time and had to return to their families for the hunting and harvest seasons. Neither the confederacies of resistance led by Tecumseh, Pontiac, or the Iroquois could field standing armies, as could the United States and the colonial governments. The absence of centralized power, the inability to command resources from lo-cal groups for the military and diplomatic actions as well as subsistence eco-nomic production did not enable the Native governments and confederacies to compete in the long run against the colonial powers, and ultimately against the concentrated state and economic power of the United States. The Found-ing Fathers gave up on the Articles of Confederation because it was not capa-ble of managing government in a world that had become increasingly competitive both diplomatically and militarily and richer through the spread of market relations. The early U.S. Confederacy failed to effectively support do-mestic national market relations and international trade relations and agree-ments, and could not command enough internal economic and trade resources to carry on national government and international diplomatic relations. The U.S. constitution regulates interstate and foreign trade relations and sets the regulations for a common national market. Without these federal regulations, the Articles of Confederation states created their own currencies and tariffs and often inhibited trade across state borders. The U.S. constitution sought to regulate chaotic trade relations among the colonies.[17]

During the colonial period before the U.S. constitution, the Native nations did not adopt new constitutional forms. Few Native nations moved to centralize and reorganize their governments to the extent of creating constitutional governments. Before the U.S. constitution there were few models of constitutional government available to the tribes, who were not familiar with European political models and for the most part not interested in adopting European or U.S. political models over their own political forms, which had the sanction of religion and history.

After the end of the War of 1812, the United States increasingly extended its power over Indian tribes. The United States dominated trade and political relations and actively worked to reform and reorganize tribal economies, culture, and political relations. The Americans suggested to many tribes that they take on a U.S. constitutional form of government. Missionaries, Indian agents, treaty commissioners, and Indian service agents introduced the U.S. model of government to most tribes. Most tribes were reluctant to accept American political models. The so-called Five Civilized tribes—the Choctaw, Chickasaw, Creek, Cherokee, and Seminole—adopted constitutional governments during the 1800s, although even these governments retained many aspects of tribal regional and village organization, especially in the Creek and Seminole governments. In the latter two, traditionally autonomous villages remained the primarily local political groups and were incorporated into the central constitutional government as political districts. While the Five Civilized tribes enjoyed a measure of success with their new governments, they were dismantled by 1907. Although most other tribes were reluctant to assume American political constitutional forms, Indian Service agents nevertheless introduced limited forms of representative government through business committees, bylaws, or constitutions. The Indian Reorganization Act (IRA) in 1934 was the most deliberate attempt by the U.S. government to introduce quasi-U.S. constitutional style governments into Indian country.

Despite the attempts at reform by the U.S. government, most Native communities remain organized by confederate and traditional forms of sociopolitical organization. In most cases, IRA constitutions, bylaws, and business committees ignored traditional social and political organization of the tribe and introduced new electoral-representative political forms, but rarely (if

ever) a full model of the U.S. constitution. In fact the Indian Service origi-
nators of the IRA and related constitutions deliberately introduced specific
forms of constitutional government that they thought would be more compatible with Native culture and social organization.[18]

Most U.S.-introduced tribal constitutions do not separate business and
government relations; there are few separations of power between tribal
council, tribal chair, and the courts. In most cases there is only one legislative power, the tribal council, and often the executive, the tribal chair, has
little power, except to manage the meetings of the tribal council, and the
courts are often not politically insulated from the council's power. These
tribal constitutions often leave plenary power in the hands of the tribal council and do not provide checks and balances on the tribal council. Since the
council members are elected by political supporters, the actions of the tribal
councils often reflect the political interests of the tribal council's political
supporters. Consequently the tribal councils have the power to act in
unchecked ways while in office and tribal members have little recourse except to vote them out of office at the next election. Such situations contribute to political instability and inconsistent policies, and the theory
propounded by the Founding Fathers rejected as unstable and conflict ridden
the forms of government which the Indian Service introduced and promoted among the Native nations.[19] Since such government forms are considered unstable and ineffective even by U.S. political theory proposed at the
time of the writing of the U.S. constitution, there is little wonder that many
tribes have not been able to make their constitutional governments work effectively for their communities.

Most tribal communities retain the decentralized religious–normative confederate organization whether or not they have a tribal constitution. Most
tribal constitutions ignore the traditional and often spiritually ordained organization of villages, families, clans, or bands. The constitutional governments separate religion and political relations, even though Indian nations did
not. The tribal constitutional governments introduced by the United States
ignored tribal sociopolitical organization by bypassing the social and cultural
organization of the tribes and delegating power directly to individuals. Even
the U.S. constitution does not bypass the early U.S. Confederate organization
by ignoring the power and authority of state governments. Consequently, the
checks and balances that could be expressed through the autonomies of actual social and political power groupings within traditional tribal communities do not play significant roles in most contemporary tribal constitutions and
governments. The cost of ignoring the traditional social and political forms
of power within the community is the absence of a set of checks and balances

on the concentration of power at the center of contemporary tribal governments and the loss of commitment to the tribal government through traditional forms of social and cultural support. By ignoring the traditional
relations of power in the tribal communities, the tribal constitutional governments have the look of modernism and secularism, but often lack the social, political, and cultural support of consensus and shared goals necessary to
maintain and lead an engaged and mobilized political community.

The religious-social confederate character of tribal communities and the
structural shortcomings of contemporary tribal government constitutions
contribute to the need for renewal in tribal constitutional governments. Like
the Founding Fathers, tribal communities and governments find themselves in
a world of increasing political and economic competition with a decentralized confederate form of social organization and a central government that
appears not fully capable of protecting the interests of the community or actively pursuing its goals, values, and interests. The situation of contemporary
tribal governments suggests rethinking of tribal constitutions and their relations to tribal communities as well as their capabilities to manage and protect
tribal interests and achieve future aspirations. Dissatisfaction with tribal government is widespread throughout Indian country, and while some tribes are
actively reconsidering their constitutions and other organic documents,
movement is slow.[20] Often constitutional changes must be approved by the
secretary of Interior and reviewed by Bureau of Indian Affairs (BIA) officials.
Furthermore, as the U.S. Founding Fathers may have predicted, many communities are divided into those who have been educated in the American cultural and political views and are more accepting of the current constitutional
governments, while many reservation community members carry on their
lives according to tribal norms and values, while not entirely accepting or supporting the current tribal governments. Differing views over the form of government and the continuity of tribal forms of social, cultural, and political
organization amounts to the presence to two concurrent and often antagonistic social and political arrangements within the same community. The
struggles between the Iroquois Confederacy and constitutional governments
on many contemporary Iroquois reservations illustrates this point.[21] Similarly
the nonparticipation by the Hopi traditional villages or the conflicts between
the tribal government and local communities and *tiyospaye* among the Pine
Ridge Lakota illustrate the conflict between social and political systems on
many reservations.[22] Community groups and individuals are free to form alliances in these conflicts according to their own interests and values. The
struggle over basic rules of social and political organization often results in
factional cleavages where there is little common ground for stable consensus

among the opposing groups. The Founding Fathers feared open factions and considered them destructive to developing a stable and effective constitutional government.

The U.S. constitution was a response to a competitive economic and political environment and involved creating a government that could establish a domestic market economy, manage international trade and diplomatic relations, concentrate power to enable the government to respond directly to changing economic and political conditions, and at the same time protect the rights of states and individuals. Contemporary tribal governments face strong forces of political and market competition and most likely will need to establish reformed political institutions that will enable tribal communities to pursue and protect their cultural and political interests while protecting the rights of subgroups and individuals. This similarity of task for the tribal governments to the situation of the early U.S. republic reflects the continuing and intensifying trends of economic and political competition in recent history.

## Human Nature, Worldview, and Institutional Relations

When the Founding Fathers proposed the U.S. constitution, they made culturally specific assumptions about human nature, about the place and role of man in the universe, and the relation of political institutions to religion that were specific to European tradition and history. Following a predominantly Protestant Christian worldview, the Founding Fathers assumed that human nature was evil and people were inherently self-interested and would take any opportunity to seek advantage even if it meant destroying the rights of others. This view was based on Christian beliefs of original sin and a reading of political history in the West, especially Roman and British history. The Founding Fathers believed that absolute power corrupts absolutely, and therefore, checks and balances are necessary to curb the interests and actions of individuals, political groups, and states in order to keep any one faction from gaining control of the government and subordinating the rights of others.[23]

Native worldviews, however, avoid self-interested views of human nature. For many Native peoples, the universe is a sacred place and the powers and beings in the world are gifts from a powerful but unknowable creator or primary force of the universe. The Creator is a benevolent gift giver who through intermediary powers and spirits provides culture and knowledge to the people and informs them of the sacred rules and direction of the universe. In many Indian worldviews, people are one of many forces and powers in the universe. People are not considered privileged in creation over plants and animals. People play a role in a divine plan within the universe but that role is not considered the most important, as there are many forces of nature that are considered more powerful than people. Humans are not destined to dominate the world or even make it into a better place because it is a sacred gift. The Western Christian tradition suggests the world is an evil place filled with death, sin, and suffering. There is a radical dualism between heaven and the secular world. The task of Christians is to reconstruct the world and make it a better place, since the secular or mundane earth is not sacred. The world is undeveloped and needs transformation, and in recent theory the social and political institutions are constructions that are made by people and have no divine or religious foundation. Therefore the world is malleable, and so are social institutions, which can be constructed and reconstructed without divine interference. In Native worldviews, the world is a sacred gift and to disturb it through remaking the earth and reconstructing social and political relations is to disturb the divine order of the universe and incur this-worldly disaster from the powers that are disturbed by such action. People prosper when they live in balance and harmony with the powers of the universe, but suffer when relations with the powers or spirits of the universe are disrupted or treated with disrespect.[24]

The Founding Fathers' assumptions included belief in individual freewill and the right to pursue self-interest within the constitutional framework. There is considerable autonomy of individual action in many Native communities, but in contrast to the U.S. view, Native individualism takes place within the cosmic order of purpose and balanced powers. Individuals have a divine task to perform in their lives. For women, that task is the creation and guidance of the next generation, while men must seek their tasks through ceremony or visions. Today many Native women also seek visions to gain knowledge and understanding that will shed light on their life tasks or will be of benefit to the tribal community. Ideally each individual is respected as an autonomous force and purpose in the universe and part of the unknowable divine plan of the Creator. Consequently, individuals, including children, are often given considerable leeway in their lives since their actions are part of a sacred purpose revealed only to them. Each individual is seen as a sacred power with the right to speak in public and be heard by their community members. Similarly social and political groups are respected as autonomous cultural and political units because they are viewed as created within the divine sacred plan and having a specific role to play. The roles played by individuals, families, clans, bands, or nations are often spelled out in creation teachings and are unique to each tribal community. Nevertheless, autonomy is a powerful principle among the relations of tribal, social, and political groups. The autonomy of the social and political groupings reflects the world-view of a universe made up of powers of varying strength that play a role in the path of the entire universe. Efforts to subordinate tribal social and political groupings to central political authorities will run counter to most Native worldviews and will engender resistance if forced on them.

While Western culture assumes a radical duality between the sacred and the mundane, this is not emphasized in Native cultures. In terms of political relations this contrast is directly relevant when considering the relation of government and religion. In the U.S. constitution, religion and government are walled off into separate domains. In many Native cultures, however, social and political institutions are part of the cosmic order, and their structure and character are often determined within the creation teachings. Native social and political relations are part of the cosmic balance of the universe, and separating religious views and political order is an alien concept. Just as individuals and social groupings such as clans, villages, or bands are often ordained as part of the cosmic order, tribal political relations are also part of the cosmic order and are subject to the same rules of balance and retaliation as are the other forces of the universe. Withdrawing political relations from the cosmic order puts the whole community in jeopardy because the rules of balance and harmony are no longer observed and therefore threaten the community with disasters such as drought, disease, and other misfortunes. From this point of view, the adoption of secularized tribal political institutions violates tribal worldviews and may be viewed as a cause for their ineffectiveness and troubles that may have emerged within them.

## The U.S. Constitution as a Possible Model

By U.S. constitutional standards, tribal governments are not well organized, since they lack checks and balances on the use and concentration of power. Furthermore, the tribal governments generally have not concentrated political power to actively defend their interests against states, the federal government, and other U.S. political interests. Economic development is a major concern for tribal communities, where unemployment rates can range as high as 80 to 90 percent. Nevertheless, few tribal governments have established legal and governmental frameworks for promoting market-driven economic development on Indian reservations. Bureaucratic constraints and tutelage further curb the possibilities of change and action for tribal governments. Tribal governments are faced with the challenges of contemporary market and political competition, but few have the institutional arrangements to meet these challenges. The present tribal governments will likely need significant reorganization in order for the tribes to meet the challenges of the twenty-first century. Furthermore, the cultures and institutional arrangements of most tribal communities are not recognized within the tribal governments and often create a dualistic and antagonistic social and political arrangement within tribal communities. Most likely, tribal governments will not gain active support from tribal communities unless they are seen to advance the culture, goals, and interests of the tribal community. The issues confronting tribal governments are even more complex in some ways than those confronting the Founding Fathers, who assumed a similar and shared common culture among the thirteen original colonies. The understandings of human nature and relations between sociopolitical institutions and the universe do not allow a direct acceptance of the U.S. constitutional model for tribal communities.

Many of the solutions adopted by the Founding Fathers in the U.S. constitution may be useful for tribal communities to consider when constructing their constitutional forms. The U.S. constitution rejects the government of the Articles of Confederation because it lacked a central authority strong enough to manage a variety of domestic and international issues. The Articles of Confederation formed the early colonies into a loose coalition of independent states. This union is analogous to many tribal confederacies, although the member groups of the religious-social Indian confederations were not state governments, but rather kinship groups, families, clans, villages, bands, or regional coalitions of villages. The U.S. constitution preserves certain rights and autonomies of the state governments because they demanded such rights and were reluctant to delegate too much power to the federal government for fear of arbitrary use of power and the threat of takeover by a dictatorial faction or military general.[25]

Since the Founding Fathers did not have a national community in support of a central government, but rather were confronted with contending colonies, the Constitution is constructed with checks and balances designed to prevent abuses of power and hostile takeover of the government by one faction or another. Many powers of the state governments were preserved in part as a check on power in the central federal government. The plan of separating legislative, judicial, and executive branches is a main source of the checks on abuse of power, but a bicameral legislature, election of senators through state legislatures, and election of representatives through popular vote were modes of preventing any one source of power from becoming dominant and also of preserving the relative powers of the states.[26]

To a large extent, tribal government institutions do not have checks and balances and do not prevent arbitrary use or abuse of power in ways that are possible within the U.S. government. Tribal governments could be made more stable with bicameral legislatures, which are almost unknown in Indian country. Secure checks between legislative, judicial, and executive branches are also almost unknown and could improve the operation and stability of tribal governments. If checks and balances are in place, then greater concentration of power in the executive, instead of the tribal council, would allow tribes to act more decisively.

The U.S. constitution divides sovereignty among federal, state, and local governments. The states have power over limited aspects of the government, while the federal government concentrates on encouraging a domestic national market, international trade and diplomacy, national defense, and national issues not delegated to states or local governments. Tribal governments or tribal councils tend to hold sovereign power in plenary fashion, which inhibits checks and runs the risk of inefficient use of political power. The states that formed the Articles of Confederation continue to have strong powers assigned to them and their powers in many areas are preserved under the Constitution.

The autonomous sociocultural subgroups of most tribal communities are not recognized in their tribal constitutions or organic documents. This in part is owing to the models of government introduced by Indian Service agents who were consciously working to abolish tribal government structures and socio-cultural organization. Most tribal governments rule directly over individual tribal members usually organized into districts that sometimes roughly correspond to tribal social groupings. Ignoring tribal sociocultural groupings does not enable the tribal government to mobilize support or utilize tribal sociocultural resources and symbols for creating a mobilized and unified political community within the tribal government. Many tribal members continue to adhere to tribal sociopolitical structures on a day-to-day basis and work with the tribal government only to the extent that it concerns their interests or interferes with their lives or social groupings. The dual character of sociopolitical relations between tribal sociopolitical groups and the government creates antagonistic relations and little support and participation among the people. Consequently tribal governments may become more effective if they follow the example of the U.S. constitution by incorporating their preconstitutional confederate organization into a revised constitution. The families, clans, villages, bands, or village coalitions, or whatever arrangement characterizes the sociopolitical power relations of the tribe, will work to mobilize political and cultural resources from the people and serve as a balance on the central tribal government in ways that are analogous to the state governments under the U.S. constitution.

Despite the prevalence of tribal constitutional governments in Indian country, most tribal communities remain organized through coalitions of relatively autonomous subgroups. The particulars of these relations vary considerably in terms of social, political, and cultural organization, and any reconstruction based on such relations must look into the specific and often unique features of each tribal community. Nevertheless, the general pattern consists of confederacy or loose coalitions of autonomous subgroups, which often still preserve considerable social autonomy despite the absence of formal recognition within the tribal government constitutions or bylaws. As the Founding Fathers argued, confederacies, and even the religious-normative confederacies of Native nations, are not capable of managing the competitive political and economic relations that have predominated over the past several centuries. The Founding Fathers would argue that the political decline and economic marginalization of Indian nations over the past centuries is due in no small part to inability of confederate-style governments to manage internal resources, market relations, and cohesive internal and international political relations.

Consequently confederated tribal governments will not entirely meet the contemporary demands of tribal communities. The U.S. constitution solves this problem with its the concentration of partial sovereignty and power in the central federal government, but at the same time preserving significant powers of state governments. The U.S. constitution creates a direct relationship between the federal government and individual citizens not mediated by the states. This creates the possibility of national allegiances in areas where the federal government has preeminent powers delegated from the states. This arrangement between federal government and individual bypasses the confederate organization on specific issues within the shared sovereignty of the U.S. constitution. The ultimate formation of a national identity and loyalties is more possible within the U.S. constitution than within confederated organization where loyalties can remain local and regional.[27]

In contemporary tribal governments, in most cases, relations between the government and individuals are direct, but without shared sovereignty or jurisdiction with the local confederate tribal social groupings. Most contemporary tribal governments avoid the autonomies of confederated organization, unlike the U.S. constitution, and present a direct relation between individual and tribal government. The principles of the U.S. constitution suggest that if tribal governments that preserve their ancient confederated subgroups and rights within a constitutional framework, such a constitutional form will have more checks on concentrated power and greater support and participation from the tribal community.

Several suggestions for constitution building can be learned from the U.S. example and may prove useful for creating stronger tribal governments throughout Indian country. Well-defined concentrations of power should be delegated to the tribal government in order that it may effectively manage contemporary political and economic issues. The concentration of power at the center needs to be balanced by the separation of powers, many of which are not currently part of tribal constitutions. Not only should there be separation of executive, legislative, and judicial powers, but also bicameral legislatures and the recognition of tribal confederated forms of social and political power within a constitutional government. The recognition and union of tribal confederate organization, discouraged by Indian Service officials but not forgotten in most tribal communities, will create checks on the necessary concentrations of power and will help mobilize community action and support for the tribal government and its work on behalf of the tribal community. The incorporation of tribal confederate organization within a tribal constitution will go far to solve the issues of cultural disjuncture between tribal social-cultural organization and the tribal government. The formation of such a tribal constitution will help develop consensual and enduring institutional relations in support of the central tribal government.

## Some Examples of Constitution Building in Tribal Communities

While most contemporary tribal governments have not adopted a full constitutional organization similar to the U.S. constitution, there are several very interesting Native constitutional examples from the nineteenth century. The Cherokee, Choctaw, Chickasaw, Creek, and, to a lesser extent, the Seminole adopted constitutional governments that were close adaptations to the principles of the U.S. constitution, but at the same time retained very significant aspects of tribal political culture and organization. These examples should be analyzed and compared to extend our knowledge about the possible ways in which contemporary tribal constitutions might be modified to further benefit and preserve tribal communities. While there are many different forms of tribal governments and some of them have operated with considerable success, two twentieth-century tribal governments, the Tlingit and Navajo, present contrasts with the so-called Five Civilized Tribes and give some indication of the issues and possible solutions confronting tribal governments in the twenty-first century.

The process of adopting an active and culturally appropriate constitutional government is not simple. Native tribal governments have had their confederate

forms of government from time immemorial and in many cases, such as the Iroquois Confederacy, the form and constitution of the government is given
through sacred teachings. Communities who believe their social and political institutions are divine gifts and part of the sacred order of the universe are going
to be very reluctant to change their form of government.[28] Native nations and
governments have been under great political and cultural pressure to change. Located in the U.S. arena of cultural and political hegemony, the tribes have few
options but to take on U.S.-influenced forms of political organization. U.S. policy in Indian country has strongly supported tribal adoption of U.S. social and
political institutions. Early Indian agents actively advised and encouraged tribal
communities to adopt U.S. political forms. The extent to which tribes accepted
U.S. political institutions varied considerably, but few Native nations wholly accepted U.S. political forms during the nineteenth century and most of the twentieth century.

While many tribes were encouraged to adopt U.S. political forms, few
were willing to do so. The mere introduction of a U.S. constitutional model
into a tribal community is not enough to ensure its acceptance. Under strong
encouragement by U.S. Indian agents, some Delaware leaders adopted a constitutional government in 1867, but it lapsed into disuse because it was alien
to most Delaware people, and the community refused to participate.[29]
Through the 1880s until the 1930s, the Indian Service actively discouraged
exercise of tribal forms of government in favor of business committees or various constitutional forms. The introduction of IRA constitutional governments during the 1930s often resulted in lukewarm participation in both the
adoption of such governments and their subsequent administration. Many
tribal communities found the constitutional IRA and non–IRA constitutional
governments alien and ignored them.[30] Participation in elections for adopting
the constitutions and for elections of officers was in many tribal communities
very spare until the 1960s, when Great Society programs and federal agencies
began to allocate significant resources to tribal governments. Tribal governments now controlled significant resources and pushed programs of economic
development. The recent success of gaming tribes compounds the issue of
constitutional crisis, since most tribal governments were not designed to manage large resources and manage market relations.

The nineteenth-century Cherokee, Choctaw, Chickasaw, and Creek are
major exceptions to this generalization that tribal governments have not easily taken to adopting the principles of the U.S. constitution. These tribes accepted constitutional governments that incorporated the principles of the
U.S. constitution in deeper ways than any tribal government in the twentieth
century. One reason the four major southern tribes formed constitutional

governments was to protect themselves from the increasing bureaucratic pressures and land expansion of the United States. Without the threat of U.S. political, economic, and land expansion, the Cherokee, Choctaw, Chickasaw, and Creek would not have adopted constitutional governments. Nevertheless, most tribal communities were subject to similar pressures from the United States and did not form constitutional governments in the same way or as early. All four southern nations were strongly tied to their traditions and in that way are similar to most contemporary tribal communities.

There are two central differences between the contemporary situation of tribal governments and the nineteenth century of the Cherokee, Choctaw, Chickasaw, and Creek. First, the United States had yet to extend administrative control over tribal communities, and therefore the four southern tribes had freedom to exercise their own political interests and work toward preserving their sovereignty. Second, there was strong cotton production for markets throughout the region of the southern tribes. The children of intermarried traders moved from trading into cotton production and formed a small agrarian capitalist class. The mixed-blood capitalists often pushed for change and ensured that the new constitutional governments protected their market and accumulative interests. The southern Indian constitutions were adopted in situations of strong market relations, and the constitutions preserved and protected the market and business interests of the small agrarian entrepreneurs. While U.S. policy and agents favored the political change and market orientations of the Indian planters, the constitutional governments of the Cherokee, Choctaw, and Chickasaw gained considerable support within their respective communities, although not without some discussion and conflict, while the Creek constitutional government remained controversial for many years. Nevertheless, strong community support and commitment to the new constitutional governments was very important for their effectiveness and stability. One reason that these nineteenth-century tribal constitutions ultimately gained strong community support was that the new governments were seen as instruments for protection of tribal nationality and land against U.S. policy and land pressures. The mobilized community support for the Cherokee, Choctaw, and Chickasaw constitutional governments stands in marked contrast to the general indifference and dissatisfaction many communities have with their contemporary tribal governments.

The so-called Five Civilized tribes established different forms of relations between community and constitutional government. The relations between community organization and political relations help us understand the different ways in which the southern tribal communities adopted constitutional governments. The Cherokee formed their constitutional government between

1808 and 1828, with relatively little conflict and with broad community support. The Choctaw, Creek, Chickasaw, and Seminole formed their constitutional governments about thirty years later and with more conflict than the Cherokee.[31]

Both the Cherokee constitution of 1828 and 1840 and the Chickasaw constitution of 1855 took on most of the principles of the U.S. constitution. Both were governments designed to protect national interests against U.S. policies and land expansion; both promoted market and business enterprise while formally separating business and government spheres. Both constitutions upheld clear separation of powers with bicameral legislatures, a chief executive officer, and relatively independent judiciary. Both the Cherokee and Chickasaw handled confederate organization in a way that did not directly incorporate the old confederate subgroups directly into the new constitutional government.[32]

The Cherokee were traditionally organized into between fifty and sixty villages and the villages allied into regional groupings, such as Overhill towns, valley towns, middle towns, out towns, and lower towns. Between 1760 and 1795 many of these villages were disrupted during wars and continuing conflict with settlers on the frontier. In 1819, the Cherokee formed political and judicial districts and the former Cherokee national council of villages representatives no longer formed the legislature of the nation. District representatives were elected and formed the lower house, while a group of appointed individuals formed a national committee that ultimately became the upper legislative house. The villages and traditional regional village coalitions were not recognized in the Cherokee constitution. Districts or geographical regions, where most likely many village communities and former village coalitions still functioned on a daily basis, became the organizational units of the Cherokee constitutions, something akin to U.S. states but with few powers allocated to the districts within the Cherokee constitution. The decision to remove the villages from the national government had much to do with their autonomy and right to sell land. The national government wanted to prevent local villages from ceding land and wanted to vest that right in the central government. In this way, the Cherokee strengthened their ability to resist U.S. land demands and treaty enticements.

Most Cherokee were traditional people who were strongly attached to their religion, land, and social and cultural institutions. Many of these traditions lived on and were politically active through political parties. The Ross Party or National Party, as well as the Keetoowah Society were well organized and favored tradition but were strongly attached to the constitutional government that was seen as an instrument for the protection of land and tribal rights and interests. The Cherokee conservatives in the Ross Party and Keetoowah Society dominated Cherokee government until the middle 1880s, when the U.S. government started policies that eventually led to the dismantling of the Cherokee government.

The Chickasaw constitution of 1855 has many similarities to the Cherokee and U.S. constitutions. It has clear separation of powers between judicial, executive, and legislative branches. There is a bicameral legislature and a separation of business and government. Market enterprise was encouraged and market relations supported by the constitution. Like the Cherokee, district political units were created over the old villages. Villages were not parts of the Chickasaw constitution. The Chickasaw constitution also bypassed the traditional clan system of the Chickasaw, which had determined political leadership, military leadership, and spiritual leadership. Like the Cherokee, the old confederate and clan organization of Chickasaw regional political districts supplanted direct relations between the individual and the central government politics.[33] However, the old kinship, spiritual, and political ties were maintained through conservative political parties. Among the Chickasaw, the Pullback Party was well organized and controlled much of the government until the late 1880s. Like the Cherokee, the old confederate characteristics of the Chickasaw government were preserved not in the new constitution but in many aspects of traditional village, and kin-based politics lived on through the conservative political parties. Again, like the Cherokee, the Chickasaw conservative parties challenged the economic, cultural, and political interests of the minority planter-rancher class that was engaged in cotton farming and, after the Civil War, cattle raising for export. The planter-rancher parties' and the conservative parties' conflict ranged on issues of national preservation and cultural preservation as well as modes of economic action. While most of the citizens of the Cherokee and Chickasaw nations were subsistence farmers with few ties to capitalist markets, the constitutions preserved and encouraged market enterprise for the planter-rancher class interests, and in this way resembled the market and property supports of the U.S. constitution.

In the sense that the Cherokee and Chickasaw constitutions did not formally incorporate traditional confederate political organizations of clans, villages, and regional coalitions of villages, they resemble many contemporary tribal constitutions. Nevertheless, the Cherokee and Chickasaw conservatives formed active and formal national political parties that united and transcended kinship and local village political allegiances. The formation of national or tribal-wide political parties is unusual in contemporary Native nations. The political parties of the Cherokee and Chickasaw were built on class relations, subsistence farmers versus capitalist planter-ranchers, as well as differing levels of acculturation, where the conservatives carried on clan, ceremonial and subsistence lifestyles, the planter-ranchers were more educated in the ways of U.S. society. The formation of active, well organized, and highly committed political parties was related to the tribal-wide clan systems of the Cherokee and Chickasaw, which fostered a broad sense of unity. During the period of strong pressures for change and land cessions pressed by the U.S. government and settlers, traditional clan relations helped mobilize the conservatives into a strong sense of nationalism devoted to preserving the nation from dissolution, protection of the tribal land base, and resistance to incorporation into the United States. In the end, during the 1890s, many within the planter-rancher classes had strong cultural and economic interests in the United States, and they were more willing to accept national dissolution in 1907 than were the conservative nationalist parties that fought very hard to preserve their tribal land and government.[34]

The Cherokee-Chickasaw experience suggests that highly mobilized nationalist political parties in support of a centralized and market-oriented constitution is possible in Indian country. Political parties, based on kinship, village, or band organization, can support a national constitutional government and market economy. The situation of the planter-rancher class with strong cultural orientations toward market economy and knowledge of U.S. life and government is currently reproduced in most Native communities by the small group of relatively well-educated tribal members and the formation of small business classes, such as ranchers in many plains reservation communities.[35] There, however, is very little political party formation in contemporary Native communities. Most do not have the tribal-wide clan systems, like among the Cherokee and Chickasaw, that might serve as a social network for maintaining national alliances and promoting a strong sense of nationalism. For those tribes with extended kinship-community relations, a strong sense of national community mobilization may be possible and useful for constructing active and responsive constitutional governments. Nevertheless, many tribal subgroupings are often very autonomous socially and politically and the path that the nineteenth-century Cherokee and Chickasaw show us may not be open to them.

The Choctaw constitutional experience suggests another path toward establishment of stronger constitutional governments. The Choctaw were early buffeted about by slave raids and trade wars starting as early as the 1680s. Out of remnants and traditional regional coalitions of villages, the Choctaw formed three autonomous districts each with a matrilineal hereditary head chief and a district council comprising village headmen. By 1750, the Choctaw had a confederated form of government made up of three regional coalitions of villages; the national government comprised all three regional chiefs and their tribal councils, consisting of about thirty leaders in each of the three districts. Decisions at the national level needed agreement from all three chiefs and their councils of village leaders. When the U.S. government moved the Choctaw west to Indian Territory after the Treaty at Dancing Rabbit Creek (1830), one provision of the treaty provided that the Choctaw form a constitutional government after they had resettled. In 1834 the Choctaw, in compliance to their treaty, met and reluctantly adopted a constitutional government that preserved the powers of the three district chiefs and provided for a unicameral legislature consisting of ten elected representatives from each district. The move to Indian Territory took a heavy toll on Choctaw village and regional organization; nevertheless, the new Choctaw constitution preserved the regional confederate organization and powers of district chiefs.

Between the Choctaw treaty of 1834 and the Choctaw constitution of 1860, the Choctaw incrementally reorganized their constitutional government. In 1842 a bicameral legislature was established to ensure fairer representation among the districts. An upper house, or senate, consisted of three representatives from each of the three districts. The lower house received representatives from the three districts according to population; one representative for every 1,000 people. In 1850 county governments were created within the district regional governments and courts were created. Considerable controversy emerged between 1855 and 1860, when a group of planter-ranchers attempted to create a centralized government that abolished the powers of the three regional district chiefs. The centralized constitution had U.S. government support, but strong resistance from the Choctaw community led to a compromise constitution in 1860, which preserved the offices of the three district chiefs while investing the central government with power over the district governments in several critical areas such as national political, legal, and economic policy. As time passed, the district chiefs, while important symbolically and socially within Choctaw society, deferred political authority to the Choctaw chief executive, or governor, and central government. The three district regions, however, remained an important organizing principle for the national Choctaw government. For example, there were three judges, one from each district, on the Choctaw supreme court. The national political government of the Choctaw also promoted market relations, accumulation of wealth, and separation of powers between judiciary, executive, and legislature.[36]

The Choctaw experience resembles in some ways the U.S. constitution-building model. The Choctaw preserved their major confederate organization of three regions within the new constitution, but also delegated concentrated power to the executive, or governor, while containing centralized power with checks and promoting a market economy. In their incremental change approach, the Choctaw abolished the autonomy of the old Choctaw villages or local Iksa. Furthermore, the old Choctaw national clan and moiety relations were not formalized in the constitutional government after 1834. Like the Cherokee and Chickasaw, the Choctaw conservatives and planter-ranchers formed opposing political parties that contended for political leadership and contested various economic issues. The incremental approach of the Choctaw and their method of incorporating the three traditional political districts into the formal organization of their constitutional government may be a path to follow for communities that want to move toward independent market protections and the concentration of political power, while at the same time incorporate regional and local political groupings within the formal organization of the constitutional government.

The Creek constitution-building experience is another possible model for contemporary tribal governments. Unlike the Cherokee, Chickasaw, and final Choctaw constitutional governments, the Creek constitutional government of 1867, to a large extent imposed by U.S. demands at the end of the Civil War, conserved the confederate organization of the Creek nation by incorporating Creek villages into the constitutional order. Creek villages were sacred, autonomous groups from the time of the creation teachings. In the 1867 constitution, the Creek villages each sent a representative to the House of Kings and a representative to the House of Warriors; the latter was the lower house. The village governments retained considerable local religious, political, and social power, while the central government concerned itself with external affairs, managing market relations, and national court issues. The central government divided powers between the courts, judiciary, and bicameral legislature. The central government managed most national affairs and issues with the U.S. government and managed national market relations and maintained a national court system, while village governments retained most of their traditional powers. Unlike the Cherokee, Choctaw, and Chickasaw constitutions, the powers of the central government did not penetrate through the local village governments, which usually operated according to traditional patterns. In Creek government, the villages mediated relations between the central government and individual citizens, thereby preserving considerable confederate powers. In many ways, the Seminole constitutional government in Indian Territory reflected a similar pattern to the Creek government. Seminole villages retained considerable autonomy and sent representatives to the national government, which operated as an executive committee for national affairs.

The Creek constitutional government was the least institutionally stable of the so-called Five Civilized Tribes. A large number (perhaps a majority in the early 1870s) opposed the constitutional government and supported returning village chiefs and religiously appointed central villages to the government. The U.S. government supported the Creek constitutional government, and the conservative challengers were not able to reinstitute the government by village chiefs.[37]

The Creek-Seminole constitutional model provided a plan for tribal communities with strong traditional village or local groups who will be reluctant to delegate authority to a central body. Many tribal communities have sociopolitical groups that will prefer to manage local affairs. The Creek-Seminole model preserves the local autonomy of villages while at the same time delegates specific nontraditional powers over national economic and political relations to the central government. The tribal governments of the Tlingit and Navajo offer further examples of possible ways to move toward stronger tribal governments. The Tlingit, who occupied the panhandle of Alaska, had a system of clans and moieties that unified the community symbolically and socially through periodic potlatch ceremonies. The Tlingit did not have a central government. There was no chief; most social, economic, and spiritual activities were organized through clan and house relations. There were about twenty-five clans in each of two moieties, Eagle and Raven, and each clan was subdivided into several houses that were usually located in different villages. Tlingit villages were collections of local houses that contained extended families or clan segments. Houses organized the main economic activities and had rights to hunting and fishing areas. The villages did not have a head chief, and each house had a leader who managed the affairs of the house with the advice of elders, including his sisters and female clan relatives.

The Tlingit had an acephalous society, with no formal council or political leadership. Centralized leadership was not created until the formation of the Alaska Native Brotherhood (ANB) in 1912, partly as a response to the loss of the Tongass forest lands to the U.S. government. The ANB had a confederate organization, with each village in the Alaska panhandle having a camp and sending representatives to the grand camp. Robert's Rules of Order were used during camp and grand camp meetings. The ANB, built on Protestant Christian principles of individual responsibility and commitment to an agreed-on charter or organizational constitution, did not recognize clan or moiety relations or obligations. The ANB formed a political center in villages and within Tlingit country that was not constructed by the clans, moieties, or villages. Many clan leaders supported the ANB, which bore the task of protecting Tlingit political and economic interests within the state of Alaska and the United States.

While pursuing compensation for the Tongass forest in a lawsuit against the United States, the Tlingit were forced to form a new political organization. Since the ANB was a voluntary association that accepted non-Tlingit members, the ANB could not represent the Tlingit in a land claims case. The ANB moved to establish a government often called the Tlingit-Haida Central Council (THCC). The Haida, a group with a similar culture to the Tlingit on the Alaska panhandle, were also plaintiffs to the land claim suit. After considerable controversy and debate the THCC was formed with a coalition of Tlingit and Haida villages. A Tlingit lawyer, William Lewis Paul, argued strongly that the clans should have rights and powers within the new government, but U.S. lawyers argued that the villages should have representative rights and not the kin-based clans and houses. The U.S. lawyers prevailed and the THCC was formed by a coalition of villages. Every two years representatives from the villages elect a president and executive committee. The THCC with the aid of the ANB successfully concluded the land claims case and was awarded $7.5 million, which was held in investments and the interest used to fund the THCC and its projects.

In 1971, the Alaska Native Claims Settlement Act (ANCSA) led to the creation of thirteen regional for-profit corporations in Alaska. In Tlingit country, Sealaska Corporation was formed and held hundreds of thousands of dollars in funds as well as land and resource assets. Sealaska is organized according to U.S. corporate structures and is managed by a board of directors who are elected by tribal shareholders. Each tribal member alive in 1971 was awarded one hundred shares in Sealaska, which went on to operate like a holding and investment company. Sealaska is very powerful economically and works to promote economic development as well as provide funds for cultural preservation and promote employment among tribal shareholders.

The Tlingit adopted an unusual method of dealing with the political, cultural, and economic issues of living in U.S. society. They established a political center with the ANB and THCC. Both organization are based on principles of U.S. and Protestant Christian organization. Both THCC and ANB have incorporated villages into their structures and do not recognize clans and moieties for political purposes. At the same time, Sealaska Corporation engages in market-oriented enterprise and manages large assets for Tlingit shareholders. Business and government are separated and the corporation runs under U.S. rules. At the same time, the Tlingit clan, house, moiety, and house complex continues to function and provides the Tlingit with spiritual and social unity. But it is separate from the political activities of the ANB and

THCC and also from the economic activities of Sealaska corporation. The Tlingit have preserved a strong sense of traditional culture and core community through their potlatch and moiety/clan ceremonies, while forming a centralized political government through village coalitions and managing Sealaska Corporation through individual shareholders. The THCC has not adopted a constitutional government; it does not have a judicial branch or a bicameral legislature but rather operates largely as an executive committee over a coalition of villages. Nevertheless the Tlingit and Haida preserve community and culture while managing their political and economic affairs in U.S. society with a variety of cultural, political, and economic organizations.[38]

During the latter half of the twentieth century, the Navajo tribal government has incrementally moved toward a culturally appropriate form of constitutional-like government. Like the Tlingit, the Navajo have an acephalous society with no regular central council or head chief. The Navajo are organized by matrilineal clans and live among local groups of extended family with a headman who served as long as he had the support of the local community. When U.S. government officials called Navajo leaders together, many leaders of local communities answered the call, and since agreements were made by consensus few decisions would be made by a large group of local leaders. In 1924 the United States created the Navajo Business Council to manage Navajo business affairs. By the middle 1930s the business council had fallen into disfavor among the Navajo, and after some negotiation, and the submission of a Navajo constitution in 1936, the Interior secretary dictated the Rules of 1938, which forms the organic document of the Navajo nation. Since the 1960s, however, the Navajo have been incrementally changing their government and courts to suit their own cultural views and interests. Starting in the 1920s, government officials created local chapters that incorporated local forms of Navajo community organization. During the 1930s and later, the chapters formed organizational points for opposition to both U.S. policy and centralized Navajo tribal government.[39]

In the 1960s in response to threats from local states, the Navajo formed a court system to prevent Navajo citizens and cases from being heard in state courts. At first the Navajo courts resembled U.S. courts, but during the 1970s and 1980s the courts became increasingly strong powers in Navajo government and increasingly incorporated Navajo peacemaking and common law into the exercise of justice.[40] The strength of Navajo local communities for political organization and influence in Navajo elections led to the establishment of about 110 Navajo local chapters into the formal structure of the Navajo tribal government. In recent years, about eighty-eight chapters or groups of chapters have enough registered voters (1,000) to have a representative in the tribal council. The Navajo created a president with some veto powers and maintain a unicameral legislature of elected representatives from the local chapters. Over the past two years, the Navajo council has passed legislation that will allocate more political power and resources to the local chapters that to a large extent represent the local kin-based community of traditional Navajo society. Always suspicious of centralized power, the Navajo are decentralizing some of the tribal government's powers and allocating them to local chapters.[41]

The Navajo have made considerable progress toward a culturally appropriate tribal government. They have incorporated their traditional confederated local communities through chapter organizations into the government framework. The Navajo have delegated greater powers to the local chapters in an effort to place greater checks on the exercise of power by the Navajo central government. The Navajo court system has become increasingly respected within the government and provides more checks on the center and has incorporated significant aspects of Navajo culture, procedure, and views of justice into the Navajo court system. While the Navajo have not separated business and government relations and provide limited support of market economy, these choice reflect the economic and cultural orientations of many of their tribal members.

## Tribal Governments in the Twenty-first Century

Tribal governments of the future will need to be more effective in protecting Native sovereignty, incorporating culture, incorporating the sociopolitical powers of tribal communities, and managing market and subsistence economies. Meeting the challenges of the next century most likely will not be accomplished with the tribal governments handed to Native nations during the twentieth century; nor will traditional confederate governments manage market economies, concentrations of power or wealth, and the rise of new economic and literate classes that carry diverse and often nontribal interests and cultural orientations.

As the writers of the U.S. constitution argued, the management of effective relations with foreign powers and management of internal affairs require enough concentration of power for the government to work effectively and actively in the interests of the nation. The government requires powers to act and command resources in order carry out actions. While specific powers and resources are granted to the central government, a system of checks is necessary to prevent tyranny or arbitrary exercise of power.

Most contemporary tribal governments have little or no power invested in the tribal chair or tribal chief executive. While many tribal chairpersons have considerable political influence and are charismatic leaders, little formal power is granted to them. Many tribal chairs have voting rights similar to the members of the tribal council and do not have veto power. Often the tribal chair votes only if there is a tie in the tribal council; the chair's main duty is to conduct tribal council meetings. Furthermore, the chair is not responsible for the administration of the tribal bureaucracy or implementation of tribal policies. Instead the tribal councils often have plenary powers and can overrule the chair and directly manage tribal administration. This form of organization violates the rule of separation of executive and legislative branches. Tribal councilpersons are elected for political purposes and their political agendas often prevail in the legislature and in the executive. Furthermore, in many tribal governments, the courts are subject to the decisions of the tribal council. The elected members of the tribal council do not have checks placed on their collective actions by the judiciary, the executive, or a second legislative body. Consequently the acts of the tribal governments are not regularly checked by other powers in the government or community and therefore lay open the possibility of misguided use of tribal government powers and resources. Tribal council domination of tribal bureaucracy politicizes administration and creates instability and uneven implementation of tribal goals and policies.

If we consider the U.S. constitution as a benchmark, then tribal governments need both greater concentrations of power and greater checks on the distribution of power. In order to create greater effectiveness, the executive branch of tribal governments needs to be invested with greater power—tribal bureaucracy without direct interference from the tribal council. The chair needs to be delegated specific powers to act in behalf of the tribe on issues and relations with federal, state, and local governments. The chair needs to have veto power over the actions of the tribal council, which should have the right to overturn a chair's veto with a two-thirds majority vote.

Tribal councils should not have de facto plenary power, since unchecked power leads to possible misuse of power and resources. Such arrangements reduce the tribe's ability to manage both internal and external political relations. A strong and relatively independent chair or executive branch will place a check on the plenary powers of contemporary tribal councils. Furthermore, like the U.S. constitution and the Cherokee, Choctaw, Creek, and Chickasaw constitutions, the tribal councils would have more checks on the concentration of powers and exercise of power if bicameral tribal councils were adopted. The tribal council can serve as a lower house, while an upper house can be constructed from elders or major confederated groups who exercise influence and authority already existing within the community. The construction of upper houses is a good opportunity to empower confederate forms of organization such as villages, clans, bands, coalitions of villages, or kinship within the tribal constitution. Such incorporation of tribal confederated groups is analogous to the strong position of states in the U.S. constitution and reflects the autonomous powers of the older confederated forms of sociopolitical organization. Furthermore, tribal symbols and sociopolitical groupings will have direct access to political power and will serve as a conservative check. Tribal cultures emphasize individual and groups autonomy, and the new constitutional form with confederated units represented in upper legislative houses will work to emphasize and preserve such tribal autonomy directly. Such an arrangement will go far to legitimate the tribal government and generate support and commitment. Two legislative houses will create checks on each other; also, if the two houses are constructed from different empowered constituencies within the community, they will more effectively represent the diverse interests and social organization of the community. The lower house could be organized through regional populations, like the 1842 Choctaw constitution, while an upper house could be constructed to reflect and represent the power and influence of tribal confederate groups. Tribal autonomy, personal and group, is a profound theme in Native cultures. Native groups and individuals fight long and hard to preserve their spiritual rights. Bicameral tribal councils based on confederate organization, like the Choctaw regional or Creek village-based governments, would do much to unite tribal and constitutional organization and philosophies.

As in the U.S. constitutional model, the tribal courts need to be constructed and should provide stable protections of cultural autonomies, reliable rulings and procedure in support of market economies, and protections for subsistence economy, and they should embody the views of and procedures of tribal worldviews that emphasize restoration of balance between individuals, families, social groups, and the powers of the universe. Just as checks need to be created between the legislative and executive branches, and within the legislative branch between two legislative houses, the courts need to be endowed within the constitution with relative independence from legislative and executive interference. The courts should have capability to overrule executive and legislative branches in constitutional issues that threaten the integrity of the constitutional agreement. Enforcement of such constitutional agreements and powers can come not only from an American-style system of checks and balances but also from a general consensus within the tribal community. Among the Navajo, while there is no written formal constitution, the separation of powers between the courts and executive and tribal council have gradually been accepted by the general Navajo population. Any effort to disrupt relations will cause widespread reaction among the people.[42]

The concentration of greater power and independence in the executive and the creation of checks on the tribal councils through formation of an upper house based on tribal confederate sociopolitical formations, as well as an independent and culturally appropriate judiciary, will go far to generate more vigorous leadership, redistribute the plenary powers of contemporary tribal councils, incorporate greater judicial stability and cultural compatibility, and generate greater commitment and protection for culturally based social and political groups. Much of this theory can be gained from the reinterpretation of the U.S. constitutional model given earlier, although applied to the cultural worldview and social organization of tribal communities. Such steps will go far to invigorate, protect, and preserve tribal communities.

Tribal communities need to meet the demands of contemporary market relations while at the same time meeting and protecting the demands of tribal members who choose to live wholly or partially within the subsistence economy. A major challenge to tribal communities and governments is to create the political and legal environment that fosters the development of market enterprise. Tribal confederacies were not well equipped to manage market relations, since they were largely constructed to conserve subsistence economies, redistribute wealth, and discourage the concentration of wealth. Market economies, however, are the predominate contemporary economic form, and tribal governments will need to foster market enterprise in order to be competitive and acquire economic resources necessary for the exercise of tribal sovereignty.

Most tribal governments directly manage major tribal business assets. Tribal councils with de facto plenary powers have direct power over tribal business decisions. This arrangement does not separate business and government decisions. Often highly politicized tribal councils with few if any checks or business qualifications make critical management and investment decisions. One tribal council's business decisions are often overturned by the next elected tribal council. This leads to unstable and overly politicized management that inhibits business. Neither business nor tribal government is well served by conflicts of business and government interest.[43]

Following the U.S. constitutional model, tribal governments should create the conditions for the accumulation of wealth and the judicial and government supports for a sustained and independent market economy. The tribal government should divest itself from managing business enterprises and maintain a general policy of noninterference in business management and relations. The Cherokee, Choctaw, Chickasaw, and Creek constitutions promoted independent market economy during the nineteenth century. Tribal governments need to create business codes that ensure stable business activities and allow courts to adjudicate disputes in predictable and relatively nonpoliticized ways. Contracts and preservation of private property need constitutional protections.

Markets and business have become specialized, competitive, and globalized. The present-day IRA corporations and business councils do not separate business and government interests and organization and are not to be regarded as enduring models for economic development. The Alaska Native Corporations, created by the Alaska Native Claims Settlement Act of 1971 (ANCSA), provide a possible model for managing tribal assets as part of an autonomous market sector. The thirteen Alaska Native corporations, such as the Tlingit Sealaska Corporation, are organized according to U.S. corporate law and are for-profit institutions. In the beginning, each tribal member is granted one hundred shares and has the right to vote for a board of directors, who are responsible for managing the corporation. Granting tribal members shares in tribal assets empowers them within a process of decision making and gives them voice, which is compatible with tribal political culture. The corporate model takes tribal assets and management out of the hands of elected government officials and puts them into the hands of those who are elected to manage collective tribal assets. Direct participation by tribal shareholders will help ensure that economic development is ecologically sound and more compatible with tribal views of balance and order with the universe. Tribal community values and culture will be preserved and implemented in tribal corporate decision making. Alaska Native leaders have nearly thirty years of experience in the management of their business corporations and could provide direct models and consultation to tribes who wish to separate business and government interests and organization. Most tribes may not want to organize under U.S. corporate law, since that may conflict with tribal trust responsibilities. Corporate laws may be created under tribal law and protections for tribal assets may be guaranteed for the holding companies of tribal assets. Furthermore, additional corporations might be created under U.S. laws when tribal trust assets are not in jeopardy.

So far few contemporary tribal governments have been able to promote and ensure market economy. Capitalist accumulation, uneven distribution of wealth, and competition are generally incongruent with tribal economic and cultural ethics. Often many tribal members continue to live within a subsistence economy with few ties to market economies. Not only are tribal governments under pressure to create viable market economies, but they need to protect tribal members who live within the hunting, fishing, or farming subsistence economies still viable in many places in North America such as the Navajo reservation, Alaska, the Northwest Coast, and in such states as Wisconsin and Michigan where tribes have succeeded in preserving tribal fishing and hunting rights. Tribal economies are often organized by both subsistence and market economies, and tribal governments will need to preserve and protect both modes of economy.

The concentration of powers, checks on power, and the guarantee of market economy will go far to prepare tribal governments to meet the political, economic, and cultural challenges of the contemporary world. Nevertheless, tribal governments will need to do more than borrow technical achievements from the U.S. constitution, since tribal cultures and confederate organizations are very different from the United States. Market values are alien to tribal communities, and consequently creating market institutions that are compatible with tribal values will be difficult. Most likely tribal economies will bifurcate into subsistence and market sectors. Tribal worldviews emphasize the autonomous powers in the universe. People, groups, and objects in nature are part of a cosmic and interrelated community. Tribal confederate organization emphasizes autonomy, and what outsiders often view as factionalism in Indian communities is usually the exercise of autonomy by individuals, families, and local or other tribal groups who are defending and acting on their beliefs. Native groups and individuals work hard to retain and exercise their spiritual autonomy. The incorporation of tribal autonomies and powers within the formal constitutional order will go far to eliminate conflict and create commitment to the new political order. Cultural understandings of social and political action will be more explicitly anchored in the new constitutional arrangements that will more accurately reflect the social and cultural powers of the tribal community.

A power that many tribal governments might consider restoring is the role of women in tribal government. Many Native nations continue to be organized through matrilineal forms of family, clan, and community organization. Among many tribes such as the Creek, Cherokee, and Iroquois, women were formally represented within the government through clans and/or had veto power over decisions of the tribal council. The all-male nineteenth-century governments of the Five Civilized tribes did not have a place for formally recognizing the political power and influence of women in matrilineal kin-based societies. The decline of matrilineal clan and family organization, encouraged by the United States, directly challenged and diluted the social and political power of women. As matrilineal tribal communities wish to consider the reconstruction of their governments, they may wish to experiment with the restoration of the political power role of women as an upper house or in ways that are compatible with their social and political position within the community.

Many tribal communities are constructed from religiously and socially confederated subgroups. Tribal members often have stronger identities to families, clans, villages, or bands, and alliances to the collective tribal group are often secondary. This is a similar situation to that confronted by the Founding Fathers. Native worldviews reaffirm that the confederate organization of the tribes be preserved and that each grouping—families, bands, villages, clans—have considerable autonomy and freedom. The Founding Fathers believed that constitutional government would be more stable and efficient if the federal government were supported by national loyalties that superseded local and state commitments.

Several tribal groups have developed mobilized national or tribal political communities, or civil societies. The nineteenth-century Cherokee, Choctaw, and Chickasaw constructed national political communities that were not primarily based on clans, villages, or regional alliances or identities. Political parties organized on national or tribal issues became the main political groupings in each of the three Indian nations. In the twentieth century, the formation of the Tlingit ANB and Tlingit-Haida Central Council, as well as the shareholder organization of Sealaska Corporation, reflect the Tlingit political identity that was based not on clans or villages but individual commitments to Tlingit collective tribal interests and goals. Unlike the Choctaw, Chickasaw, and Cherokee, the Tlingit have not formed political parties nor have they adopted a formal constitutional government. Nevertheless, the formation of tribal-national identities and civil societies composed of a mobilized community of tribal citizens who have strong loyalties and identities is a possibility, as the experience of both historical and contemporary communities show. A constitutional government may require a supporting national political community. As is indicated by the Tlingit case, the formation of a national political identity does not necessarily imply the denial to traditional tribal forms of social organization. The Tlingit retain their moiety, clan, and potlatch institutions, which provide a strong sense of community that supports the political unity of contemporary Tlingit government. Similar observations could be made for the Cherokee national identity that formed between 1808 and 1828, supported by a tribal-wide clan and village alliances. The Choctaw and Chickasaw also had tribal-wide kinship organizations for ceremonial purposes; this kind of organization may be a base for developing national political communities with loyalties to a central constitutional government.

Nevertheless, not all tribal communities have followed the path of developing national political communities or civil societies based on individual commitments and mediated through confederated sociopolitical groupings. The Creek and Seminoles did not allow their constitutional governments to reach into village and local clan affairs. Villages remained the primary political units of Creek and Seminole societies, and political relations were mediated through village governments. Similarly, the early Choctaw constitution was based on village and regional coalitions but gradually over a twenty-five-year period the Choctaw moved to regional and county political organization and abolished the village prerogatives in Choctaw government. The path of gradual transition from confederate organization toward a district- or territory-based political community may appeal to some communities, but others may wish to preserve their confederate organization since in many cultures, such as the Creek and Seminole, villages or other confederated groups have sacred political, religious, and social rights. Similarly, the Iroquois Confederacy is given by the teachings of Deganawidah, and the Iroquois confederate constitution preserves the rights of families, clans, and nations to choose leaders and vote in the confederate council. Many tribal communities will prefer to retain confederate organization, since it reflects the distribution of social, economic, political, and spiritual power within the tribal communities. The incorporation of such confederate organization into the constitutional government will more accurately reflect the cultural values, norms, and commitments of the tribal community and have a greater chance of mobilizing the tribal community to support a centralized constitutional government. If a tribal community wishes to preserve its confederate organization and religiously ordained political rights, it needs a system of checks to ensure the autonomy of the confederate units while preserving the concentration of central political power necessary for effective action in tribal and extratribal affairs.

The national political communities of the nineteenth-century Cherokee, Choctaw, and Chickasaw were not based on a wholesale borrowing from the U.S. example. Like most tribal communities, the Cherokee, Choctaw, and Chickasaw were reluctant to change their political and community organization. The strong pressure for land and increasing legal and economic encroachments from U.S. society helped motivate tribal citizens to mobilize in unified resistance to U.S. political and economic encroachments, and in many ways the new constitutional governments were instruments of protection against further U.S. demands. The development of national collective orientations and commitments were intended to preserve land, community, and culture. Centralized constitutional governments were seen as instrumental means for protecting tribal rights from threats from the U.S. government and society. Tlingit national identity formation followed a similar pattern as the ANB was formed in response to loss of land, as well as loss of social rights and freedoms. The ANB's collective goals were aimed at protecting Native educational, political, fishing, and social rights.

Many contemporary tribal communities include highly educated tribal members, businessmen, and professionals employed by the federal or tribal government. Many of the new professional and business groups are familiar with U.S. institutions and political culture. Among the nineteenth-century Cherokee, Choctaw, and Chickasaw, the planter-rancher classes formed similar political formations of well-educated individuals who had market interests within the U.S. and world markets. These groups had economic and cultural interests and views similar to U.S. government officials and were often instrumental in introducing and supporting constitutional forms among the Cherokee, Choctaw, and Chickasaw. The southern tribal planter-ranchers were strongly nationalistic through most of the nineteenth century. Because they were barred from entering southern society, most cast their political allegiance to their tribal groups and worked hard to preserve tribal governments, land, and sovereignty. During these periods, the southern tribal constitutional governments thrived. Toward the end of the century, however, many in the educated and business classes acquiesced to U.S. demands for dismantling the tribal constitutional governments.[44]

The educated professional and business classes will play significant roles in the reformulation of tribal governments, and their loyalty and commitment to tribal sovereignty and indigenous rights will be critical for the survival of the tribal governments. During the nineteenth century, the planter-rancher classes formed a small proportion of the entire community and could not enforce political change over the highly mobilized communities in the Choctaw, Chickasaw, and Cherokee nations. The planter-rancher classes formed agreements with the tribal community about the organization of the constitutional governments, which could not have been constructed unless the tribal communities gave their consent and commitment.[45] Some members of the planter-rancher classes took on leadership of the more traditional tribal membership, but their leadership represented the interests of the general community in regard to sovereignty, land, and cultural preservation.

Contemporary tribal communities will also need to forge agreements and understandings among the tribal community and newly emergent professional, business, and educated groups. The new groups will not be able to construct stable and enduring constitutional governments without the consent and commitments of the tribal community. The tribal community will need skilled leaders in order to protect and support their goals of community and cultural and political preservation. Tribal governments can be renewed only through agreements and consent within the tribal communities over issues such as the construction of centralized, culturally sensitive, and market-based constitutional governments. National alliances among professional and business classes and the tribal communities will be crucial to the development of mobilized political communities in support of active tribal constitutional governments.

## What Can Tribal Communities Do?

Concentrating political power with appropriate checks is a major step toward creating vigorous, effective tribal governments. Incorporating tribal confederate organization and/or forming national political communities committed to tribal rights and cultural preservation will go far to provide a match between the constitutional government and the values, goals, and interests of the tribal community. Effective, vigorous government that represent the aspirations of the tribal community are necessary for the future and long-term protection of tribal sovereignty, land, and preservation of the tribal cultural community. The efficient exercise to tribal sovereignty and community aspirations will provide the political infrastructure necessary for exercising and preserving tribal rights. If tribal governments do not effectively defend their rights, then federal, state, and local governments will move to fill the vacuum. Economic development will be a critical factor in the future to tribal communities. Dependency on federal programs and administration does not foster the cultural understanding, political freedom, and economic standards that tribal communities might achieve if they were more effectively managed with stronger constitutional governments. Stable, vigorous, and culturally supported constitutional governments will provide the organization and commitment necessary for exercise of tribal sovereignty and promotion of culturally appropriate and community-based market participation.

The U.S. constitutional model is proposed here as a benchmark for managing the challenges of the present political and economic world. It is a model that can be regarded as relatively successful over the past century, and its principles of organization should get careful consideration from tribal leaders and communities. Nevertheless, the issues of concentration and centralization of political power, promotion of a market economy, and accumulation and inequality of wealth are activities that are generally in direct contrast to tribal organization and culture. The U.S. model is one solution for providing a stable and vigorous government in an age of competitive politics and economy. Tribal communities that do not find the U.S. model agreeable may wish to experiment with other solutions based on their tribal organization and cultures. The next century may mark a period of broad movement among tribal communities for building on tribal organization and culture in ways that will meet the economic, political, and cultural challenges of the contemporary world.

In many ways the present-day Navajo tribal government exemplifies how one tribal community has borrowed many aspects of U.S. constitutional principles but has retained many critical aspects of Navajo culture and decentralized confederate organization. While not wholly adopting the U.S. constitutional model, the Navajo have incrementally adopted some principles of the U.S. constitution while at the same time including Navajo decentralized political organization and culture within the tribal council and courts. As in the Navajo case, many tribes have the opportunity to strengthen their governments with knowledge and principles gained from contemporary political theory, but at the same time retain features of their own social and political organization that embody the culture and values of their ancestors.

The challenges of the twenty-first century are upon us. It is a world of globalized markets, competitive political relations, technological change, and cultural diversity. The preservation of tribal sovereignty demands that tribal communities participate in this world at least to the extent that tribal communities need to preserve their rights and communities. Restoring tribal constitutional governments and reinvigorating them with strong community support give them the political and economic tools necessary to preserve tribal political, economic, and cultural interests.

# Notes

An earlier version of this chapter appeared in Duane Champagne, "Renewing Tribal Governments: Uniting Political Theory and Sacred Communities," *Indigenous Peoples' Journal of Law, Culture, and Resistance,* April 2004, pp. 24–66.

1. Donald A. Grinde and Bruce E. Johansen, *Exemplar of Liberty: Native America and the Evolution of Democracy* (Los Angeles: UCLA American Indian Studies Center, 1991), pp. 61–72; Jeffrey Alexander, "The Paradoxes of Civil Society," *International Sociology,* June 1997, pp. 118–20.

2. William Kelloway, *The New England Company, 1649–1776* (London: Longmans, 1973), p. 276.

3. Duane Champagne, "American Bureaucratization and Tribal Governments: Problems of Institutionalization at the Community Level," in *Occasional Papers in Curriculum Series* (Chicago: Newberry Library, 1987), pp. 176–77.

4. Richard Clemmer, *Roads in the Sky: The Hopi Indians in a Century of Change* (Boulder: Westview, 1995), pp. 144–61.

5. Richard Clemmer, "Hopis, Western Shoshones, and Southern Utes: Three Different Responses to the Indian Reorganization Act of 1934," *American Indian Culture and Research Journal,* Spring 1986, pp. 29–31.

6. Tom Holm, "The Crisis in Tribal Government," in *American Indian Policy in the Twentieth Century,* ed. Vine Deloria Jr. (Norman: University of Oklahoma Press, 1985), pp. 142, 186; Robert Porter, "Crisis Pending: Governance in Tribal America," *Native American Law Digest,* August 1999, 5–7; Ian Wilson Record, "Broken Government: Constitutional Inadequacy

Spawns Conflict on San Carlos," *Native Americas,* Spring 1999, pp. 10–16; Gerald Monette and Robert Lyttle, "The Crisis Is Constitutional," *Native Americas,* Spring 1999, p. 64.

7. Alexander Hamilton, James Madison, and John Jay, *The Federalist: The Famous Papers on the Principles of American Government,* ed. Benjamin Fletcher Wright (New York: Barnes & Nobles, 1996), pp. 155–62, 186–96; Dave R. Palmer, *1794: America, Its Army, and the Birth of the Nation* (Novato, CA: Presidio, 1994), pp. 5, 55, 65–73.

8. Benjamin Fletcher Wright, introduction to *The Federalist: The Famous Papers on the Principles of American Government* (New York: Barnes & Nobles, 1996), pp. 49–59.

9. Hamilton, *The Federalist,* pp. 92, 98, 113.

10. Hamilton, *The Federalist,* pp. 171–90.

11. Hamilton, *The Federalist,* pp. 199, 302–5, 318, 329–30.

12. Hamilton, *The Federalist,* pp. 336–47.

13. Hamilton, *The Federalist,* pp. 164, 184.

14. J. Leitch Wright, *Creeks and Seminoles* (Lincoln: University of Nebraska Press, 1986), pp. 2–4, 30; Michael D. Green, *The Politics of Indian Removal: Creek Government and Society in Crisis* (Lincoln: University of Nebraska Press, 1982), pp. 11–13.

15. Barbara Graymont, *The Iroquois in the American Revolution* (Syracuse, NY: Syracuse University Press, 1972), pp. 45–48, 128, 147, 163, 218–19, 285.

16. Paul Wallace, *Indians in Pennsylvania* (Harrisburg: Pennsylvania Historical and Museum Commission, 1970), pp. 91–97; Paul Phillips, *The Fur Trade* (Norman: University of Oklahoma Press, 1961), 1: 314, 464, 500–4, 553–54; Henry Schoolcraft, *The Indian Tribes of the United States* (Philadelphia: Lippincott, 1884), pp. 224–26; Paul Phillips, *The Fur Trade* (Norman: University of Oklahoma Press, 1961), 2:20–26, 69, 80, 197–208.

17. Hamilton, *The Federalist,* pp. 302–5, 318–38.

18. Clyde Kluckhohn and Robert Hackenberg, "Social Science Principles and the Indian Reorganization Act," *Indian Affairs and the Indian Reorganization Act: The Twenty-Year Record,* ed. William Kelly (Tucson: University of Arizona Press, 1954), p. 32.

19. Hamilton, *The Federalist,* pp. 336, 347, 355, 479.

20. Porter, "Crisis Pending," p. 20; Record, "Broken Government," pp. 13–16; Monette, "The Crisis," p. 64.

21. Robert B. Porter, "Building a New Longhouse: The Case for Government Reform within the Six Nations of the Haudenosaunee," *Buffalo Law Review* 46, no. 3: 805–945; Bruce Johansen, *Life and Death in Mohawk Country* (Golden, CO: North American Press, 1993).

22. Clemmer, *Roads in the Sky,* 163–65; William K. Powers, *Oglala Sioux* (Lincoln: University of Nebraska Press, 1977), pp. 119–20; Raymond J. DeMallie, "Pine Ridge Economy: Cultural and Historical Perspectives," in *American Indian Economic Development,* ed. Sam Stanley (The Hague, Netherlands: Mouton, 1978), p. 276; Delmer Lonowski, "A Return to Tradition: Proportional Representation in Tribal Government," *American Indian Culture and Research Journal,* Winter 1994, 148–61.

23. Wright, introduction, pp. 26–41.

24. Duane Champagne, "Renewing American Indian Nations: Cosmic Communities and Spiritual Autonomy," in *Diversity and Community: A Critical Reader,* ed. Philip Alperson (Oxford: Blackwell, 2003), pp. 167–281; Duane Champagne, "The Cultural and Institutional Foundations of Native American Conservatism," special issue on North American Indians: Cultures in Motion, ed. Elvira Stefania Tiberini, *L'Uomo: Societa, tradizione, sviluppo* 8, no. 1 (1995): 17–43.

25. Hamilton, *The Federalist,* pp. 336–47; Palmer, *1794,* pp. 94–108.

26. Hamilton, *The Federalist,* pp. 355–59, 407–12.

27. Hamilton, *The Federalist,* pp. 158–62.

28. Champagne, "Conservatism," pp. 17–43.

29. William W. Newcomb, "The Culture and Acculturation of the Delaware Indians," *Anthropological Papers* (Ann Arbor, MI: Museum of Anthropology. 1971), pp. 95–104; C. A. Weslager, *The Delaware Indians* (New Brunswick, NJ: Rutgers University Press, 1972), p. 419.

30. Laurence Hauptman, *The Iroquois and the New Deal* (Syracuse, NY: Syracuse University Press, 1981), pp. 9, 179; Lawrence Kelly, "The Indian Reorganization Act: The Dream and the Reality," in *The American Indian Past and Present,* ed. Roger Nichols (New York: Knopf, 1986), p. 250; Peter Blaine Sr., *Papagos and Politics* (Tucson: Arizona Historical Society, 1981), p. 81.

31. Duane Champagne, *Social Order and Political Change: Constitutional Governments among the Cherokee, Choctaw, Chickasaw, and Creek* (Stanford, CA: Stanford University Press, 1992), pp. 137, 184–93, 198, 228–30.

32. Champagne, *Social Order,* pp. 137–43, 198–99.

33. Champagne, *Social Order,* pp. 198–99.

34. Champagne, *Social Order,* pp. 217, 221–22, 225–27, 236.

35. Castle McLaughlin and Tracy Andrews, "Introduction," *American Indian Culture and Research Journal,* Summer 1998, 9.

36. Champagne, *Social Order,* pp. 189–93.

37. Champagne, *Social Order,* pp. 228–37.

38. Duane Champagne, "Culture, Differentiation, and Environment: Social Change in Tlingit Society," in *Differentiation and Social Change: Historical and Comparative Perspectives,* ed. Jeffrey C. Alexander and Paul Colomy (New York: Columbia University Press, 1990), pp. 52–87.

39. Aubrey Williams, *Navajo Political Process* (Washington, D.C.: Smithsonian Institution Press, 1970), pp. 19–23, 35–40, 60–62; R. W. Young, *A Political History of the Navajo Tribe* (Tsaile, AZ: Navajo Community College Press, 1978), pp. 59–67, 107–18.

40. Peter Iverson, *The Navajo Nation* (Westport, CN: Greenwood, 1981), pp. xxiii, 10, 74, 201–11.

41. Office of Native Government Development, *Navajo Nation Government Book* (Window Rock, AZ: Navajo Nation, 1998), pp. 33–40; David E. Wilkinson, *The Navajo Political Experience* (Tsaile, AZ: Dine College, 1999), pp. 146–50.

42. Robert Yazzie, personal communication, November 10, 1999. See also and compare the patterns of cultural change among the Navajo in Jerold Levy, *In the Beginning: The Navajo Genesis* (Los Angeles: University of California Press, 1998).

43. Stephen Cornell and Joseph Kalt, *Sovereignty and Nation Building: The Development Challenge in Indian Country Today* (Cambridge, MA: John F. Kennedy School of Government, 1998), 15–20; Stephen Cornell and Joseph Kalt, "Reloading the Dice: Improving the Chances for Economic Development for American Indian Reservations," in *What Can Tribes Do? Strategies and Institutions in American Economic Development,* ed. Stephen Cornell and Joseph Kalt (Los Angeles: American Indian Studies Center, UCLA, 1992), pp. 1–66.

44. Champagne, *Social Order,* pp. 217, 221, 226–28, 235–37.

45. Champagne *Social Order,* pp. 101–7, 188–93, 195–99, 202–5.

# Self-Government
from Time Immemorial

## 5

ROM WHERE did the Indian nations come? The belief that Native nations have inherent rights to self-government and territory derives from the tradition that Native peoples lived on this continent from time immemorial. Many tribes claim to have lived in a region for as long as 10,000 years, while many nations have creation stories that say the Creator placed them on their lands at the beginning of the world. An immediate issue arises here about how to characterize Indian nations before Columbus. The term "Indian nation" does not apply, since no Native person would have used this term in the way we understand "nation" in the contemporary sense, which implies a unified and mobilized political community. The concept of mobilized political community does not describe the communities of Native America before significant European contact, just as many communities around the world and throughout history could not be described as nations.

Native communities are better described in their own terms and from the understanding of the people themselves. The term *oyate* among the Lakota is often used to indicate the Lakota nation or community. But the term means more than the unity of the Lakota people or even their unity with the Dakota and Nakota peoples. It also means community of the Lakota with the spirit beings of the universe, including the plants, animals, water, wind, fire, and the entire collection of beings that make up the universe. There are hundreds, even thousands, of Native communities prior to European contact, and they all deserve to be understood as specific cultural microcosms, all with powerful interpretations of the universe and of their relations and role within the direction of the universe. Just as there are hundreds of Indian nations or communities, there are hundreds of specific Native American understandings of community, the relation of human community to politics, and to the order and beings given by the Creator. Native nations generally have a strong sense of community embedded in powerful visions of the order of the universe. Western nations tend to be secular, based on social relations, and focused on the human dimension, while Natives view their communities as part of a cosmic order or cosmic community that includes all the beings or powers of the universe, including interdependent human and natural worlds.

Native communities usually had a concept of land, although the concept of personal ownership of land was alien to the Indian nations. The concept of ownership in fee simple, without government or other private encumbrances, a European medieval concept, was unknown to the Native peoples and made little sense in their cultures or worldviews. Many Native peoples understand land as sacred space that was given in creation stories. Land was used for hunting, fishing, and gathering of wild plants in support of human subsistence. Among many Algonkian-speaking people and among many of the southeastern nations such as the Choctaw, Chickasaw, Creek, Cherokee, and Seminoles, families or clans often used portions of the common territory for hunting, fishing, gathering, and planting. A family had rights to use a fishing or hunting territory for as long as they worked the land for their subsistence. If the people left and went to hunt somewhere else on a regular basis, another family might move to the area and use it for their hunting or fishing camp. This type of land use if often called usufruct by Western legal authorities. Nevertheless, Native nations had a distinct understanding of their territory. One major reason for large-scale military clashes between Indian nations was disputed hunting territories, which most nations carefully guarded and defended against intruders. Although using the land for their subsistence and material needs, Native people did not believe the land belonged to them as private property. Certainly Native people possessed tools, clothes, weapons, and other material necessities that were owned by a person or by the women of the family. But land was collectively held, not necessarily in ownership but in stewardship.

Land was often given in creation stories or through migration stories to the community as a collective gift. Among the Cherokee, Choctaw, and Chickasaw there are migration stories where priests seek direction and advice from the leaning directions of a sacred pole. Each morning the sacred pole points in the direction the Creator wants the people to travel in order to direct them to the land that is to be given to them. When one morning the sacred pole does not bend to show the direction of travel that day, then the people have arrived at their new homeland. The migrations are considered sacred instructions for the people to live at a certain place. The Native nations honor and thank the Creator for his benevolence and wisdom in their ceremonies, and believe that the Creator has put the nation at a certain place for a purpose within the divine plan or unfolding of the universe.

The birthplace of the Osage people is a sacred and mysterious place. One day the Osage passed down through the sky world searching for a physical body in which their spirit could live. The Osage people were also searching for goodness and knowledge that would help them have peace among all living things.

One day the Tsi shu (Peace Clan) were living in what was known as the mid-world. There the Osage had spirits or souls, but they had no bodies. They had heard of a place where spirits had been given form in the physical world, so the Elder Brother sent the Younger Brother to find this place. Younger Brother continued his search through the second and third worlds but found them unlivable for the Osage People. Finally, Younger Brother came to the place of the fourth and lowest world. As Younger Brother walked through the lower fourth world, he found beautiful cloud beings, echoes of thunder beings, and powerful lightning beings. Younger Brother called out to this place, and soon the Man of Mysteries appeared to him. Younger Brother asked the Man of Mysteries how the Osage could live in the fourth world as do the cloud beings, the thunder beings, and the lightning beings. The Man of Mysteries told the Younger Brother that the Osage People would need names and bodies. So the Man of Mysteries gave the Osage People the names Little Hawk and Hawk Woman. Younger Brother then went back to the midworld to tell the Elder Brothers what he had discovered. "Elder Brother, I have found in the fourth world a sacred place where we can live," said Younger Brother.

Younger Brother then needed a way for the Osage People to make this journey to the fourth world, called Earth. Younger Brother began to sing and soon three eagles appeared. Each eagle gave the Osage People wings. When the Osage People passed down through the sky and came close to Earth, the first eagle landed on the branches of a red oak tree, the second landed on the branches of an alder, and the third placed his feet on the stem of little yellow flowers. Those who had landed on the red oak were given the power to have many descendants. Those who landed on the alder tree were given power to make medicine, and those who had landed on the little yellow flowers were given the power of peace. . . .

Younger Brother again began to sing, and soon the cedar tree spoke to the Osage People. "Brothers, you have made a long and courageous journey. And you have done what has been asked of you. For this I want you to make from my roots medicine so that your children will be well and live a long and good life. See that my branches are old and bent. Use these as signs and symbols to have respect for the old, and let the little children grow old with knowledge of peace and respect."[1]

Stories of trickster figures and great power beings usually determine the topology of the land and create places in the land where cosmic events of sacred and ceremonial significance take place and for which they are revered and honored by the people.

The Pueblos and the Dine have creation stories that describe the ascent of the nation out from lower world beneath the present earth's surface. Among Pueblos and the Navajo, the rise to the present, fifth world, is marked by the emergence of the ancestors and sacred beings into the present world marked off by four sacred mountains. Purposeful human life and community relations are perceived to take place within the boundaries of the four sacred mountains. The seven sacred mountains of the Navajo are created soon after their emergence into the fifth world after escaping a flood that destroyed the fourth world.

> It is also said that soon after the Pueblos moved away, the First Man and the First Woman decided to embellish this new world.
>
> So together with the Black Body, and with the Blue Body, they first set out to build the seven mountains sacred to the Navajo people to this very day. They built those mountains out of things they had brought with them: things they had taken from similar mountains in the fourth world below . . .
>
> After they had secured the mountains that marked the four cardinal points, they built the three central mountains.[2]

The land is sacred and the present fifth world can be destroyed if the people are immoral and do not honor the sacred laws and ceremonies given to them to restore and maintain social and cosmic harmony. Where the people come from and how they acquired their land is very important in most Native cultures. Most Native communities believe that their land is a sacred gift, and there is some purpose for the Native people to live a specific place. Therefore Native people were reluctant to give up land for religious reasons as well as economic or political ones.

Most Indian nations know why and for how long they have lived on their land. Since many of these stories are based on creation, Native people believe they have occupied their land from the beginning of time or from time immemorial. Scholars have a different view of Native American origins; the most prevalent theory is that the Indians came across the Bering Strait, a relatively short gap between Siberia and Alaska. More recently some have argued that Europeans, Polynesians, Iberians, Egyptians, and Africans migrated to North and South America around the end of the last Ice Age, when water levels were lower, since much of the earth's ocean water was captured as ice in the north and south poles. Scholars argue that proto–Native Americans traveled across a land bridge when ocean levels were low and made their way quickly through the continents and reached the tip of South America. About 12,000 years ago the world began to warm. The large ice glaciers receded north, and water from the ice poles began to raise the ocean levels. Thereafter it was more difficult to cross over from Siberia, although we know that Inuits, who live in both Siberia and Alaska, crossed the Bering Strait in kayaks. Some peoples may have used small boats to travel along the coast line across from Siberia and then south to South America.

Some historians state that all peoples migrated to North and South America at some time over the past 20,000 years. They argue that all people in the New World are migrants, implying that Native peoples do not have significant claims of priority to territory or self-government. However, the view that Natives are also immigrants is not shared by many Native peoples. Some Native migration stories may be generally compatible with the Bering Straits argument, since most of the migrations are from west to east. The Creek or Muskogee people believe their migration east was a sacred pilgrimage to find the abode of the sun, an embodiment of order and knowledge. Similarly, many of the Algonkian-speaking nations, such as the Anishinabe, Potawatomi, and Odawa, believe that they migrated to the east coast of North America, and some groups of Anishinabe and Cree later migrated back into the interior and onto the western plains. The sacred lodge of the Anishinabe, the Midewiwin, is created through the journeys and experiences of a man in the eastern country within the lodge of Seven Grandfathers. The Midewiwin is a ceremony about healing and relations with the beings of the cosmos.

> This teaching of the first Midewiwin ceremony and how the boy was cured of his sickness establishes the order of the priesthood of the Midewiwin. It established the relationship that should exist between elders and youth among all people. This relationship provides a link between the knowledge that must flow between generations. It provides the links for an unbroken string of lives all the way back to our origin as a people.
>
> As the Midewiwin developed, it gave the people new meaning to their lives. It became a strong and guiding force. Men, women and children were inspired by it. . . .
>
> Through these ways the people were able to develop a rapport with all the other beings of the Earth who shared the same space and time. They were able to communicate with all the other things in the Ish-pi-ming' (Universe). They understood that they belonged to the Four Levels of the Earth: the Mother Earth, the plant life, the animal life, and the human beings. In this chain, the human beings were the last to come. It was understood that human life could not survive without any of the preceding levels, while the other levels could survive very easily without the human beings.[3]

The Lakota believe that they migrated to the east coast to areas such as present-day Virginia and the Carolinas and then returned west, leaving some groups of their people in the region. The present-day states of Virginia and the Carolinas have Siouan-speaking peoples, which corroborates the Lakota historical tradition.

Nevertheless, most Native nations do not have a view saying that they traveled over the Bering Straits or had some similar experience. In most of the stories, the origins of the migrations eastward are not clearly spelled out, and some scholars have argued that the migration stories may indicate origins in Asia or Siberia. The Natives themselves do not usually indicate such specific origins to the migrations, but it is possible that the stories are thousands of years old and the precise originating point is lost in memory.

Most Native nations, however, have creation stories that determine the origins of the people and often the territory in which they live. Often the origin stories (or associated stories) determine many aspects of culture such as annual ceremonies, kinship relations, political leadership, and gender relations. The creation stories usually indicate that the country the Native people live in, here in the New World, was given to them as a gift by the Creator. Thus most Native people reject the Bering Straits in favor of their own creation stories, since their origin stories provide them with a worldview and understanding of place in the universe that the Bering Straits theory does not. The Navajo believe that their ancestors emerged from the earth from the fourth world into the fifth world in the present-day southwestern United States between four sacred mountains that define Navajo land. Scholars have discovered that the Athapascan-speaking nations of Alaska and western Canada speak a language related to the Navajo language. Other researchers argue that it is possible to trace Navajo migration from the north to the south starting around A.D. 800. Despite the scientific evidence, most Navajo reject this view of migration, since there are no migration stories in their tradition, and the creation stories supply them with a powerful worldview that is compatible with their understanding of the universe and their place and role in it. Some debate has emerged between Natives and American scholars over the migration and origins theories, but for most Indian communities, the Native people hold to their traditional views and do not take the arguments of the scholars as significant challenges to their way of life or their origins. The interpretation I am presenting in this book relies heavily on the interpretations of the Native nations, and I present as much material as possible through their interpretations, since I believe this method will give insight into why Natives insist on preservation of nations, culture, land, and self-government.

# Change and Diversity in Native Nations

Much of the history of the Indian Nations was written by Europeans during the early colonial period, mostly males with limited training or interest in ethnography as we know it today. Today archaeological evidence complements our knowledge but is hard-pressed to provide reliable cultural interpretations. Native peoples always had to adapt to the changing climate and conditions of North America. When the last Ice Age ended about 12,000 years ago, the Native people hunted mastodons, camels, horses, and other large game. About 10,000 years ago much of the large game died off, and many animals like mastodons and horses disappeared from the New World. Native peoples became more mobile and exploited their environment by hunting small game, sometimes fishing, and gathering roots, berries, and other plants. They apparently experimented with plant domestication, abandoning some plants that did not yield reliable sources of nutrition. Since women generally gathered plants for food, they likely were the early experimenters in plant domestication. Corn from Mexico, which was developed there at least by 2000 B.C., found its way into the Mississippi and Ohio Valleys and supplemented food supplies in those regions. Around 2500 B.C., there is archaeological evidence of pipes, which we now recognize as having spread to many Native cultures. Since Native peoples did not smoke for pleasure, the pipe and its religious significance within Native cultures and religions was already established at this early date. For several thousand years, productive communities in the eastern woodlands created earthen sculptures and, by 500 B.C., conical burial mounds. The communities of this early mound builder culture are called the Adena, an Ojibway word that means village, and dates from about 1000 B.C. to 100 B.C. The sculptures and earthen mounds had sacred significance: often the mounds are laid out in relations that allowed Native interpreters to determine the timing of the summer and winter solstices, and other ceremonial events about which we know little.

The Hopewellian Mound Builders flourished in the Ohio and upper Mississippi Valleys and undoubtedly mixed with or elaborated the cultures of the Adena period. The Hopewellian cultures were partially based on corn and relied on hunting and gathering and sometimes fishing for subsistence. Platform mounds with temples and priest classes emerge between A.D. 800 and 1600 and characterize the Mississippi Culture, which covered most of the Mississippi Valley and Ohio Valley as well as considerable portions of the present-day eastern United States. The platform mounds constituted an increased hierarchy in socioreligious organization. Platform mounds and conical mounds continued to be constructed in cosmological order recognizing major changes in seasons and star constellations. These nations were very religious and conducted many ceremonies in their annual cycles, and most likely had a centralized religious-political leadership. Archaeological evidence indicates that some of the Mississippi Culture towns had as many as 30,000 people. The ancient city of Cahokia, across the river from present-day St. Louis, was perhaps one of the largest towns in North America, with about 30,000 people around A.D. 1100. The people planted corn, beans, and squash, the famous three sisters of the Haudenosaunee and eastern woodlands peoples. They grew a few other crops and also hunted, fished, and gathered wild plants and fruits.

We have only archaeological evidence and hints about the beliefs and cultural organization of the Mound Builders. The Natchez people living along the Mississippi River were led by a Great Sun, who was honored as the representative of the Creator on earth and for the Natchez people. The Natchez told early English traders that at one time all along the Mississippi River and its tributaries there were five hundred Great Suns. The Great Sun represented the presence of the Creator on earth. When Hernando De Soto visited the Chickasaw about 1540, the Chickasaw leader was carried about and was not allowed to touch the ground. Apparently the leader's body was sacred, and perhaps he was considered a being of the upper world. According to one Choctaw oral creation story, the Creator and his wife came to earth and created the animals, plants, and different groups of people on the earth. The Creator and wife instructed the people in religious and moral issues, and he was honored in the great Temple of the Sun. The sun and fire are powerful images in many cultures and often constitute one of the four basic elements of the universe, the others being the water, earth, and wind. The sun signifies knowledge, the source of life, and warmth. The connection between the individual, fire, and the life-giving sun is through the fire or warmth that burns in a person's heart. The Great Suns were representatives or even embodiments of the power of the sun and the power of the Creator. Therefore the Great Suns were honored and attended to by priests. As the Choctaw story indicates, the Great Suns were accompanied by a female consort, which among the Natchez was the Great Sun's sister. Women and the balance of male and female forces were probably symbolic in this relation of Great Sun and female consort, but we have little information. Often in southeastern cultures such as the Creek, the upper regions of the universe (e.g., sun and wind) are symbolic of male powers, while the earth and water are symbolic of female powers. The sun is a male power, while the moon is a female power. The universe is engaged in a struggle for balance between male and female principles, and upper and lower world forces.

The peoples in the present-day southwestern United States developed analogous religious and social centralization as the Mississippi Valley Mound Builders. Around A.D. 500, most of the peoples living in the present-day Arizona and New Mexico areas were hunters and gatherers living in pit houses, where the foundations were dug into the ground and then the roof covered. These people, known as the Mogollan Culture, were introduced to ideas and technologies from the powerful cultures of Central America. The cultures there had already been growing crops and developed many cities with complex religions and architecture. Pottery and religious practice, as well as agriculture, were adopted from traders and colonists from the Central American cultures. The Pima and Tohono O'odham descended from these Central American immigrants, who had a profound effect socially and culturally on the Mogollan peoples, who adopted and incorporated many practices of the new peoples and began to create complex architecture and plant corn and other crops. The period from A.D. 500 to nearly 1200 saw the emergence of the Pueblo peoples and the formation of settlements and villages throughout the southwestern area, which was tied in trade with the peoples on the western ocean coast as well as the trade and cultures of Central America.

Nevertheless, while the emergent Pueblo villages and cultures began to farm and build beautiful religious centers such as Pueblo Bonito, the Pueblos developed and retained distinct religious, cultural, and political identities. The Mogollan–Pueblo peoples did not adopt the culture or religion of the central American traders and colonists, but rather extended and used the new architecture and food supplies to support larger settlements and build distinctive religious structures such as kivas. For the Pueblo peoples, humans emerged from four worlds located underground. The kivas are underground because people enter the kivas for ceremonies and prayer aimed at honoring and reenacting the creation story of the people from the worlds beneath the earth. During ceremonial occasions the kiva represents a conduit for prayer and communication with the spirit beings of the lower worlds, through which people traveled in previous times and received aid and advice.

The village and religious organization of the pueblo peoples differs considerably from those of the immigrant Central American traders and colonists. A central religious ceremony among the Mayan culture and many cultures that it influenced, including the Aztecs, is the story surrounding the ball game, which to contemporary sports fans might look like a cross between soccer and basketball. The game was played with a rubber ball, and the goals were round hoops placed vertically at each end of a court, which was often lowered partially into the ground. In Mayan and related cultures, the ball game signifies a struggle between life and death, and the effort of a set of twins who wish to descend to the world of death in order to do battle with the lords of death, in revenge for the taking of their father. On ceremonial occasions the game symbolizes the battle against the lords of death. The winners of the game signify the honor of descending to the land of the dead to do battle with the lords of death. In some situations, the winners of the ceremonial ball game may have been put to death with the idea they would replay the role of the twins and seek to battle the lords of death in the underworld. On other occasions the losers may signify the ultimate futility of battling the lords of death, who must win in the end and use dishonorable means to take the lives of humans. The living people have consolation, in this worldview, that their bodies and spirits are reborn in the form of plants that nourish the living world.

The Mayan–Central American religions and pueblo religions have different interpretations of the underworld, and their ceremonies and community organizations differed as well. The Mogollan-Pueblos borrowed technologies, architecture, and plant food production methods such as irrigation, but maintained distinct cultural and social communities in which they used innovations to elaborate and support their own values, religion, and way of living.

Most of the pueblo peoples of present-day Arizona abandoned the area because of a severe drought starting about A.D. 1175. Between A.D. 500 and 1175, the environment in present-day Arizona was wetter than the desert conditions that exist there now. As the land became hotter and drier, crops failed and many began to move eastward to live near the Rio Grande River in present-day New Mexico. These migrations took place during the 1200s and 1300s. When the first Spanish explorers found them, the pueblos numbered at least fifty in the Rio Grande region, while the Hohokam speakers, Pima, Ak-Chin, and others, tried to eke out an existence along the rivers or turn to living in the desert. The Hopi villages concentrated along the Colorado River and in northern Arizona. When the Spanish encountered the Pueblos, they already had a history of change and migration in a difficult ecological environment.

The peoples and cultures of North America, like all human groups, were undergoing change long before the European intrusion. Change can be a product of environmental changes, new technologies, generational differences, cultural and spiritual events, or interpreted revelations. We know that there were changing patterns of social and cultural life among the Native nations of the pre-Columbian period, but we know little about exact ethnographic details. Archaeological evidence provides some interesting clues to historical events in some cultures, especially if we can identify their present-day descendants. Nevertheless, archaeology is not a science with complete information and much theorizing on cultural and ethnographic matters is necessary.

Native communities, like all human groups, are not static and unchanging. Social and cultural institutions are upheld by committed social action by individuals and the community. Not all members of the community will agree on the interpretation of a group's history or its ceremonial life. Native communities include many spiritual leaders, with different apprenticeships and spiritual teachers. The ceremonies and prayers may vary from teacher to teacher, and each apprentice may have his own experiences and special relations to the sacred. Native traditions are negotiated with families, clans, and communities and adapt to changing ecological conditions as well as through changing political and religious relations. As we shall see later, although there is a strong sense of tradition or conservatism in Native nations, this does not mean that Native nations have been the same for thousands of years. Social and cultural change in highly religious and conservative communities often takes place through visions and dreams, and through contact and instruction with the spirit world. In very religiously oriented Indian communities, where the sacred permeates social and political relations, change comes through new insights and knowledge from the sacred world. Sacred law is changed often by insight or knowledge gained through visions, ceremonies, or portents. Often a leader will emerge with a vision and a new way of doing things, and those who believe him follow, while others will remain as before. The separation of the Crow nation from a mound-building nation along the southern Mississippi River and their migration from the southern to the northern plains, starting the 1400s, is told in this way: No Vitals, brother to leader of the people, had a vision that proposed a splitting in leadership between the two brothers. Those willing to follow No Vitals left on a sacred quest that ultimately led to establishment of the Crow Nation and to a new homeland in the north.

Immediately after the first encounters with Europeans, Indian nations were changed in ways that distinguished them from their predecessors. The pre-Columbian Native world was more populous, and the southern nations more sedentary and perhaps more religiously and politically centralized in the years between A.D. 800 and 1500. Some estimates give between 3 and 12 million Native people living in the present-day United States around 1500. The most immediate impact from first European encounters during the 1500s was the spread of diseases such as smallpox, cholera, and others. Throughout North and South America millions of Native people perished. The new diseases were not treatable with Native medicines and few Natives had natural resistance.

It is difficult to gauge the effect of the destruction of life to the social and political communities of Native nations. The pueblo communities declined from about fifty to nineteen, while archaeological records indicate that some mound-building communities suffered losses as high as 90 percent. The diseases were spread from intermittent contact with Europeans in the coastal areas into the interior through trade routes and normal social relations. The decline of populations owing to disease in the interior and northern regions is difficult to estimate. Native populations started a rapid decline that did not stop until 1910. The effect of the diseases on communities led to losses of elders and spiritual leaders, people who carried the history and knowledge of the community. Among the mound-building peoples, during the 1500s, losses of life led to scarcity of food and increased conflict among nations. Sporadic Spanish records indicate that political and religious centers, once centralized and powerful, experienced rebellion from subordinate communities, who took advantage of the turmoil to throw off the yoke of political and spiritual domination. During the 1500s, the entire mound-building culture declined. People moved out of the large towns and abandoned their sacred mounds and sacred centers to move into scattered and independent villages. In the Choctaw tradition, the people abandoned their town and sacred mound, Nanih Waya, and the various kinship and village groups spread out to live in more isolated areas. The cause, according to the Choctaw oral history, was the scarcity of hunting around Nanih Waya. The Great Suns disappeared, and political leadership became less based on religious relations and more based on kinship group, village organization, and warrior skills.

Because of the dramatic population losses and resulting turmoil, many elders and spiritual leaders who kept the knowledge of the traditions died and many of the traditions were not passed on. When Europeans first saw the mounds and remnants of religious sites in many places in eastern North America, they were very impressed, but many of the local Indian nations could tell them very little about the mounds. This led the Europeans to doubt that the Native Americans built the mounds, and a variety of theories to explain the mound building were developed, such as the views that the mounds were build by the lost tribes of Israel or travelers from European antiquity. From among the Indian nations, we have only fragments of stories and traditions about the mound-building period, although we know for almost certain the Cherokee, Choctaw, Creek, Chickasaw, Caddo, and many other peoples were part of the Mississippi mound-building tradition. Several Indian nations have traditions about the fall of the mound-building period. Among the Cherokee there are several stories about a time when there was a priesthood that led the nation in religious and political matters. According to the Cherokee creation stories, priests were leaders of all seven of the Cherokee clans. Cherokee stories indicate there was a priesthood that led ceremonies and honored the rise of the sun each morning. Prayers were made from the platform mounds to encourage the sun to rise and have a safe journey across the sky each day. Because of oppressive and immoral actions by the priesthood, in some stories the raping of women, the Cherokee priesthood was overthrown by warrior and village leaders. Priests continued to play a role in the Cherokee nation but were subordinate to village chiefs. Thereafter the Cherokee social order is less a centralized theocracy and more of a coalition of about sixty relatively independent villages. Priests are different from shamans in that priests are usually trained for their profession from childhood and, as among the Cherokee, the priests belonged to special families. A shaman does not inherit his calling through his lineage, but rather has a vision or spiritual experience that provides him with a calling. A shaman can travel to the spirit world to bring back recently deceased or very sick individuals. When a priest cures, he tries to restore moral and cosmic relations, which are believed to be out of balance and in need of restoration. The spiritual leaders among the Mound Builders were most likely priests, but many of the more northern and western hunter and gather nations probably had shamans.

The Choctaw have a long oral history of the struggle between priests and clan, or Iksa, leaders. In the beginning, the priests, who attended to the Temple of the Sun, managed a relatively harmonious society within a sacred town. The people gave thanks to the sun for nourishing and creating the earth and the annual cycle of life. The Choctaw leaders, the Inki and Ishki, husband and wife, were appointed by the Great Spirit to lead and instruct the people. Then the Great Spirit and his wife ascended to the upper world after creating the City of the Sun for the people on earth. When the priests interpreted the Europeans as gifts from the Creator, their policies based on this interpretation led to European domination and abuse. The warriors and clan leaders increasingly challenged the theocracy and assert political leadership within the nation. The Choctaw priests were excluded from political leadership and they turned toward fortune-telling, occasional political advice, and healing. A similar pattern is noted among the Chickasaw. When De Soto visited them about 1540, the Chickasaw leader was treated as a sacred person and carried on the shoulders of men. Documents from English traders working among the Chickasaw in the 1690s still mention a principal Chickasaw leader based on clan affiliation. However, he was not a sacred personage carried about by others but a first among political equals within a gathering of village and clan leaders.

The diseases that spread to the interior nations caused disruption and change. The mound-building nations were destroyed and turned toward more secular and decentralized political and religious organization. By the time of first consistent contact with Europeans for many nations in the 1600s, many Indian nations had already undergone dramatic changes and were not living in the ways that they had lived for thousands of years before. We have little information and can only guess at the effects of the early devastation, much of it taking place before many of the Native peoples even saw a European. The information and knowledge we have about Native nations starts, to a large extent, with early European contacts and records collected mostly after 1600. There are indications that even the Powhatan Confederacy, which met the Jamestown colonists in 1607, had been undergoing change and conflict for many years. The descriptions by European settlers and explorers are often about Indian nations enduring or having endured considerable change and stress.

Scholarly knowledge about Native life and nations starts to a large extent with the colonization and settlement of Indian lands. Generally the condition and situation of the Indian nations in about 1600 is considered the starting point or long-standing condition of the Indian nations at the time of European contact and interest. How the Indian nations were living during this early colonial period is often believed to be the way they had always lived, and the images of early contact come to define Indian peoples, their characteristics, and their place in American history. Nevertheless, European contact intensified the processes of change and disruption among the Indian nations. The colonization period introduced new markets, greater political and military competition, diseases, and resulting demographic changes, and led to faster and more dramatic change than during the pre-Columbian period. The Wampanoags, led by King Philip in New England between Puritan colonization in 1620 and 1675, believed that their world had been severely corrupted and rebelled against the Europeans in a desperate effort to set their world in order. Failing in the military effort, the Wampanoags were relegated to Puritan political and cultural domination.

Despite the increasingly rapid and often destructive change among Indian nations during the 1500s and 1600s, scholars often attempt to use historical, archaeological, and oral history information in order to best construct the way the Native peoples lived in the period before and immediate to European contacts. The cultural and social reconstructions are often illustrative of how a typical Indian nation and its communities might have looked in particular times in history. Anthropologists often use the concept of culture area to indicate the relative similarity of cultures that occupy large ecological zones.

The eastern woodland cultures contain many Iroquoian- and Algonkian-speaking nations that live in a similar ecological area and have similar forms of economic organization and methods of securing food and medicinal plants and exploiting the environment.

The culture area concept helps organize and classify a large number of Indian nations according to geography and environmental circumstances that condition their way of life. This method, while useful, has some drawbacks because it tends to be ahistorical and presents cultures at different times in their histories and in relation to European contact, without making the reader aware of such difficulties. For example, the Indian nations of the plains cultural area have become widely known. The horse, Sun Dance, buffalo hunts, and the dress and style of the plains Indians have become almost synonymous with the public image of Indian. Nevertheless, before the 1500s and 1600s, few Indian peoples lived on the plains. Horses were introduced into the area after the middle 1500s by Spanish explorers. Before the horses, while some buffalo hunting took place on foot, the main economic resources were not buffalo but horticulture, supplemented by hunting, carried on by Indian Nations living in villages along the river beds. The Indian nations that make up the public image of the plains tribes such as the Lakota, Blackfeet, Assiniboine, Gros Ventre, Cheyenne, Kiowa, and others were not living on the plains areas in the 1500s or 1600s, but were pushed into the plains by the force of European colonial expansion. Many of the commonly understood northern plains Nations were living in woodland regions before more eastern nations like the Iroquois or Ojibway invaded their territories armed with European weapons and supplies. Some woodland nations were forced onto the plains, where they encountered other Indian nations, like the Kiowa and Pawnee, and with whom the plains territories became places of active competition and military engagement.

While the culture area classifications are useful, Native peoples do not view their nations in this way. Most Native peoples prefer to be identified as nations or "tribes." Native people generally identify with a family, clan, village, or moiety, depending on the particular social and cultural organization of the group. Many might identify with subgroups within the nation, such as a regional coalition of villages, like the Cherokee Overhill towns, or with a clan and moiety, such as the Tlingit Kiksadi (frog) clan within the Raven moiety. The terms "nation" and "tribe" are not words that belong to any indigenous Native community. While the term I use to describe Indian peoples is nation, the concept is Western, and Indian communities have a much more cosmic understanding of their community organization and their relations to the power beings in the universe.

All plants are our brothers and sisters. They talk to us, and if we listen we can hear them. Arapaho proverb[4]

Nation is a concept that developed from political and legal competition between the Canadian and U.S. governments in order to place the struggle for self-government and cultural preservation within legal and political terms understood in American and Canadian policy and legal discussions.

Native terms of identity are often local and kin-based, and concepts of tribe, nation, or confederacy are often created through religious ceremony and creation stories. Among the Creek a person belonged to the clan and sacred square and village of one's mother. One's primary social and religious and political allegiances were to the village and kinship group and only secondarily to the coalition of villages that made up the Creek political community. The body politic of Indian nations is generally decentralized, and local and kinship obligations often take precedence over commitments to national groups. The collective commitment of subgroups or individuals to the nation is often a defining characteristic of nationality among modern European nations, but Indian nations in the pre-Columbian period, and to a significant extent up to the present, do not exhibit such collective political allegiances. Sometime between A.D. 1000 and 1400, five Iroquois nations formed a confederacy based on the visions of Dekanawidah, a Huron wise man.

> I, [the Peacemaker], . . . with the statesmen of the League of Five Nations, plant the Tree of Peace. . . . Roots have spread out. . . . Their nature is Peace and strength. We place at the top of the Tree of Peace an eagle. . . . If he sees in the distance any danger threatening, he will at once warn the people of the League. If any man or any nation outside the Five Nations shall obey the laws of the Great Peace . . . they may trace back the roots of the Tree . . . [and] be welcomed to take shelter. The smoke of the Council Fire of the league shall ever ascend and pierce the sky so that other nations who may be allies may see the Council Fire of the Great Peace [the eternal flame of liberty at the center of the United Nations]. Dekanawidah, the Peacemaker[5]

Although the law of the confederacy is the word of the Great Spirit, the rules of the confederacy preserve the political autonomy and power of families and clans. The council of the confederacy was composed of forty-nine leaders drawn from families and clans within the five nations. Nevertheless, the confederate council could not make decisions that were binding on the rest of the Iroquois people without gaining unanimous consent from all the families, clans, and nations. Consensual political decision making is a key characteristic of many Indian nations. Individuals, kin groups, villages, and other groups have the right to voice their views on issues affecting the entire community. In order for there to be a collectively binding agreement, all the people and subgroups must agree; if not, then each group carries on as it sees fit. This decentralized and consensual decision making requiring unanimous consent often upset European officials who preferred majority rule or centralized authority and quick decisions, while the Indian method requires considerable time and discussion before decisions can be made and recognized. If considerable agreement on an issue was not achieved, it was often tabled and not acted on. Local groups acted as they saw best, and often Indian communities and nations did not act concertedly according to European expectations. European colonial administrators often attempted to create more centralized and powerful organization within Indian nations by recognizing certain chiefs or creating kings or emperors, but these efforts often were largely ignored by the Indian people, who continued to carry on their political and social relations according to their own cultural principles of individual and subgroup autonomy.

Indian nations' identity and political process are not like European political understandings or traditions. Native peoples self-identify as Haudenosaunee, Anishinabe, or Muskogee, and each has a distinct social and cultural organization that constitutes their national community. With the hundreds of Indian nations in North America, there are hundreds of ways in which communities are organized and carried on. Anishinabe clans, language, and social and political organization differ drastically from the Iroquois Confederacy, or the Cherokee, Creek, and other Indian nations. Indian nations do not form homogeneous cultures, and they do not form homogeneous political systems, kinship groups, or national communities. Indian nations are uniquely organized. They represent hundreds of languages, hundreds of independent cultural groups and nations. Because of this distinctive history of unique cultural, political, and national organization, the Indian nations do not form a common ethnic group; the internal diversity is too great. The uniqueness of each community or nation laid the seed for the struggle with colonial and government officials about Native nationality. Out of Native political process and organization, social and cultural community, and the sacredness of space and territory, Native peoples have endured with their unique forms of community and nationality. Natives have carried on their own social, cultural, and political traditions from time immemorial, they have lived on the land provided to them from the Creator, and they have a purpose to serve in the universe given to them by the Creator. They serve their divine purpose by carrying on ceremonies honoring the Creator, giving thanks for his gifts, and fulfilling the sacred instructions and missions given in the teachings to the nation.

## Native Values and Worldviews

There was no one Native American religion or worldview. Each Indian Nation had its own creation stories and religious beliefs and understandings. The ceremonies differed, and even though there was much trade and exchange of cultural songs, dances, and even ceremonies, a borrowing Nation usually placed a new cultural item within its own cultural traditions in ways that were not intended by the donor nation. A song about creation might be borrowed and used as a love song by one borrowing nation and as a funeral song by another borrower. Peoples in one Native culture, just as Europeans would later do, did not always understand the context of the religious items they borrowed from another Indian nation and usually reinterpreted them from within the context of their own cultural understandings. Even though religions and ceremonies differed considerably among the Indian nations, there were some common patterns of values and themes in Native cultures that can be instructively compared with Western religious views in order to better understand Native worldviews, values, and perspectives. The more we can gain insight into the way Natives understood the world—their goals, values, assumptions about human nature, assumptions about the universe, and about the role of community, individual and political process—the better we will be comprehend the Native struggle for land, self-government, and community preservation over the past five hundred years.

If there is one bald generalization one could make about Indian nations over the past five hundred years of colonialism, it would be that Indian Nations have sought to preserve themselves despite colonial efforts to assimilate them into Canadian or U.S. society. Although Native nations have resisted unwanted change in their communities, they have not always survived in the ways they wanted to; the forces of colonialism arrayed against them at times have been mighty and formidable. The strong emphasis on cultural and community preservation is no accident; it is deeply embedded in the way that Native peoples understand the world and the place of people in the universe.

There are strong orientations of conservatism inherent in Native religions and worldviews. Most Native religions view the universe as holistic, as one whole composed of many powerful beings, but with an ultimate unified purpose. Unlike Christian worldviews, Natives do not make radical distinctions between this world and the otherworld, or earth and heaven, or between the sacred and profane worlds. In Christianity and Platonic philosophy, there are two worlds, the sacred or real world and the profane, which is full of contingency, suffering, death, sickness, and misfortune. In Christianity, this world is a dark and profane world, while the real world is heaven, where saved people are reunited with Jesus and God. The goal in Christianity is salvation in heaven, so we call it an otherworldly religion. The earth is considered an evil and corrupt place, and salvation comes not in this world, but in the next world.

Native views on these issues are very different. For many Native religions, the Creator is a benevolent gift giver who provides the plants, animals, waters, and other forces in the universe for some unknowable purpose or plan. Humans and the Indian nations are part of this plan, but the plan is not comprehensible to humans. Life is seen as a gift, and all the powers and forces in the universe are also part of the Creator's plan. The Creator, or Great Spirit in some traditions, is an unknowable force. Sometimes the Creator is anthropomorphized, but this might show the influence of Christianity or the diversity of views among the Indian religions. The unreachable Creator communicates with the universe and humans through intermediary forces and powers, such as animals, lightning, rain, or portents. Since the universe is a gift and part of the Creator's plan, every power and force is part of this plan and, therefore, has a divine mission to undertake. Thus all beings are to be respected and honored, for they are part of the sacred plan. The earth is a gift and a sacred place and is to be thanked and honored for providing sustenance to the people and other beings. The only real world is the present world, and there is much less emphasis on heaven as a distinct reality from this world. In many traditions, after death people traveled west to new land much like the one people lived in when alive. Salvation in the next world is not strongly emphasized in Native religions. Many Natives religions have views of rebirth, such as the Tlingit, and people often prefer rebirth into this world rather than endless bliss or punishment in the worlds after death. Since this world is a sacred place, there is relatively little interest in reorganizing or changing the world, since that may disrupt the plan of the Creator. In the Christian view, this world is an evil place; it is not seen as sacred but profane and therefore can be made better by human efforts. Progress is making the world a better place by transforming the raw materials of the earth into the products of human civilization. In some Christian Protestant sects, humans have a moral obligation to make heaven on earth and transform the world through work and moral action. Progress and utopia at the end of history are symbols of transformation in Western culture.

In many Native views, transforming or changing the world is dangerous. Humans are not the center of the universe in Native religions, but are usually one of many power beings that make up the universe. There are many powers greater than humans, and humans must be careful not to upset them. Disrupting other forces in the universe can have dire consequences because the offended forces or beings will retaliate and cause harm in the form of sickness, death, defeat in battle, failure of crops, bad luck in the hunt, or other misfortunes within the community. The consequences of disruptive or disrespectful actions are not sin or guilt or punishment in hell in the afterlife, but rather retaliation and harm in this world, not in the next world. The Creator is a benevolent gift giver and does no wrong. When humans break sacred law, inaccurately perform ceremonies, disrupt and disrespect other powers in the universe, they bring retaliation and harm on themselves in this world. The harm can be corrected by ceremonies appealing to the offended forces and attempting to restore harmony and respect. In the creation stories of many northeastern woodland cultures like the Iroquois and Anishinabe, a character known as Sky Woman is cast out of the upper sky for quarreling with relative spirit beings, and she lands in the great water. Several animals sacrifice themselves by diving deep into the water to bring up land, which Sky Woman transforms into the earth. The animals make a pact with Sky Woman and the people that they will sacrifice their bodies for the sustenance of humans. A female turtle volunteers to carry the land on her back so that the people can live, hence the expression Turtle Island, often used by woodland Indians in speeches to designate North America. In return for their services and animal bodies, the humans must honor their agreement with ceremonies and respect. If the humans do so, the spirit of the animals killed in the hunt will be preserved and will be reborn, ensuring that game will be plentiful. Animals are not killed for sport because that would disrupt the sacred covenant relation between humans and animals and the animals would refuse to give themselves to humans for food, and the people would suffer. Indian people must eat plants and animals and must exploit their environment to live. By conservationist methods and taking only what is needed for life, Indians honor the powers of plants and animals and help ensure their survival and their own survival as well. In this way, humans try to maintain sacred and spiritual relations with the powers of the universe.

A long time ago the Deer People (a wi yv wi) came together. They saw that the human beings or the Tsalagi (Cherokee) were the weakest of all living beings. They knew that the Tsalagi needed food, they needed shelter, they needed clothes, and they needed knowledge. The Deer People came together in a great council, and they agreed to give themselves in order to help the Tsalagi stay alive, live a good life, and understand the ways of the Good Mind (o slguu oda nv dv). The Deer People told the Tsalagi that hunters (ga no hi li to hv) could hunt deer and use their flesh to nourish their bodies; use their skin for clothes, shelter and sinew; and use their bones for tools.

The deer people would sacrifice themselves so the Tsalagi could live. But, said the Deer People, the Tsalagi hunters can never take more than what they need and must use all that they take. In this way the Tsalagi would show respect and honor for the Deer People. And so it was. For many years the Tsalagi would pray and sing before they hunted. There was plenty to eat. None of the Tsalagi ever went hungry or became cold or needed government welfare. Life was good.[6]

Just as the order of the Native universe is given and sacred, so are the social institutions, clans, and norms of community. Ceremonies are often ways of acknowledging thanks to the Creator and other power beings for their guidance and protection. Many annual renewal ceremonies like the Green Corn Ceremony among the eastern and southern nations encouraged the purification and renewal of the world. In the Sun Dance, the Lakota, Cree, Cheyenne, and other plains nations encouraged restoration of the world by honoring the thunderbird, who is appeased to make lightning and rain, which will make the grass grow and feed the buffalo, on which the plains peoples depended for food. Ceremonies, social institutions, and political organization were often seen as part of the divine order of the universe. Therefore, disrespectful performance of ceremonies, or religiously nonsanctioned change in social and cultural relations, led to upsetting the balance of relations in the universe and this-worldly retaliation from powers or spirits that were disturbed in the process. The emphasis in most Native nations was not dominating, controlling, or reordering the world, but learning from it and finding one's place and carrying out one's prescribed task within the grand plan of the Creator. Actions against the plan of the universe lead to this-worldly harm, and ceremonies are necessary to recreate harmony with the offended power beings. Most Indian nations and people had conservative orientations toward the world, religion, and social and political relations. Change required portents or religious sanctions in order not to disturb the balance of forces and plan of the universe. Consequently, most Indian peoples strongly emphasized preserving their religion, kinship, and political relations despite strong ecological change and, after A.D. 1500, the powerful forces of colonialism. The continued efforts of Indian nations to preserve their communities, territories, and cultures also derive at least in part, if not wholly, from their views of the nature and power relations in the universe.

In the Christian Western culture, human nature is seen as self-interested. People seek material gain and political and cultural advantage. Since all are assumed to behave this way, life is seen as competitive, active, and personal.

Native cultures share a sense of cultural individualism, but it is cast within the context of their worldviews and hence is very different from the Western view of self-interested individualism. Each individual in most Indian nations is considered a power being given from the spirits or Creator. Like all beings in the universe, each human must be respected as an autonomous spirit power who has a role to fulfill within the Creator's plan. Similarly, kinship groups, villages, clans, bands, or other social groupings are seen as autonomous collective human forces within the same sacred plan. Since the plan of the Creator is unknown to humans, each group and individual is given respect and autonomy to carry out their plan through their life and collective group tasks. For women, a main life task is bringing new spirit beings into the community. Women often are seen as creator beings who are a portal to the spirits and who bring children or new spirit beings to the community. In many traditions, such as Sky Women in the northeastern woodland, or Changing Women among the Dine, women are creator beings who help bring the earth and people into existence. Men, on the other hand, are less directly tied to the spirit powers, and they search for their sacred life task or instructions through visions, dreams, and ceremonies. Women can participate in dreams, have visions, and participate in some ceremonies. An individual's instructions usually are not shared with all the people in the community, but sometimes told to elders who help interpret the visions or dreams in order to guide the individual in the right direction. Powerful spirit helpers assist and instruct the individuals through life and help them understand their role within the sacred order of the universe.

The sacred autonomy of social groupings and individuals is generally reflected in the political processes of most Indian nations. Decisions are made through a process of discussion and must have unanimous consent in order to be binding on the entire group. There is no majority rule, since then the majority will force its will over the minority. Each individual is a member of the cosmic order and is living to carry out their sacred life tasks and cannot subordinate his calling to the demands of other human forces. Thus in Indian councils, all people, often including women and young men, have the right to address the council and express their views. Those decisions that do not gain unanimous consent are either tabled, discussed further on future occasions, or abandoned, and each individual or group does as it sees as best. Similarly kinship groups, villages, bands, and clans often enjoy the same sacred and political autonomy, depending on the rules of the particular Indian Nation, and each group is given respect and autonomy. This decentralized and highly consensual political order was difficult and frustrating for European officials to understand, since they usually preferred more centralized decision-making and power relations.

The individuals in an Indian nation often did not give their primary allegiance to the collective nation, as in the contemporary view of nationality. Rather, religious commitments and kinship or local group commitments often took precedence. In the pre-Columbian period and to a large extent to the present day, Native nations are constructed on the consensual union of individuals, social groups, and religious commitments. The Indian nations, social groups, and individuals see themselves not only living among other nations but as part of a cosmic community of power beings. Individuals, social relations, and nationality are embedded and interacting with the forces of the animals, plants, elements such as fire, water, earth, and wind, all of what the Western world calls the natural world. The Indian nations, however, do not make a distinction between the natural and human world. There is only one world of power beings, and people must strive to maintain purpose and harmony within the powerful forces within the universe. Native peoples do not separate human life or sociopolitical life from the forces of the cosmic order. Native people, social groups, and nations are active forces within a universe of many powerful forces with which constant attention must be given to maintain good and respectful relations.

## Land, Government, and Cosmic Community

Native worldviews let us make a few observations about Native values and motivations, which will help us interpret their social actions during the history of colonialism and to a large extent at the present time. The reciprocity of beings in the universe and the danger of disrupting powerful forces suggests that Native nations will strongly emphasize social, cultural, and religious preservation, despite powerful forces for change. This conservative orientation is inherent in their worldview. Native peoples trade and barter, but they are not capitalists in the sense of producing goods according to the demands of the market place. Native peoples have strong religious injunctions against wasting food or exploiting the environment for uses beyond their subsistence needs. Native individuals and communities will strive to preserve their sacred autonomy and purposes within a cosmic community of power or spirit beings. There will be strong emphasis on individual and group autonomy and group preservation. Native political relations will be decentralized and largely consensual for groups and individuals. Like relations within the universe at large, justice relations in Indian nations will be restorative. If a crime is committed, then efforts will be made to make restitution, if possible, for the harm, and the individuals or groups will then be restored to their original condition, which will rebalance community and individual relations. Cases of murder sometimes are restored with goods or services, but often a spirit is demanded for a spirit, since the victim's spirit cannot be restored. Balance and harmony in social relations reflect those in the cosmic community.

Native nations have sacred tasks to perform in the universe, and they will strive to preserve themselves and fulfill those visions. The Creator made the Native nations, gave them their land, sacred places, cultures, and ceremonies, and the Native peoples will strive to preserve them. Native nations did not necessarily own land in the Western sense, but they were granted land by the Creator as part of the cosmic plan and relations and for their care and subsistence. Native peoples are the designated caretakers of the land and it is their duty to preserve the resources or sacred gifts of the land and environment. Indian nations have a sacred role to play in the cosmic plan of the universe; otherwise the Creator would not have put them on earth. Understanding and knowledge of that sacred role is gathered through ceremonies, dreams, and the collective wisdom and experience of the individuals who make up the nation. Native nations and people must preserve the gifts of the Creator and pass them onto future generations.

> So Grandson, this is why our People have reverence for the Earth and all living things. We must have balance and harmony guide us. If you want to live many years, then live in this way. Keep your words that you make between People, understand that your mind is your spirit, respect our Mother Earth, for she is the only force we have to keep us healthy, and she will reveal the mysteries and powers to grant us long life.[7]

# Notes

1. Eddie Webb, *Generations Our People Say . . .* (Sacramento: California Department of Education, 2000), pp. 21–23.

2. Paul G. Zolbrod, *Dine Bahane: The Navajo Creation Story* (Albuquerque: University of New Mexico Press, 1984), pp. 86–89.

3. Edward Benton-Banai, *The Mishomis Book: The Voice of the Ojibway* (St. Paul, MN: Red School House, 1988).

4. Webb, *Generations,* p. 91.

5. Webb, *Generations,* p. 208.

6. Webb, *Generations,* p. 208.

7. Webb, *Generations,* p. 91.

# A Multidimensional Theory of Colonialism: The Native North American Experience

**6**

THEORIES OF COLONIALISM emphasize materialist domination and are analyzed from the point of view of the colonizer. The primary focus is on the powerful forms of political, economic, and cultural domination, and sometimes the effects of disease. Yet the views of the colonized deserve greater attention. In North America, Native communities survived five hundred years of colonialism. How? Why? In what ways? Theories that emphasize colonial domination cannot answer such questions. This chapter presents a theory and method that place the colonized at the center and view them as historical actors with pliable cultures and communities. The theory also incorporates the processes of cultural exchange between colonized and colonizer. Such a multidimensional theory provides a more accurate and powerful understanding of the processes of colonization and of social change in general.

## The Colonial Context of North America

Political competition, economic incorporation, cultural exchange, and biological resistance are major features of the colonial context. By political competition, I mean the strategic and diplomatic bargaining between nations by which they ensure their own protection and effect and protect their strategic interests. Geopolitics is the study of international relations or diplomatic national policy.[1] As to economic incorporation, world systems theorists and economists have long argued for the relative autonomy of markets, or a pattern of relations based largely on material interests, which drives the expansion of markets or explains exchange and market relations. Economists, and many economic anthropologists, believe that the urge to truck and barter is part of human nature.[2] Cultural exchange refers to the transfer and internalization of symbolic codes between colonized and colonizer. Such symbolic codes include language, information, norms, economic ethics, worldviews, religion, and many other aspects of culture.[3] Biological resistance refers to the capability of the colonized to resist the diseases of the colonizer.[4]

While there have been colonial systems in many historical periods and in many places, the colonization of North America exhibits several characteristics that can shed some information on processes of colonialism in general. A major distinguishing feature of North American colonialism was the competitive colonial rivalries among European powers. Multiple European powers struggled for control of North America. The British, French, Spanish, Dutch, Swedes, and, to some extent, the Russians struggled for control of land and trade. The situation of competitive rivalries reflected the situation of competing nations in Europe, and these rivalries usually resulted in armed conflicts and wars in North America.[5] The intense political and economic competition led to treaties of alliance with Native nations, which held important trade, diplomatic, and military assets capable of tipping the tide of European colonial relations. Native leverage on rival European contenders ended by about 1820. The Europeans made trade and diplomatic agreements and treaties of alliance with Indian nations, and thereby gave these nations international recognition. These early treaties later became the precedent for more treaties and especially the treaties negotiated for land by the United States and Canada with their respective Native peoples. There are few other places in the world where colonizing nations negotiated similar treaties.

Like that of many non-European peoples over the past five hundred years, the colonization of Native North Americans occurred in association with the rise of capitalism in Europe and with the emergence of world markets. Furthermore, the United States ultimately emerged as a central player among the core capitalist countries. Consequently, Native North Americans were economically colonized by a major capitalist economy in the world system. This close proximity to the capitalist core is not the same experience as the African nations, the Native peoples of Latin and South America, Australian Aborigines, or the peoples of India, China, Japan, and other non-Western nations who were forced to respond to the world expansion of capitalism. In some ways, the future of non-Western peoples, increasingly incorporated into a world capitalist market, can be seen in the experience of Native North Americans.

Cultural exchange in the colonial situation was carried by interpersonal interaction with missionaries, traders, colonial officials, slaves, and other colonists. To varying degrees both the indigenous peoples and colonizers get to know each other's language, culture, economy, political norms, and social relations. Each Native nation selectively appropriates ideas, words, economic techniques, forms of dress, and many other cultural and normative items.[6] In recent years, some cultural theorists have focused attention on the effects of cultural domination on subject peoples.[7] Nevertheless, it also is critical to understand the extent to which the colonized internalize selected aspects of the colonizer's culture. The cultural knowledge gained from the colonizer by the colonized was used to build resistance to colonization and/or promote acceptance and participation in the colonizer's new order.

Diseases killed millions of Natives throughout the Americas, and this large and rapid decline had major demographic, political, economic, and social impacts on many Indian nations. The rapid demographic decline of the Aztecs and Latin American Indians enabled the Spanish to subordinate them more easily. In North America, disease weakened many Indian communities throughout the colonial period, and Native health continues to be abysmal to this day.[8] The diseases lasted throughout the colonial period, striking deep into the interior, before many Europeans ever visited the people there, causing extremely large demographic losses as well as undocumented destruction of culture and social institutions.

## The Autonomy of Colonial Forces

For the purposes of conceptualization and analysis, I have identified geopolitics, economy, culture, and biology as major but relatively autonomous dimensions of the colonial situation. Each operates under an internal logic that is not determined by the forces of any one or all three of the others. I argue that during the 1690s, the strategic bargaining between France and England for control of North America east of the Mississippi River is not reducible to their interests to control the fur trade in North America, or to their interests to extend their religions over the region, or to assimilate the Native North Americans, or to their interest in controlling or spreading disease. The strategic bargaining relations of the colonial powers had their own primary end—to control territory for the glory, protection, and future political interests of their sovereign nations. Colonial political expansion, economic expansion, and cultural exchange operate at different and relatively independent levels in the colonial situation. In general, none is necessarily the by-product of the other, and thus each has to be investigated simultaneously in order to understand the overall pattern of colonial actions. By isolating these three arguments, specific historical colonial situations can be described and certain features of colonialism explained. Taking each argument one at a time will explain only part of the colonial situation. Therefore, the three major dimensions (or four if the biological dimension is included) can be reconstructed by weaving the arguments together over the same historical context. Such a discussion of colonialism in the American Southwest would concentrate on the features of Spanish, then Mexican, and after 1848 American colonial administration, on features of market relations and incorporation, the internalization of Western religion, as well as any epidemics that had a significant impact on the demography of the Native peoples of the Southwest.[9] The four analytical dimensions of colonialism provide a model for understanding the historical processes of colonialism. By isolating the patterns of colonial relations through the four dimensions, an integrated model including all four dimensions helps provide a more holistic explanation for the outcomes of colonial relations.

## Colonial Forces and Their Threats to Indigenous Communities

Each of the three dimensions of colonialism, geopolitics, market incorporation, and cultural exchange presents a critical threat to indigenous or colonized communities. In response to geopolitical threats, each indigenous nation seeks to protect territory and political autonomy. The threat of political domination by one or more colonizing nations is undesirable. Indeed, the indigenous nations sought to retain political independence as long as possible. The rights to self-government and control over territory increasingly became symbols of national, political, and cultural identity. In the precontact period, such concepts were developed in the context of colonial threats to territory and self-government. During the U.S. period, the increasingly powerful U.S. government redefined Indian treaties and government to deny Indians' status as foreign nations.[10] Nevertheless, much law concerning American Indian issues is centrally focused on treaty and legislative acknowledgment of Indian rights to limited self-government. Contemporary Indian reservation communities continue to assert rights to self-government and limited sovereignty based on law and treaty. A primary goal of tribal governments is building stronger government and community institutions as well as protecting land and indigenous rights. Indian communities have not given up their right to preserving a self-governing community. Each community moves to protect its territory and political autonomy from encroachment by colonizing entities. The issue of preserving political independence or limited powers of self-government is confronted by each indigenous nation. Naturally, the ways in which particular Indian nations try to preserve territory and political autonomy will vary according to the power of the colonizing nation as well as the resources and political organization of the colonized nations. Nevertheless, all indigenous nations are confronted with the same dilemma of preserving political independence, and therefore they are comparable in an analytical sense. Although the historical situations and the organization and resources of the indigenous nations vary empirically, the need to preserve land and political independence confronts each nation and, therefore, can be a fruitful point of comparison for understanding the range and possibilities of mobilization and change within colonizing political environments.[11]

Similarly, the increasing economic globalization of the world and the penetration of markets and trade confront each nation. If indigenous peoples are going to engage in trade, and if they are to achieve any comparative advantage in the trade, the price they must pay is increased economic dependency and loss of self-sufficiency. The movement from relative self-sufficiency to market dependency implies that Natives will need to compete or at least participate in the marketplace. Global market incorporation is a new form of economic relation for indigenous nations; once involved, each nation is confronted with the issues of producing for exchange, which often involves economic specialization of labor, production, and entrepreneurship. Native nations that cannot achieve reorganization in social and economic relations according to the demands of the marketplace will be forced into economic impoverishment. The observed result over the past several centuries has been the economic marginalization of many indigenous nations. Thus, once captured in the trade and market networks and dependent on market relations for basic goods, each indigenous nation is confronted with the requirement to maintain production for the market and change economic output according to its demands. The survival of any indigenous nation in the world market system depends partly on local available markets, but also on the organization of labor, skills, and resources, and the economic culture of the indigenous group. The possibilities of change or marginalization are not wholly given within the colonial situation of market relations and resulting dependency.

A third requirement faced by indigenous nations within a colonial context is cultural pluralism. Through cultural exchange, new values, norms, political models, economic ethics, religious worldviews, language, and other cultural aspects will be transferred and internalized by some members of the indigenous nation. These new forms of cultural understanding may be compatible with indigenous culture, may be tolerated, or may lead to division as well as to cultural and political factionalism. The Christian-pagan conflicts of the Iroquois since the 1820s illustrate the clash of Western religious and political models leading to internal political and cultural strife.[12] Other nations have tolerated new cultural elements, such as the Northern Cheyenne, who practice a variety of religions such as Catholicism, Native American Church, and traditional religion with ceremonies such as the Sun Dance.[13] Others may reject Western influences, as did many Creeks such as the Red Sticks, or followers of the Shawnee Prophet.[14] Nevertheless, many nations have incorporated Western political models, such as the constitutional governments of the Cherokee, Choctaw, Chickasaw, and Creek, and the Tlingit Alaska Native Brotherhood. And some among the Cherokee, Choctaw, Chickasaw, and Creek became agrarian capitalists with strong market orientations for profit making during the 1820s and later. The economic ethic of market profit making came not from indigenous cultures but from the interactions and transfer of market orientations to members of indigenous nations from members of colonizing nations. Each colonized nation confronts the dilemma of how to manage multiculturalism. The response of the community members of the colonized nations may depend on the organization and exclusiveness of the indigenous worldview, the compatibility of indigenous cultural elements with the culture of the colonizers, or the degree of indigenous control over the socialization of children and other elements.

In the colonial situation, each indigenous nation is confronted with protecting self-government, economic viability, and cultural continuity. If the biological dimension is added, then protection of physical health is yet another responsibility for colonized communities. Given the situation of colonial expansion, each indigenous nation must develop, from within its own institutional order, a strategy that will ensure meaningful survival, despite drastic change and unfavorable situations. Since each nation confronts similar issues of maintaining self-government, economic viability, and preserving cultural communities, it is possible to make systematic comparative empirical descriptions and historical analyses of the ways in which indigenous nations have tried to solve the demands of colonization.[15]

## Toward a Multidimensional Theory of Colonialism

The four major dimensions of colonial domination have been described as having a single impact on colonized nations. Such a view gives only a limited understanding of colonial relations, as none of the dimensions by itself provides a complete explanation of the outcome of colonized nations in terms of institutional change and survival. The geopolitical context or state domination of a colonized nation can explain much about the political possibilities of a colonized nation, but an argument based on power and strategic relations tells us little about the processes of change in a colonized nation, other than those forced on the colonized. For example, expansionary political pressures by the United States set the context for the Handsome Lake movement (1799–1815), a religious revitalization movement among the Iroquois, while at roughly the same time the Cherokee formed a constitutional government (1805–1828).[16] The geopolitical context cannot explain the different forms of institutional change among the Iroquois and Cherokee. The geopolitical argument, however, does explain the increasing political subordination of both the Cherokee and Iroquois during the early American period.

Similarly, the argument of global market incorporation does not explain why, in the south, only a small number of Cherokee, Choctaw, Chickasaw, and Creek took up producing cotton for profit, while over 95 percent did not. The opportunity of the cotton market was a precondition to participation in the market but not a sufficient condition. Nevertheless, market incorporation can explain many changes in Indian labor patterns and processes of economic marginalization. To illustrate, the rise of agrarian capitalists is better explained with the two arguments of transfer of market values through trader families and the cotton market opportunity. Thus the dimension of cultural exchange is critical to understanding the rise of southern Indian agrarian capitalism.[17]

A multidimensional theory of colonialism should include an integrated argument of geopolitics, transsocietal economy, and cultural exchange. Each dimension provides a powerful but fragmentary explanation on its own, yet yields more powerful explanatory possibilities within an integrated argument. One way to develop such an integrated argument is to analyze colonial situations in terms of geopolitical, market, and cultural exchange over the same historical period and region. In one sense, a theory prescribes where to look, and this theory prescribes to look at geopolitical, market, and cultural exchange relations in order to explain processes of political subordination, economic dependency, and cultural change. For example, in the southeast, the Cherokee, Choctaw, Chickasaw, and Creek were subject to similar political and land pressures from the United States, and were incorporated into the same sequence of markets on the world system, the fur trade, and after 1810 the cotton market, and a small portion of members of each nation took up producing cotton for the market. During the period from 1828 to 1867, all four of the southern nations adopted constitutional governments. The constitutional model for the government came from U.S. agents and was internalized by members of the entrepreneurial planter classes in each Indian nation. Thus mere force of geopolitical pressures did not induce the southern nations to adopt constitutional governments, since similar pressures were placed on the northern nations, such as the Iroquois, Delaware, and Ojibway, yet no enduring constitutional governments emerged among them over the same historical period. The rise of the cotton market in the south helps explain the rise of entrepreneurial Indians. In the northern country, on the other hand, although there were intermarriages as well as cultural transfer of trader skills and values, no capitalist class structure developed among the northern Indian nations. Consequently the southern Indian capitalists are a product of the cotton market opportunity and market organization as well as the new market values imported by trader families. The integrated argument of geopolitical pressures from the United States and the entrepreneurial, pro-constitutional classes of the southern Indian nations helps explain the rise of constitutional governments among the southern nations. The southern Indian nations moved to preserve self-government through political centralization and by forming constitutional governments; remained economically viable through plantation production and subsistence farming; and incorporated many elements of the colonizers' culture—constitutional government, market values, some Christianity—to reorganize their political, economic, and cultural institutions in order to enhance their overall goal of national survival within the colonial context.

The south is only one of many geopolitical, economic, and cultural localities within North America. Other regions may be analyzed in similar ways, although there will be considerable variation in geopolitical pressures, market relations, and form and content of cultural exchange. Such regions are known as the northeast, the plains, the Pacific northwest, the arctic, subarctic, California, the Great Basin, and the southwest. Even finer local or subregional areas might be defined. In the end, each nation confronts a unique set of geopolitical, economic, and cultural forms of colonialism.

Nevertheless, even the integrated argument of geopolitical, market, and colonial cultural relations provides an incomplete picture of the colonial process. All such arguments are external to the organization and culture of the indigenous nations, and unless these arguments are so powerful as to forcibly determine the response of the colonized nations, attention must be given to the institutional and cultural organization of the indigenous nations themselves.

# Beyond an External Model of Colonialism

Focusing on geopolitics, world economy, cultural exchange, and biology does not provide a complete model of colonial processes. Desperately missing from most interpretations of colonialism are the communities of the colonized and the colonized as actors. A more complete model should take into account the normative, political, economic, and cultural dimensions of the Indian communities themselves.[18] Furthermore, the heavy reliance on analytical features of the colonizers and the colonized can take an argument only so far. At some point, more precise understanding has to be gained by analyzing historical contingent processes within the context of the relations between colonizer and colonized. Thus the geopolitical, economic, cultural, and biological features of colonialism, set in context with the normative, political, economic, and cultural dimensions of colonized communities, create the situational context that informs actors and communities in specific historical situations. Such a position is consistent with Jürgen Habermas's view of "system" and "lifeworld," although the lifeworld concept does not help explain the individual possibilities of survival and change among indigenous communities. Colonized actors will adhere to the normative, political, economic, and cultural imperatives set out from their societal institutions and relations, while the political, economic, and cultural features of the colonial context will constrain and inform group and individual decisions. Those resulting patterns of action, whether processes of institutionalized change or adherence to tradition, are not reducible to political competition, economic incorporation, cultural exchange, or biological resistance.

# Explaining Processes of Institutionalized Change

The proposed argument is designed to explain patterns of institutional change and continuity. Institutionalized change occurs when an innovation becomes an enduring feature of the normative and cultural order of a community or society.[19] For example, most Hopi in the American Southwest rejected the Catholicism offered by Spanish missionaries, and thus Catholicism did not become a permanent or major feature of Hopi society. The adoption of a constitutional government by the Cherokee in 1828 is an example of major political institutional change. Aspects of Cherokee political centralization probably started as early as 1751, and other features, such as the abolition of the blood revenge in favor of courts, emerged over the 1799 to 1810 period. Between 1819 and 1828, the Cherokee increasingly centralized their government and formed a constitution that lasted until 1907, when their government was abolished by the U.S. government. The Cherokee constitution was institutionalized. The large majority of Cherokee accepted the new form of government and most adhered to it until the end of the Cherokee state. The Choctaw and Chickasaw also formed constitutional governments that were ultimately accepted and preserved by their societal members. Other examples of institutionalized change are the cultural and economic features of the

Handsome Lake movement (1799–1815) among the Iroquois, the Native American Church, the Shaker Church, the community and cultural changes of the Kickapoo Prophet, and others.[20]

Institutionalization requires sustained normative, political, economic, and cultural support within the community.[21] To the extent that the colonized accept and use cultural items borrowed from the colonizing regime, the greater the likelihood the colonized society will have to struggle with the emergence of multicultural views and consider issues of change based on views borrowed from the colonized society. Carriers of new cultural values, worldviews, economic ethos, and/or political models often advocate change in colonized communities. Whether the carriers of the new cultural values succeed in carrying out their new cultural imperatives depends on their political influence or power, their leadership, and their ability to organize and mobilize others in favor of change. The ability to mobilize groups for change will depend also on the form of community and political solidarity as well as on the specific modes and relations of differentiation among the major societal institutions, such as polity, community, economy, and culture. In general, more institutionally differentiated and well-integrated communities will be more capable of adopting consensual change than less differentiated and less socially and politically integrated societies or communities. Indigenous communities with institutional relations and cultural orientations similar to those of the colonizer will have greater possibilities for change in the direction of the colonizer's institutional and cultural order than those indigenous communities with greater institutional and differences from colonizing culture and institutional relations.

Significant cultural exchange with colonizers can have serious consequences for the continuity and survival of the communities and cultures of the colonized peoples. The cultural exchange and impact take place in the struggle over defining the basic orientations and ground rules of the social order. The struggle for the cultural preservation of religion and values, as well as of institutional, normative, and community order, is threatened by the introduction of potentially competing values, institutional models, religion, and ideals of community order and personal conduct. The cultural exchange aspects of colonialism can be profound. Either they provide new cultural resources for the institutionalization change that will enhance community survival in the colonial context, or, in some cases, they lead to internal cultural cleavages and community conflict.

Innovations are often introduced into communities during the turbulent colonial period but may be rejected or left unsupported. For example, the religions of the Shawnee Prophet, the Winnebago Prophet, the 1890 Ghost

Dance, the Cherokee movement of 1812–1813, and many others did not generate cultural, normative, political, or economic change. Some movements, such as the 1890 Ghost Dance, after a brief period of attention were left to small and scattered adherents. Why movements or innovations fail to take hold can be an interesting explanatory question in many colonial situations where political, economic, cultural, and biological pressures may press heavily and seem to indicate that change is likely.

## Conclusion

Colonialism is a complex phenomenon in which geopolitical relations, market incorporation, and cultural exchange vary considerably over historical periods and regional context. Analyzing the major dimensions of colonial relations as relatively autonomous forces will provide a more complete understanding of the impact of colonial forces on colonized nations. Each nation is forced to seek the means of preserving cultural values, political self-government, and economic viability within the changing context of colonial relations. By focusing on the issues and strategies of the colonized nations and understanding the colonial context through the cultural, political, and economic requirements of self-preservation forced on the colonized by the colonizer's power and interests, the present theory avoids the deterministic and coercive explanations usually given to colonial contexts and the view that the colonized are helpless victims of the inevitable domination. The external forces of colonization will have significant but incomplete capability for explaining the historical and institutional strategies of indigenous cultural, political, and economic survival. A theory that focuses on forces external to the institutional organization of the colonized nations can provide only limited explanatory power for understanding institutional change and historical action. Theories of colonization must move in the direction of detailed conceptualization of the institutional—political, economic, community, cultural—order of indigenous nations, and analyze their countermovements of institutional change and historically contingent strategic action in order to develop a more complete and balanced understanding of the complexities of life among the colonized.

## Notes

An earlier version of this chapter appeared as Duane Champagne, "A Multidimensional Theory of Colonialism: The Native North American Experience," *Journal of American Studies of Turkey*, Spring 1996, pp. 3–14.

1. George Rawlinson, *Ancient History* (New York: Barnes & Noble, 1993), pp. i–iv.

2. Andre Gunder Frank, *Capitalism and Underdevelopment in Latin America: Historical Studies of Chile and Brazil* (New York: Monthly Review Press, 1967); Immanuel Wallerstein, *The Modern World System: Capitalist Agriculture and the Origins of European World Economic in the Sixteenth Century* (New York: Academic, 1974); Joseph G. Jorgensen, *The Sun Dance Religion: Power for the Powerless* (Chicago: University of Chicago Press, 1972).

3. Duane Champagne, "Transsocietal Cultural Exchange within the World Economic and Political System," in *The Dynamics of Social Systems,* ed. Paul Colomy (London: Sage, 1992), pp. 120–53; Emile Durkheim, *The Elementary Forms of the Religious Life* (London: Allen & Unwin, 1915); Talcott Parsons, *The Evolution of Societies* (Englewood Cliffs, NJ: Prentice-Hall, 1977), pp. 25–31.

4. Henry Dobyns, *Their Number Become Thinned: Native American Population Dynamics in Eastern North America* (Knoxville: University of Tennessee, 1983); John Duffy, *Epidemics in Colonial America* (Baton Rouge: Louisiana State University, 1953); Russell Thornton, *American Indian Holocaust and Survival: A Population History since 1492* (Norman: University of Oklahoma Press, 1987).

5. Otto Hintze, "Economics and Politics in the Age of Modern Capitalism," in *Historical Essays of Otto Hintze,* ed. Felix Cohen (New York: Oxford University Press, 1975), pp. 160–88; Hintze, "Military Organization and State Organization," in *Historical Essays of Otto Hintze,* ed. Felix Cohen (New York: Oxford University Press, 1975); Theda Skocpol, *States and Revolution* (New York: Oxford University Press, 1970), pp. 19–24.

6. J. Weatherford, *Indian Givers* (New York: Crown, 1988); Donald A. Grinde and Bruce Johansen, *Exemplar of Freedom* (Los Angeles: UCLA American Indian Studies Center, 1991).

7. John M. Findlay, "An Elusive Institution: The Birth of Indian Reservations in the Gold Rush California," in *State and Reservation,* ed. George Pierre Castile and Robert L. Bee (Tucson: University of Arizona Press, 1992), pp. 18–32; Michel Foucault, *Power/Knowledge: Selected Interviews and Other Writings, 1972–1977,* trans. Colin Gordon, Leo Marshall, John Mepham, and Kate Soper (New York: Pantheon, 1980); Tom Biolsi, *Organizing the Lakota: The Political Economy of the New Deal on the Pine Ridge and Rosebud Reservations* (Tucson: University of Arizona Press, 1992).

8. Dobyns, *Their Number;* Duffy, *Epidemics;* Thornton, *Holocaust.*

9. Edward Spicer, *Cycles of Conquest: The Impact of Spain, Mexico, and the United States on the Indians of the Southwest, 1553–1960* (Tucson: University of Arizona Press, 1962); Thomas Hall, *Social Change in the Southwest, 1350–1880* (Abilene: University of Kansas Press, 1989); Richard Perry, *Apache Reservation: Indigenous Peoples and the American State* (Austin: University of Texas Press, 1993).

10. Frank Pomerscheim, *Braid of Feathers: American Indian Law and Contemporary Tribal Life* (Berkeley: University of California Press, 1995), pp. 37–56.

11. Skocpol, *States,* pp. xi, xiii, 14, 18.

12. Robert L. Berkhofer, "Faith and Factionalism among the Senecas: Theory and Ethnohistory," *Ethnohistory* 12 (1965): 99–112.

13. Personal communication, 1983.

14. Champagne, "Transsocietal Cultural Exchange," pp. 143–46.

15. Skocpol, *States,* pp. 33–40.

16. Anthony F. C. Wallace, *The Death and Rebirth of the Seneca* (New York: Vintage, 1972); Duane Champagne, *Social Order and Political Change* (Stanford, CA: University of Stanford Press, 1992), pp. 128–43.

17. Champagne, *Social Order,* pp. 128, 283–85.

18. Jeffrey C. Alexander, *Theoretical Logic in Sociology,* 4 vols. (Berkeley: University of California Press, 1983); Talcott Parsons, *The Structure of Social Action,* 2 vols. (New York: Free Press, 1949).

19. Talcott Parsons, *The Social System* (New York: Free Press, 1951), pp. 39–45.

20. Joseph Herring, *Kenekuk: The Kickapoo Prophet* (Lawrence: University Press of Kansas, 1988); Omer C. Stewart, *Peyote Religion: A History* (Norman: University of Oklahoma Press, 1987); Champagne, "Transsocietal Cultural Exchange," pp. 146–48.

21. Neil Smelser, *Social Change in the Industrial Revolution* (Chicago: University of Chicago Press, 1959), pp. 7–49; Jeffrey Alexander and Paul Colomy, "Toward Neofunctionalism," *Sociological Theory,* Fall 1985, 13–16; Paul Colomy and G. Rhoades, "Toward a Micro Corrective of Structural Differentiation Theory," *Sociological Perspectives* 37, no. 4 (1994): 547–83.

# Native-Directed Social Change
# in Canada and the United States

## 7

ARE THE PATTERNS OF SOCIAL CHANGE and social movements different between Canadian and U.S. Native nations? I am interested in Native-directed change where a community has control over decisions, although not necessarily control over many circumstances of change. We can call this self-directed or voluntaristic change. Why take this viewpoint when, especially in Native history, change is imposed externally by colonial powers or institutions? Looking at patterns of voluntaristic change, as opposed to coerced change, provides some insight into the long-term possibilities of institutionalized change. Institutions that have general consent and are congruent with the values and culture of a community will have broad support, and the rules and goals will generally be obeyed and upheld. Consensually based institutions endure as long as there is a general community consensus. Coerced forms of change or institutional arrangements are unstable in the sense that whenever the supporting power resources are withdrawn, there is no consensus to continue in the same way. Institutional arrangements and forms of change that are supported through processes of consensus and compatibility with a Native community's culture and values will generate enduring and stable change. The history of Native nations is rife with patterns of both voluntaristic and coerced change.

Most of the patterns of change observed in contemporary and recent historical Native communities tend to encompass changes that reflect patterns of institutional order in U.S. or Canadian society. This is neither an accident or a bias among researchers. Many contemporary patterns of change and organization in Native communities result from economic, political, and cultural colonial pressures over the past several centuries. Social change in Native communities is a negotiation between the Native community, its values, interests, and institutional organization, and the demands of markets, nation-states, and Canadian or U.S. cultural or religious objectives.[1] At certain times in history Native nations retained control over those processes, but at other times U.S. or Canadian policies and power led to coerced change in Native communities. Major patterns of change include market enterprises, centralized governments with elected officers, Christianity, capitalist values, and changing gender roles and community organization. The latter institutional arrangements are not an exhaustive list, but are a manageable group of central institutional arrangements to focus our present analysis.

## Comparative Methodology

An analysis of social change for the U.S. and Canadian Native nations includes study of coercive and consensual change. For purposes of national and comparative analysis, the historical period from 1600 to the present can be broken into eras defined by the relation of Native groups to the colonizing powers or nation-states. Increasingly, the conditions of indigenous peoples are defined (although not entirely) by their cultural, political, and economic relations to the emerging nation-states in the United States and Canada. In both the United States and Canada, we need to compare the relations of power and autonomy between in the indigenous nations and the colonies and nation-states. When colonizing powers allow greater governmental powers and cultural choice among the indigenous nations, then they will choose to make change according to their current cultural interests, institutional arrangements, and values.

Several historical periods can be defined for comparative analysis. First is the precontact period, for which I will characterize and compare the worldviews and institutional arrangements of Native communities in the future United States and Canada. The second period extends from 1600 to 1760, and is a period of competitive colonialism. Several rival European powers are competing for control over land, trade, and Native diplomatic and trade alliances. The third period is British hegemony from 1760 to 1777. A period of hegemony is characterized by the dominion of one European colonizing power. The Native nations are not under the direct administrative control of the hegemonic power, but the hegemon controls trade and diplomatic relations and other foreign powers don't interfere. The period from 1777 to 1820 is again characterized by colonial competition among the Americans, British, Spanish, and to a certain extent the French. The period from 1820 to 1871 is characterized by both U.S. and Canadian hegemony. The 1872 to 1968 period of U.S. and Canadian administrative colonialism is defined by nearly absolute control over Native communities, land, governments, language, culture, and education. The period from 1969 to the present is self-determination, named after the U.S. policy, and is defined by enhanced decision-making autonomy and control over land and resources for Native communities.

## Native Communities before Colonization

Are Natives capitalists? This may depend on the definition of capitalism, and the one I want to use comes from Max Weber, who defines rational capitalism as the continuous organization of the means of production (land, labor, capital) according to the demands of the marketplace.[2] According to this definition, Native peoples are not capitalists. Capitalism, according to this definition, presupposes a formally free labor force, people who are selling their labor because they have been wholly or partially separated from the means of production. Natives do not sell their labor to others and are not separated from the means of production. All Natives have access to land, hunting and gathering areas, and work for their families, clans, or bands. Furthermore, Natives do not have a capitalist spirit, where wealth is accumulated as an end in itself or for investment in profit-making enterprises.[3] Natives generally redistribute wealth, and there are strong injunctions against accumulating and hoarding wealth.[4] While some researchers have argued that the potlatch of the Pacific Northwest nations was a form of capitalism, according the definition here, the Northwest cultures are practicing elaborate ceremonial ways of redistributing wealth and gaining prestige and social esteem, sometimes gathering political influence, but they are not engaged capitalism and accumulating wealth for reinvestment according to the demands of a market.[5]

Native cultures and worldviews do not condone exploitation of the environment, plants, animals, or resources for production or sale or use beyond the immediate needs of the person or community. To do so will generate retribution from animals that will not sacrifice themselves in the hunt or overexploitation of plant life that will not grow back and support the people.[6] Unlike the Christian and capitalist interpretation of the world as an inert resource to be made better, Natives believe that the universe is composed of spiritual beings who are potential relatives or helpers and who need to be respected and honored. Otherwise they will retaliate or withdraw any aid to humans.[7] The world is a powerful and sacred place, and humans have no mandate to reform or change it but hold stewardship to preserve the world as given and maintain the environment for future generations of humans and beings that compose the community of the universe.[8] Relations with the environment are considered sacred, and the institutions of the nation and community, often given in creation stories or through an intermediary, sometimes a trickster, are considered gifts from the Creator. Native social and political institutions are part of the sacred world and therefore need to be honored and respected. Ceremonies, governments, gender relations, and community organizations are gifts with a sacred beginning and continuous sacred meaning.[9] Change can come only through permission from sacred beings acting as intermediaries from the Creator. This change may come in the way of omens, dreams, or visions. In terms of culture, Natives must maintain and respect the sacred balance and order given by the teachings and the Creator. Native nations are conservative and will accept change only within their own understandings and worldview.[10] Left to their own devices, they are reluctant to accept change in the form of capitalism, delegated democracy, or individualized community, or an absence of balance between genders.

Many nations in North America are matrilineal, meaning that descent is reckoned through the mother. In most communities, there are teaching that give respect and honor to women, and women are generally considered powerful beings who represent one principle of the universe, while male forces dominate the other alternative force. Women often have power and influence through extended families or clans.[11] There are reports and controversies about the role of women in numerous Native communities. For example, there is a long-standing academic debate about the role of women among the Ojibway of the United States, since the bands are patrilineal. However, many Algonkian-speaking communities, of which the Ojibway are one, argue for powerful relations for women and matrilineal organization.[12] The information is not conclusive. Similarly, some nations (e.g., Santa Clara Pueblo and the Ho Chunk) changed from matrilineal to patrilineal during the colonial period. Again, most California Mission Indians say they are patrilineal, but this may be the influence of the missionaries and Spanish interpreters, and there is little available evidence for the early kinship relations or matrilineallity. The general trend after colonialism is toward patrilineality.

The general pattern toward conservatism should hold for both Canadian and U.S. Natives. Thus there are few differences in social change orientation and we would not look there for differences, as long as the communities continue to adhere to their worldviews. Where Canadian and U.S. Natives may vary is in the diversity and range of social, political, and cultural organization. The Canadian territory lies north of the United States and is populated by egalitarian, decentralized hunter and gather communities. The main exceptions are the Northwest Coast communities of British Columbia, where there are elaborate clan and families structures and potlatch or giveaway ceremonies. In the United States, decentralized and egalitarian social and political relations characterize many Algonkian-speaking peoples of the northeastern wood-land, which stretched into Canadian territory. But there are Northwest Coast peoples in the United States too, as well as pueblos and Mound Builders, who provide variation in social and economic organization. There are more seden-tary communities that are more dependent on farming than in Canada. The diversity of social organization in the United States should yield more diver-sity of social change responses to colonialism than found in Canada.

## Competitive Colonialism, 1600–1760

The period of competitive colonialism sees intense political and military ri-valries, Native dependency on the fur trade, and some missionaries, but few institutional changes among Native North American nations. North America is subject to colonization by the French, English, Dutch, Spanish, and Swedes. There is nearly constant warfare and backwoods strategic trade and military maneuvering. The period ends with the French and Indian War and British control over much of eastern North America. Trade relations characterize economic relations in eastern North America, and the Natives quickly be-come engaged as hunters in the fur trade. Soon they become dependent on European metal goods, guns, powder, and ball. Nevertheless, Natives do not adopt capitalist values or actions; they continue to hunt for the goods they re-quire for maintaining their way of life and do not accumulate wealth.[13] Na-tives are now incorporated and dependent on markets and European manufacturing, and are no longer able to reproduce their own material needs. This trade dependency accentuates their military and diplomatic dependen-cies to one or more of the European colonies. Natives begin to hunt more and trade more, because of their trade dependencies, but continue to hunt and trap to satisfy their own and new trade needs.[14]

The competitive colonial period is not characterized by direct colonial control over most Native nations, and therefore treaties, diplomacy, and com-mercial agreements are used to manage relations with Natives. Sometimes colonial governments tried to introduce more centralized political authority among the tribes, such as the Choctaw and Cherokee, where the French and British established emperors. These new leaders, while eventually accepted by the Cherokee and Choctaw, were reclaimed and understood from their own terms. The new centralized leadership was a response to new trade and diplo-matic demands but did not change significantly the social and political organ-ization of the two nations.[15]

Perhaps the most remarkable changes were the formation of confederations among the Creek and Iroquois. After the Beaver Wars (1645–1700), the Iroquois believed that the English taking of parts of the Mohawk Valley created a significant threat to their territory, and having suffered greatly in the Beaver Wars, the Iroquois decided to ally to both the French and English and thereby play one off against the other in trade and diplomatic terms. The Iroquois proceeded to make commercial alliances with many interior nations, including many in New France. The Iroquois claimed to have the alliance of fifty nations, which they could use for military purposes. This claim might have been a diplomatic threat, but the Iroquois forged a large alliance of Native nations in the northern Great Lakes area. This alliance, which stayed together until after the War of 1812, resisted European and later American expansion. The Creeks, located in present-day central Georgia, created a confederacy by inviting many nations, often partially disrupted because of war, disease, or colonial expansion, to join their alliance of towns and villages. The Creeks sought to strengthen their diplomatic, trade, and military presence with the Europeans, and negotiated with the British, French, and Spanish colonies. Throughout the late competitive colonial period, the Creek and Iroquois maintained relative success for protecting their interests and asserting their nationality.[16]

The extension of competitive colonial relations, however, was uneven and more direct and coercive for many coastal nations and in the Spanish colonies of Florida and New Mexico. Many Native nations in the original thirteen English colonies and the Spanish colonies were forced to migrate or accept colonial law.

Overall there was little voluntary institutional change during the competitive colonial period. The fur trade did not lead to capitalist values or institutions but did lead to dependency. Europeans preferred men over women in politics and trade. The traders preferred to work with young men, and hence the role of women was undercut through the general nonrecognition of women in trade and politics. Elders tended to lose respect and power, as the younger men gained trade and diplomatic attention and power, because hunting, trade, and military skills were valued by the Europeans. In many communities, women and elders lost their place in Native communities. Although there was some political centralization and alliance building during this period, the changes involved the reallocation of preexisting institutional relations to form coalitions or support more centralized leadership.[17] Native worldviews, values, and institutions remained intact for many Native nations, although Christian teachings were becoming known to many, and Christian Indian communities appeared among the Mohawk, among the New England

Indian nations, the Delaware, and others. Outside the Christian (or praying) towns, Native community remained based on family, clan, or band, and there was no clear movement to individualization or nuclear families. The patterns for the future Canadian and U.S. Native nations are not remarkably different.

## British Hegemony, 1760–1777

For the eastern Native North American nations, British hegemony created a crisis. After the Seven Years War ended in 1763, and the French and Indian War, the British won New France from the French and Florida and West Florida from the Spanish. Now the British controlled all eastern North America, although they had yet to establish direct control over the Native nations. For many tribes, this new situation of hegemony, where a single colonial power held political and trade dominion by international agreement with other European competitor nations, was cause for concern. Most were not willing to submit to British control or possibly suffer British military retaliation. This situation led to the emergence of the Delaware Prophet movement, which became associated with the Odawa Pontiac. The teachings of the Delaware Prophet combined elements of Christianity, particularly salvation and heaven, and taught a fundamentalist view that the Europeans had corrupted the world through their trade and land expansion. The Natives needed to drive the Europeans from the continent and restore the old way of life, and then well-being would be restored to the nations.[18] Pontiac used the Prophet's teachings to organize many groups from the old Iroquois confederacy, including nations from the future U.S. and Canadian sides. The confederacy, sometimes called the Western Confederacy, could not push the British from the forts in the Great Lakes region and were ultimately forced to make treaties acknowledging British dominion by 1765.

Less well known during this period is the movement among the Delaware people, who formed a centralized religious organization, the Big House religion, and created for the first time three chiefs to lead them. The Delaware movement was created by a prophet through a vision and was believed to be the will of the Creator. The movement centralized political authority and formalized and three divisions of clans, which had ceremonial and religious significance.[19] A similar centralization was observed among the Cherokee in the 1760s after a war with the local British colonies. The Cherokee attempted to centralize greater control over their traders and people to avoid conflict and trade disputes with the British. The Cherokee, like the Delaware, did not propose new forms of government but centralized and empowered existing social and political forms.[20]

# Competitive Colonialism, 1777–1820

The American Revolution ushered in another period of colonial competition. The British retained British America, later to become Canada, and the Spanish retook the Floridas and Louisiana in the 1780s. The new American republic found itself surrounded by hostile European powers and Native nations leery of U.S. expansion. The Natives and their European allies worked to prevent U.S. expansion westward, and the Western Confederacy under the leadership of Little Turtle fought the Americans in the Ohio and Indiana region during the 1790s, and again later in 1812, Tecumseh inherited leadership of the Western Confederacy and led it against the Americans during the War of 1812. In the middle and late 1790s, the Native nations were forced to agree to treaties with the United States recognizing U.S. dominion in the region. Dominion meant that the other European powers, Spain and Britain, agreed not to interfere with the Natives in the lands recognized by the Europeans as belonging to the United States. The Americans were about to establish hegemony over the eastern part of present-day United States, but the Native nations resisted, and the troubles in Europe and the Napoleonic Wars continued to plague British and American relations.

In early 1806, the Shawnee Prophet emerged among the Delaware villages in present-day Indiana. In spring of 1805, the Munsee Prophetess was preaching new doctrines and ceremonies that were incorporated into the Delaware Big House religion. When the Shawnee Prophet (the brother of Tecumseh who lived in the same village) emerged, the Munsee Prophetess stepped aside. The Shawnee Prophet taught a fundamentalist message that the Europeans and Americans had corrupted the lives of the Natives, and disavowal of alcohol, manufactured goods, and a return to the ways of the ancestors was necessary for the Natives to regain their health, lands, and community.[21] The Prophet and Tecumseh worked to develop an alliance of Native nations to resist the westward expansion of the United States. The two brothers gathered individuals and groups from the Great Lakes nations. Tecumseh sought an alliance with the southern Native nations such as the Cherokee, Choctaw, Chickasaw, and Creek, but with limited success. When the War of 1812 broke out, Tecumseh was elected to lead the Western Confederacy but was killed in battle in 1813. The Shawnee Prophet was discredited after the Battle of Tippecanoe in 1811. After the War of 1812 the Western Confederacy was in disarray and the Native nations subject increasingly to nation-state control on both sides of the border.[22]

Other than the coalition building of Tecumseh and the Shawnee Prophet, there was little movement toward institutional change during this time. A primary exception is the Handsome Lake religion (1799–1815), which in-corporated both Jesuit and Quaker elements, while synthesizing with tradi-tional religious elements to form a religious movement that aided the Iroquois in making accommodations to life on a small reservation in upstate New York. The Iroquois found themselves increasingly under U.S. control, and they did not share the relative autonomy of the more western nations. The Handsome Lake movement is an example of voluntaristic change, but it oc-curred largely under local U.S. hegemonic conditions.[23] Generally, Christian teaching emphasized patriarchy, and colonial officials and traders continued to value men and young men for trade and military alliances. Men began to con-trol more resources and may have diminished the control over land, houses, and food that the women enjoyed in matrilineal nations.

## American and Canadian Hegemony, 1820–1871

After the War of 1812, both British America and the United States gained in-ternationally recognized dominion over their territories in eastern North America. International powers would no longer negotiate treaties with Na-tives, who were forced to recognize the dominion of the United States. Na-tives in Canada were no longer useful as military allies, and the fur trade starting in the 1820s declined and moved north. This decline had devastating effects on eastern North American nations who depended on the fur trade. The Industrial Revolution, especially in textiles, greatly reduced demand for furs, and many Native people and communities became impoverished as they could no longer trade for necessities. Impoverishment often led to land sales and cessions in both Canada and the United States as both governments were eager to treat or buy Indian land whenever it was offered, or whenever the Natives could be induced to sell. This trend continued out into the plains, and by 1840 most of the beaver east of the Rocky Mountains had been trapped. By 1869, American hunters destroyed the southern buffalo herd, and by 1880 the northern herd was gone. The plains tribes lost both trade source and sub-sistence. The prairie bands, as they are called in Canada, suffered a similar fate. As in the United States, agriculture and manufacturing were more important than the fur trade. Isolated Native nations in upper and western Canada stayed intact because there was less pressure for land sessions and less contact with British citizens and government.

The Canadian hegemonic period is marked by the formation of the Do-minion of Canada in 1867. Canada seemed more secure in its Native policy than the Americans, and began to regard its Native groups as economically and politically marginal by the 1790s. By the 1820s and 1830s Canadians were creating assimilationist programs for educating and Christianizing the eastern Native communities.[24] The early day schools were considered failures, and by the 1850s the Canadian government was establishing residential schools. Canadian agents wanted to transform Native culture; Native leaders agreed to education but not to the directions of assimilative change of Canadian policy.[25] There is little information on Native Canadian resistance and change, outside the change implemented by the external and coercive policies of the Canadian government. Canadian policies during the 1850s and 1860s continued to emphasize assimilation, framing, residential schools, individual property over Native community property, and Indian status as opposed to Canadian citizenship. After 1868 Native women who married non-Indians lost Native status and became Canadian citizens.[26] The first Métis Rebellion of 1869–1870 established Manitoba as an independent province on the French model, but the Métis and Indian allies were crushed by the Anglophile Canadian government. The Métis, usually mixed-blood Native and French, were allied to some Native nations in the present-day Saskatchewan and Manitoba region. The Natives and most Métis were experiencing declining economic fortunes on the plains as the buffalo declined and land tenure was not assured.[27] The Canadian government sent troops and the Métis leadership was forced to flee to the United States.[28] The British did not foster leadership development of the Native nations but rather introduced policies of assimilation into British Canadian society. Coercive or directed change in culture became the strategy of Native affairs. Impoverished and living under conditions of directed assimilation, the Native communities of British America had few opportunities or resources for voluntaristic change, and were subject to changes in education and religion that were designed to make them culturally British and ultimately British subjects.

While there was little Native-directed institutional change among Canadian nations, there was much diverse activity among U.S. Natives. Most remarkable is the formation of the constitutional governments of the Choctaw, Chickasaw, Cherokee, and Creek. The Cherokee adopted a constitutional government in 1828 after many years of reforms. The Chickasaw formed their constitutional government in the 1850s, the Choctaw and the Creek in the 1860s. Each government was modeled after the U.S. constitution but adapted to each community's history and culture. The so-called Civilized Tribes were located in the South, where the price of cotton rose several times after the War of 1812, and many mixed-blood families who were long engaged in the fur trade moved to producing cotton for market. They bought slaves, organized plantations, and produced cotton, corn, and cattle for market. Small groups of entrepreneurs emerged among all four nations, and economic classes formed among 2 to 3 percent of the families. These families were interested in Christianity and business education, and were familiar with American culture and government. They introduced the model for American government, often with the help of U.S. agents, and proposed change to their communities. Although there is often controversy, the communities of the four nations ultimately gave consent and adopted constitutional governments. The rise of the Native constitutional governments required assistance and competition from, but not control by, the U.S. government. Capitalist values and constitutional governments were not indigenous to the four nations but were introduced from the outside by European traders who intermarried into the Native nations.[29]

The 1820–1871 period was active with treaty making and Native responses. There are several religious movements such as the Winnebago Prophet in the 1820s and 1830s, the Cherokee movement in 1812, the Creek Red Sticks in 1812, the first Ghost Dance movement in 1869–1870, California Ghost Dance in the 1870s, and the Wishat movement on the Northwest Coast starting in the 1850s, although most of these movements were fundamentalist, suggesting sacred or ceremonial ways to bring back the old ways and the old world without interference from the Americans.[30] Some movements such as the Peyote religion, the Handsome Lake church, and the Kickapoo Prophet, Kenekuk, resulted in new religions and community commitments that helped people adapt to changing social and economic conditions.[31]

## Administrative Colonialism, 1872–1968

The newly formed Dominion of Canada and the end of U.S. treaty making ushered in a long period of directed and coercive change and administration in both countries. Increasingly Native communities were settled on reservations and put under direct and nearly total control by Indian agents.[32] Major efforts through the allotment acts and the Canadian eleven numbered treaties withdrew large portions of land from Native control. The agents controlled schooling, language, culture, government, and everyday life. The policies were to prepare Native people for assimilation into Canadian or U.S. society by educating the children, teaching working skills, dividing the land and placing it in private hands, establishing bureaucratic control over Native government, changing Native governments, discouraging Native cultural expression and life, and ultimately planning for the end of Native reserves and reservations. The Canadians were already experimenting with residential schools in the 1850s and established more schools throughout the western regions. The 1876 Indian Act in Canada divided Native nations into separate bands and reserves according to land, identity, culture, language, and government. The Native communities were subjected to detailed administrative supervision by the Canadian Indian service. The act dismantled traditional Native governments and rights to self-government. In 1885, armed resistance in the Second Métis Rebellion in Saskatchewan was put down. Louis Riel, the Métis leader, attempted to settle long-standing land issues for the Métis and establish claims to collective Métis territorial possession, nationality, and services based on aboriginal rights, although with Christian organization.[33] The Métis and Natives wanted to establish rights to territory and political autonomy and inhibit Canadian expansion and the extension of agriculture to the prairies.[34]

While there was some loosening of administrative policy in Canada in the 1950s, with the 1951 Indian Act opening the door for more self-government, progress was slow.[35] In the United States, the Indian Reorganization Act of 1934 ended the allotment policy after the loss of at least 90 million acres of land and provided for new constitutions, some funds to buy land, education funds, and other issues. But the IRA was not well funded and World War II intervened. In the later 1940s and 1950s assimilationist policies such as termination, a policy to abolish reservations, emerged. With a few exceptions, IRA governments and non-IRA tribal governments with constitutions or bylaws were generally powerless and often had little or divided support from their communities. Many Native communities and leaders expended considerable efforts fighting against allotment, about treaty rights, and against termination.

There was little voluntaristic institutional change during the colonial administrative period in Canada and more diversity in the United States, although much of this activity was an early religious and social response to reservation life and changing economic and political conditions. The Cherokee, Choctaw, Chickasaw, and Creek governments were dismantled and their estates allotted; the U.S. president was appointed their leader until the 1970s. In the early 1900s, conservatives among the four tribes organized movements to resist dismantling of their governments and break up land: the Redbird Smith movement or non-Christian Keetoowah, the Four Mothers movement among the Creek and others, and the Creek Snake or Chitto Harjo movement, and resistance from the Chickasaw Pull Back Party.[36] During the nineteenth century there was a flurry of religious movements in the United States, some seeking to organize resistance, such as a movement among the Apache in the 1880s.[37] Others used ceremonies to seek a return to the old ways, as was the case with the Ghost Dance of 1889–1890 and the California Ghost Dance or Earth Lodge religion.[38] Other movements sought to create modified religions with both Christian and

Native elements, such as the Indian Shaker Church and the Peyote religion that created new moral and religious communities that would provide support for Native people under the new political, economic, and cultural environments.[39] Many Native beliefs and ceremonies went underground and some reemerged during the 1970s.[40]

Perhaps the administrative colonial period is best understood for the emergence of a variety of organizations that lobbied and fought for Native rights and issues. The movements were not directly based within Native communities. The Indian Defense League of America engaged in Native rights issues in both the United States and Canada and struggled to place Native issues before the United Nations. The Society of American Indians established in 1911 consisted of relatively well-educated Native Americans and advocated on a variety of Native rights issues. The Alaska Native Brotherhood and Sisterhood (ANB-ANS) was established in 1912 and 1915 and sought to protect and extend Native economic and civil rights issues in Alaska. The National Congress of American Indians (NCAI) was established in 1944 and played a central role in the struggle against termination in the 1950s and 1960s. The NCAI lobbied Congress on a variety of issues in behalf of Native nations. Some of the main activists, like David Sohappy Sr. in the Oregon and Washington State fishing rights issues of the 1960s and 1970s, were adherents to the Seven Drums, or Washat. The National Indian Youth Council of the 1960s proposed new avenues of American Indian policy. The ANB-ANS played a role during the 1960s in organizing Alaska Native land claims that resulted in the politically negotiated Alaska Native Claims Settlement Act of 1971. Urban Indian centers and groups organized Native community centers, and the American Indian Movement (AIM) emerged in Minneapolis. After the takeover of Alcatraz Island by students in November 1969 until June 1971, many who visited or participated at Alcatraz Island joined AIM and took part in a series of movements and takeovers during the 1970s.[41]

Canadian Natives were migrating to urban areas and established Native centers in many towns and cities. A counterpart organization to the ANB-ANS, the Native Brotherhood of British Columbia (established in 1931), protected the fishing rights for Native fishermen and sought to advance Native welfare and interests. In 1961, largely at the instigation of the prairie Native communities, the National Indian Council (NIC) was established and advocated economic development and social change, but with retention of Native rights and identity.[42] NIC engaged the Canadian government in policy discussions and proposed alternatives, for example, challenging the assimilationist white paper of the Trudeau government in 1969.

# Self-Determination Policy, 1969–2004

The post-1968 period saw considerable activity among Native nations in both the United States and Canada. Land claims and treaties were central issues for many Canadian indigenous nations but were less promising in the United States, where most issues are settled in courts or ignored. In the United States, politically negotiated land claims experienced greater success, such as the Alaska Native Claims Settlement Act and the Maine or Passamaquoddy settlement. The affected Native communities had greater opportunities for economic success, but perhaps with increased risk. The Native communities in Canada after long legal struggles gained Canadian government recognition of land claims in the 1982 constitution for territories located outside the eleven numbered treaties negotiated from 1871 to 1921. Since the 1970s, Native communities across Canada have filed treaty and land claims with the Canadian government, and while the process is slow, several nations have gained agreements, such as the Inuit of Labrador, Gwich'in of the Northwest Territory and Yukon, Yukon Indians, Inuit in the Northwest Territory, and others.[43] In *Delgamuukw v. The Queen* (1997), the Canadian Supreme Court recognized Native oral history as evidence and recommended that the province of British Columbia and the Canadian government negotiate land claims and rights to self-government with the Native nations of British Columbia. *Delgamuukw* suggested that Native title was not extinguished in British Columbia, and therefore the First Nations retained rights to the land and resources. After some continuing legal maneuvering by opposition to the ruling, British Columbia has initiated treaty negotiations with fifty-three First Nations, about two-thirds of the nations eligible. The treaty process involves not only recognition of land and resources, but also self-government and the right of Natives to choose the institutional forms of government that suit their culture and values. Whether the new tribal governments will be subject to the province or have a government-to-government relation with the federal Canadian government remains controversial.

In Canada, the process of land claims negotiations and settlements create greater possibilities for economic self-sufficiency and Native management of future economic and institutional developments.[44] For example, the James Bay and Northern Quebec Agreement of 1975 provide a form of self-government to the Natives of northern Quebec and exclusion from the restrictive Indian Acts. Recent treaty negotiations among the British Columbian Native nations will provide many opportunities for gaining control over land and economic assets that will enable greater decision making by Native communities and leaders. The combination of commercial fishing supports among the coastal British Columbian Native nations and the new treaty arrangements that will provide greater economic and institutional diversity promise to create a period of active institutional change based on Native interests and values. The British Columbian nations, given their distinct cultures and institutional organizations and current economic and political opportunities, may set the stage for culturally based and unique Native innovations in social, political, and economic organization.[45]

Perhaps one of the most dramatic institution reorganizations is the recent establishment of Nunavut. The new government combines Canadian parliamentary democracy with Inuit values and emphasizes processes of consensual decision making and participation of the traditional villages in the government process and organization. The formation of Nunavut started with the Inuit Tapirisat of Canada (ITC), which identified Inuit territorial claims and in 1976 proposed the creation of Nunavut as part of a comprehensive settlement of Inuit land claims in the Northwest Territories. Working with Canadian governments and enjoying strong community support, the Inuit land claim and territorial settlement was adopted by parliament and given royal assent in 1993, and established on April 1, 1999.[46]

The Nunavut story is analogous to events leading to the formation of the North Slope Borough in Alaska by the Inuits and villages in that region. Having lost access to gas and oil reserves under the Alaska Native Claims Settlement Act of 1971 (ANSCA), the Inuit decided that their local village organizations needed to be augmented with establishment of a state borough, similar to a county or a municipality. The Inuit are the majority on the North Slope, and by organizing the North Slope Borough they could tax oil and gas companies that worked offshore and on the land. The North Slope Borough then joined the Inuit villages, regional association, and regional for-profit corporation created by ANCSA, as Inuit organizations that manage much of the political and economic development in the area.[47]

In the post-1968 period, many national and regional organizations emerged representing Native interests. In 1968, the National Indian Council separated into the National Indian Brotherhood (NIB) and the Canadian Métis Society. The NIB pursues Native rights issues from treaties and Canadian government policy, while the Canadian Métis Society pursues rights of Métis and non-status Natives. In 1982, the NIB reorganized as the Assembly of First Nations (AFN), an association of chiefs rather than an alliance of bands. In addition to the AFN, which represents status Natives on reserves, there arose the Native Women's Association of Canada (NWAC) representing Native women in Canada, the Congress of Aboriginal Peoples representing off-reserve Indians and Métis, the Métis National Council representing prairie Métis, the Aboriginal Youth Network serving the interests of Native youth, and others. Canadian Natives have been increasingly active in urban and national organizations and have developed a presence in international indigenous issues.

Native women's rights became visible because of the differential treatment in the Indian Acts, which disbar from band membership Native women who marry non-Natives. After much controversy, Canada enacted C-31, which restored band status to people who lost it under the Indian Acts, where Native women who married non-Natives lost Native status and so did their children.[48] This act and its implication for band membership and access to resources have produced continuing controversy.[49] The act led to many people to reclaim Native status and return to the reserve communities. The NWAC played a major role in the passage of C-31 and challenged many other national Canadian Native organizations, which were led by men. The crystallization of gender issues, membership, and identity issues around C-31 created a national issue and movement toward upholding and restoring indigenous women's rights in Canada. There is no similar organization or movement in the United States, although the restoration and reclamation of Native women's indigenous rights and status are very current issues.

Many Native nations in the United States are rethinking their constitutional governments, which are not well suited for managing community democratic governments, promoting economic development, incorporating Native culture, and managing political or bureaucratic relations with the U.S. government. As more Native communities believe they need to rethink and reclaim their governments, a variety of interesting efforts to build culturally informed and more functional Native governments will emerge. For example, the development of the Navajo court and recent decentralization of the Navajo government is a long process of change, still not yet completed, toward developing a democratic Navajo government.[50] The new government forms promise to be diverse, according to the specific traditions and histories of the specific Native communities. Many Native governments and communities are aspiring to gain greater economic self-sufficiency and thereby become less dependent on federal funds and regulations. U.S. policy is moving toward establishing Native governments as a fourth government branch with limited jurisdiction within the federal, state, and local system. Within the U.S. system, Native governments have rights according to treaties, congressional acts, court decisions, and executive orders.

One of the most significant trends in recent Native history is the effort to regain control of education. Since the 1970s many reservation communities have assumed control over local K-12 schools, and thirty-four tribally controlled community colleges have been established in the United States and

Canada.[51] Canadian bands are also beginning to seek control over local schools in their communities.

While over two hundred Native nations are engaged in gaming for profit in the United States, only twenty-five nations make large amounts of money. Proximity to a large local market is a key factor in determining whether a casino will do well. In southern California, there are over forty Native nations and they are located within driving distance of San Diego or Los Angeles. Current estimates say that those nations are grossing about $12 billion. The gaming business has helped relieve poverty in many communities and has enhanced Native visibility and political access. Funds from gaming are not distributed evenly throughout Indian country, since isolated tribes, say in the plains area, have fewer customers and do not earn enough money to make a significant difference within their communities.[52]

There has been a proliferation of national organizations among Native groups. In the United States, these include academic and professional groups such as the National Indian Education Association and the American Indian Higher Education Consortium (AIHEC), as well as political groups such as the NCAI and economic groups such as the Consortium of Energy Resource Tribes (CERT). Native communities and groups are active in lobbying for funding and for recognition of Native issues and rights in Congress.

## Autonomy, Markets, Community, and Change

Voluntaristic change, which is created by the values and institutions of the Native communities, depends on the controls of nation-state policies, access to markets, acceptance of education, and non-Indian cultural and institutional models. During the periods of administrative colonialism, when both the U.S. and Canadian governments exerted tight controls over Native governments and resources and introduced mandatory change in education, economy, and lifestyle, there were few opportunities for Natives to make change according to their own values and interests. While many Native communities were interested in education, markets, Christianity, and institutional innovations, they wanted to make change on their own terms, and in their own ways according their values and institutional relations. The periods of coerced change introduced new ideas, Christianity, and education in Native communities, but at the expense of Native control over the direction of change.

The cultural and institutional order of most Native communities does not indicate a path of change similar to European change paths toward bureaucratization, nation-states, free market systems, and individualization. When coming into regular contact with European colonial regimes, their directions of change, and the emphasis on Natives taking these directions of change, then Native communities were obligated either out of interest or political and cultural hegemonic environments to adopt institutions that were compatible with the European nation-states and economy. As in the precontact and competitive colonial periods when Native communities had considerable political autonomy, they changed gradually, as their institutions and holistic cultures emphasized balance and order in the present world; there were no cultural or religious mandates for change, at least not according to European patterns.

The most dramatic change consistent with Native interests and values occurred during the U.S. hegemonic period and the most recent self-determination period. The four southeastern nations, the Choctaw, Chickasaw, Cherokee, and Creek, formed constitutional governments from 1828 to 1870 and formed small planter-capitalist classes based primarily on the cotton market. Many gradually accepted syncretic forms of Christianity and American constitutional government organization. All four adopted these institutional patterns as a means to strengthen their ability to remain self-governing and protect their land and culture. All four Native nation-states were abolished during the administrative colonial period. The U.S. tribes before 1900 exhibited a variety of religious movements during the hegemonic and competitive colonial periods after 1760. While many Canadian Native nations participated in some of the movements, most originated in U.S. Native communities. Some, like the Handsome Lake movement, the Kickapoo Prophet movement, Native American Church, the Shaker Church, and Seven Drums religion, remain movements to the present and have helped Native people accommodate to the changing cultural, political, and economic conditions. These movements and the southeastern nations are examples of voluntaristic institutional change.

Since 1968, U.S. Natives have been asserting greater rights to sovereignty and seeking greater autonomy through economic development and government reorganization. Some nations have gained a measure of economic autonomy through gaming, manufacturing, and natural resource exploitation. U.S. Native communities control education at the K–12 level and through tribally controlled community colleges. Many National Native organizations have proliferated and pursued Native interests at the national and internal levels. Many U.S. Native nations are experimenting with new constitutional and judicial forms, attempting to incorporate Native culture and values into their governments. The Navajo, for example, have been relatively active in this way. Others, like the Ho Chunk of Nebraska and the Pechanga of California, have established tribally controlled corporations to manage casinos and tribal businesses. Alaska Natives have been managing twelve tribally owned corporations since the early 1970s. The present policy periods hold out possibilities for self-directed social change, at least for communities that have opportunities for relative economic self-sufficiency.

Before 1968, there was relatively little voluntaristic institutional change among Canadian Natives. The decentralized and hunter and gather social organization of the Canadian nations, except on the Northwest Coast, tended inhibit change, and Native worldviews did not outline a pattern of change similar to European patterns. The fur trade enabled many Canadian and U.S. nations to engage in trade but did not demand a change in economic values, so Natives did not become capitalists. They continued to hunt and trap according to their needs, although young men began to control the means of production and trade, and that gave them more social and political power that shaded the influence and roles of elders and women. The decline of the fur trade led to impoverishment and economic and political marginalization for many nations in the United States and Canada. Where alternative markets emerged, like the cotton market in the U.S. southeast or commercial fishing among the Northwest Coast peoples in Oregon, Washington State, British Columbia, and Alaska, the Native nations retained some continuing economic base and had resources to avoid bureaucratic dependence and, therefore, greater possibility for self-directed institutional change. However, during periods of direct administrative controls, the Native communities with viable market economies were inhibited from managing their own institutions or making change according to their values and interests. In both the United States and Canada, the fur trade was not associated with sustained institutional change. Many northern Canadian Native communities continue in the fur trade to the present, although the market is down since the antifur movement of the 1980s. While many northern and isolated Canadian Native communities were not directly challenged for land and resources as were their southern neighbors, the combination of conservative values, the fur trade, and less pressing conditions to dictate change allowed the northern communities to retain their language, culture, and community organization. The fur trade, however, introduced economic dependency on the fur trade market and on manufactured goods and external foods that changed patterns of consumption and created some necessity for trade or cash economy.

The post-1968 period showed dramatic increases in institutional change, national organizations, and possibilities for change. While the most recent period continues to acknowledge the dominion of the Canadian and U.S. nation-states, Native peoples have won and have been granted greater control over their own communities, and they have adopted change that is consistent with their institutions, values, and interests. In the United States and

Canada, there has been considerable national organizational change, new economic possibilities, and new movements toward greater political and cultural autonomy.

In Canada, Native gender relations owing to the Indian Acts and C-31 have gained greater attention and national organization than in the United States. Native women are seeking to regain their place in Native cultures, although male dominance has been fostered by markets and colonial administrative and cultural preferences in both countries.

Canada generally showed greater control over Native affairs, more decentralized Native communities, and fewer possibilities for self-directed Native change before 1968. During periods of direct administrative control, U.S. Natives showed few events of self-directed change. The diversity of U.S. Native social organization and markets tends to generate more religious and social movements, and examples of self-directed social, cultural, and institutional change than occurred in Canada. Since 1968, there has been considerable activity and enhanced possibilities for self-directed institutional change among Natives in the United States and Canada.[53] Contemporary Canadian land claim settlements and new treaty making may generate greater and perhaps different possibilities for Native-directed change than in the United States. Issues of generating economic self-sufficiency through access to markets may inhibit change for many Native communities and create unevenness among the nations about the directions and possibilities self-directed change. The recent negotiability of government restrictions over tribal governments enables greater expression of Native leadership and community building in both countries.

## Notes

An earlier version of this chapter will appear as Duane Champagne, "Native-Directed Social Change in Canada and the United States," *American Behavioral Scientist,* special issue on Indigenous Peoples: Canadian and U.S. Perspectives (forthcoming).

1. Duane Champagne, "A Multidimensional Theory of Colonialism: The Native North American Experience," *Journal of American Studies of Turkey,* Spring 1996, pp. 3–14.

2. Max Weber, *Economy and Society,* ed. Guenther Roth and Claus Wittich (Berkeley: University of California Press, 1978), 1: 160–68; Weber, *General Economic History* (New Brunswick, NJ: Transaction, 1981), pp. 275–78, 352–69; Weber, *Max Weber on Capitalism, Bureaucracy, and Religion,* ed. Stanislav Andreski (London: George Allen & Unwin, 1983), pp. 21–29.

3. James Treat, *Around the Sacred Fire: Native Religious Activism in the Red Power Era* (New York: Palgrave Macmillan, 2003), pp. 41–42, 136, 181.

4. Frank G. Speck, *The Iroquois:A Study in Cultural Evolution,* Cranbook Institute of Science, Bulletin no. 23, 1945, p. 33; Isaac Hope, "Orenda and the Concept of Power among the Tonowanda Seneca," in *The Anthropology of Power,* ed. Raymond Fogelson and Richard Adams

(New York: Academic, 1977), pp. 168–92; Theda Perdue, *Slavery and the Evolution of Cherokee Society, 1540–1866* (Knoxville: University of Tennessee Press, 1979), pp. 13–15.

5. Gregory Cajete, *Native Science: Natural Laws of Interdependence* (Santa Fe, NM: Clear Light, 2000), pp. 212–13, 226–41; Richard J. Perry, *Apache Reservation: Indigenous Peoples and the American State* (Austin: University of Texas Press, 1993), p. 91; Max Weber, *The Protestant Ethic and the Spirit of Capitalism* (New York: Scribner's, 1958), p. 59.

6. Gregory Cajete, *Look to the Mountain: An Ecology of Indigenous Education* (Skyland, NC: Kivaki, 1994), pp. 46–47, 97–98, 122.

7. Vine Deloria and Daniel Wildcat, *The Power and Place: Indian Education in America* (Golden, CO: Fulcrum, 2001), pp. 69, 121.

8. Melissa A. Pflug, *Ritual and Myth in Odawa Revitalization: Reclaiming a Sovereign Place* (Norman: University of Oklahoma Press, 1998), pp. 66–78; Deloria and Wildcat, *Power,* pp. 58–64.

9. Cajete, *Mountain,* pp. 46–47; Deloria and Wildcat, *Power,* pp. 92–99; Cajete, *Native Science,* pp. 103–5.

10. Duane Champagne, "The Cultural and Institutional Foundations of Native American Conservatism," special issue on North American Indians: Cultures in Motion, ed. Elvira Stefania Tiberini, *L'Uomo: Societa, tradizione, sviluppo* 8, no. 1 (1995): 17–43.

11. Nancy Bonvillain, "Women in Traditional Native Societies," in *The Native North American Almanac: A Reference Work on Native North Americans in the United States and Canada,* ed. Duane Champagne (Detroit: Gale, 2001), pp. 745–48.

12. Shirley Dunn, *The Mohican World, 1680–1750* (Fleischmann, NY: Purple Mountain, 2000), pp. 267, 271.

13. Thomas Norton, *The Fur Trade in Colonial New York, 1686–1776* (Madison: University of Wisconsin Press, 1974), p. 70; Roul Narrall, "The Causes of the Fourth Iroquois War" *Ethnohistory* 16 (1969): 58–59; E. E. Rich, "Trade Habits and Economic Motivation among the Indians of North America," *Canadian Journal of Economics and Political Science* 26 (1960): 53; Arthur Ray, *Indians and the Fur Trade* (Toronto, ON: University of Toronto Press, 1974), p. 68; Weber, *Protestant Ethic,* pp. 59–60.

14. Paul Phillips, *The Fur Trade* (Norman: University of Oklahoma Press, 1961), 2:524; Sherman Uhler, *Pennsylvania Indian Relations to 1754* (Allentown, PA: Donecker, 1951), p. 61; Dean Howard Smith, *Modern Tribal Development: Paths to Self-Sufficiency and Cultural Integrity in Indian Country* (Walnut Creek, CA: AltaMira, 2000), pp. 80–82.

15. Edmond Atkins, *The Revolt of the Choctaw Indians* (London: London Museum Landowne Manuscript 809, 1750s); Charles William Paape, "The Choctaw Revolt: A Chapter in the Intercolonial Rivalry of the Old Southwest" (Ph.D. diss., University of Illinois, 1946), pp. 95–96, 119, 159–60; Duane Champagne, *Social Order and Political Change: Constitutional Governments among the Cherokee, the Choctaw, the Chickasaw, and the Creek* (Stanford, CA: Stanford University Press, 1992), pp. 56–62.

16. Champagne, *Social Order,* pp. 64–67; Duane Champagne, "Politics, Markets, and Social Structure: The Political and Economic Responses of Four Native American Societies to Western Impacts" (Ph.D. diss., Harvard University, 1982), pp. 80–84.

17. Atkins, *Revolt.*

18. Pflug, *Ritual and Myth,* pp. 48–54.

19. Geroge Croghan, "George Croghan's Journal, Feb. 28, 1765–October 8, 1765," in *The New Regime, 1765–1767,* ed. Clarence Walworth and Clarence Edwin Carter (Springfield: Illinois State Historical Library, 1916), p. 7; Frank G. Speck, *A Study of the Delaware Big House*

*Ceremony* (Harrisburg: Pennsylvania Historical Commission, 1931), p. 75; Vernon Kinietz, *Delaware Culture Chronology,* Prehistory Research Series, vol. 3 (Indianapolis: Indiana Historical Society, 1946), p. 93; William W. Newcomb Jr., "The Culture and Acculturation of the Delaware Indians," *Anthropological Papers* (Ann Arbor, MI: Museum of Anthropology of Michigan, 1956), pp. 125–27; Duane Champagne, "The Delaware Revitalization Movement of the Early 1760s: A Suggested Reinterpretation," *American Indian Quarterly* 12, no. 2 (1988): 107–26.

20. Champagne, *Social Order*, pp. 67–74.

21. Lawrence Gipson, ed., "The Moravian Indian Missions on White River; Diaries and Letters, May 5, 1795 to November 12, 1806," in *Indiana Historical Collections* (Indianapolis: Indiana Historical Bureau, 1938), 23:183, 392–453, 562; Roger James Ferguson, "The White River Delawares: An Ethnohistorical Synthesis, 1795–1867" (Ph.D. diss., Ball State University, 1972), pp. 52, 112; Champagne, *Politics*, pp. 238–45.

22. R. David Edmonds, *The Shawnee Prophet* (Lincoln: University of Nebraska Press, 1983).

23. Anthony F. C. Wallace, *The Death and Rebirth of the Seneca* (New York: Vintage. 1972), pp. 182–86, 202–8.

24. Roger James Miller, *Skyscrapers Hide the Heavens: A History of Indian–White Relations in Canada* (Toronto, ON: University of Toronto Press, 1989), p. 95.

25. Miller, *Skyscrapers*, pp. 108–11.

26. Miller, *Skyscrapers*, pp. 114–15.

27. Fritz Pannekoek, "Some Comments on the Social Origins of the Riel Protest of 1869," in *Louis Riel and the Metis,* ed. A. S. Lussier (Winnipeg, Manitoba: Pemmican, 1991), pp. 69–73.

28. Miller, *Skyscrapers*, pp. 159–60.

29. Champagne, *Social Order*, pp. 128–43, 184–205.

30. Peter Nabokov, *A Forest of Time: American Indian Ways of History* (New York: Cambridge University Press, 2002), pp. 99–100.

31. Joseph B. Herring, *Kenekuk: The Kickapoo Prophet* (Lawrence: University Press of Kansas, 1988); Wallace, *Seneca*; Steve Talbot, "Pluralistic Religious Beliefs," in *The Native North American Almanac,* 2d edition, ed. Duane Champagne (Detroit: Gale, 2001), pp. 724–27; Kenneth M. Morrison, "Native American Religious Life: Creating through Cosmic Give-and-Take," *The Native North American Almanac,* 2d edition, ed. Duane Champagne (Detroit: Gale, 2001), pp. 693–96.

32. Treat, *Sacred Fire*, pp. 174, 180–85.

33. Thomas Flanagan, "The Political Thought of Lous Riel," in *Louis Riel and the Metis: Riel Mini-Conference Papers,* ed. A. S. Lussier (Winnipeg, MB: Pemmican, 1991), pp. 121–27.

34. Miller, *Skyscrapers*, pp. 170–71.

35. Treat, *Sacred Fire*, p. 186.

36. Champagne, *Social Order*, pp. 218, 227, 236.

37. Perry, *Apache*, pp. 133–34.

38. Nabokov, *Forest*, pp. 100–104.

39. Omer C. Stewart, *Peyote Religion: A History* (Norman: University of Oklahoma Press, 1987).

40. Treat, *Sacred Fire*; Morrison, "Religious Life," p. 699.

41. David Anthony Tyeeme Clark and Joanne Nagel, "U.S. American Indian Activist Movements," in *The Native North American Almanac,* 2d edition, ed. Duane Champagne (Detroit: Gale, 2001), pp. 597–610.

42. Miller, *Skyscrapers*, p. 225.

43. Ted Binnema, "Chronology of Canadian Native History, 1500–2000," in *The Native North American Almanac*, 2d edition, ed. Duane Champagne (Detroit: Gale, 2001), pp. 126–48.

44. Ian Getty, "An Overview of Economic Development History on Canadian Native Reserves," in *The Native North American Almanac*, 2d edition, ed. Duane Champagne (Detroit: Gale, 2001), p. 1140.

45. Alan L. Hoover, ed., *Nuu-chah-nulth Voices, Histories, Objects, and Journeys* (Victoria, BC: Royal British Columbia Museum, 2000).

46. Nunavut Government, 2004; www.gov.nu.ca/Nunavut/English/about/road.shtml.

47. Gerald A. McBeath, *North Slope Borough Government and Policymaking* (Anchorage: University of Alaska, 1981); Gerald McBeath and Thomas Morehouse, *The Dynamics of Alaska Native Self-Government* (Lanham, MD: University Press of America, 1980).

48. Katherine Beaty Chiste, "Aboriginal Women and Self-Government: Challenging Leviathan," in *Contemporary Native American Cultural Issues*, ed. Duane Champagne (Walnut Creek, CA: AltaMira, 1999), pp. 71–72; Mary Jane Jim, "Role of Indigenous Women in Decision-making," *Indigenous Peoples, Racism, and the United Nations*, ed. Martin Nagata (Sydney, Australia: Common Ground, 2001), pp. 124–25.

49. Chiste, "Aboriginal Women," pp. 71–87.

50. Navajo Government Office of Native Government Development, *Navajo Nation Government Book* (Window Rock, AZ: Navajo Nation, 1998), pp. 33–40; David E. Wilkinson, *The Navajo Political Experience* (Tsaile, AZ: Dine College, 1999), pp. 146–50.

51. Karen Swisher and Tarajean Yazzie, "Primary and Secondary U.S. Native Education," in *The Native North American Almanac*, 2nd edition, ed. Duane Champagne (Detroit: Gale, 2001), p. 1000.

52. Eve Darian-Smith, *New Capitalists: Laws, Politics, and Identity Surrounding Casino Gaming on Native American Land* (Belmont, CA: Wadsworth/Thomson Learning, 2004), pp. 53, 59.

53. Rebecca Tsosie, "Land, Culture, and Community: Envisioning Native American Sovereignty and National Identity in the Twenty-first Century," in *The Future of Indigenous Peoples: Strategies for Survival and Development,* ed. Duane Champagne and Ismael Abu-Saad (Los Angeles: UCLA American Indian Studies Center, 2003), p. 11.

# Border Towns

**8**

WHEN I FIRST CONSIDERED an assignment from the editors of a book collection to look at border towns, I thought about the border towns that were near my home reservation, the Turtle Mountain Reservation in north central North Dakota. One border town that came to mind was Rolla, North Dakota, as well as Rolette, St. John, and Dunseith. I began to think about how border towns were a more prominent part of my life than I had ever thought before. I lived with my family in Devil's Lake, North Dakota, until I was ten years old. Devil's Lake is the primary border town for the Spirit Lake Dakota, then known as the Devil's Lake Sioux Reservation. My experiences as a fieldworker, professor, researcher, and consultant gave me other contacts with border towns, although I did not think about them in this way before. If we put Native communities at the center of our work in Native studies, then there are many border towns everywhere. I have come to think of Los Angeles, California, as a regional border town for not only Southern California but also the western half of the United States. Since I lived and worked in Los Angeles on Native issues for nearly twenty years, I have gained a perspective about the role in contemporary Native life that a major city and county like Los Angeles has on many Native people and communities. In my experience, border towns are generally places of transition, assimilation, economic and political marginalization, and social breakdown; but they are also places of opportunity, regeneration, creativity, and education. Either way, the path was difficult and generally not in a direct line.

Let me start from the beginning and develop the thoughts as they arose through my experience with border towns. I will present my experiences of border towns in chronological order. I interpret border towns in the way I do in part because the assignment to discuss and analyze border towns as a phenomenon worthy of attention. Border towns are part of the experience of all Natives who have lived on reservations, and we should record this experience and make it part of our intellectual and political consciousness in order to explore as fully as possible our experiences and understandings. Information about the images and social and political effects of border towns should be recorded, analyzed, and discussed.

## Devil's Lake: My Father's Sojourn

My first memories of life are in Devil's Lake, a town named after a remnant glacial lake consisting of saltwater and called Minne Wakan, or Spirit Lake, by a band of Dakota who made the area their home and where they retained a reservation. The saltwater lake (one of only a few in the world, such as the Dead Sea in the Middle East) makes the area remarkable. Maps from the 1860s give the Minne Wakan interpretation to the lake, but the American or Christian interpretation has been transformed into Devil's Lake, with a sinister connotation not found in the original. While Devil's Lake, a town of about eight thousand in the 1950s, was a border town for the Devil's Lake Dakota, that was not my experience. I am sure many of the Dakota from the nearby reservation could recount their understandings and interpretations of the border town from the point of view of their lives and reservation experiences, but I cannot, since I was a small child then and did not have the consciousness of understanding Native reservations and relations with nearby communities. My understandings of the Devil's Lake experience come through my father and family. My father sought employment at Devil's Lake and worked in an automobile body repair shop for about a decade, before returning home to work for the Bureau of Indian Affairs (BIA) in Belcourt, North Dakota, on the Turtle Mountain Reservation.

My father was born in the 1920s and was educated in Catholic Indian boarding schools from his early grades and finished high school during World War II. His parents, my grandparents, spoke one of the languages of the Turtle Mountain Band of Chippewa Indians, a hybrid language locally called Mitchif, sometimes called "Cree" and known as Saulteaux among scholars. The language, a mixture of English, Cree, Ojibwe, and French, was probably a trade language developed in the northern Great Lakes region, perhaps near Sault Ste Marie, and hence the name Saulteaux. The Mitchif language follows Algonkian language rules and forms of declination but uses many borrowed French and English terms. My father's parents sent their two children, my father and his sister, to boarding schools, since they had a hard time supporting their children during the difficult reservation days of the 1930s and

1940s. My father learned the Mitchif language from his grandfather, my great-grandfather, who died about six years before I was born. My dad's parents encouraged him to speak English, since they believed that their children needed to learn English in order to work off the reservation. My father took an accelerated high school program at St. Stephan, a Catholic boarding school on the Crow Creek Reservation in South Dakota, in order to join the service and support the war effort. He joined the navy and served in the Aleutian Islands. He was briefly assigned to Admiral Nimitz, for whom he sorted mail and played on a specially assembled navy basketball team against an air force team. After a couple weeks of successfully serving on the admiral's basketball team, he was reassigned back to his normal duty monitoring Japanese submarine activity.

After the war, my father married my mother. He worked for several summers harvesting grain in the small farm towns around the Turtle Mountain Reservation. The reservation since 1892 is composed of two townships and measures six by twelve miles. According to the 1860 treaty, the Turtle Mountain Chippewa retained thirty-two townships of land, or 1,152 square miles, mostly in the northern quarter of present-day North Dakota. In the 1880s, the Office of Indian Affairs wanted to move the Minnesota and North Dakota Chippewa bands to the White Earth reservation in Minnesota. Although the Turtle Mountain Chippewa had many relatives among the Minnesota Chippewa, they did not want to give up their homeland in northern North Dakota and parts of eastern Montana. After considerable discussion, the so-called Ten Cent Treaty was formalized by an act of Congress, leaving the Turtle Mountain Chippewa a small six- by twelve-mile reservation and individual trust allotments in western North Dakota and eastern Montana. The act was called the Ten Cent Treaty because the tribe received ten cents per acre for the ceded land. The tribe retained beautiful land in the Turtle Mountain area, filled with game, trees, and lakes, and was good for hunting and some cattle raising, but generally not able to support more than subsistence farming. Soon many farmers moved into the newly vacated lands of northern North Dakota. Migrants from Scandinavia, Germany, and Russia came to the newly vacated lands of North Dakota in the 1890s. Hard economic conditions in northern Europe and political pogroms in Russia prompted their migrations. With the establishment of railroads, many towns sprouted up, including Devil's Lake, where the primary economy focused on collecting and shipping grain, mostly wheat, to eastern markets. The Chippewa took the Turtle Mountain area because it resembled the hunting lands of Minnesota and the rest of the northeastern woodland area. Turtle Mountain, always singular, is a glacial formation of hills about sixty miles across and extending into

Canada. The hills are an unusual formation in an otherwise flat plain. According to some Chippewa stories the hills have the shape of a turtle when viewed from the northeast. The Turtle Mountain Band of Chippewa did not retain the fertile plains areas, since they did not intend to farm the land or export wheat for railroads and eastern American markets.

After 1892, the land on the Turtle Mountain Reservation was allotted to individuals and held in trust by the tribe. The people continued to hunt, fish, pick berries and nuts, maintain small gardens, and raise some cattle for meat and dairy production. My great-grandfather, Louis Baptiste Champagne, took an allotment of 160 acres on the western edge of the reservation. My father's father inherited eighty acres, and my father inherited forty acres of trust allotment land.

Beginning in the 1890s, many Turtle Mountain residents began to look for cash income by working in the grain harvest for neighboring farmers. Tribal members annually went to provide labor for the harvest, and "thrashing," as the work was called, became a sign of initiative and ability to earn a livelihood. The farmers needed labor to gather their harvest, and the tribal members needed the cash income. Working the harvest became an annual event, and many families went farther away to work on the beet harvest in the Red River Valley. The Red River, which separates North Dakota and Minnesota and has the unusual feature of running north, was known to the Turtle Mountain Chippewa from the days when they hunted, traded, and claimed the territory. Many tribal members came to rely on seasonal farm labor to support their families.

In the late 1940s, when my father left the service, the grain harvest in North Dakota became increasingly mechanized and fewer laborers were needed. Over time, Native laborers in the Red River Valley were replaced by Mexican seasonal laborers. The Bureau of Indian Affairs (BIA) encouraged tribal members to acquire skills as carpenters, electricians, welders, construction labor, and other skilled workman jobs. Many tribal members moved to seasonal construction employment, working during the warm months in larger cities as far away as Minneapolis and returning to the reservation to live with their families during the colder months when work was not available. My father spent a couple of summers with the old pattern of harvest labor, but the work was eliminated by harvesting machines. By the 1950s there was little harvest labor left. In order to gain more stable employment, my father used the GI Bill and spent two years at a junior college in southern North Dakota, where he learned to repair car bodies. He obtained a job in Bottineau, North Dakota, a small farming community about sixty miles west of the Turtle Mountain Reservation. He worked there for about a year, making short visits home. In 1952 he took a job in Devil's Lake, working in an auto body shop on a piece rate. He was paid a percentage of the profit for each car that he finished. This method was strongly reminiscent of sharecropping, where the sharecroppers are allowed to use land but must pay the owner a percentage of the agricultural production.

Devil's Lake, a market town and grain shipper, was a border town for my family and me, although I was not conscious of it at the time, as well as for the nearby Dakota and for us as Turtle Mountain tribal members. The Turtle Mountain Reservation was about one hundred miles north. My father regularly visited his parents and relatives there, as well as my mother's, who lived off the reservation north of Dunseith. My mother, who completed the eighth grade, worked alternately as a waitress and a nurse's aide. In order to make more money, she often worked nights. These circumstances often led to us children having a considerable amount of freedom. We spent much of our time playing sports with children in the neighborhood and throughout the town. During the 1950s everyone played and lived baseball. Our family grew to seven boys, six while we lived in Devil's Lake and the seventh when we moved to Rolla in 1960. Our neighborhood was on the west side, which was the poor side of town. I was not aware of this until I visited the houses of my friends in the first and second grade. Our neighbors on the west side were generally Germans and Russians, who were actively assimilating into American life. One neighbor across the alley was a Mitchif, a mixed-blood Chippewa who had married a non-Indian. During my childhood in that neighborhood and at that time, we had little consciousness of a Native identity, despite occasional family discussions of Native identity and issues.

My father loved to work on cars and create special edition vehicles, but he did not like the routine work or pay. The work involved sanding and painting, which filled the air with particulate matter. Occasionally equipment failed, and my dad would sustain an injury that put him out of work without salary. Sometimes workmen's compensation helped, but I remember those periods as hard times. Ultimately my father applied for a clerk job with the maintenance department at the Turtle Mountain BIA agency office. My grandfather eked out an existence as a seasonal farm laborer, hunter, fisherman, and dairy farmer, but he still occupied the remaining forty acres of his allotment, having transferred forty acres to my father's sister. Living off the land, supplemented by seasonal farm labor, was no longer sustainable, and my father was directed by circumstances into wage-labor activities. He accepted a position as clerk (GS-3) working for the BIA around 1960. He remained a clerk for many years until after the *Mancari v. Morton* decision in the early

1970s, which upheld Indian preference in BIA hiring and promotions; thereafter he rose steadily to become manager of his department.

## Rolla and Other Border Towns in Rolette County

We moved to Rolla, North Dakota, located about three miles off the eastern border of the reservation. My folks could not find housing in Belcourt, and found an apartment in Rolla. Since my folks did not want to pay for tuition in Rolla, the school-age children rode to work every day with my father and started school at the Turtle Mountain Community school. Then the school contained K-12 in one old solidly built BIA building, which remains a landmark. I started the third grade and eventually went on to complete high school there. We lived in Rolla for several years and then moved to BIA housing in Belcourt, the village on the Turtle Mountain Reservation.

Rolla was the county seat and location for the county court, sheriff, and government. The town had about 2,000 people generally of Scandinavian descent, and many were successful farmers. A railroad went through town and was connected to the granaries, where the farmers sold their wheat, barley, and other grains. The railroad connected to St. John, a town to the north of the reservation, and probably was named by Métis, or mixed-blood Chippewa and French, who made up most of the Turtle Mountain Reservation community. Although the train may have carried passengers during the early part of the twentieth century, in the 1950s it carried mainly grain and only at harvesttime. Although there were other farming towns in Rolette County, such as Rolette, Dunseith, and St. John, most of the people on the reservation frequented Rolla for business, shopping, groceries, and recreation. There were few stores on the reservation, and Rolla had banks, a movie theater, a pool hall, grocery stores, a bowling ally, several restaurants, and several hotels. Rolla was a town to visit and carry on business, but one never felt welcome or at home there. Dunseith, about seven miles to the west of the reservation, had fewer stores and fewer opportunities for recreation or shopping. North of Dunseith lived many tribal members, including my mother's family, who had trust allotments or owned land in fee simple. Most were dairy farmers and hunted, but the land was full of trees, lakes, and hills, and while beautiful, not quite suitable for commercial farming. Dunseith was smaller than Rolla. Although the more conservative and traditional families held powwows there and other ceremonies in the hills and woods north of the town, Dunseith was not an Indian town. Rolette was farther away to the south of the reservation and people from the reservation, until recent years, rarely went there. The town was small with a few stores but was mainly a farming depot for goods and shipment of grains. South of the reservation stretched the great plains with fine farming land.

As children and students we had contact with the surrounding towns through athletics. We participated in baseball, football, basketball, and wrestling with teams from many of the towns in the region. In those days, the schools were about the same size in terms of students, but in recent years the population of the reservation has grown rapidly, while the population of the surrounding farming communities has stagnated or declined. Family farming in North Dakota is changing; with mechanization and globalized agricultural markets, small farms are at a disadvantage. North Dakota family farmers supported laws that discouraged corporate farming. With increased mechanization, fewer family members are needed to tend a family farm, and larger farms tend to be more productive and profitable. Children of farmers started to attend colleges and moved out of the state, and in recent decades the population of North Dakota has been slowly declining. Fewer family farms mean declining economics and demographics for the small farming towns. Some disappear completely, and others remain as granary and railroad stations. Rolette and Rolla both declined economically as their populations declined or remained stagnant.

When I was a child growing up in the 1960s, Rolla was the center of the county. Businesses on the reservation began to develop with efforts from the tribe and federal government during the 1970s. A mall was constructed and several convenience stores owned by tribal members appeared, reducing dependency on Rolla's stores. Before then, most shopping was conducted off the reservation, and most income on the reservation was spent in Rolla or other off-reservations towns. Banks were all off the reservation. I remember the anguish my father expressed in the 1960s when he was turned down by a Rolla bank for a $300 loan. Natives were viewed as high credit risks, and our accounts were carefully watched.

Over the past fifty years Rolette County demographics changed considerably. The clear majority of county residents are tribal members. As many as 12,000 tribal members live in the county, not all on the reservation, and there are over 28,000 enrolled members at Turtle Mountain. Many have come back to live and the reservation looks more densely populated and more affluent than I remember as a child. Rolla, still the county seat, seems to have declined economically, demographically, and in symbolic significance. Tribal members seem to consider Rolla not as the main border town but as a neighboring town. More businesses have been successful on the reservation, and many tribal members are willing to travel to larger regional towns such as Devil's

Lake or Minot to make large purchases. Rolla seems to have lost the importance it once had, and it seems less formidable, as tribal members now live in Rolla; some have intermarried, and some Rolla businesses are owned by tribal members.

The rising reservation population has led to greater political and economic power for tribal members. The North Dakota state assembly representative from Rolette County is usually a Turtle Mountain tribal member. State and county representation enhances Native political voice in county, state, and federal government relations. The tribe opened a small casino and hotel and manages several business, although seasonal work tends to persist among many reservation residents. The reservation population continues to grow, there are plans for building another new high school—the third new high school since all grades were housed in the old BIA building in the early 1960s. The farming market and trends in North Dakota indicate that small farming towns and family commercial farming will decline further, and corporate farming may be introduced in the foreseeable future. Corporate farming would present new challenges to the Turtle Mountain community.

## Border Towns in My Research

I left the Turtle Mountain Reservation when I was eighteen and have not lived there since, except for a few summers at home. My college and graduate studies brought me first to Fargo, North Dakota, and then to Boston, Massachusetts. Most of my graduate and undergraduate work was book work, and I had little direct contact with Native communities outside my own. In Boston, I had occasional consulting or community projects at the Boston Indian Council (BIC), which was the main Indian community center, and frequented by Micmacs, Passamaquoddy, Wampanoags, and other northeastern Indians. For many Native students who came to Boston's many colleges, their sojourn was primarily for gaining an education. Many northeastern Indians looked to Boston for seasonal employment, usually during the winter, and they often returned to their home reservations for ceremonial purposes during the summers. This was particularly true of Micmacs and Passamaquoddies. Native students at the colleges and universities usually did not remain in Boston and left soon after graduation to pursue careers and other plans. In those days there were few Indian studies programs, but there were active student organizations where students congregated.

After graduating with a sociology Ph.D. in 1982 from Harvard University, I had the opportunity to take a postdoctoral fellowship from the Rockefeller Foundation, which enabled me to spend a year preparing and doing fieldwork among the Tlingit and Northern Cheyenne. During that year, I traveled to the Alaska panhandle, the home of the Tlingit, Haida, and Tsimshian, as well as to Montana to spend several months among the Northern Cheyenne. Among the Tlingit and southern Alaska Natives there are several border towns. Juneau, the state capital, and Anchorage are the local trade centers, and Seattle is the regional major trade center for Alaska and for the panhandle of Alaska. Sitka was the home of some of the leading Tlingit clans and the Alaska Native Brother-Sisterhood (ANB-ANS). The Alaska Natives of the panhandle lived in isolated fishing villages along the coast and islands. The Natives have been commercial fishermen for well over a century; consequently they have close economic dependencies on fish markets and the fish canneries. Alaska Natives have long provided fish to the cannery industry and also supplied labor to work in the canneries. The men fished and the women worked the canneries. Natives often traveled to Juneau, Ketchikan, and Seattle for business and employment. Since Juneau, Sitka, and Ketchikan were located near traditional Tlingit villages, they continued to serve as ceremonial centers, where potlatches and ANB-ANS meetings were regularly held.

My visit to the Northern Cheyenne also underscored the relation the reservation had to Billings, Montana, as the largest trade center in the southeastern part of the state. Many activities required business and travel to Billings. The Northern Cheyenne reservation is relatively isolated on marginal farming land. A few families can make a living by cattle ranching, but most families cannot. The most striking border town issue when I visited there in the beginning of 1983 was a bar located just off the northern reservation line. Although the reservation was dry (no alcohol was allowed), the bar was only a quarter of a mile off the reservation line and provided the opportunity for any adult Northern Cheyenne to purchase alcoholic beverages. The place was called, I believe, Tiny Town and was a typical rural bar. Many members of the Northern Cheyenne community did not have high regard for the establishment, which tended to be frequented by binge drinkers and alcoholics. Many Northern Cheyenne felt the community would be better off without the bar, but they were powerless to do anything about it, since it was off-reservation land owned by non-Indians. From a distance the Tiny Town building did not look remarkable—except for the pile of beer cans behind the building that towered several times higher than the building itself. According to one story, Boy Scouts from Billings made periodic trips to Tiny Town to mine the pile of beer cans for recycling.

## Los Angeles as Regional Border Town

After finishing graduate school in Boston, I taught for one year at the University of Wisconsin–Milwaukee and then moved to Los Angeles to join the sociology department at UCLA. Milwaukee has some characteristics of a regional border town, with an urban Indian population and students at its universities and colleges, but I will leave that story for another time. Los Angeles County has the most Indian people of any urban county in the country; about 132,000 people claim at least some Native descent. Los Angeles County also has the most businesses by far of any urban metropolitan area, with over 7,000 Indian businesses, while the next largest city with Indian businesses has less than 3,000. There are more than one hundred tribes represented in Los Angeles County, and there are numerous Native peoples from Mexico who have large and thriving populations there. Indigenous Gabrielino/Tongva people have been living in the Los Angeles basin for thousands of years, and several groups and communities, while not federally recognized, are active in Native rights and community issues and strive to protect their rights, sacred sites, and burial places of their ancestors. Most Natives, however, living in the Los Angeles metropolitan area are not from California. Thousands of Natives are migrants from reservations throughout the country, although many from the Southwest, such as Dine, Hopi, Pueblos, and Apaches, make up a considerable part of the Los Angeles Native community. Many Natives from the northern and southern plains carry on an active powwow culture, and one can find one or more powwows on any given weekend. Cherokees, Choctaws, Creeks, and other Natives from Oklahoma are well represented. Many people migrated to Los Angeles starting with the BIA relocation programs in the 1950s, most were seeking work since reservation economies did not provide enough support for tribal members. Some came to Hollywood and wanted to break into various aspects of show business.

Los Angeles in many ways is a place of ethnic freedom. There are people from all over the world, and there are few people who will question your identity just by looking at your appearance. Since the city and county is so diverse, few people question identity and few people are pejorative about a person based solely on ethnic issues. An American Indian may be regarded with some interest, but most Natives, like everyone else, tend to invisible at the individual level. Few people are prejudiced regarding ethnic origins. There is no mainstream domination of identity, since the environment is diverse and tolerates different cultures and identities. Saying that you are Native American may generate mild interest but not the relatively hostile reaction one often receives from off-reservation communities.

The many tribal peoples of Los Angeles form a pan-Indian community, although many retain strong tribal identities and ties. Some Native folks have been in the city for several generations, and some are becoming relatively affluent and accustomed to urban life. Many Los Angeles born or raised Indian children have little contact with their tribal communities, although many are interested in investigating their Native identities. Most Los Angeles Native children are given few opportunities for direct contact with their tribal communities, although they may retain tribal membership. Many Native migrants have economic and social difficulties when they first arrive in the urban environment. Those who have been in the city for several generations have many education skills and are gaining economic affluence but tend to be invisible. While many relocation migrants were placed in certain parts of Los Angeles County, Native people are too few and eventually too dispersed to gain notice or concentration. Native peoples in Los Angeles are spread thinly throughout many locations in the county. This dispersion perhaps reflects cultural as well as economic preferences in the sense that peoples of different tribes do not congregate in the same neighborhoods, and more economically successful Natives move to more upscale neighborhoods. The dispersion of the Native community makes it difficult to form a coherent community, and the community tends to be decentralized.

Los Angeles is a regional economic and cultural center attracts many Native people, including professionals, students, homeless, workers, artists, actors, drunks, Christians, and powwow people. The Native community is diverse culturally and economically. Los Angeles is a place of hardship for many, but for others it is a place of opportunity and possibility. Native entertainers, actors, intellectuals, activists, spiritual leaders, professionals, and educators have the opportunity to meet and work on urban and tribal issues through universities, community organizations, and reservation communities. Some of these interactions may lead to creative social and political strategies and solutions that may benefit Native peoples and communities and further the causes of Native rights.

At UCLA I have had the opportunity to work with many colleagues and participate in a variety of programs and community-oriented activities that directly benefit Native communities. Much of our scholarly work is devoted to understanding and implementing issues of Native rights and understanding the history of policy and culture in Native communities. Both research and fieldwork have been oriented toward issues that are of central significance for tribal communities and Native policies. The *American Indian Culture and Research Journal* publishes many articles about Native history, culture, and policy. The Native Nations Law and Policy Center (NNLPC) is home to a joint degree program in law and American Indian studies, the Tribal Legal Development Clinic, Project Peacemaker, and the newly formed Tribal Learning Community and Education Exchange (TLCEE). The joint degree program developed because we observed that many bright students and practitioners in the Indian law field did not have good understandings of tribal culture, government, and policy. The joint degree program provides both law training and exposure to theories and fieldwork with Native communities. Students who benefit from both Indian studies and law training, we believe, will make more capable and understanding lawyers for Indian country. The Tribal Legal Development Clinic provides training to students through working on projects with tribal communities and organizations. The clinic does not take legal cases but assists tribes in writing and reforming constitutions, writing code, and supporting tribal courts.

Project Peacemaker creates tribal legal studies curriculum for tribally controlled community colleges and is introducing web-based online courses so that students, tribal government employees, and professionals can have access. Through Project Peacemaker, we hope to provide both traditional understandings of law as well as knowledge about state and federal law in order to educate better tribal citizens, administrators, legal advocates, and new Indian lawyers. TLCEE is a new project building on the philosophies of the previous work. It combines both traditional information and knowledge with academic knowledge, and provides courses to Native reservation and college students that directly address reservation issues. Many Native students do not finish high school, partly because they do not find contemporary education relevant or focused on issues and values that are important in the Native community. By taking training and courses that address Native issues, such as Federal Indian Law, Introduction to Tribal Legal Studies, Cultural Resource Preservation, Introduction to Native Theater, and other courses focused on community issues and providing guidance for Native nation building, Native students and communities become the center of the curriculum, rather than marginalized to invisibility.

At UCLA, several of us believe that our program has many important benefits for Native governments, communities, and students. The program depends heavily on working in reservation communities, with community and urban Indian groups and organizations, with Native studies students, and utilizing academic and university resources. These programs help transform Los Angeles and UCLA from indifferent border town or "border institutions" to active programs aimed at supporting Native governments, legal rights, and providing culturally and academically appropriate support to reservation communities and to Native policy and issues. In this way, at least some negative aspects of the Los Angeles Indian border town can be turned on its head. Institutions like the UCLA Native Nations Law and Policy Center can be frameworks for positive and supportive work within Native governments and communities, and for policy and educational purposes. Border towns often control many more resources than are available to reservation governments and communities. By gaining access to the powerful resources available in off-reservation border towns and institutions, and using those resources for protecting and enhancing tribal sovereignty and culture, the border town can become a resource rather than a place of exploitation and despair. Working within border town institutions while retaining Native identities and viewpoints will help Native individuals, organizations, and allied colleagues to focus off-reservation resources toward protection and assistance to tribal governments, communities, and individuals.

## Border Towns: Opportunity or Exile

Border towns are everywhere. They are usually the first step removed from the reservation community, and they are often hostile economic and social places. A border town is a social construction of the Native migrant or visitor; the Native has entered foreign territory, and the homeland is somewhere else. Psychologically, culturally, and politically the Native migrant may have his heart and mind within the Native community, but economic and creative opportunities in the contemporary world must often be sought in places off the reservation. Border towns can be engines of assimilation and ethnicization of Native peoples, but they also can be places for the development and experimentation of new concepts and coalitions for preserving Native rights and culture. Over two-thirds of Native Americans now live in urban areas that have border town relations to reservations. We ourselves must choose how we meet the challenges of preserving Native communities and culture. Border towns have been forces of change, but it is up to us to forge the direction of change toward positive benefits to Native communities by taking advantage of the opportunities and resources offered in border towns.

# Ramona Redeemed? The Rise of Tribal Political Power in California

## 9

IN THE 1884 NOVEL *RAMONA* by Helen Hunt Jackson and the annual California state play by the same name, Ramona is a woman of Native Californian (perhaps Luiseno) ancestry living during the early post-Mexican period. She learns of her Indian ancestry and marries a Native, settling with him on his ancestral lands in Temecula, California. Soon American settlers forcibly occupy the entire territory, chasing Ramona and her family into the hills and eventually killing Ramona's husband. Ramona moves to Mexico, leaving the country to the newly arrived U.S. settlers who make California their home.

The Ramona story symbolizes the marginalization and mistreatment of California Indians during the second half of the nineteenth century. California Natives struggled greatly throughout this period of California history. Because treaties negotiated during the 1850s were never ratified by the U.S. Senate, many went landless until the rancheria and reservation acts of the 1890s provided tiny, economically undesirable land bases. The population declined from approximately 300,000 at the beginning of the American period to only 15,000 at the turn of the twentieth century.

Federal policy toward California Indians during the twentieth century continued this disregard for tribal sovereignty and well-being. Beginning in the 1920s, land claims settlements targeted individual California Indians rather than tribes, suggesting the extinction of tribal existence. Approximately forty California Indian reservations and rancherias were scheduled for termination during the 1950s and 1960s. The passage of Public Law 280 in 1953 extended concurrent state jurisdiction over criminal matters and led to state and local intrusion into tribal affairs and sovereignty. Public Law 280 also served as the excuse for federal withdrawal of services and support for California tribes, contravening the federal trust responsibility.

For much of twentieth century, California Indians were administratively, culturally, economically, and politically disadvantaged, even compared with tribes elsewhere in the United States.[1] Most California Indians lived on small reservations with few economic prospects and little supportive attention from the Indian administration. As late as 1990, when tribal self-determination was professed federal policy, most California Indian tribal governments received limited funds from the BIA or other federal agencies. Few schools were created for Indian children in California, and most Native children attended local public schools that did not receive supplemental funds from federal Indian programs. No support was provided for tribal law enforcement or tribal courts. Allocations from the Indian Health Service were seriously inadequate for the size of the service population.[2] Although the rationale for federal withdrawal was the availability of state services, state and local governments did not serve Indian populations effectively, with resulting high rates of crime, school dropouts, and substandard housing. Through most of the twentieth century, California Indian economic and political conditions were very bleak, with little hope or opportunity on the horizon. Although the tribal population was relatively large statewide, it was distributed among one hundred federally recognized tribes, making concerted action and influence difficult. California tribes seemed poorly positioned to join in the nationwide resurgence of tribal sovereignty that began in the late 1960s.

The advent of tribal gaming in the 1970s hinted at a different prognosis, however. The influx of non-Indians into California that had nearly doomed tribal sovereignty also provided one of the largest markets for casino gaming in the United States. If tribes could capture that market, they could create economic opportunities for their people and use their newfound wealth to reverse the deterioration of their cultural and political fortunes. However, California had some long-standing legal restrictions on gaming, particularly on slot machines and house-banked card games. Nearby Nevada had a strong interest and informal alliance with California designed to perpetuate these restrictions. Furthermore, California had become accustomed to dominating Indian country within the state and did not take Indian nations seriously as governments. Thus achieving the tribes' goal required working in concert to confront and resist state government.

Against the odds, California tribes succeeded in establishing casino gaming as a lucrative form of economic development. Repeated litigation, passage of two separate statewide ballot propositions, and often acrimonious negotiations with state government were required to reach this end. Through these efforts, California Indian leaders learned how to gain the attention of political leaders, and soon they had access to the political process and sympathetic support for the first time in California's political history. Today California Indian tribes have greater political access to and influence in state and federal government than ever before.[3] Political power, accumulation of significant capital, reinvestment into community preservation, and large resort casinos are now major activities among many California Indian tribes.

The rise to political access and influence by many California tribes is a recent and unusual situation in Native history. The long struggle and result of uncertain duration is the topic of this chapter. I will analyze the rise to political access and power through the struggle for establishing legal Indian gaming in California, focusing on how ideas of tribal sovereignty contributed to this rise and the consequences of tribal gaming for the future exercise and development of tribal sovereignty.

## California Indian Tribes before Gaming

California is a large state with many Native communities representing diverse language and cultural groups. Currently there are 106 federally recognized tribes, and at least another fifty Native communities seeking recognition. Native California communities are restored from termination or recognized through legislation or legal cases nearly every year.[4] Many Native Californians live in isolated locations, often deep in the mountains or out in the desert. Such locations do not bode well for economic market development, and most are too small to support their Native populations through traditional subsistence methods or local farming. Communities located far from urban centers and tourist sites have difficulty making significant returns from gaming.[5] Most California Indian tribes do not have gaming establishments, and many that do are not realizing a significant income from gaming. Nevertheless, with the right location, many tribes have done quite well and the gross take on California Indian gaming is in the billions of dollars.

The primary motivation for California Native communities to take up gaming was the long-standing impoverishment and enduring poverty of their communities. With so few economic prospects, many California Indians were forced to migrate from their homes in search of gainful employment. Native communities and culture could not be maintained if all the tribal and community members left to live in distant places where they could find employment opportunities.

Federal self-determination policy of the 1970s, coupled with court decisions affirming tribal sovereignty and immunity from state laws, suggested new possibilities for economic development.[6] Tribal communities tried to establish businesses that capitalized on tribal sovereignty, for example, opening smoke shops that exploited differences in the price of cigarettes or gasoline when the Native vendor did not have to charge state taxes. An important U.S. Supreme Court decision, *Bryan v. Itasca County*, established that Indian lands in California and other Public Law 280 states are *not* under greater state jurisdiction for purposes of taxation or regulating business.[7] California tribes with some locational advantage thus adopted this same economic development strategy. However, the possibility of turning reservations into sites of large-scale retail sales to non-Indians disappeared when the Supreme Court ruled that tribal sovereignty did not protect tribes from having to collect state sales taxes imposed on non-Indian buyers.[8] This ruling greatly decreased any advantage Native businesses might have had in Indian country.

With smoke shops offering very limited economic advantages, the Cabazon tribe, located in the resort area of Palm Springs, decided to open a high stakes bingo hall and card parlor. California law allowed bingo and card games to be played under very limited conditions; but the Cabazons believed that the state could not force them, a sovereign Indian nation, to abide by these restrictions. Local authorities soon challenged the Cabazon bingo and card room establishment, and the Cabazons sued to retain their right to maintain the high stakes bingo and card games. The state of California took up the challenge against Cabazon, and the case went to the U.S. Supreme Court (*California v. Cabazon Band of Mission Indians*).[9] In 1987, the court upheld the Cabazon's right to maintain high stakes bingo and card games so long as the state had no strong public policy against gaming. Given that California had instituted a state lottery in 1984, had long approved pari-mutuel horse racing, and allowed bingo and card games in some form, the state was in no position to infringe on tribal sovereignty, even if nearly all the patrons were non-Indian. The high court noted, however, that states could acquire jurisdiction to regulate tribal gaming if Congress enacted a law clearly manifesting that intent.

The *Cabazon* case and other Indian and state gaming conflicts around the country led the tribes and states to the Indian Gaming Regulatory Act of 1988 (IGRA).[10] For all games other than traditional Indian games and bingo (known as Class III gaming), this act established two major restrictions on tribal gaming enterprises: (1) the games involved had to be allowed in some form under state law and (2) the state and tribe had to negotiate a compact, approved by the secretary of Interior, authorizing the games. If the state refused to negotiate a compact in good faith, the act provided an elaborate set of remedies for the tribes, including suit in federal court to compel compact negotiations, appointment of a mediator to recommend compact terms, and imposition of terms by the secretary of Interior.[11] A new federal agency, the National Indian Gaming Commission, was established to regulate tribal games and gaming management contracts.

While some tribes opposed the ultimate form of the legislation because it limited their sovereign power to control reservation gaming, others supported the bill because it provided a method of creating agreements with state governments that would deflect anticipated legal challenges to their right to establish gaming casinos. Casino gaming, in particular slot machines, accounts by far for the highest return and profitability among commercial gaming enterprises. Nevada gaming interests lobbied heavily for IGRA because they saw tribal powers to establish gaming enterprises acknowledged in the *Cabazon* case as a threat to their industry and profits.[12] Tribal opponents argued that IGRA restricted tribal sovereignty because the state could regulate tribal government and community activities through the compacts, and the tribes were required to negotiate with the state over whether certain types of gaming were permitted on reservations.

## The Failure to Negotiate Gaming Compacts

Shortly after passage of IGRA, California entered into compacts with several tribes regarding off-track betting. However, when tribes requested compact negotiations concerning the far more lucrative video gaming machines, the state, led by Republican Governors George Deukmejian and later Pete Wilson, refused to deal. Invoking the century-old state ban on slot machines and house-banked card games, Governor Wilson vetoed three separate bills that would have established compacts. In the meantime, local authorities raided Indian casinos and confiscated video gaming machines, at least until a federal court held in 1993 that under IGRA, only federal authorities had the power to challenge tribal gaming that violated state laws.[13] Within a short period, most of the affected tribal casinos returned to business with new machines.

So long as there was some doubt about whether the state was obliged to negotiate compacts, federal law enforcement officers were reluctant to close down Indian casinos. The prospect of lucrative gaming enterprises both motivated and enabled the tribes to hire sophisticated lawyers who could raise just such doubts. These lawyers argued that video gaming machines were just another form of bingo, a game permitted without a compact; that the video machines were operating as lotteries, not as slot machines; that the California Lottery's recently instituted Keno game was a state-authorized slot machine, rendering such gaming legal under state law; and that under IGRA, a state that allowed any kind of gaming other than bingo (such as horse racing) had to negotiate in good faith as to all kinds of high stakes gaming, including slot machines. A 1996 decision by the United States Supreme Court, *Seminole Tribe v. Florida*, made it difficult for tribes to take the offensive in advancing these arguments against the state.[14] The *Seminole* decision invalidated the provision in IGRA allowing tribes to sue states in federal court for failing to negotiate compacts in good faith, severely undermining the political compromise embodied in the act. The tribes still found creative ways to keep their arguments alive in the courts, and they continued to insist that the state was acting in bad faith and that they were entitled to operate their casinos under the circumstances.[15] Nonetheless, in the absence of compacts, tribal casinos operated under a pallor of illegality, which discouraged outside investors who were not sure of the legality of the gaming establishments.

Between 1994 and 1996, the federal and state courts rendered several rulings that rejected the tribes' legal arguments.[16] At this point, the tribes could have backed down and accepted the state's position. By this time, however, the tribes could see the dramatic gains in tribal employment, housing, education, return of tribal members, and revitalization of tribal cultures possible from gaming. Notwithstanding the legal cloud that hovered over the tribal casinos, many continued operation during this time and tribal governments earned considerable amounts of capital, which were invested in community development, and is some cases passed out to tribal members in per capita payments. Tribal communities such as Sycuan invested in housing, support for elders, cultural events, and support of tribal members. In the gaming communities, new jobs were available for tribal and nontribal members, and great increases in local business enterprise. Many tribes like Barona and Agua Caliente made philanthropic donations to local charities and organizations. In the Native traditions of sharing wealth, the tribes redistributed their good fortune to local community groups, many of which were very grateful for the recognition and support. According to IGRA, a significant amount of gaming revenues, 70 percent, must be reinvested in community infrastructure and support. California Indian communities were extremely poor and disenfranchised, and gaming funds enabled the tribes to start building tribal social and economic infrastructures that had never been possible with federal funding. Tribal governments made decisions for their communities with the use of their own funds, and could better reflect and uphold the culture and interests of their cultures and communities. Furthermore, the new capital enabled the gaming tribal governments to diversify their economic base by buying businesses and making investments in the local economy. Cabazon, for example, made significant investments in real estate and construction in San Diego County.

With these new opportunities within their grasp, California gaming tribes were unwilling to accept the limited vision of their sovereignty presented in the unfavorable court decisions and state positions. An alternative political strategy within the framework of state government presented itself, but it required a substantial financial commitment. The relatively sudden access to significant amounts of capital allowed tribes to expand their government activities, including support of state and local political leaders and candidates. The tribes began contributing to political campaigns. While most tribal leaders favored Democrats, some tribal leaders also supported Republican candidates and issues.[17] Tribes began to support candidates who were favorable to their issues, and some long-standing political friends began to emerge and held steady in their support of California Indian issues, especially those surrounding the negotiation of gaming compacts.

By the middle 1990s, some California gaming tribes were seeking political alliance and support from both state and national leaders and political parties. In 1994, gaming tribes contributed disproportionately to Democratic candidates with contributions of about $2.5 million while Republican candidates received about $300,000. Since the tribes leaned heavily to Democratic candidates, Governor Pete Wilson began returning donations to his campaigns from California gaming tribes.[18] In the 1996 elections, some gaming tribes strongly supported national candidates for president and took clear positions among political candidates within the state of California. The tribes' early attempts at supporting candidates for high office in California, however, were not successful. Many tribes supported the campaign of Kathleen Brown in the 1996 governor's race against incumbent Pete Wilson, and many tribes also strongly supported the opponent of Dan Lungren, attorney general. Both Lungren and Governor Wilson strongly opposed casino style gaming in California and were reluctant to grant compacts that would enable California tribes to benefit from the highly lucrative slot machines.[19] Both Wilson and Lungren won their offices in statewide elections with comfortable margins. The clear financial support and preference for their opponents by most Indian gaming tribes did not engender warmer or more cooperative relations between the California tribes and the state government over gaming issues. The tribes were neither able to gain an agreeable compact from Governor Pete Wilson nor gain enough support in the state assembly to implement a compact over the governor's objections or veto. Negotiations with Wilson's representatives were often hostile, and many tribes despaired of ever gaining an acceptable agreement. Wilson opposed significant Indian gaming activity, wanted to restrict the number of machines, and insisted on local and state regulation of Indian gaming on reservations. Most tribal leaders considered his position a violation of tribal sovereignty and did not wish to submit tribal sovereignty to such extensive state regulation of tribal activities and restrictions on gaming.

While both sides negotiated, the tribes carried on casino-style gaming which members of the Wilson administration, in particular Attorney General Dan Lungren, considered illegal. State officials continued to pressure the local U.S. attorneys to bring actions to shut them down. Finally the Wilson administration proposed a model compact with the Pala reservation, which restricted the number of gaming machines for each reservation and statewide, and enabled local and state regulation of health, labor, and other regulatory activities associated with the business of gaming. The model compact also banned the most common forms of slot machines, insisting that prizes be paid from a pool created by the players, and that machines themselves avoid features such as hand levers and coin payouts that made the games most attractive to customers. Pala was a reservation that wanted to enter into gaming, but was inhibited from establishing a casino by the absence of a compact agreement. The governor's plan was to negotiate with Pala and hold all other tribes to the Pala Compact. Although he had initially promised to let all tribes participate in the negotiations, only Pala was allowed at the table.

The other tribes strongly criticized the Pala Compact as too intrusive into tribal government and sovereignty and too restrictive of the type and number of gaming machines allowed. The tribes would be limited to 975 video gambling machines with a statewide limit of 19,000 machines. The legal gaming age was raised from eighteen to twenty-one, and the tribes would have to permit the unionization of casino workers. In addition to the restrictions on video gaming machines, some popular games such as blackjack would be prohibited altogether. Under Wilson's plan, all tribes in California would have to accept and abide by the Pala Compact. Eleven tribes accepted the Pala Compact, while thirty-one tribes opposed. Many tribes already had more than 1,000 slot machines and wanted to expand their operations.[20] State officials, however, threatened tribal governments with closure of their casinos if they did not comply with the Pala Compact; in 1997, the U.S. attorneys gave the tribes until May 1998 to accept the Pala Compact or shut down their casinos and negotiate alternative compacts with the state.[21]

Rather than accede to these unpalatable choices, the dissenting tribal governments formed a coalition and decided to appeal to California voters in a statewide initiative for more favorable and respectful compact terms. Many

California Indian tribes did not believe that Governor Wilson's administration would ever negotiate an acceptable compact. Surveys showed that about 65 percent of the California general public had favorable opinions of Indian gaming, and the tribes hoped to use their positive image to gain approval of a more satisfactory compact with the state. Statewide propositions become the equivalent of statutory law if they are passed with a majority vote.

The tribes drafted Proposition 5 with the help of longtime lawyer friends and firms. The decision to draft the proposition and put the vote before the public was made quickly, and the proposition was drafted in haste. At a minimum, the proposition needed at least 800,000 voter signatures to be placed on the November 1998 ballot as a legislative initiative measure. There was some discussion that the proposition should be presented as a constitutional amendment in order to avoid possible conflict with a 1984 state constitutional provision that prohibited "casinos of the type currently operating in Nevada and New Jersey," but some tribal leaders thought it would be difficult to get the required 1.2 million voter signatures before the deadline for placing the proposition on the ballot.[22] The tribes, led by San Manuel and Pechanga, hired consulting firms to canvass voters to support Proposition 5 as a legislative initiative measure. Pressed for time, they poured $10 million into the qualifying effort, almost ten times the amount normally spent for this purpose. Besides traditional petition signature gatherers, the tribes used television and direct mail to achieve qualification.[23] The canvassing went faster than expected and more than the required number of voter signatures were gained. Even though the petition for placing Proposition 5 on the ballot had more signatures than required for a California state constitutional amendment, the tribes had already decided not to seek a constitutional amendment, thinking that it was too ambitious. So the campaign went forward as a legislative measure. Without the "war chest" supplied by the continued operation of casinos with video gaming machines, none of this activity would have been possible.

# The Proposition 5 Campaign

In October 1998, at the request of the state of California, a federal judge requested that tribal video gaming machines be shut down by December 4, 1998, if they were not operating under a tribal-state gaming compact. The deadline was conveniently placed after the November 1998 election and so the outcome of Proposition 5 would be known by time the U.S. marshals would have to act if no tribal-California gaming compacts were agreed to by then.

The Proposition 5 campaign coincided with the state and federal election of November 1998. Both the California Indian tribes and the Nevada gaming interests invested heavily in the campaign. The Indian tribes invested over $66 million while the opposition invested $25 million. Opposition also came from labor unions, California casinos, horse racing tracks, card clubs, and the Walt Disney Company.[24] The campaign had a significant effect on the election. Democratic candidates gained the governor's and lieutenant governor's offices, and the assembly gained a Democratic majority. This election was influenced by the record campaign spending on the Proposition 5 campaign. No other initiative measure in California history attracted as much attention and campaign financing as did Proposition 5.

The tribes organized a very effective campaign. They hired professional campaign firms that used state of the art techniques for producing television and publicity advertisements.[25] Most of the campaign by the tribes and the opposition were aired on short television spots of thirty seconds or less. The Proposition 5 team conducted numerous surveys throughout the state to gain an understanding of underlying support and focus on issues that were important for the voters to judge the issues. Initial focus groups concentrated on issues of tribal sovereignty and Native self-government. However, early results underscored the point that few California voters understood tribal sovereignty issues and they quickly grew disinterested and even hostile to the argument. For many voters, sovereignty smacked of images representative of the English king, which did not engender favorable views since the history of the United States is premised on the separation from British authority. Stronger responses in the focus groups were gained from presentations from Natives that gaming promised to move California Indians out of poverty, that many jobs would be created, that casinos would contribute to the California tax base, and that Indians would gain considerable opportunities for economic self-reliance. Provisions in the proposition that created trust funds for the benefit of nongaming tribes and for local government services supported this point. The issues of economic self-reliance, paying of taxes, more jobs, and self-help gained the attention and support of the voting public, so the television campaign drummed away at these themes.

In addition, the focus groups and sample surveys were used to highlight key figures in the campaign. Mark Macarro, chair of the Pechanga Band of Luiseno Indians, and Carole Goldberg, professor of law at UCLA, emerged as spokespersons for Proposition 5 commercials. These commercials were short and forthright, and urged support Proposition 5 as a means to gaining Indian economic self-reliance. The opposition placed a series of misleading and argumentative television commercials. The tribes and allies responded to each commercial with gentle, informative, and reasoned positions often emphasizing the human side of the issues. They also missed no opportunity to mention the hypocritical and self-interested role of Las Vegas gambling interests in funding the anti–Proposition 5 campaign. The responses to issues raised by the opposition often were aired within forty-eight hours of any strong challenge. While this campaign was extraordinarily expensive for the tribes, they perceived that nothing less than the future well-being of their communities was at stake. What made this encounter with dominant California non-Indian political interests so different from the past was the availability of tribal funds to fight back. These funds could be tapped because the tribes had defied state and federal authorities by continuing to operate their casinos without a compact.

The record campaign financing and expensive television campaign put Proposition 5 into the homes of most Californians for several months. The advertisements were plentiful and attention grabbing for both sides. There was both strong support for the issue and significant opposition. At least 30 percent of the voters were opposed to casino-style gaming under most conditions. Early surveys gave a 65 percent approval rating to Indian gaming, but would such support melt away when people went to the voting booths? The active campaign by both proponents and opposition aroused considerable attention not only to the Proposition 5 vote but also to the general election at large. Democrats swept the major positions in the California government and gained control of the legislature. Over 60 percent of Latino and Chicano voters voted for Proposition 5, and undoubtedly the interest generated by the Proposition 5 campaign stirred many Californians to take part in the vote and contributed significantly to the Democratic sweep in many offices within state government. Gaming tribes contributed heavily and worked to support Democratic candidates. Attorney General Dan Lungren ran against Lieutenant Governor Gray Davis, and most tribes supported Davis, who was elected after a difficult campaign. Proposition 5 won a solid endorsement with 62 percent of the vote in favor of allowing Indian tribes the right to pursue many of the most lucrative forms of gaming in California.

The vote gave California Indian tribes some relief from threats by the state and federal governments to close down their casinos as illegal gaming establishments. The opposition, composed largely of organized labor, California card rooms, and Nevada casinos, with the consent of Governor Wilson's administration, proposed a lawsuit, claiming that the proposition was unconstitutional under state law and in conflict with IGRA. On November 20, 1998, the opposition filed its suit and requested an injunction against the initiative's implementation. In *International Union (HERE) v. Davis*, the opposition argued that the proposition, a law by initiative, violated the 1984 state constitutional amendment prohibiting Nevada and New Jersey style gaming in California as well as inconsistent with IGRA.[26] In a vote of 6 to 1, the California Supreme Court ruled that Proposition 5 was unlawful under the state constitution and declined to reach the IGRA issue.[27] Lawyers for the tribes had pointed out the many differences between tribal casinos and those operated in Nevada and New Jersey; but the Court showed no interest in those arguments. Although the 1984 anticasino provision was vague and the debate over its enactment shed little light on its meaning, the court insisted that the language was designed to constitutionalize the state ban on slot machines and house-banked card games.

## The Proposition 1A Campaign

The tribes were delivered a setback by the California Supreme Court decision, but as the Court heard the case, the transfer of political power based on the November 1998 elections took place. A new and more favorable California legislature and gubernatorial administration took office. Governor Davis, while not entirely supportive of casino-style gaming, campaigned that he would respect Native rights to sovereignty and would support California Indian tribes in their decisions to create gaming agreements with the state. Governor Davis's administration, with strong support from the California legislature, crafted a new compact, after long negotiations with most of the Indian gaming tribes. Representatives from about sixty tribes gathered in Sacramento to work out an agreement. The new compact was a compromise that avoided many of the restrictions of the Pala agreement relating to numbers and types of gaming machines, but was also more limiting than the provisions of Proposition 5, which gave the tribes considerable autonomy from state regulation. In particular, it gave the state gambling control agency some input into tribal hiring decisions, required tribes to create mechanisms for workers' compensation and liability to customers for personal injuries, and allowed local communities to voice environmental objections to proposed casinos. Most significant, it required tribes to adopt ordinances that facilitated union organizing. After difficult negotiations, most California gaming tribes agreed to put this compact before the California voters as a constitutional amendment known as Proposition 1A.

The tribes invested $20 million in a campaign reminiscent of Proposition 5, but this time the opposition did not raise the requisite $100,000 to qualify for campaign financing. Nevada gaming interests probably did not believe that Proposition 1A could be defeated, since the proposed constitutional amendment was supported by the governor and state legislature and contained significant concessions to labor interests. The campaign message for Proposition 1A was very similar to Proposition 5. Rather than engage in complicated arguments about tribal sovereignty, the campaign emphasized Indian self-reliance, jobs, tax payments, and Indian community and hospitality. The election was held during the primary election of March 7, 2000, and won with 64.5 percent of the vote. Passage of Proposition 1A created a constitutional amendment that avoided the ruling of the California Supreme Court.

Proposition 1A created terms for agreements between the Indian tribes of California and the state of California. The proposition allowed casino-style gaming on reservations, but the state enforced several compromises on tribal governments. Apart from the provisions relating to labor, licensing, and customer suits, tribes were restricted to 2,000 slot machines each and two casinos per tribe. Banking and percentage card games such as blackjack were allowed, tribes were to share $1.1 million per year with nongaming tribes, a joint state-tribal oversight agency was created with two representatives from each gaming tribe, tribal funding was provided for compulsive gaming treatment, and the tribes were required to adopt ordinances for environmental protection, worker safety, building codes, and were required to waive limited sovereign immunity for injuries to patrons.

Some tribes, such as Tule River and the Coyote Valley Band of Pomo Indians, did not sign the new compacts, believing that they intruded too far into the internal sovereignty of their tribal governments and addressed matters that were outside the scope of compacting set forth in IGRA. Particularly offensive were the provisions requiring tribes to adopt a code regulating labor relations and to pay a fee (tax) for machines in excess of 2,000. For example, the mandatory tribal labor ordinance included provisions guaranteeing casino employees the right to organize, guaranteeing unions the right to gain access to employees for purposes of organizing, and allowing secondary boycotts under some circumstances. Some of the employee rights specified in the mandatory ordinance actually exceed those granted under the National Labor Relations Act.[28]

The complaints of the nonsigning tribes were advanced through a lawsuit, originally filed in 1997, that charged the state with refusing to negotiate compacts in good faith.[29] Many tribes were favorable to the struggles put forth by Tule River and Coyote Valley, but most were pragmatic and accepted the compromises of Proposition 1A. For example, Agua Caliente signed the compact but filed an amicus curiae brief supporting Coyote Valley in its litigation.

The passage of Proposition 1A was derived from considerable public support, as well as strong support from the Davis administration and California legislature. Already by the election of November 1998, gaming tribes had gained considerable experience and actively supported candidates who worked in their behalf and were generally favorable to their interests and needs. Tribal leaders gained considerable access to state leadership and many state assemblypersons and senators began to pay closer attention to tribal leaders and tribal communities. Gaming tribes supported political candidates and issues, but also gained considerable support from local groups and organizations through significant redistribution of gaming profits for the benefit of local issues, causes, and organizations.

Both Republican and Democratic political leaders sought and often gained support from gaming tribes. Some tribes were led by Republican tribal chairs, such as Agua Caliente, and sometimes negotiations and strategies among the Southern California tribes split along Democratic and Republican leadership. Not only did the governor and state legislature place Proposition 1A on the March 2000 ballot, but several prominent state office holders also began to sponsor and support bills and issues that tribal leaders and Indian communities wanted and needed. Some assemblypersons, often not understanding issues of tribal sovereignty, proposed bills meant to help tribal governments build courts and law enforcement capability, but subordinated tribal government operations to state regulation.[30] While tribal leaders and communities appreciated the good intentions, most tribal communities and leaders opposed bills that threatened or weakened tribal government powers against the state of California. State officials, as well as local and county law enforcement agencies and officers, began to take more seriously longstanding issues and conflicts over providing court actions and law enforcement on California Indian reservations and rancherias according to the concurrent criminal jurisdiction of PL 280.[31] Tribal leaders can gain the attention and interest of California local and state officials, and state bills have passed in realms such as Indian child welfare that are important to tribes.[32] Long-standing grievances, such as the flooding of the Torres-Martinez reservation when the Salton Sea formed, are being addressed through federal enactments.[33] There are increasing efforts to create more cooperative agreements between state and tribal governments.

After passage of Proposition 1A, many Nevada and New Jersey investors became more interested in California Indian gaming tribes. Previously, gaming investors feared that California Indian gaming might be ultimately ruled illegal, and therefore they curtailed investments in California Indian gaming. However, after the election many gaming investors started negotiating investment plans with California Indian tribes, and several tribes announced plans for significant expansions in larger casinos, new hotels, and recreation centers. The most seasoned gaming tribes are undertaking these new enterprises entirely on their own. Some of the new casino and resort developments are in the $200 to $300 million range. For the immediate future, many gaming tribal governments are investing heavily in their gaming enterprises. The Proposition 1A compact will last ten years, giving the tribes significant time to accumulate capital and make new investments and economic diversification that will help create stronger reservation economies and help ensure community cultural and social survival. Gaming tribes are actively seeking to comply with Proposition 1A, which requires greater security and protections for non-Indian gaming guests. Tribal governments will need to strengthen their courts, ordinances, and law enforcement capability. Many tribal governments are stronger and will be stronger in the future because of resources gathered from gaming enterprises.

Tribal governments and courts in California have been weakly supported by the Bureau of Indian Affairs for the past 150 years. Tribal governments are faced with new demands from state, federal, and local governments, and from an increasingly globalized and competitive market system. Until the last decade of the twentieth century, California Indian tribal governments languished in neglect and powerlessness and with little capital to gain access to American or global markets. The gaming funds have not only created new opportunities for political access at the local, state, and federal levels, but also provide the tribal governments with independent funds for community improvement.[34] Most California Indian gaming tribes manage their own casinos and reinvest the profits by direct per capita monthly payments to tribal members and by investments in tribal programs and education. California Indian tribes most likely will gross billions of dollars in the next decade, investing much of it into community strengthening, cultural preservation, tribal government reorganization, and economic diversification.

## Sovereignty and Political Power

Seneca law professor Robert Porter has challenged tribes to consider whether they can sustain their sovereignty while simultaneously participating in state politics.[35] In Porter's view, it is inconsistent for tribes to assert their governmental status and yet to function as state citizens. He counsels against tribal members voting in state elections, out of concern that this involvement will weaken claims of tribal sovereignty. From Porter's perspective, the rise of California's tribes within California politics, fueled by gaming revenues, should be nothing short of a catastrophe for tribal sovereignty. The fact that the two state proposition campaigns developed themes of tribal economic well-being and self-sufficiency rather than tribal sovereignty would only confirm this prediction. Provisions in the gaming compacts, such as those addressing labor and licensing, that allow state involvement would provide further support. According to this view, the price of achieving economic development opportunity would be sacrifice of the very governmental status that gave rise to that opportunity. Tribes might gain economically in the short-term but lose politically and culturally in the longer term.

Yet the interplay between sovereignty and political power seems far more complex and multidirectional in the case of California tribes. Before gaming, they had a tenuous hold on sovereignty at best. There was only one tribal court, and it had limited jurisdiction. The tribes had no meaningful control over child welfare, environmental degradation, or cultural resource protection. Without federal funding or independent sources of revenue, the tribes could not provide for or educate their members, leaving most to find their way to urban areas. Maintaining culturally distinctive communities was nearly impossible under these circumstances. The tribes seemed to accept the fact that Public Law 280 rendered them less sovereign than tribes elsewhere in the United States.

In attaining political power through gaming, California tribes may have developed a stronger conception of their sovereignty that may affect future encounters with the state. Even though the proposition campaigns were not framed in terms of sovereignty, sovereignty was key to the tribes' success. When the gaming tribes refused to shut down their casinos in response to state and federal demands, disregarding court decisions that rejected their legal position, they enacted their sovereignty. A separate government asserts the right to define its own sovereignty, and that's precisely what the California gaming tribes did. Propelled by the high stakes for their communities, they refused to accede to non–Indian claims of limited tribal sovereignty. Without these defiant acts of sovereignty, the tribes would not have been able to accumulate the financial resources they needed to mount two extraordinarily expensive proposition campaigns as well as costly litigation. For tribal leaders who had been raised to believe that their communities were subject to state domination, this insistence on sovereignty signaled a new and more robust understanding of their status and powers that may trigger future assertions of sovereignty.[36] For example, the Cabazon tribe has challenged application of state law to tribal police vehicles traveling on state roads while passing from one part of their noncontiguous reservation to another.[37] State law allows only state and local government authorities to operate vehicles with light bars and sirens, making it impossible for tribal police to use necessary equipment when their reservations are split by state lands. In challenging the application of this state law, the Cabazons are advancing leading edge claims of tribal sovereignty. The tribes also secured passage of state legislation that rejected the "existing Indian family" doctrine for child welfare cases.[38] As former Viejas tribal leader Anthony Pico stated, "The real issue is not gaming, and tribal leaders know this in a profound way. The issue is that Native American tribes are governments and gaming is hooked up to the tribes' right to self-government."[39]

The California tribes' political battle over gaming also created an economic base that makes it easier to implement their sovereignty, establishing sovereign realities "on the ground" that change options for both state and federal governments. For example, tribes can use and have begun using their revenues to establish court systems, police departments, and cultural resource protection commissions. They are also establishing cultural centers and language preservation programs, taking advantage of the fact that many of their most educated and talented members have reason to return home. Some uses of the funds, for example, creating fire departments that serve adjacent non-Indian as well as tribal communities, also establish political capital. Of course, gaming tribes may choose instead to distribute their handsome revenues in the form of per capita payments, an option that will not produce many of these sovereignty benefits. But the California gaming tribes seem savvy about the fact that their monopoly on gaming may not last indefinitely, and they must invest their earnings in community development and sovereignty.

Even gaming tribes' payments into the fund for nongaming tribes can work to enhance sovereignty. If the nongaming tribes use their allocations to develop long-needed government infrastructure, they will be demonstrating that even small, newly restored, and newly recognized tribes are sovereign governments.

Finally, California tribes' new political influence as a result of gaming may positively affect sovereignty because of the coalitions and modes of cooperation that sprang forth from the gaming campaigns. Before gaming, the scores of diverse and geographically dispersed California tribes found it difficult to join political forces. Gaming created both the incentive and the financial means to forge coalitions. Of course, tribal differences still emerge, as evidenced by the fact that eleven tribes signed Governor Wilson's Pala Compact, and some of those tribes went on to oppose Proposition 5. However, the vast majority of tribes worked together on the two proposition campaigns, and these combined efforts established new lines of communication and possibilities for development of trust. In addition, gaming has triggered the formation of new organizations, such as the California Indian Nations Gaming Association, that provide regular occasions for tribal leaders throughout the state to convene and discuss common concerns. These networks have persisted after the two proposition campaigns, giving rise to concerted efforts on issues such as law enforcement and education that matter to a broad base of tribes.[40] In coalition with one another, tribes have a much greater chance of prevailing in contests and negotiations with the state over sovereignty and other issues.

## Ramona Redeemed?

Helen Hunt Jackson's novel indicted Americans for dispossessing California Natives and generated considerable sympathy for the Indians' losses. At the same time, however, it provided a convenient myth supporting American set-tlement of California—the Indians had been so mistreated that they either died or fled south of the border, leaving behind empty lands for the Ameri-cans to occupy. This myth of the disappearing Indians put them out of the consciousness of non-Indian Californians for over a century.

Ironically, gaming brought many non-Indian Californians onto reserva-tions for the first time, raising awareness of tribes' continued existence. Gam-ing also provides a form of entertainment that most non-Indian Californians want to be able to enjoy and have ready access to. The two proposition cam-paigns over tribal gaming, funded by gaming revenues, further expanded this non-Indian awareness. The tribes benefited from this new consciousness through political support and significant patronage. More than one hundred years after *Ramona* was published, the descendants of the American settlers have helped restore California Indians to a place within the state's political and social landscape, at least for the near term.

## Notes

An earlier version of this chapter was published as Carole Goldberg and Duane Champagne, "Ramona Redeemed? The Rise of Tribal Political Power in California," *Wicazo Sa Review,* Spring 2002, 43–64.

1.  Duane Champagne, Leroy Seidel, and Carole Goldberg, "The ACCIP Community Ser-vice Report: A Second Century of Dishonor: Federal Inequities and California Indians," *Final Report: Advisory Council on California Indian Policy Submitted to Congress on September 1997* (Washington, D.C.: Bureau of Indian Affairs, 2002), pp. 1–80.

2.  *Rincon Band of Mission Indians v. Califano,* 464 F. Supp. 934 (N.D. Ca. 1979).

3.  Ioana Patringenaru, "Tribes Come of Age," *California Journal* 8 (1999).

4.  During the 1970s and 1980s, litigation succeeded in reversing the termination of dozens of California tribes. See, for example, *Hardwick v. United States,* No. C-79-1710 SW (U.S. Dist. Ct., N.D. Ca., July 20, 1983); *Big Sandy v. Watt,* No. C-80-3787 MHP (U.S. Dist. Ct., N.D. Ca.); *Smith v. United States,* 515 F. Supp. 56 (N.D. Ca. 1978); *Duncan v. Andrus,* 517 F. Supp. 1 (N.D. Cal. 1977). Federal legislation restoring or recognizing California tribes includes Public Law 103-434 and Public Law 103-454. The most recent restoration bill to pass the Congress involves the Coastal Miwok of Graton Rancheria, Public Law 106-568 (2000). Most of the

"unterminated" tribes lost their land bases during termination. The recently recognized tribes often have no land base and must seek congressional or U.S. Department of Interior assistance to acquire one.

5. Claudia Buck, "Life without a Casino," *California Journal* 16 (1999).

6. *Williams v. Lee,* 358 U.S. 217 (1959); *McClanahan v. Arizona State Tax Commission,* 411 U.S. 164 (1973).

7. *Bryan v. Itasca County,* 426 U.S. 373 (1976).

8. *Washington v. Confederated Tribes of the Colville Reservation,* 447 U.S. 134 (1980).

9. 480 U.S. 202 (1987).

10. 25 U.S.C. §§ 2701–2721.

11. 25 U.S.C. § 2710.

12. W. John Moore, "A Winning Hand?" *National Journal* 25, no. 9 (1976).

13. *Sycuan Band of Mission Indians v. Roache,* 54 F.3d 535 (9th Cir. 1994).

14. *Seminole Tribe v. Florida,* 517 U.S. 44 (1996).

15. See *Western Telcon Inc. v. California State Lottery,* 13 Cal. 4th 475 (1996) (tribes unsuccessfully argued that California Lottery's Keno game was a state-authorized slot machine ); *Rumsey v. Wilson,* 64 F.3d 1250 (1994) (tribes unsuccessfully argued that a state must compact for all Class III gaming if it allows any such games); *Chemehuevi Indian Tribe v. State of California* (No. 97–04693, N.D. Ca.) (tribes argue that state of California has not negotiated over compact terms in good faith).

16. The Chemehuevi case is still pending.

17. Patringenaru, "Tribes Come of Age."

18. April Lynch, "Gambling Industry Aces Out Reforms," *San Francisco Chronicle*, October 8, 1996, p. A1.

19. *Washington Post,* April 12, 1998, p. A9.

20. "The Recent History of Indian Gaming in California: Why Proposition 1A (2000 Primary Election) Was Necessary" (2000), draft copy.

21. The tribes responded with a lawsuit alleging that the state was refusing to negotiate in good faith and seeking to compel compact terms (*Chemehuevi Indian Tribe v. State of California,* No. 97–05693, N.D. Ca.). To get around the Seminole restrictions, the plaintiffs sought to compel the U.S. government to sue on their behalf. In the meantime, the Ninth Circuit ruled that the Class III gaming restrictions in IGRA could not be enforced unless the state agreed to waive its Eleventh Amendment sovereign immunity. *U.S. v. Spokane Tribe,* 139 F.3d 1297 (9th Cir. 1998).

22. Ca. Const. IV § 19(e). This provision was included in the constitutional amendment that authorized the state lottery, but did not receive much public comment or interpretation at the time it was adopted. Proposition 5 was drafted with this prohibition in mind. For example, the proposition did not authorize certain casino games such as roulette and craps. It banned alcohol at tribal casinos and made efforts to characterize the video gaming as a lottery rather than as slot machines. See Joseph G. Nelson, "California High Court Strikes Down Indian Gaming in *Hotel Employees and Restaurant Employees International Union v. Davis,*" in Angela Mullis and David Kamper, eds., *Indian Gaming: Who Wins?* (Los Angeles: UCLA American Indian Studies Center, 2000), pp. 35, 43–44.

23. Steve Scott, "Proposition 5's Legacy," *California Journal* 30–31 (1999).

24. Christopher E. Skinnell, *The Opponents of Proposition 5: An Analysis of Campaign Expenditures in Opposition to Proposition 5* (Claremont, CA: Rose Institute of State and Local Government, 1999).

25. See Steve Scott and Melissa Mikesell, "Following the Money," *California Journal* 26 (1999). The chief campaign consultants were from the firm of Winner/Wagner and Mandabach.

26. 21 Cal. 4th 585 (1999).

27. James P. Sweeney, "Indian Gaming Opponents File Lawsuits over Proposition 5; Constitutionality of Measure Is Questioned; Foes Also Request Stay," *San Diego Union-Tribune*, November 21, 1998, p. A3; Tom Gorman, "Who Would Be Winners, Losers If Prop. 5 Passes?" *Los Angeles Times*, October 19, 1998, p. A1; James P. Sweeney, "Court to Hear Issues Today on Gaming Initiative," *San Diego Union-Tribune*, June 1, 1999, p. A3; Copely News Service, "Proposition 5 Called Unconstitutional," *San Diego Union-Tribune*, October 13, 1998, p. A; "The Recent History of Indian Gaming in California" draft, p. 14. For a discussion of the federal law issue, see Carole E. Goldberg et al., "Amici Curiae Brief of Indian Law Professors in the Case of *Hotel Employees and Restaurant Employees International Union v. Wilson*," in *Indian Gaming: Who Wins?* ed. A. Mullis and D. Kamper (Los Angeles: UCLA American Indian Studies Center 2000), pp. 54–66.

28. Chad Gordon, "From Hope to Realization of Dreams: Proposition 5 and California Indian Gaming," in *Indian Gaming: Who Wins?* ed. A. Mullis and D. Kamper (Los Angeles: UCLA American Indian Studies Center 2000), pp. 3, 10.

29. Eventually Tule River agreed to the compact terms. Coyote Valley is still resisting being shut down by the United States Attorney, pinning its hopes on a lawsuit that alleges failure of the state to negotiate in good faith. *Chemehuevi Indian Tribe v. State of California* (No. 97-04693, N. D. Ca.).

30. See, for example, A.B. 2353 (Honda), which died for lack of tribal support. This bill would have provided funding for tribal court development through the California Judicial Council.

31. For a discussion of these conflicts, see Carole Goldberg, "Public Law 280 and the Problem of 'Lawlessness' in California Indian Country," in *Contemporary Native American Political Issues,* ed. Troy Johnson (Walnut Creek, CA: AltaMira, 1999), p. 197.

32. Cal. Family Code § 7810. This legislation, adopted in 1999, rejected the "existing Indian family" doctrine as applied to Indian child welfare proceedings in California.

33. Benjamin Spillman, "Clinton's Signature Seals Deal for Tribe," *Desert Sun*, December 28, 2000.

34. "Casino Donations Flow for Top State Law Officer," *San Jose Mercury News,* March 16, 2000; Jonathan Serrie, "Tribes Flex Political Muscle of Casino Wealth," *Fox News*, June 3, 2000, www.foxnews.com/060300/Indian_fnc.smi.

35. Robert B. Porter, "The Demise of the Ongwehoweh and the Rise of the Native Americans: Redressing the Genocidal Act of Forcing American Citizenship upon Indigenous Peoples" *Harvard BlackLetter Law Journal* 107, no. 15 (1999).

36. In our encounters with California tribal leaders, we have observed that many did not believe they could not establish tribal courts with concurrent civil or criminal jurisdiction because of Public Law 280.

37. *Cabazon Band of Mission Indians v. Smith,* 34 F. Supp. 2d 1201 (C.D. Cal. 1998), appeal pending.

38. "Casino Donations Flow for Top State Law Officer."

39. Patringenaru, "Tribes Come of Age," p. 14.

40. The Coalition for Enhanced Tribal Law Enforcement, initiated by the Cabazon Band, has been pressing for state legislation that would enable tribal police to exercise the powers of state peace officers, thereby enabling them to arrest non-Indians for on-reservation crimes. At least sixty-seven California tribes have joined this coalition, and state officials have met with the tribes in a summit to begin working out this and other related law enforcement issues. Benjamin Spillman, "Policing Summit Proving Complex," *Desert Sun*, November 28, 2000.

# Toward a Multidimensional Historical-Comparative Methodology: Context, Process, and Causality

**10**

I N 1856, THE CHICKASAW FORMED A constitutional government modeled on principles similar to the U.S. government. This nineteenth-century Indian society, however, was an unlikely case for such a transformation if one considers structural arguments only. The Chickasaw occupied the present northern Louisiana–Alabama and western Kentucky region. Between 1700 and 1820, they engaged the fur trade with European traders. From the early 1800s, a small percentage of Chickasaw families organized black slave labor and produced cotton and other agricultural products for market and export. The Choctaw, Cherokee, and Creek also occupied territory in the South and therefore suggest natural comparisons with the Chickasaw. All four Indian nations encountered the same sequences of world-system incorporation, formed capitalistic planter classes, and experienced increased U.S. political pressure for removal west during the 1820s and 1830s.

Social order among the four nations, however, differed significantly. Although socially and symbolically unified by seven national clans and associated ceremonial relations, villages and regions formed the primary political units in the Cherokee national polity. Under U.S. pressure for land, the Cherokee formed a unified political nationality between 1809 and 1810 and adopted a democratic constitution in 1827. Under similar conditions, the Chickasaw, Creek, and Choctaw did not follow the Cherokee plan of forming a nation-state in order to preserve territory and national independence. Chickasaw clans organized and celebrated national ceremonies, which indicated a greater degree of centralized national ceremonial order than among the Cherokee. Unlike among the Cherokee, however, the Chickasaw polity was embedded within kinship and ceremonial institutions, since specific clans held rights to national religious and political offices. Thus the Chickasaw had greater institutional obstacles to adopting a secular, non-kin-based nation-state than the politically better integrated and institutionally differentiated Cherokee. These institutional differences between the Cherokee and Chickasaw help explain why the Cherokee were more likely to adopt political change, while the Chickasaw were more reluctant. A polity with overlapping kinship, solidary, religious, and cultural institutions is difficult to change by consensual social action. In such situations innovators contend with multiple overlapping group prerogatives and often must introduce fundamental changes in traditional orientations between polity and cultural order. All else being equal, a polity is more amenable to consensual change when it is more autonomous from kinship, social solidary, and religious institutional relations. In such cases, innovators contend with fewer overlapping group prerogatives and need not introduce fundamental changes in cultural and normative order.[1]

Thus there are institutional antecedents for explaining Chickasaw traditionalism compared to Cherokee change within their common geopolitical and world-system contexts of the 1820s and 1830s. Given similar world-system and geopolitical contexts as the Cherokee, overlapping political, cultural, and kinship institutions help explain Chickasaw reluctance to adopt political change. An anomaly, however, arises as this juncture. If we rely on the structural arguments given earlier, then we cannot explain the formation of the Chickasaw democratic government in 1856. We therefore must appeal to other factors and/or different levels of analysis in order to give an explanation for Chickasaw traditionalism in one context and political change in another. We can move beyond the structural explanation by including the analysis of historically contingent group struggles within the context of institutional and transsocietal relations. This approach implies that an appropriate vision of causality includes the effects of interdependent transsocietal and institutional contexts and historically contingent group interactions that lead to enduring change in a social order. Before continuing analysis of Chickasaw political change, I discuss institutional and transsocietal context, microgroup processes, and multidimensional (or cybernetic) causality as central to theoretical and empirical progress in comparative-historical analysis.

## Issues in Historical Comparative Methods

Much contemporary comparative work focuses on cross-sectional survey comparisons among nation-states. Underlying this approach are positivist assumptions about methods and social action. Positivist methodologies and epistemologies encourage collection of survey and statistical data, which yield static slices of social phenomena. When attention turns to the study of process, change, and institution building, then the positivist assumptions are less suitable. Positivism tends to look past normative and cultural contexts and group interpretations and actions in historically contingent events.[2] The researcher who seeks to explain change in institutional order must ultimately refer to the historical sequences and human actions that account for such events. In my view, positivism and statistical methods cannot satisfactorily explain processes of institutional change. I am not willing to constrain my analysis with the assumption that historical sequences conform to one or more probability functions that underlie statistical theory. Explanation of institutional change in historical social orders demands a more multidimensional epistemology and method than contemporary positivism now bears.[3]

My explanatory goals dictate the use of a multidimensional method. I seek to explain processes of institutionalized change, and in my view this may require interdependent change in culture, values, social solidarity, political solidarity, political order, and/or economic order. From the outset I assume that consensual social change requires interdependent adjustments among normative, organizational, and material conditions of life. Parsons argues that economy and polity condition relations of normative order, values, and culture, while the latter control social action within the polity and economy.[4] In Parsons's model, control means that norms, values, and culture inform and motivate social action within (and sometimes beyond) the context of political and economic situations or conditions. The relative primacy of normative or material relations is a major issue in macrosociological theory. Parsons argues that in long-term evolutionary change, culture and normative systems control social action within the systems of polity and economy. Although many contest this argument, Parsons insists that normative and cultural primacy is less applicable to short-term historical change, where explanatory emphasis may take a variety of interdependent configurations among material and normative factors.[5] For the student of historical comparative methods, the shorter-term historical period is of most interest. In the shorter run, Parsons's theory leaves open the question of interdependent relations among normative and material factors.

In my view, researchers should set aside the materialist-normative debate in favor of studying historically interdependent normative and material conditions that help explain processes of institutional change. Such a method requires specification of empirical interdependencies between material and normative factors (or environments) and transsocietal conditions. Furthermore, the explanation should not be reduced to a single factor or variable but retain as part of the explanation the interdependent relations among institutional, transsocietal, and material conditions. A multidimensional view of causality will indicate necessary but not sufficient causes (parameters or preconditions) and sufficient conditions (effective causes or cybernetic controlling factors or environments).[6]

As the Chickasaw example shows, structural factors do not necessarily give a complete explanation for change. Analyses of social change should take into account the microlevel group processes that negotiate, reconstruct, and maintain the institutional order.[7] Group actions and historically contingent events, which occur within the context of interdependent material and institutional relations, however, provide an additional dimension of analysis. Contemporary theory suggests a social movements approach to institutional change and focuses attention on concrete actors and groups (elites, classes, class segments, local communities). Outcomes are determined through conflicts and/or consensus formation among pro-change, conservative, and accommodationist leaders and groups.[8] Institutional, transsocietal, and material conditions provide a context for group struggles and negotiation. Nevertheless, processes of change depend on group interactions as they break down, maintain, and/or create and legitimize new forms of institutional organization. In the explanation of social change, microlevel group processes and historically contingent events complement and extend explanations based on interdependent macrolevel transsocietal and institutional contexts.[9] In the following sections I expand on these arguments.

## The Transsocietal Context

Transsocietal context refers to geopolitical relations, world-system relations, and global cultural and normative interchanges. Skocpol argues that geopolitical relations are analytically independent from world-system economic relations.[10] In other words, interstate competition has autonomous effects on processes of social change. World-system and neo-Marxist theorists, however, often assume that geopolitical context is reducible to economic class interests.[11] Similarly group acceptance of colonial or transsocietal institutional models, religions, and new cultural and normative views are potential elements for an explanation of change. Again arguments can be made to reduce transsocietal cultural and institutional influences to economic incorporation or geopolitical-colonial hegemony. For example, do missionaries follow their national flag (colonial hegemony) or does the flag follow missionaries? These situations can vary by case, region, and historical period. Therefore I prefer to handle transsocietal cultural and normative interchanges as analytically independent from world-system incorporation and geopolitical context. The interdependent relations among transsocietal impacts are left to empirical study within historically specific contexts. Each transsocietal factor is potentially dominant. The relative causal effects of transsocietal relations on any particular society is a matter for empirical investigation.[12] Such questions should not be decided before the historical and/or comparative analysis begins.

Let's return to the example of the Chickasaw and outline their transsocietal context. The Chickasaw traded regularly with the English and French by the early 1700s and were subject to trade and diplomatic entreaties from both colonial powers. Like most other eastern Native American societies, the Chickasaw quickly became dependent on trade. They bartered furs and skins—usually deerskins, but beaver primarily among the northern Indian nations—in exchange for European manufactured goods. Being dependent on European trade for guns, ammunition, metal goods, and other industrially manufactured materials, the Chickasaw sought alliance with one or another of the European colonial powers. During the early 1700s, the French planned to forge a line of forts and Indian alliances along the Mississippi Valley and restrict the English colonies to the eastern seaboard. The English countered the French plan by attempting to win over the strategically located Chickasaw with more abundant, cheaper, and better trade goods. From 1730 to 1760 the Chickasaw engaged in almost constant warfare with the French colonies and Indian allies. The Chickasaw usually allied with the British, although some clans formed a minority pro-French faction. After 1763, in a treaty that confirmed French defeat in the Seven Years War, the British assumed hegemony over present eastern North America. During the American Revolutionary War, however, the Spanish recaptured West Florida from the British.

During the late 1780s and early 1790s, the Spanish and the Americans vied for Chickasaw trade and military alliance. By the late 1790s the pro-American party (old pro-English clans) gained the upper hand in favor of trade and alliance with the U.S. government. Between 1800 and 1820, the fur trade steadily declined owing to falling prices and declining demand. As a result, most Chickasaw adopted subsistence agriculture and husbandry during the 1820s. A small percentage of families who exploited black slave labor moved from trade and/or merchandising into plantation production and export of cotton, corn, and cattle. The Chickasaw, like the Cherokee, Choctaw, and Creek in the Southeast, increasingly stratified into two culturally and economically distinct classes—a small market-oriented planter class and a large majority of culturally conservative subsistence farmers.

After 1795 and even more so after the War of 1812, the United States gained hegemonic power over the territory east of the Mississippi River. By the late 1820s the American government and newly created southern states were pressing the southern Indians to move west of the Mississippi River. Before 1817 there were few missionaries among the Chickasaw and before removal west in the late 1830s, the missionaries had little success among most Chickasaw. The Chickasaw planter class welcomed teachers, who taught literacy and business skills to their children, but did not necessarily encourage their children toward Christian conversion. The availability of Western cultural orientations had little significant effect on Chickasaw institutional order before 1837. The Chickasaw and other major southern Indian nations participated in the southern export economy and were subject to strong pressures from the United States to sell their homelands and migrate west. Furthermore they were exposed to U.S. models of education, Christianity, and economic and political organization. These latter relations constitute the transsocietal context for the Southern Indian nations between the 1817 and 1840.[13]

## The Institutional Context

Theoretical assumptions influence the selection of variables, their relative weights, and relations of interdependence. Assuming the analyst strives for an argument of interdependent conditions and factors, it is advisable to adopt fewer reductionist arguments, since they entail simplification of institutional relations that may not hold in many empirical situations. For example, an orthodox Marxist analysis might reduce culture and moral order to an ancillary role with respect to capitalist class interests. Such an argument, however, may overlook the empirical influence of culture and normative order in historical processes of institutional change. Most theories and epistemologies make reductionist assumptions at some level. For example, positivism underemphasizes faculties of the human mind for interpreting cultural, normative, and situational contexts. Advocates of the so-called rational model also understate the causal effects of cultural, normative, and institutional contexts.[14] The tendency toward reductionist assumptions about social action and institutional order has been a great stumbling block to developing a sophisticated cross-cultural comparative analysis.

My particular theoretical biases suggest analytical separation of cultural and normative relations from economy, polity, and personality. In an analogous way, the disciplines of psychology, economics, political science, sociology, and anthropology have staked out their principal analytical terrains. Without doubt, the social sciences have progressed with this academic division of labor. In the study of institutional change, however, even more significant are the interdependent relations among cultural, political, solidary, economic, and personality institutions. Theoretically it is possible to specify interchanges between various subsystems as Parsons has done.[15] Rather than pursue abstract systems analysis, I prefer to analyze concrete historical configurations of interdependency among culture, polity, normative order, economy, and personality (or configurations of institutional differentiation). Furthermore, I seek to know how these empirical configurations vary throughout the world and across history. After determining the configuration of institutional differentiation of a society, the next step is to study its processes of change through time. Observing patterns of change shown by empirical institutional orders within the various historical contexts will provide data for understanding a broad range of social change processes.

I disagree fundamentally with the comparative method of Arthur Stinchcombe, who disregards transsocietal and institutional context and compares organizations and social action across contexts.[16] As Stinchcombe and others say, totalistic units of analysis such as nation-state, society, or empire are too diffuse and need analytical decomposition.[17] Nevertheless the units of analysis (i.e., units of institutional differentiation) should decompose totalistic units into comparable subunits, yet retain the sui generis character of the totalistic order or unit of analysis.[18] Others, like Geertz, use contextual analyses for elaborating differences among societal orders that share some common institutions or traditions such as Islamic religion.[19] Unlike Weber, Geertz does not present causal arguments for explaining institutional change. In Weber's comparative studies, he investigated social, economic, political, and cultural differences in order to explain how they comparatively or directly helped explain the rise of Western capitalism.[20] Understanding the institutional and transsocietal context of a causal argument is a prerequisite for providing a meaningful and adequate explanation; otherwise researchers risk abstract applications that disregard important features that may contribute to or refine an explanation.

Comparative conceptualization of institutional orders, however, requires a common analytical language capable of expressing and defining relations within all social orders.[21] A corollary to this premise suggests that the analytical principles of institutional order are similar for all human societies. In other words, a comparative understanding institutional order and processes of change posits that human societies are analyzable by a common set of organizational principles. Variations in institutional order derive from permutations generated by a set of fundamental principles. The assumptions made about the principles of institutional order thus have bearing on the analysis of institutional order and processes for change. I argue that the theory of differentiation and associated arguments of social and political solidarity provide fundamental principles and a universal language for comparative analysis of institutional change.

The arguments for social and/or political solidarity are required for explaining consensual institution building and institutional stability and continuity. As emphasized previously, processes of stable, consensual institutional change require adjustment not only in economic and political order but also in normative and cultural order. Groups that impose major institutional change (i.e., the formation of a state) without accompanying changes in cultural, normative order and values will have to maintain order through vigilant coercion. Coercively controlled institutional orders can persist for extended periods. Such societies or institutions, however, will experience instabilities caused by groups that are resistant to the imposed order.[22] Analysis of stability and consensual change in institutional orders requires investigation of processes of solidarity formation and cultural legitimacy.

Since I have argued the necessity of observing interdependent relations among cultural, normative, political, and economic institutions, Parsons's functionalist paradigm comes to mind. Parsons, however, presents a paradigm consisting of four functions: pattern maintenance, integration, goal attainment, and adaptation. The four functions, however, do not have a one-to-one correspondence to empirical institutions.[23] Parsons did not make a concentrated effort to apply his analysis to empirical processes of social change. He therefore leaves the historical comparativist at somewhat of a loss. Nevertheless, Parsons emphasized systemic interdependencies within the institutional order. For those who seek to understand processes of institutional change, this key insight sets the stage for transcending more reductionist views of institutional order and change. Instead of Parsons's emphasis on systems theory, however, I prefer returning to Weber's emphasis on concrete empirical institutional orders, but aided by an empirical version of Parsons's differentiation theory.

The theory of differentiation is implicit within Parsons's interdependent functional paradigm, and it argues that more differentiated societies have greater generalized capacity to manage relations with their environments. For Parsons, environments are multiple, consisting of cultural, social, and organic as well as the physical environment. This level of analysis, however, is not usually one that interests the comparativist, especially since Parsons's evolutionary theory does not focus on concrete historical processes of change.[24] Nevertheless, the theory of differentiation provides a set of principles for understanding institutional relations within societies. The theory hypothesizes, everything else being equal, that more institutionally differentiated societies will exhibit greater capacity for change and adaptation than less differentiated societies. As a historical comparative sociologist, I find the latter statement somewhat general and without due respect for historical contingency. Nevertheless I accept the argument as a guiding hypothesis but withhold my final judgment awaiting further empirical evidence.

In terms of institutional context, the theory of differentiation directs attention to relations of autonomy and interdependence among major societal institutions. In order to start an analysis of institutional context, we need to describe a society's primary features: cultural worldview, political organization, normative order, and economic order. We also need to know the degree of mutual autonomy or interdependence among political, cultural, solidary, and economic institutions. The first step in analysis of institutional context is conceptualizing the cultural, normative, political, and economic order and, just as important, describing the relations of differentiation among the same major institutions. When having done this, the researcher has a benchmark institutional configuration from which to gauge change.

Now we can again return to the Chickasaw case study. In the introduction, I briefly outlined early Chickasaw institutional order. While there is no space to give an elaborate description, I extracted the information from documents, oral histories, ceremonies and myths, and observations by travelers and traders.[25] The Chickasaw study, as I have conceived it, seeks to explain the formation of a differentiated constitutional government. Therefore the analysis of early Chickasaw society concentrated on the organization of the Chickasaw polity and its relations of differentiation with culture, normative order, and economy. As mentioned earlier, the Chickasaw held traditionalistic cultural orientations that predisposed well-socialized Chickasaw to prefer preservation of the old institutional order.[26] The early Chickasaw polity was embedded within local clans and religious–ceremonial organization.[27] By the early 1800s one report states that the Chickasaw national council no longer met in a sacred ceremonial square, indicating a trend toward secularization of Chickasaw political order.[28]

Hence the Chickasaw had traditionalistic cultural orientations and a relatively nondifferentiated polity and we expect them to resist major institutional change. Interestingly enough, the Chickasaw acted in accordance to the previous theoretical prediction during the pre-removal period. During the 1820s and 1830s, the Chickasaw polity did not change significantly, despite strong U.S. geopolitical pressure, incorporation into the southern export economy, the presence of a market-oriented planter class, and American agents and missionaries who worked to convince the Chickasaw to adopt U.S. forms of agriculture, Christianity, and U.S. forms of democratic political order.[29] Thus the Chickasaw case upholds an argument that institutional order—a traditional worldview and a polity embedded in kinship, solidary, and religious relations—helps explain Chickasaw resistance to change despite intense pressures for adaptive change.

So far so good, but now we meet the dilemma presented in the introduction. The Chickasaw formed a differentiated constitutional government in 1856, when the intensity of U.S. pressure for land temporarily receded and while many Chickasaw preferred the old institutional order. How can we use the same transsocietal and institutional arguments to explain Chickasaw traditionalism before 1837 and political change in 1856? The answer to this question is that we cannot. Such arguments work better for explaining Chickasaw traditionalism than for explaining change. Sole reliance on geopolitical context, class formation, nondifferentiated political order, and world-system incorporation cannot explain Chickasaw state formation. Nevertheless, empirically this is what happened, and therefore we must look to other modes of analysis, since sole reliance on structural arguments fails.

## Group Interaction, Historical Contingency, and Causality

Turning again to theory, macrosociological arguments have often relied heavily on structural arguments. In particular, Parsons's evolutionary theory understates the issues of process and change between levels of societal differentiation. Even to understand processes of evolution there must be historical causes for major changes in institutional order. A serviceable theory of social change must explain change and transition between types of institutional order. Such explanations will necessarily involve actions by groups and contain narratives of group actions played out within transsocietal and institutional contexts. Several theorists have contributed arguments toward a theory of institutional change based on social movements theory.[30] In this view changing structural or contextual conditions can create dissatisfactions or opportunities for the introduction of institutional innovations. These innovations may lead to a path of increased institutional differentiation or they may lead to less differentiated institutional orders. Several groups may offer competing innovations, but the mere introduction of a particular innovation will not necessarily lead to its adoption. The mere desire for change does not mean that institutional entrepreneurs will succeed in gaining adoption of their innovation. The likelihood that an innovation becomes institutionalized will depend on a variety of conditions, including the strength and interests of opposition groups and organizations, cultural acceptability of the innovation, the level and configuration of preexisting institutional differentiation, the social solidarity of the innovators, the form of social and political solidarity of the society, and the ability of the innovators to gather widespread support, commitment, and resources from the major groups in the society. It is quite likely that more traditional social movements' literature can extend and broaden the institutional change perspective, but we will not explore that possibility here.[31] This view of institutional change indicates that we must look to group interactions and sequences of historically contingent events to explain processes of institutional change.

Now we have analytical tools for analyzing Chickasaw state formation. Until the late 1830s the Chickasaw were reluctant to make major changes in their political system, where kinship groups and hereditary chiefs held traditional rights to political office. Under similar transsocietal conditions, the Cherokee, with a more politically solidary and differentiated society, formed a differentiated constitutional government in 1827. The other two major southeastern nations, the Creek and Choctaw, however, did not follow the Cherokee path of political centralization and increased differentiation. In the late 1820s, a small group of Christianized Choctaw planters attempted to form a centralized constitutional government. This attempt, however, failed owing to the political resurgence of traditional regional leaders, who mobilized considerable support against centralization and differentiation of the Choctaw polity. The decentralized and nondifferentiated Choctaw political order helps explain their resistance to political change. The Choctaw polity relied on social and political loyalties to kin groups and consisted of a federation of local clans and regions. Similarly the symbolically ordered and politically and culturally decentralized Creek responded much like the Chickasaw and willfully and collectively refused to adopt the plan of change taken by the Cherokee.

The Choctaw and Creek formed centralized constitutional governments in 1860 and 1867, respectively. In both cases, an alliance between the U.S. government and a small group of pro-change planters imposed differentiated constitutional governments over reluctant conservative majorities. Planters supported by the United States applied force to create the Choctaw and Creek constitutional governments, while Cherokee constitution building was more consensual and thirty to forty years earlier. Earlier and more consensual political change was possible within the more politically solidary and differentiated Cherokee society, than among the locally solidary and less differentiated Creek and Choctaw societies. With U.S. support, Creek and Choctaw institutional entrepreneurs created constitutional governments without strong support from conservatives, who preferred less differentiated and decentralized political and institutional orders.[32] Similarly, Chickasaw planters, with backing from U.S. officials, dismantled the kin-based political order. Nevertheless, after these events greater national political solidarity supported the formation of a Chickasaw constitutional government than among the Creek and Choctaw. A historical narrative of group interests, struggles, and contingent events that transpired within the institutional and transsocietal conditions of the 1840s and 1850s will illustrate this turn of events. The Cherokee, Creek, and Choctaw movements toward political change also deserve treatment, but here we concentrate on the critical Chickasaw case.

By the early 1830s Chickasaw society stratified into a majority of subsistence farmers, and minority of market-oriented planters, merchants, and cattlemen. The market-oriented groups did not challenge the old political authorities, in part because some leading planters had access to political decision making by means of inherited political office and honorary chiefdoms. The conservative majority allowed the planters and merchants to benefit privately from managing Chickasaw relations with the United States. In exchange, the conservatives hoped to gain protection against American land and removal pressures. In the late 1820s the planters engineered the adoption of laws regulating market relations, but the political order remained organized by a hereditary principal chief and hereditary subordinate chiefs. The Chickasaw, under federal and state pressure, reluctantly agreed to sign removal treaties in 1830, 1832, and 1836, but they could not find a suitable homeland in the west. The Treaty of 1834 established a Chickasaw Commission and delegated to it management of Chickasaw legal issues arising from removal. The Chickasaw Commission acted as a de facto government and administered to Chickasaw grievances that emerged during the removal period. In fact the Chickasaw Commission contained the most important hereditary chiefs, including the principal chief, or "king" as the English and Americans called him. Nevertheless, the king led a majority of Chickasaw, who before 1837 had little interest in changing the kin-based political order.[33]

Between 1837 and 1845 a series of events led to the official dismantling of the Chickasaw kin-based government. Desperate for a place to settle after suffering the intrusion of American settlers and legal harassment from nearby states, a group of planters negotiated a treaty with the Choctaw in 1837. By this time most Choctaw were living in the west. In the early 1830s, the United States pressured the Choctaw to resettle in present-day eastern Oklahoma. Previous negotiations ended in failure because the Choctaw would not cede land but were willing to grant citizenship to the Chickasaw. Most Chickasaw, however, did not wish to surrender their independent nationality, and they therefore refused the Choctaw offer. By 1837 conditions in the east deteriorated so far that the Chickasaw agreed to surrender their nationality and become citizens of the Choctaw nation.

Under U.S. pressure, the Choctaw formed a decentralized constitutional government in 1834. The new Choctaw national council consisted of thirty delegates elected from three districts. The three traditional regional chiefs formed the national executive branch, but none had jurisdiction outside his own district.[34] According to the 1837 treaty, the Chickasaw created a fourth district within the Choctaw nation. In 1838 the Choctaw revised their constitution, which now included the Chickasaw. Thereafter, the Choctaw and U.S. governments expected the Chickasaw to conform to Choctaw law and political order. This, however, required the Chickasaw to abandon their old political system and adopt the electoral system of the Choctaw. By 1843, a group of Christians and planters took up residence in the Chickasaw district and elected a district chief in conformity with Choctaw law and the treaty of 1837. Most Chickasaw, however, hesitated to settle in the Chickasaw district during the early 1840s. The area was subject to intermittent raids from plains Indians who still claimed the land.[35]

A large group of conservative Chickasaw, probably a small national majority at this time, refused to accept abolition of the kin-based government and were disheartened over the loss of national autonomy. Between 1843 and 1845, three interconnected groups vied for official U.S. recognition and control over Chickasaw affairs—the king and his conservative following, the Chickasaw Commission, and the Chickasaw district chief. The American government refused recognition to any Chickasaw government other than the Chickasaw district government. Planters led in the district and they actively campaigned against the old government and for adoption of the Choctaw constitutional government. Despite this setback the conservatives openly advocated nationalist separation from the Choctaw government.[36]

In the late 1840s, the planters of the Chickasaw district agreed to pursue nationalist separation, while the conservatives agreed to accept a constitutional government if established independently of the Choctaw government. In 1846, the Chickasaw district government adopted a early constitutional declaration. In 1848, the constitution was revised to include separation of powers between executive and legislative branches and the election of a unicameral national council composed of thirty captains—the old name given to clan headmen by the Spanish. The thirty captains were elected from throughout the districts of the Choctaw nation, since many Chickasaw did not reside in the Chickasaw district. Seventeen out of the thirty elected delegates were elected from the Chickasaw district. The Chickasaw district chief was named "the Chief of the Chickasaw People," and he had the right to convene the national council whenever necessary. The constitution went on to create laws for the organization of the governmental bodies and stated that the Chickasaw government strongly supported education and economic development for its citizens. With this constitution the Chickasaw declared that they had the right to make their own laws and to manage their own financial affairs. At this time, the U.S. government recognized the Chickasaw district within the Choctaw government and delivered funds from treaty agreements to the Chickasaw district chief.[37] The constitution of 1848 shows a clear break with past political organization. While the name "captain" was retained, men no longer occupied offices according to clan and heredity. All offices were now elective, and the polity was formally differentiated from kinship ties and from Chickasaw religious ceremonial order.

In 1850 they again revised the constitution of their "unofficial" government, this time taking a more nationalist turn by electing a chief—"the financial chief"—who was independent of the U.S. and Choctaw-supported Chickasaw district chief. In late 1850 the Chickasaw council elected a chief with superior authority over the Chickasaw district chief, who served the Choctaw government. The delegates to the unicameral national council were reduced from thirty to twelve. After election of the new chief, the national council convened in secret session and considered the question of nationalist separation form the Choctaw government.[38]

Between 1850 and 1855, a united movement to secede from the Choctaw nation and create an independent national government galvanized a new Chickasaw political nationality. As among the Cherokee, the formation of a mobilized and unified national political identity preceded the consensual formation of the differentiated constitutional government. In October 1851, the Chickasaw held a convention to further revise their constitution. The new constitution declared that the general council under the provisions of the Chickasaw constitution had plenary powers to manage Chickasaw funds. This was the Chickasaw solution to the struggle dating from the early 1840s over who controlled Chickasaw funds and governmental authority. The United States, the Choctaw, and many Chickasaw planters then agreed that the Chickasaw district chief control the funds. By 1851, the Chickasaw conservatives and planters were united within a constitutional government and were pursuing control over their own national affairs from the Choctaw and United States. The Chickasaw constitution of 1851 created a bicameral legislature composed of thirteen captains and thirteen representatives. Eleven captains were elected to four-year terms, and two prominent conservative leaders were granted office "for life and always entitled to be members of the council."[39] The chief was elected by the general council for two-year terms and was granted a salary. From 1852 to 1855, the "financial chief" was granted powers to appoint a committee and seek separation from the Choctaw nation. In early 1852 the Chickasaw council declared, "Be it enacted by the Chickasaw in General Council that the Chickasaws will no longer submit to the oppression of the Choctaws or the enforcement of the Choctaw laws in the

Chickasaw District until our rights are acknowledged that the expenses of the Chickasaw District, as a district of the Choctaw Nation, shall not hereafter be paid out of the funds of the Chickasaws."[40]

The formation of a Chickasaw constitutional government, however, depended on U.S. officials who forced the Choctaw to grant national independence to the Chickasaw in the Treaty of 1855. Negotiations with the Choctaw for separation repeatedly failed, since they saw such a movement resulting in permanent loss of Choctaw national territory. U.S. officials ultimately intervened on behalf of the Chickasaw and arranged the Treaty of 1855.[41] The Treaty of 1855 allowed the Chickasaw to form an independent government, after paying the Choctaw substantial amounts for land and withdrawal from Choctaw citizenship.

In August 1856 the Chickasaw convened a constitutional convention. The financial chief, the elected captains under the Chickasaw constitution, and elected delegates from the Chickasaw precincts composed the body of the convention. They adopted a differentiated constitutional government formally modeled after U.S. federal and state constitutional governments. The new Chickasaw government included a bill of rights, separation of church and state, freedom of speech, right to trial, equality before the law, and separation of powers among executive, legislative, and judicial branches. The constitution also included a slave code that prohibited the government from emancipating slaves without agreement and compensation from the owners. The slave code was struck down after the American Civil War, in which most Chickasaw allied with the South.[42]

The Chickasaw constitution of 1856 defined a polity that was differentiated from religious and kinship organization. The election of delegates to office indicated a differentiation of polity from society. The new government also included separation of executive, judicial, and legislative powers, all of which increased institutional differentiation within the organization of the polity itself. By the middle 1870s, the Chickasaw created formal political parties, another indication of further organizational differentiation within the polity and further differentiation of polity from society. If we were to continue the analysis, it could be shown that although the Chickasaw adopted a highly differentiated polity, there was considerable continuity of Chickasaw culture, values, norms, political culture, and social organization that gave social and political relations a very different dynamic than found within the U.S. polity.

In the Chickasaw case there was no evolutionary or systemic progression from the kin-based political order to a differentiated constitutional government. An alliance of U.S. officials and Chickasaw planters willfully dismantled the old Chickasaw political order. U.S. and planter repression of the kin-based political order removed overt religious and kin-based resistance to the consensual acceptance of a constitutional government in the 1850s. A new and more centralized national political solidarity emerged from the Chickasaw movement to regain nationalist independence. The new national solidarity contributed to a political consensus that was relatively independent of the old nondifferentiated religious-kinship-political consensus that supported the kin-based political order. The mobilization for nationalist separation by the Chickasaw conservatives included planter leaders who carried and supported a U.S. model of political organization. Chickasaw planters eventually supported separation but not a return to the old political system. The conservatives, however, were forced to abandon the traditional political order in face of U.S. and planter opposition. Conservatives enlisted the aid of Chickasaw planters and U.S. officials in their quest for national independence by submitting to U.S. and planter interests in forming a constitutional government. Ultimately groups and organizations are the creators and modifiers of institutional orders. The outcomes of struggles between the major social groupings are the effective causes of institutional change, although always conditioned by their transsocietal and institutional contexts.

## Discussion and Conclusion

I have advocated an inductive and empirical method for studying processes of social-institutional change. To be sure, this method must be informed by theoretical arguments in order to identify significant controls and salient features of cultural and social order and to define the process of change itself. But theory must not dictate results to research and method, as I believe has been the case in macrohistorical studies of social change, which in sociology have tended to implicitly incorporate evolutionary or modernist teleologies. The method I propose here curbs some of the more strident and predictive claims of current theory and forces sociologists to show how their theories fare within concrete historical situations. By considering institutional, cultural, world-system, and geopolitical contexts, I expect to obtain a healthy respect for analyzing processes of stability and change within varying situations. Our theories should not abstract past historical contexts but enlighten us as to how societies change and/or remain stable from context to context. This can be done with specific analysis of cases studies and comparative studies of societies within regions within the modern world-system and throughout history. This is the work for a discipline over long periods of scholarly activity. Certainly there are many obstacles, since much historical data is missing and the magnitude of the project is large, but I believe such a project promises us a better and more thorough understanding of human societies, their variations, and likely future. Therefore, I believe that such a difficult undertaking is well worth the effort and will pay great rewards in understanding the past and future of human societies.

Encroached in the method is a strong antievolutionary and antistructuralist bent. A multidimensional method demands much care in understanding political, cultural, social, geopolitical, and world-system contexts and consideration of their relative conditioning and effective cause for explaining social change. This method seeks to understand the variation in institutional orders among societies and to explain their differential paths of social change. Hence there can be no inherent teleology of modernism or evolution or convergence. An inductive empirical approach can isolate historical trends of centralization, bureaucratization, market expansion, and increased institutional differentiation, but such trends should not be extrapolated into evolutionary principles for all time or for the next several centuries. Knowledge of history should give the researcher and theorist a healthy respect for the decline and fall of great civilizations. Similarly, it should not be posited, as Parsons does, that the modernization of U.S. society will continue into the next several centuries. Such a position ignores the possibility that world and domestic economic conditions may change drastically, and that U.S. democracy is upheld by a continually negotiated process and is not a structural ordained, and that just as the Roman republic passed to centralized authoritarian leadership, specific historical conditions may yet arise that foster similar authoritarian developments within the U.S. polity. It should be our task to understand how specific historical societies and their constituent groups behave under varying contextual conditions. A primary objective of historical-comparative sociology should be to develop grounded generalizations about group action and institutional change within varying historical contexts. Our methods and theories should seek ways to understand the complexity and diversity of all human societies and study the variations in their trends in stability and change. Hence small societies such as the Chickasaw of North America or the Pygmies of Africa become as worthy of study as the larger-scale societies that are currently featured in sociological studies. Only after completing many empirical studies about the social change processes of historical and contemporary societies can we formulate a general theory of social change that more accurately reflects the diversity of the human institutional order and more accurately account for the diverse possibilities of future societal change.

Transsocietal conditions and institutional contexts identify the parameters of institutional change, but they do not by themselves necessarily account for processes or causality in institutional change. Processes of change take place within transsocietal and institutional contexts. Change in transsocietal contexts condition group action and is analyzable as sequences of group actions and historical events effecting change in institutional order. Application of this method will help identify a variety of historical and contemporary institutional configurations and sequences of change. By studying group processes of institutional change within their transsocietal and institutional contexts, we can accumulate empirical knowledge about historically specific processes of social change. Based on this evidence, theory can be generated by inductive means; through comparison of results from accumulated historical and comparative studies. Researchers who combine empirical investigation of transsocietal and institutional contexts with group processes of change will necessarily address fundamental theoretical issues of social order and social change. For example, the arguments for institutional order, social movements, world-system, and geopolitics draw on theories current within macrosociology. Consequently, both empirical and theoretical analysis will extend hand in hand. Not only will a multidimensional method include interdependent material and normative arguments, macro- and microarguments, but also will help reconcile theory and historical comparative data.

## Notes

This chapter appeared earlier as Duane Champagne, "Toward a Multidimensional Historical-Comparative Methodology: Context, Process, and Causality," in *Race and Ethnicity in Research Methods*, ed. John H. Stanfield and Rutledge H. Dennis (Hollywood: Sage, 1993), pp. 233–53.

1. Duane Champagne, *American Indian Societies: Strategies and Conditions of Political and Cultural Survival* (Cambridge, MA: Cultural Survival, 1989); Champagne, *Social Order and Political Change: The Constitutional Governments among the Cherokee, the Choctaw, the Chickasaw, and the Creek* (Stanford, CA: Stanford University Press, 1992).

2. Adam Przeworski and Henry Teune, *The Logic of Comparative Social Inquiry* (New York: Wiley Interscience, 1970), pp. 144, 182–83; Gunther Roth, "Max Weber's Comparative Approach and Historical Typology," *Comparative Methodology in Sociology*, ed. Ivan Vallier (Berkeley: University of California Press, 1971), pp. 80–82; Stanislav Andreski, *The Uses of Comparative Sociology* (Berkeley: University of California Press,1965), pp. 66–67, 82–83.

3. Jeffrey C. Alexander, *Theoretical Logic in Sociology*, 4 vols. (Berkeley: University of California Press, 1983); Talcott Parsons, *The Structure of Social Action* (New York: McGraw-Hill, 1937); Mattei Dogan and Dominique Pelassy, *How to Compare Nations: Strategies in Comparative Politics* (Chatham, NJ: Chatham House, 1984), p. 18; Roth, "Max Weber," p. 80; Alan Sica, *Weber, Irrationality, and Social Order* (Berkeley: University of California Press,1988).

4. Talcott Parsons, *The Evolution of Societies* (Englewood Cliffs, NJ: Prentice-Hall, 1977).

5. Parsons, *Evolution*, p. 240.

6. Dogan, *Comparative Politics*, pp. 16, 164–65; Andreski, *Comparative Sociology*, p. 83; Roth, "Max Weber"; Neil J. Smelser, *Comparative Methods in the Social Sciences* (Englewood Cliffs, NJ: Prentice-Hall,1976), pp. 131–34.

7. Sheldon Stryker, *Symbolic Interactionism* (Menlo Park, CA: Benjamin Cummings, 1980); Randall Collins, *Theoretical Sociology* (San Diego: Harcourt Brace Jovanovich, 1988), pp. 264–300.

8. Jeffrey C. Alexander and Paul Colomy, "Social Differentiation and Collective Behavior," *Sociological Theory* 3 (1985): 11–23; Colomy, "Uneven Structural Differentiation: Toward a Comparative Approach," in *Neofunctionalism,* ed. Jeffrey C. Alexander (Beverly Hills, CA: Sage, 1985), pp. 131–56; Colomy, "Uneven Differentiation and Incomplete Institutionalization: Political Change and Continuity in the Early American Nation," in *Differentiation Theory and Social Change: Comparative and Historical Perspectives,* ed. Jeffrey C. Alexander and Paul Colomy (New York: Columbia University Press, 1990), pp. 119–62; Colomy, "Strategic Groups and Political Differentiation in the Antebellum United States," in *Differentiation Theory and Social Change: Comparative and Historical Perspectives,* ed. Jeffrey C. Alexander and Paul Colomy (New York: Columbia University Press, 1990), pp. 222–64; S. N. Eisenstadt, "Institutionalization and Social Change," *American Sociological Review* 29 (1964): 235–47; Eisenstadt, "Social Change, Differentiation, and Evolution," *American Sociological Review* 29 (1964): 375–86; Eisenstadt, "Modes of Structural Differentiation, Elite Structure, and Cultural Visions," in *Differentiation Theory and Social Change: Comparative and Historical Perspectives,* ed. Jeffrey C. Alexander and Paul Colomy (New York: Columbia University Press. 1990), pp. 19–51.

9. Phillip Abrams, *Historical Sociology* (Ithaca, NY: Cornell University Press,1982).

10. Theda Skocpol, *States and Social Revolutions* (New York: Cambridge University Press, 1979); Otto Hintze, "Economics and Politics in the Age of Modern Capitalism," in *The Historical Essays of Otto Hintze,* ed. Felix Cohen (New York: Oxford University Press, 1975), pp. 422–52; Hintze, "Military Organization and the Organization of the State," in *Historical Essays of Otto Hintze,* ed. Felix Cohen (New York: Oxford University Press, 1975), pp. 178–215.

11. Immanuel Wallerstein, *The Modern World System* (New York: Academic, 1974); Eric Wolf, *Europe and the People without History* (Berkeley: University of California Press, 1982).

12. Duane Champagne, "Culture, Differentiation, and Environment: Social Change in Tlingit Society," in *Differentiation Theory and Social Change: Comparative and Historical Perspectives,* ed. Jeffrey C. Alexander and Paul Colomy (New York: Columbia University Press, 1990), pp. 52–87.

13. W. David Baird, *The Chickasaw People* (Phoenix: Indian Tribal Series, 1974); M234 *Letters Received by the Office of Indian Affairs, 1824–81,* Chickasaw Agency 1824–1870, rolls 135–42. Choctaw Agency, 1824–1876, rolls 169–83 (Washington, D.C.: National Archives, n.d.), roll 135, pp. 154–58; Guy B. Barden, "The Gilberts and the Chickasaw Nation," *Tennessee Historical Quarterly* 17 (1953): 249; J. H. Eaton, "The Progress Made in Civilizing the Indians for the Last Years and Their Present Conditions," *Report From the Secretary of War,* 21st Congress, 1st sess., vol. 2. (Washington D. C.: U. S. Government Printing Office, 1830), p. 110; Champagne, *Societies,* pp. 59–61.

14. Robert Marsh, *Comparative Method: A Codification of Cross-Societal Analyses* (New York: Harcourt, Brace & World, 1967), pp. 18–20; Andreski, *Comparative Sociology*, pp. 66–67, 82–83; Smelser, *Comparative Methods,* pp. 65–67; Przeworski, *Comparative Social Inquiry,* pp. 182–83.

15. Parsons, *Evolution;* Talcott Parsons, *Economy and Society* (New York: Free Press, 1956).

16. Arthur Stinchcombe, *Theoretical Methods in History* (New York: Academic, 1978).

17. Przeworski, *Comparative Social Inquiry,* p. 169–71, 208.

18. Emile Durkheim, *The Division of Labor in Society* (New York: Free Press, 1984).

19. Clifford Geertz, *Islam Observed: Religious Development in Morocco and Indonesia* (Chicago: University of Chicago Press, 1971); Reinhard Bendix, *Nation-Building and Citizenship* (Berkeley: University of California Press, 1977); E. P. Thompson, *The Making of the English Working Class* (New York: Vintage, 1966); Theda Skocpol, "Emerging Agendas and Recurrent Strategies in Historical Sociology," in *Vision and Method in Historical Sociology*, ed. Theda Skocpol (New York: Cambridge University Press, 1984), pp. 356–91.

20. Max Weber, *The Protestant Ethic and the Spirit of Capitalism* (New York: Scribner's, 1958); Weber, *General Economic History* (New Brunswick, NJ: Transaction, 1981); Weber, *The Sociology of Religion* (Boston: Beacon, 1963).

21. Bendix, *Nation-Building*, p. 52; Marsh, *Comparative Method*, p. 6; Przeworski, *Comparative Social Inquiry*, p. 10; Dogan, *Comparative Politics*, p. 10.

22. Durkheim, *Division of Labor*, pp. 310–22; Parsons *Evolution*, p. 25.

23. Talcott Parsons, *Social Systems and the Evolution of Action Theory* (New York: Free Press, 1977).

24. Parsons, *Evolution*.

25. Champagne, *Social Order*.

26. James Adair, *The History of the American Indians* (New York: Johnson Reprint, 1968), pp. 34–46, 99–101; Thomas Nairne, *Nairne's Muskhogean Journals: The 1708 Expedition to the Mississippi River*, ed. Alexander Moore (Jason: University Press of Mississippi, 1988), pp. 40–42; Arrell Gibson, *The Chickasaws* (Norman: University of Oklahoma Press 1971).

27. Adair, *History*, pp. 31–33; Gibson, *Chickasaws*, pp. 12–30; James Malone, *The Chickasaw Nation: A Short Sketch of a Noble People* (Louisville, KY: John P. Morton,1922), pp. 211–13; Baird, *Chickasaw*.

28. Jesse Jennings, ed., "Nutt's Trip to the Chickasaw Country," *Journal of Mississippi History* 9 (1947): 34–61.

29. M234 *Letters*, roll 135, pp. 135, 155, 194, 259, 693–95; Barden, "Gilberts," pp. 222–29.

30. Alexander, "Social Differentiation"; Colomy, "Uneven Structural Differentiation," pp. 131–56; Colomy, "Uneven Differentiation," pp. 119–62; Colomy, "Strategic Groups," pp. 222–64; Eisenstadt, "Institutionalization," pp. 235–47; Eisenstadt, "Social Change," pp. 375–86; Eisenstadt,"Modes of Structural Differentiation," pp. 19–51.

31. R. H. Turner and L. Killian, *Collective Behavior* (Englewood Cliffs, NJ: Prentice-Hall 1972); A. Morris, *The Origins of the Civil Rights Movement: Black Communities Organizing for Change* (New York: Free Press, 1984); A. Oberschall, *Social Conflict and Social Movements* (Englewood Cliffs, NJ: Prentice-Hall, 1973); Neil Smelser, *The Theory of Collective Behavior* (New York: Free Press, 1963).

32. Champagne, *Social Order*; Champagne, *American Indian Societies*.

33. M234 *Letters*, roll 135, pp. 281–82; M234 *Letters*, roll 136, pp. 21–22; Gaston Litton, ed., "The Negotiations Leading to the Chickasaw-Choctaw Agreement, January 17, 1837," *Chronicles of Oklahoma* 17 (1939): 417–27.

34. M234 *Letters*, roll 170, pp. 414–20, 880; Grant Foreman, ed., *Indian-Pioneer History Collection* (Oklahoma City: Oklahoma Historical Society, n.d.), 25:330; W. David Baird, "Peter Pitchlynn and the Reconstruction of the Choctaw Republic," in *Indian Leaders: Oklahoma's First Statesmen*, ed. H. Glenn Jordan and Thomas M. Holm (Oklahoma City: Oklahoma Historical Society. 1979), pp. 12–28; M234 *Letters*, roll 171, pp. 452–53.

35. M234 *Letters*, roll 172, pp. 278–80; Angie Debo, *The Rise and Fall of the Choctaw Republic* (Norman: University of Oklahoma Press, 1934), pp. 64–77; Muriel H. Wright, "Brief Outline of the Choctaw and Chickasaw Nations in the Indian Territory 1820 to 1860," *Chronicles of*

*Oklahoma* 7 (1929): 388–418; M234 *Letters*, roll 137, pp. 144, 296–98; Gibson, *Chickasaws*, pp. 216–19, 223, 242.

36. Baird, *Chickasaw*, pp. 52–55; M234 *Letters,* roll 139, pp. 142, 148–49, 153–54, 219, 227, 236–39; Gibson *Chickasaws*, pp. 246–48; Wright *Brief Outline*, pp. 401–2.

37. CKN *Chickasaw National Records,* microfilm rolls 1, 4, 7, 8–9 (Oklahoma City: Oklahoma Historical Society, n.d.), roll 4, 1848–1856.

38. M234 *Letters*, roll 139, pp. 253–54, 456, 522; M234, roll 140, pp. 171–77, 502–5; Gibson, *Chickasaws*, p. 248; Wright, *Brief Outline*, pp. 401–2; CKN *Chickasaw National Rolls*, roll 4, 1848.

39. CKN *Chickasaw National Rolls*, roll 4, 1851.

40. CKN *Chickasaw National Rolls*, roll 4, 1852; CKN *Chickasaw National Rolls*, roll 4, 1850, pp. 33, 45; CKN *Chickasaw National Rolls*, roll 4, 1851; M234 *Letters*, roll 140, pp. 296–97, 340-342; M234 *Letters*, roll 141, pp. 193; M234 *Letters*, roll 142, pp. 139, 300–302, 304, 308.

41. CKN *Chickasaw National Rolls*, roll 4, 1855; Gibson *Chickasaws*, pp. 225-228, 231, 249-257; Wright *Brief Outline*, pp. 400–403.

42. M234 *Letters*, roll 142, pp. 139–69; CKN *Chickasaw National Rolls*, roll 4, 1856; CKN *Chickasaw National Rolls*, roll 8; Wright, *Brief Outline*, pp. 409–10; CKN *Chickasaw National Rolls*, roll 8, 1856–1889.

# The Delaware Revitalization
Movement of the Early 1760s:
A Suggested Reinterpretation

## 11

THE DELAWARE REVITALIZATION MOVEMENT of the early 1760s strengthened the political, religious, and social integration of Delaware society.
While the Delaware Prophet, one of the several Delaware prophets who
emerged during the early 1760s, was centrally involved with Pontiac's Rebellion
in 1763, the militant teachings did not lead to military success or to a lasting political coalition of Indian nations. The revitalization movement that occurred between 1760 and 1763 within Delaware society, however, had much longer lasting
effects on Delaware social, political, and religious organization. Consequently
more attention needs to be directed toward the aspects of the revitalization
movement that led to the internal reordering of Delaware society rather than to
the short-lived militant movement. The internal Delaware revitalization movement defined the primary political and religious institutions of tribal Delaware
society for the remainder of the time that the Unami Delaware enjoyed political autonomy as a nation.

Several arguments have been tendered for explaining the rise of the
Delaware revitalization movement and for explaining the consequences and
goals of the movement. Wallace gives a relative deprivation argument for the
rise of the Delaware revitalization movement, arguing that the period
between 1730 and 1740 was the period of maximum deprivation for the
Delaware in terms of loss of land and forced migration from what is now eastern Pennsylvania. Between 1740 and 1760 various prophets emerged who did
not try to restore the land but rather attempted to restore moral order and create a Delaware national identity.[1] Furthermore, it is argued that the religious
change of the 1760s was not centrally concerned with the political and economic issues of the period, but rather was concerned primarily with creating
morality, morale, and group identification. Wallace interprets the delay of the

Delaware social and religious reorganization in the 1760s, some twenty years after the period of maximum deprivation, as being due to delayed deprivation. For Wallace, economic and military stress did not precipitate the Delaware revitalization movement; the central feature leading to the movement was the disruption of social relations that contributed to a state of psychological deprivation among the Delaware. The critical form of deprivation was the loss of confidence in the usefulness of existing societal relations; this kind of deprivation can have an impact years after the conditions of economic and military pressures are manifested. Consequently Wallace argues that the rise of the Delaware revitalization movement was instigated not by the immediate political and economic situation of the early 1760s but rather by the delayed deprivation of increasing loss of confidence by the Delaware in their social relations years after suffering their highest level of economic and political deprivation.

Other theories of Delaware political and social integration have not focused directly on the delayed deprivation argument. Newcomb argues that until the 1750s the Delaware were composed of about forty decentralized and politically autonomous bands.[2] Delaware political integration emerged because the Iroquois and the Europeans treated the Delaware bands as a single cohesive tribal entity. And given the competitive geopolitical situation of the 1750s, the Delaware needed some political agency to manage the strong political and economic currents of the period. Similarly, Weslager argues that Delaware political change resulted from the period of migrations, association with other tribes, and especially the influence of colonial authorities.[3] Kinietz, in a related argument, suggests that Western contact caused the political and cultural integration of the three Delaware sociopolitical divisions (turkey, wolf, and turtle). According to the latter argument, external colonial political pressure created the conditions that led the Delaware to form a political union of mutual protection.[4]

The arguments of Wallace, Newcomb, Weslager, and Kinietz each have merit, but they are not sufficient to explain the rise of the Delaware revitalization movement that led to the formation of Delaware tribal level religious and political institutions. Wallace's emphasis on psychological deprivation as a result of the loss of confidence in the usefulness and viability of existing social relations under conditions of objective deprivation (i.e., loss of land, decline in population, and physical displacement) has had some analogues in the revitalization literature.[5] Certainly, at a theoretical level, the Delaware people must have at some time interpreted their existing social relations as inadequate to meet the conditions of absolute deprivation consisting of threatened political subordination, economic marginalization, population decline, and physical migration. If there never was a sense of dissatisfaction with the existing sociopolitical order, then there would not be any strong motivation for making or accepting change in the existing social arrangements. Some of the Delaware must have come to an understanding that their existing social relations were not sufficient to manage the complexities of a changing political and economic environment must have sought to organize or adopt alternative institutional arrangements.

Recent theories of revitalization movements focus more closely on conditions of absolute deprivation, especially conditions of cultural and political domination by colonizing powers.[6] The current emphasis is to focus on the specific conditions that lead a group of people to see a particular social movement as a solution to their problems. Worsley and others argue that revitalization movements can act as a politically unifying force for segmentary and decentralized groups when they are subordinated to colonial powers.[7] Jorgensen and Tilly, however, argue that weakly organized groups will not necessarily respond to conditions of economic and political deprivation with a movement toward political centralization. Jorgensen points out that when several indigenous societies are subject to similar conditions of colonial subordination, there is often variation in the responses of the indigenous societies. Some groups may form revitalization movements, while others will not. The conditions of domination themselves are not sufficient to explain the frequency or variation in the formulation of culturally and politically unifying revitalization movements. Both Tilly and Jorgensen indicate that some elements of sociocultural organization, leadership, and resources must be available to the subordinated group before a concerted political movement or revitalization movement will be possible.[8]

In what follows, an argument and historical data are presented that suggest that the Delaware revitalization movement of the early 1760s was a response to the threatening British hegemonic political and trade situation during the period between the defeat of the French in the French and Indian War in 1759 and Pontiac's Rebellion in 1763. Furthermore, while the movement emphasized moral and ethical revitalization, there were also political, antieconomic dependency, and anti-European themes associated with the movement. Before 1762 the Delaware did not have and did not regularly participate in tribal-level political, religious, or social institutions. The revitalization movement led to the formation of tribal political institutions and to religious and social integration. First, I will argue that there was little social and political unity within Delaware society before 1762; second, I will make the connection between the geopolitical environment and the revitalization movement; and finally I will investigate the changes and orientations that emerged in Delaware society as a result of the movement.

## Social and Political Unity before 1762

When Lewis Morgan visited the Delaware in Kansas in 1859, they were organized by three kinship groups, commonly called the turkey, wolf, and turtle divisions. Each of these three phratries were subdivided into twelve smaller kinship groupings, so there were in total thirty-six kin-based subgroups. Lewis's informants indicate that the thirty-six subdivisions were an ancient or traditional form of social organization among the Delaware.[9] We know that after the 1760s the three major kinship divisions formed the primary political units in Delaware society, and later reports indicate that the three major divisions are the primary social units in the Delaware Big House religion. Furthermore, the twelve subdivisions within each of the three phratries are highly suggestive of a symbolic tie between the Delaware worldview and social organization. There are twelve levels to the Delaware version of heaven, and a major ceremony of the Big House religion takes twelve days, each day approaching closer to direct communication with the Great Spirit.[10] Nevertheless, despite the suggestiveness of a traditional Delaware tribal or national sociocultural organization that might have its origins in the pre-Columbian period, the available historical evidence does not substantiate the presence of regular or institutionalized national political, religious, or social organization among the Delaware before 1760.[11]

Early Delaware society was composed of about forty politically and economically autonomous bands that were local settlements of several related families. During the seventeenth century, the Delaware suffered three major smallpox epidemics. While the Delaware population declined, they were forced to migrate into the interior and leave their traditional coastal territories in the present states of New Jersey, Delaware, and eastern New York. The westward migration was necessitated by the overexploitation of game necessary for barter in the fur trade. The expansion of European settlements and agriculture also contributed to the decline in availability of fur-bearing animals that could be exchanged for European goods.[12]

Between the early 1640s and 1675, the Delaware did not have access to beaver hunting territory and were forced to sell meat, corn, and land to the

Europeans to obtain manufactured goods on which the Delaware were dependent. The depletion of local game induced many bands to sell their land and hunting territories and to migrate to inland hunting areas. By the 1670s the Delaware were being dispossessed by piecemeal land sales. Game was scarce among the southern Delaware bands, who sold their land and migrated to the vicinity of Shakamaxon, near present-day Philadelphia. When the Pennsylvania colony was established in 1682, most Delaware bands had migrated into the present state of Pennsylvania. By the 1680s the Delaware had overexploited the fur-bearing animals in the Delaware Valley, and William Penn purchased the land as the Delaware retreated westward in search of deerskins and beaver for trade and subsistence.

By 1700 some Delaware bands had migrated to the Susquehanna Valley and during the early 1720s, some Delaware bands gathered on the west side of the Delaware River. The Shakamaxon Delaware and other Delaware bands migrated to Tulpehocken near present-day Reading, Pennsylvania. Tulpehocken was "the land of the turtles" and belonged to a band of Delaware who were of the turtle totem. The chief of the turtles held a special position of importance among the Delaware.[13] In the colonial records, Sassoonan represented the bands at Tulpehocken, but it is not clear that he was chief of the turtle clan or phratry since his political successors, who were his nephews and therefore his clansmen, are not identified, some forty years later, as members of the turtle phratry. A second Delaware group on the Brandywine River joined the Delaware at Tulpehocken. The bands gathered at Tulpehocken were greatly reduced in number and began to lose their individual band characters as they merged together. A third Delaware group, the Unami, was located at the forks of the Lehigh and Delaware Rivers. The Unami had their own sachems and considered themselves politically autonomous from the other Delaware bands.[14]

By the end of 1724, the Delaware at Tulpehocken, under pressure from settlers, emigrated west. A small group of Delaware under Sassoonan's leadership migrated to Shamokin, present Sunbury, Pennsylvania, while the majority of the Tulpehocken bands migrated to the Ohio and Allegheny region. The Shamokin Delaware migrated to the Ohio and Allegheny region in 1747 after a dispute with Pennsylvania over succession to Delaware political leadership. The Unami Delaware, at the forks of the Delaware River, were dispossessed by Iroquois and Pennsylvania collusion in 1742. The Iroquois resettled their Unami Delaware dependents in the Susquehanna and Wyoming Valleys. After 1747, however, most of the Delaware population was located in the Ohio and Allegheny Valleys.

From 1718 to 1747, Sassoonan was acknowledged by Pennsylvania officials as "king of the Delaware," although Sassoonan's authority over internal Delaware political affairs was nominal. He had little political authority over the Delaware bands, despite Pennsylvania's support for his authority and efforts to extend control over the Delaware through him. After the death of Sassoonan in 1747, Pennsylvania authorities and the Iroquois refused to recognize Pisquetomen as the Delaware successor to Sassoonan. From 1747 to 1751 the Delaware were reluctant to present another candidate for succession to Sassoonan, and Pennsylvania authorities could not induce any prominent Delaware leader to assume the Pennsylvania-supported title "King of the Delaware." In 1751 the Iroquois claimed the right to appoint a king for the Delaware and together with the colony of Virginia and with the approval of Pennsylvania, Shingas, a nephew of Sassoonan, was appointed king.[15] In 1755 Shingas led a group of Delaware into alliance with the French in the French and Indian War, and he forfeited his title in favor of his brother, Beaver. Beaver thereafter represented the Delaware in the peace negotiations that eventually terminated Delaware participation in the war as a French ally.

Despite the creation of a Delaware king by the Iroquois, Virginia and Pennsylvania did not create a national political organization for the Delaware. As Kinietz, Weslager, and Newcomb have argued, there were extensive colonial pressures on the Delaware to form a centralized leadership over the decentralized bands and pressures to force the Delaware to act as a unified political unit. But in fact before 1762 the Delaware did not adopt any such political framework despite the efforts and impositions of the Iroquois and the English colonies. The colonial-appointed Delaware kings did not extend more than nominal influence over the Delaware bands. In the late 1750s, Beaver was recognized by the Delaware as an official intermediary appointed by the British to transact Delaware business with colonial officials, but the Delaware themselves did not accord him political leadership of the Delaware Nation.[16]

The three Delaware sociopolitical groupings, the turkey, wolf, and turtle divisions, become recognizable in the written records only in the 1750s, but at this time they had yet to take on the identifications and formalized political relations that characterized them in the post-1765 period. The three embryonic Delaware divisions surfaced in the Ohio and Allegheny Valleys. The Delaware bands led by Shingas and his brother Beaver, the successors of the colonially backed "kingship" of the Shamokin–Tulpehocken Delaware bands, eventually formed the turkey division.

The origins of the two other major Delaware divisions are much more obscure. As early as 1754, Netawatwees, the man who eventually assumed leadership of the turtle division, was identified as a prominent man in Ohio Delaware affairs. In 1754 Netawatwees was identified as a chief, and in 1757 he was reported to be one of two principal leaders of the Ohio Delaware. Custaloga let the third major group, and he is identified as a leading Delaware chief as early as 1753. In 1757 Custaloga's group is identified as "the tribe of Wolfs," who dwelled in the Ohio Valley during the mid 1750s.[17] Many writers have assumed that both Netawatwees's and Custaloga's bands were subject to Beaver's leadership. Eventually all three Delaware groups adopt the Unami name, but before 1762 the Delaware divisions led by Netawatwees and Custaloga did not recognize more than a cultural or ethnic affiliation with the band led by Shingas and Beaver. An entry dated May 1762, in James Kenny's journal stated, "Informed by Keecaise that the Beaver King & ye Indians about Tuscarawas though of ye Lennape Nation, yet are not Delaware properly, likewise that ye Beaver never was made king by ye Indians, but by ye people of Virginia, and the Neat-hat-wheline was ye Delaware king & Tuscologa-a half king-being half a Mingo."[18] The political ties between Netawatwees's and Custaloga's bands were stronger than their ties to the division led by Shingas and Beaver, while the Unami Delaware appear to have had ties to Custaloga's wolf division and eventually joined them.[19]

The three major Delaware divisions were cognizant of each other but did not make political decisions on a regular basis or act in concert. During the 1750s Shingas and Beaver were recognized in successive reigns as "king of the Delaware" by the British and Iroquois, but most Delaware did not recognize the leadership of Shingas and Beaver, except as diplomatic intermediaries appointed by British officials. The historical evidence indicates that by 1762 the Delaware had yet to form national political, social, or religious institutions. Colonial officials backed by the Iroquois Confederacy attempted to impose a centralized political leadership onto the Delaware, but it did not gain recognition from two of the major Delaware divisions. Consequently the formation of Delaware national political institutions cannot be attributed to the fact that colonial officials treated them as a unit and in response they became more politically unified. Throughout the 1750s the Delaware were under colonial pressures to form a central chieftainship, but this pressure did not lead to direct or immediate change in Delaware political organization.

Furthermore, the Delaware suffered from deprivation conditions such as population loss owing to epidemics, economic deprivation in loss of land, loss of fur trade territories, and political subordination to the colonies and the Iroquois. Yet these deprivation conditions during the first half of the eighteenth century did not precipitate a social, political, and culturally unifying revitalization movement. As Wallace argues, various religious figures emerged among the Delaware before 1760, but none of the preaching of the early Delaware "prophets" gained widespread support among the Delaware people, and these abortive movements did not lead to significant change in Delaware social, cultural, or political institutions. The argument of delayed deprivation does not have direct historical support; it is difficult to show from the available evidence that before 1760 the Delaware psychologically experienced relative deprivation about the adequacy of their social and political institutions. On the contrary, during the period before 1762 both colonial officials and the Iroquois attempted to institute a more centralized chieftainship among the Delaware, but the Delaware themselves were reluctant to take such a step. The social and political unification of Delaware society occurred between 1762 and 1764. We must look at the conditions immediately before and during the 1762 to 1764 period for the effective causes of the social and political unification that resulted from the Delaware revitalization movement.

## British Hegemony and the Delaware Revitalization Movement

Early in the French and Indian War, the Delaware shifted their alliance to the French but were forced to return to the British when the French failed to supply the Delaware with enough trade goods. Many Delaware retained French sympathies and resented British occupation of the French forts in the Ohio and old Northwest region. Delaware leaders were dismayed by the French defeat and withdrawal from territory east of the Mississippi River. The English were too powerful for the indigenous nations, which were now threatened with hegemonic British political domination and economic control of the fur trade. The Delaware and western Indian nations feared the British were deliberately withholding powder and lead to weaken Indian capability for military resistance, after which they believed the British would destroy them in a war of retaliation for their alliance to the French in the late hostilities. The Delaware leaders were cognizant of the implications of British hegemony and joined in Pontiac's military confederacy to help drive British troops from the forts in the northwest. During the period between 1759 and 1763, the Delaware and other northwestern nations believed that British political and trade domination embodied direct threats to their political autonomy and national existence.[20]

Delaware national political and religious institutions were forged between 1762 and 1763 during the early years of British political hegemony. As late as May 1762, the Delaware still did not form a unified national political group. Two bands were politically allied with Netawatwees as their principal chief, while Beaver led the other major Delaware band. Although all three major Delaware groups occasionally met in council and sent representatives to conduct discussions of mutual concern, the Delaware were not engaged in formalized political relations with the other Delaware political groups. The initial response to British hegemony was the emergence of a revitalization movement that culminated in the formation of a national religion in 1763.

The Delaware revitalization movement began at the end of the French and Indian War in North America; between 1760 and 1763 the revitalization movement quickly spread to all three Delaware political groups.[21] In March of 1763, while the Ohio and western nations were preparing to launch an offensive against the British occupied forts, the Delaware formed a national religion. The trader James Kenny recorded this event in his journal:

> James Mohesin a Delaware man informs me that its agreed to by their whole nation to follow their new plan of religion, . . . to quit all commerce with the white people and cloth themselves in skins, he also said that none of the other nations have fell to the scheme. only the Delawares, . . .[22]

Newcomb rejects the argument that the Delaware Big House ceremonies originated with the creation of a Delaware national religion.[23] He argues that the Big House religion or variants were practiced and performed separately among the different Delaware phratries and bands before the formation of the national religion. The formation of a national religion entailed the centralization of local ceremonies and traditions of the Delaware bands, villages, and possibly the traditions of lineage groups.

The Delaware national religion consolidated the three major Delaware political groupings into a religiously and politically unified national government. The Delaware Prophet(s) had a direct hand in the formation of religiously legitimated chieftainships. One Delaware prophet stated, "Our Father has likewise spoke to my chiefs, by me, giving them advice, in what manner to behave as kings, and now they will act as kings."[24]

The first recording of a national Delaware political organization appears in November 1764. The Delaware were then organized by a three-division confederacy with a principal chief. The three phratry groupings are now recognizable. The principal Delaware chief was Netawatwees, who led the turtle division, while Beaver led the turkey division, and Custaloga was chief of the wolf division. Besides a chief, each of the three divisions also had a head warrior.[25] Unfortunately there does not seem to be any recorded reference to the thirty-six subdivisions that Morgan was to record about a century later. Although the three phratries now became institutionalized parts of Delaware society, the historical data does not inform us as to whether the thirty-six phratry subdivisions were in existence before 1762, or whether they may have been created during the movement of the 1760s or during the later movement of 1805.

In the years before the beginning of the American Revolutionary War, the details of the Delaware political system became more discernible. The chief of the turtle phratry was the principal chief. He was responsible for preserving the peace and managing diplomatic relations with other indigenous nations and with the Europeans. His decisions were subject to the advice and consent of the other two phratry chiefs. The principal chief was entrusted with the national wampum belts, which were historical and diplomatic records. The turtle chief presided over the national council and called the council together whenever an issue of national importance arose; in effect he was responsible for the well-being of the Delaware nation. The principal chief, however, did not have coercive powers and was bound by the decisions of the national council. The Delaware chiefs and councils consulted "holy men," the Delaware Prophet and his successor, on important national and foreign issues. The Delaware phratries retained considerable autonomy over local affairs and reserved the right to negotiate peace and declare war. The major Delaware groupings continued to occupy separate villages and separate geographical location, and retained separate hunting territories. By the beginning of the American Revolutionary War, however, the three Delaware political divisions were acting with greater corporate unity in international affairs, although the major political cleavages continued to persist.[26]

Most students of the Delaware revitalization movement of the early 1760s have focused their attention on the formation of the new moral and ethical system that the Delaware Prophet(s) syncretized from both Christian and traditional elements. This interpretation considers the formation of a national religion to be a reaction to the disintegration of Delaware moral and cultural community.[27] It is undeniable that a primary goal of the Delaware Prophet was to create a new moral order. The teachings of the Delaware Prophet prohibited the use of alcohol, stealing, murder, polygamy, and intertribal conflicts. Only individuals who followed the directives of the prophets would be allowed to gain access to heaven. Sin could be purged by taking a special drink and by fasting and abstinence. The prophets introduced the conception of a personified deity and preached that only by a return to traditional moral and social order could the Delaware and other indigenous nations find salvation from their troubles. All conscious European influences were to be purged from Delaware lifestyles, and the people were to return to the ancient customs and manners of their ancestors. The economic and political calamities that had befallen the Delaware were attributed to the failure of the Indians to adhere to and preserve traditional customs and were a consequence of their adoption of European customs and material goods.[28]

While the Delaware Prophet(s) did teach moral regeneration through a return to traditional culture, a primary theme of the moral regeneration was aimed at removing the Delaware from economic dependency on the British and from British political domination. One of the prophets instructed the people to hunt for subsistence and stop hunting furs for trade with the Europeans, and he also instructed that they give up use of European manufactured goods. The Delaware were to learn to live like their early ancestors and reject trade relations with the Europeans. The prophets encouraged the Indians to throw off economic dependency on European manufactured goods and to return to ancient modes of economic self-sufficiency.[29]

While some of the Delaware prophets preached economic independence from the Europeans, one prophet was also active in mobilizing military resistance against the British occupation of the old French forts in the northwest. He preached that the indigenous nations could defeat the English in war and made theological arguments for initiating hostilities against the English. It was argued that the corrupting influence of the Europeans had made the path to heaven difficult and treacherous for the Indians. The Indians had neglected their traditions and ceremonies and had allowed the Europeans to settle and live among them. The prophet taught that if the Indians reclaimed their traditions and renounced the use of guns, powder, alcohol, and other European materials, then the Great Spirit would grant the Indian warriors power to defeat the English, grant a plentiful supply of game, and clear the path to heaven. The well-being and harmony of the Indians could be restored only if the Europeans were driven off the continent and the old traditions of their Indian ancestors were reestablished. Pontiac and the western nations were influenced by the prophet's militaristic revelations, which helped mobilize a confederacy of Indian nations for an attack on the British forts in the Northwest. The Delaware Prophet traveled and preached among the western nations and villages with the intention to organize the Indians into a military force that would drive the English from the Ohio and northwest region.

These militaristic tones and antidependency doctrines suggest that the Delaware revitalization movement had political and economic ends. The ethical and moral regenerative aspects of the movement are clearly present, but they seem to be the means by which the Delaware Prophet mobilized sufficient social and political integration and influenced personal motivation, all of which were necessary to achieve the political, economic, and culturally fundamentalist goals of the movement. The purpose and goals of the movement indicate that the Delaware revitalization movement was a political, economic, and cultural response to the emergence of British trade and military hegemony.

# Discussion and Conclusion

Several writers have tried to explain the formation of the three-division Delaware political system as a response to the general conditions of European colonial administration and land pressures. Throughout the early 1700s, colonial officials and their allies, the Iroquois, tried to impose a more centralized form of political organization onto the Delaware, but no such political system emerged among the Delaware before 1762. The arguments that emphasize the desire of colonial officials to treat the Delaware as a single political unit as the primary cause of Delaware political centralization and formation of tribal institutions are not able to explain why the Delaware political unification occurred only after 1762, nor do these arguments specify the links between the Delaware revitalization movement and British political and economic hegemony in the formation of Delaware tribal society. The normative, social, and political integration of Delaware tribal society occurred during the religious revitalization movement of 1763, and only thereafter did the Delaware themselves recognize tribal-level political leaders and institutions. The centralized political leadership that was imposed by colonial officials and the Iroquois was not considered legitimate by all the major Delaware political groupings and did not unify Delaware society into a collective political unit as the colonial officials hoped it would.

Wallace reinterpreted the relative deprivation argument in order to explain the rise of the Delaware revitalization movement in the early 1760s. He argues that the period of maximum deprivation for the Delaware occurred between 1730 and 1740, when the Delaware were forced to migrate west and lost their old territories. In Wallace's terms, a straightforward deprivation argument does not account for the rise of the Delaware revitalization movement; therefore Wallace argues that new religions emerge not in periods of maximum deprivation, but rather in the period after the deprivation has subsided. The new Delaware religion was aimed not at restoring the land but at creating a new moral order and national identity. He argues that economic and military threats can create disorder but are not the effective cause of the formation of new religions. In a postcrisis period, however, there can arise a sense of psychological deprivation over the ineffectiveness of existing social relations to respond adequately to economic and political threats. For Wallace, the new Delaware religion arose in response to the loss of confidence by the Delaware in their existing social relations.

Certainly Delaware dissatisfaction with their social relations must be a precondition for change, but there does not seem to be historical evidence to indicate that is why the Delaware waited over twenty years after their maximum period of deprivation in the 1730s and 1740s before deciding to mobilize for social and political change. During the early 1750s, the Delaware did not seem dissatisfied with their decentralized political institutions and resisted colonially imposed political centralization. If the Delaware experienced understandings of relative deprivation in relation to their societal institutions, their dissatisfaction must have come to maturity between 1762–1764, when the new religion and tribal social and political institutions were adopted. Unfortunately the historical evidence is not adequate to measure Delaware dissatisfaction, but if it occurred, as I believe it did, it most likely occurred during the intensely threatening political and economic environment that arose during the period between the defeat of the French and the mobilization for Pontiac's Rebellion. I believe the latter argument is more closely grounded with the available historical evidence than is the delayed deprivation argument.

One reason that Wallace tenders the delayed deprivation argument is that he suggests the primary purpose and goals of the new Delaware religion was to revitalize morale, morality, and group solidarity. While undoubtedly the moral and social integration of Delaware society was a major outcome of the movement, the teachings of the prophets were also aimed at alleviating Delaware political and economic dependence on the Europeans. The moral teachings of the prophets contained clear economic and political tenets. Only through the rejection of European material dependency and trade relations could the Delaware return to the simple, prosperous, and moral life lived by their ancestors before the coming of the Europeans. One of the Delaware prophets actively engaged in mobilizing military opposition to the British and tried to convince the western Indian nations to boycott European goods. Thus it appears that the delayed deprivation argument, with its emphasis on social integration, does not sufficiently appreciate the political and antidependency themes of the new Delaware religion.

At first sight the Worsley hypothesis finds some support from the Delaware case that decentralized tribal societies subject to colonial domination are prone to forming politically and culturally unifying revitalization movements. But Worsley's theory is too vaguely stated to identify precisely the conditions that led to the Delaware cultural and political unification. While the Delaware movement did occur under conditions of colonial political domination, such conditions were not new in Delaware history. The more specific causes of the Delaware movement must be identified with the threatening conditions of British political and economic hegemony after 1760, and not with the general conditions of colonial subordination and dependency. Furthermore, the Worsley argument cannot explain why only the Delaware, and not the other Indian Nations who shared similar Algonkian culture with the Delaware, developed revitalization movements during the same period of perceived British threats. Nor do arguments that emphasize the availability of leadership, material, and organizational resources work well in explaining the rise of the Delaware revitalization movement. During and preceding the movement, the Delaware were both politically and economically subordinated and had few free-floating material resources or political options. Consequently, the Delaware had few resources for building a political movement. The resource of Delaware leadership and organization appear decentralized and lacking unity before 1764, and there seems little unusual about Delaware social organization or leadership that greatly distinguished them from the other Algonkian groups that participated in Pontiac's Rebellion and were subject to the same threats of British political and trade hegemony. Why Delaware society experiences a revitalization movement between 1762 and 1763 can be answered only with a comparative study of the history, cultures, and social structures of the Indian nations in the region. A comparative study might identify clues to why only the Delaware movement emerged and not any others.

One possible hypothesis for a comparative study might be that some of the other nations (e.g., the Iroquois) already had tribal-level political and religious institutions. Another possibility is to focus directly on differences in worldviews and the influence of Christian religions on Indian cultures and worldviews. The Delaware contacts with Christian religions were from Protestant Presbyterian and Moravian denominations, while the western French-allied Indian nations had contact with primarily French Catholic priests. The differences in Catholic versus Protestant doctrines as they infiltrate and become reinterpreted by the Indians may help account for the Delaware propensity for revitalization, as opposed to the absence of such movements among the French allied nations during the same period. The Protestant doctrines demand disciplined individual moral and ethical action, and the Delaware Prophet's emphasis on moral and ethical behavior as a means of mobilizing social action and achieving collective and spiritual ends seems analogous.[30] The argument of the differential influence of Catholic and Protestant doctrines on the Indians of the old northwest must be considered only a rough hypothesis that needs further conceptual development and systematic investigation.

In the absence of significant economic and organizational resources, perhaps the major resource for the social and political mobilization of change in Delaware society during the revitalization movement was the particular doctrines and religious conceptions that were taught by the prophets. The Delaware prophets appear to have been, at least partly, influenced by Christian religion, since the ethical and lawgiving prophet is found in the early Judeo-Christian tradition. More specifically, however, the teachings of the prophets emphasized that individual attainment of otherworldly existence and collective this-worldly well-being were both jeopardized by the failure to adhere to traditional moral codes and lifestyles. By emphasizing that the achievement of this-worldly political and economic goals and the achievement of otherworldly goals were contingent on moral and ethical behavior, the prophets were able to mobilize their adherents to pursue moral, political, economic, and spiritual ends. If the Delaware purified themselves from sin, abstained from sexual relations, lived as their ancestors did before the coming of the Europeans, and followed the instructions of the prophets, then they would be able to drive the Europeans out of the country in a few years. The Delaware Prophet based his authority on direct revelation from the supernatural being Keesh-she-la-mil-lang-up, who according to myth, brought the Delaware people into existence.[31] The doctrines of the revitalization movement legitimated the integration of social, religious, and political institutions in Delaware society by directing Delaware social action toward alleviating economic dependency and political subordination, as well as providing a vision for achieving otherworldly existence.

In the end, however, only a select group of doctrines survived the early movement and became institutionalized in Delaware society and culture. The militant teachings disappeared after the failure of Pontiac's Rebellion, and the overwhelming majority of the Delaware found that they could not do without the fur trade and European manufactured goods. Consequently, the Delaware remained economically dependent, and the doctrines against the fur trade seem to have had little enduring effect. Nevertheless, the movement made an enduring impact on Delaware society. Most important was the cultural and political integration of Delaware society. The Delaware formed a national unit with recognized chieftainships, a principal chief, head warriors in each phratry, and a national council for collective decision making. The three phratry divisions define the basic political and social units in Unami Delaware society throughout the rest of their history. The teachings of the prophets created a national religion, of which we have few organizational details and which seems to have been subject to reform during the subsequent revitalization movement of 1805. Finally, the early revitalization movement embedded a strong sense of cultural fundamentalism within Delaware culture, which sanctioned deliberate doctrines and proscriptions to avoid acceptance of Western political, religious, economic, and social patterns and innovations. In the subsequent years before political dissolution in 1867, the strategy for cultural survival for most Delaware, despite increasing political and economic marginalization, was to cling to Delaware traditions, refuse take up agricultural farming or American political institutions, and reject Christianity. The revitalization movement of the 1760s provided cultural support for the fundamentalist ideology that was to inform the Delaware resistance to American attempts to change Delaware economic, political, and cultural institutions.[32]

In conclusion, the rise of the Delaware revitalization movement cannot be sufficiently explained by conditions of delayed deprivation or by the general disruption of social relations among the frontier Indians. Nor did

Delaware political centralization result from the desire of colonial officials to appoint a unified Delaware leadership; the movement arose and Delaware political centralization occurred under the specific conditions of threatened British military, trade, and political hegemony that resulted from the defeat of the French in 1759. The primary end of the movement was to regain Delaware political and economic autonomy from European domination and dependency. While the political and economic goals of the movement could not be entirely achieved, the movement resulted in enduring changes in Delaware political, moral, and cultural organization, and led to a more unified political accommodation to subsequent colonial political and economic pressures.

# Notes

I gratefully acknowledge research assistance from the American Indian Studies Center at UCLA, a UCLA academic senate grant, and grant RII8503914 from National Science Foundation. Special thanks go to Nandini Gunewardena for her help on this research project. An earlier version of this chapter appeared as Duane Champagne, "The Delaware Revitalization Movement of the Early 1760s: A Suggested Reinterpretation," *American Indian Quarterly* 12, no. 2 (1988): 107–26.

1. Anthony Wallace, "New Religions among the Delaware Indians, 1600–1900," *Southwestern Journal of Anthropology* 12 (1956): 18–19.

2. William W. Newcomb Jr., "The Culture and Acculturation of the Delaware Indians," *Anthropology Papers* (Ann Arbor, MI: Museum of Anthropology of Michigan, 1956), pp. 50–53, 125, 175.

3. C. A. Weslager, *The Delaware Indian Westward Migration* (Wallingsford, PA: Middle Atlantic, 1978), pp. 10–43.

4. Vernon Kinietz, "European Civilization as a Determinant of Native Indian Customs," *American Anthropologist* 42 (1940): 116–17; see also M. Thurman, "Delaware Social Organization," in *A Delaware Symposium,* ed. Herbert Kraft (Harrisburg: Pennsylvania Historical and Museum Commission, 1974), p. 112.

5. Bernard Barber, "Acculturation and Messianic Movements," in *Comparative Perspectives in Social Change,* ed. S. N. Eisenstadt (Boston: Little, Brown, 1968).

6. P. M. Worsley, *The Trumpet Shall Call* (London: MacGibbon & Kee, 1957); Roy Wallis, ed., *Sectarianism: Analysis of Religious and Non-Religious Sects* (London: Owen, 1975); Vittoria Lanternari, *The Religions of the Oppressed* (New York: Knopf, 1963). See also Russell Thornton, *We Shall Live Again: The 1870 and 1890 Ghost Dance Movement as a Demographic Revitalization* (New York: Cambridge University Press, 1986).

7. Worsley, *Trumpet,* p. 227; Norman Cohn, *The Pursuit of the Millennium* (London: Secker & Warburg, 1970), p. 141.

8. Joseph Jorgensen, *The Sun Dance Religion* (Chicago: University of Chicago Press, 1972), p. 5; Charles Tilly, *From Mobilization to Revolution* (Reading, MA: Addison-Wesley, 1978), p. 82.

9. Lewis Henry Morgan, *The Indian Journals, 1859–1862* (Ann Arbor: University of Michigan Press, 1959), pp. 51–54; Lewis Henry Morgan, *Ancient Society* (New York: Gorder, 1977), pp. 176–77. The text follows the Unami Delaware who eventually migrated to Oklahoma and joined the Cherokee nation in 1867. The Canadian branch of Munsee Delaware do not report a thirty-six-member clan system. The Six Nation Reserve Delaware have two phratries, the turtle and wolf, but the phratries do not have a tradition of twelve subdivisions. Frank Speck, *The Celestial Bear Comes Down to Earth* (Reading, MA: Reading Public Museum and Art Gallery, 1945), pp. 21–25.

10. Frank Speck, *A Study of the Delaware Indian Big House Ceremony* (Harrisburg: Pennsylvania Historical Commission, 1931), p. 75; Sam D. Gill, *Native American Religions: An Introduction* (Belmont, CA: Wadsworth, 1982), pp. 29–30.

11. Newcomb, "Culture and Acculturation of the Delaware Indians," pp. 48–50. Newcomb argues that the thirty-six clans are not mentioned in the early colonial documents, and consequently he doubts whether they are traditional or ancient. He says the three major phratries are probably formed by remnant Delaware and other peoples who joined the tribe, and were considered kinship units and later swelled into clans, which form the three phratries. While the historical evidence is scant and Newcomb's argument has some plausibility, the argument put forth in the text suggests that the three phratries existed in embryonic form before 1760 and were politically, socially, and religiously unified by the revitalization movement. Unfortunately there is little data to shed light on the details of Delaware social structure to verify when the thirty-six subgroups came into existence. The symmetrical organization of the three phratries and the twelve subgroups in each phratry does not seem to be a likely result if one adopts Newcomb's argument of more or less random formation. The Delaware social organization of three phratries and thirty-six clans begs for an explanation based on a strong tradition or institutionalization during the Delaware revitalization movement of the 1760s or the movement of 1805.

Herbert Kraft makes the plausible argument that the three phratries existed in prehistoric times. He states that both the early Delaware and the Munsee were organized by matrilineal, matrilocal turtle, wolf, and turkey phratries. He argues that the three phratries appear in modified form in the 1760s. In the prehistoric period, the phratries were interspersed throughout the Delaware and Munsee bands, but after 1760 the three phratries have their own villages that are distinct from those of the other phratries. Kraft, however, does not support this argument with citation of sources that report observations earlier than 1760. While his argument is interesting, he does not provide direct evidence that will determine whether the phratries are an ancient form of social organization or whether they were formed or reorganized during the historical period. See Herbert K. Kraft, *The Lenape: Archaeology, History, and Ethnohistory* (Newark: New Jersey Historical Society, 1986), pp. xv–xvi, 133–36, 235, 245 n. The number twelve had ancient symbolic significance in Delaware culture and was used in the organization of an annual ceremony that predated the new religion of 1763. James Kenny wrote on April 10, 1763:

> The Delaware had held a General feast, there the provision for it was 24 Bears, 24 Dears, 24 turkeys, & 24 Squirrels, by report. They hold this feast yearly, but last year had mist So this year they provided double the quantity of provision, the yearly allowance being but 12 of a sort & the manner of performing it is. They choose 6 men head councilors & 6 young men, 12 in number which bring 12 stones & make them red hot in a fire, on which stone they burn the creatures, in this manner they bring 12 poles or long rods.

Then the older men went into a sweat bath and sang songs and prayed and admonished the people to remember the worship of the old people and to perform the ritual annually. The ceremony was finished with dancing and singing. James Kenny, "Journal of James Kenny, 1761–1763," *Pennsylvania Magazine of History and Biography* 31 (1913): 193.

Unfortunately the text does not indicate whether kinship group was important in the selection of the twelve men who performed the ceremony. For additional references to the ceremonial use of the number twelve among the Delaware, see M. R. Harrington, "Religion and Ceremonies of the Lenape," *Indian Notes and Monographs,* no. 19 (New York: Museum of the American Indian, 1921), pp. 31, 52, 88; Kraft, *The Lenape,* 162.

After 1805 there are reports that each of the three Delaware divisions had twelve "select men" who were considered spiritual and gifted. Consequently there was a total of thirty-six select men who led religious rituals, advised the chiefs, held a good deal of civil authority, undertook important missions, and executed men who were condemned to death. Paul Wallace, *Indians in Pennsylvania* (Harrisburg: Pennsylvania and Museum Commission, 1970), pp. 63–73; Harrington, "Religion and Ceremonies of the Lenape," pp. 52, 80; Speck, *Celestial Bear,* p. 57. The latter reports, however, do not directly link the thirty-six spiritual–civil leaders to the thirty-six kinship groups recorded by Morgan.

12. George Loskiel, *History of the Mission of the United Brethren among the Indians of North America,* trans. Christian Ignatius Latrobe (London: Brethren's Society for the Furtherance of the Gospel, 1794), p. 124; Donald Kent, *Iroquois Indians I: History of Pennsylvania Purchases from the Indians* (New York: Garland, 1974), p. 239.

13. Francis Jennings, "Incident at Tulpehocken," *Pennsylvania History,* October 1968, 337–40.

14. Much of the discussion of early Delaware social organization and migration patterns is taken from C. A. Weslager, *Delaware Indians: A History* (New Brunswick, NJ: Rutgers University Press, 1972), pp. 174–80; Henry Schoolcraft, *Indian Tribes of the United States* (Philadelphia: Lippincott, 1857), 6:178; Albright Zimmerman, "European Trade Relations in the 17th and 18th Century," in *A Delaware Symposium,* ed. Herbert Kraft (Harrisburg: Pennsylvania Historical and Museum Commission, 1974), p. 68; Weslager, *Westward Migration,* pp. 14–27; Roger James Ferguson, "The White River Delawares: An Ethnohistoric Analysis, 1795–1867" (Ph.D. diss., Ball State University, 1972), pp. 2–27.

15. Weslager, *Delaware Indians,* pp. 177, 226–32; William Hunter, "The Ohio: The Indians' Land," *Pennsylvania History* 21 (1954): 342; "The Treaty of Logg's Town, 1752," *Virginia Magazine of History and Biography,* July 1905, 167. The Delaware were reluctant in spring of 1751 to appoint a principal chief. Beaver spoke for the Delaware when he said:

> all their wise men were not gathered together it would take some time to consider on a man that was fit to undertake to rule a Nation, but as soon as possible they would make a full answer, which they hoped would give full satisfaction to their Brothers the English and Six Nations. *Pennsylvania Colonial Records,* vol. 5, 1745–1754, ed. Samuel Hazard (Philadelphia: State of Pennsylvania, 1851–1852), p. 537.

16. Kenny, "Journal of James Kenny," pp. 157, 175; Anthony Wallace, "Women, Land, and Society: Three Aspects of Aboriginal Delaware Society," *Pennsylvania Archaeologist* 17 (1947): 6.

17. Hunter, "The Ohio," 348; *Pennsylvania Colonial Records,* vol. 7, pp. 1756–58, 514, 660, 725; Charles Hanna, *The Wilderness Trail* (New York: Putnam's, 1911), 1:370, 375. A

report dated June 1757 states that "the Indians who live near Fort Mahault are chiefly Delaware of the tribe of Wolfs, many of whom, who before lived on Belle River (the Ohio River), moved away (after the English attack on Kittanning)." *Pennsylvania Archives*, vol. 3, 1756–1760, 307. After 1753 the Delaware towns in the Cuyahoga and Muskingum regions were central to the Delaware. In 1756 Netawatwees's town was located near Cuyahoga Falls. Helen Hornbeck Tanner, "The Greenville Treaty, 1795," in *Indians of Ohio and Indiana Prior to 1795* (New York: Garland, 1974), p. 70; Weslager *Westward Migration*, p. 27.

18. Kenny, "Journal of James Kenny," p. 157.

19. Kenny, "Journal of James Kenny," p. 186.

20. John Heckewelder, *History, Manners, and Customs of the Indian Nations* (Philadelphia: Historical Society of Pennsylvania, 1876), pp. 290–93; Charles Hunter, "The Delaware Na-tivistic Revival in Mid-Eighteenth Century," *Ethnohistory* 18 (1971): 40, 44; Randolph Downes, *Council Fires on the Upper Ohio* (Pittsburgh, PA: University of Pittsburgh Press, 1940), pp. 117–18; Paul A. W. Wallace, *Conrad Weiser: Friend of Colonist and Mohawk* (Philadelphia: University of Pennsylvania Press, 1945), p. 563. An Indian speech to George Croghan underscores the conditions that led to Pontiac's Rebellion: "Now, Brethren, do not act as you have done for a year or two before the late troubles (Pontiac's Rebellion) when you prohibited the sale of powder, lead and rum. This conduct gave all nations in this country a suspicion that you had bad designs against them." George Croghan, "George Croghan's Journal, Feb. 28, 1765–Oct. 8, 1765," in *The New Regime, 1765–1767*, ed. C. W. Alford and C. E. Carter, Collections of the Illinois State Historical Library, vol. 11, 1916, p. 16. In December 1762 Netawatwees was reportedly dismayed over the French defeat. He feared that the English would be too powerful now that the French were forced to move west of the Mississippi River. Netawatwees seemingly did not favor the complete defeat of the French. On March 26, 1763, James Kenny noted, "The Indians seem under great con-cern that the advantage the English has gained, by the peace being under jealousy that we will revenge their former insults" (Kenny, "Journal of James Kenny," pp. 187, 192).

21. Kenny, "Journal of James Kenny" p. 173; Erminie Wheeler-Voeglin, "An Ethnohis-torical Report on the Indian Land Use and Occupancy of Royce Area 11, Ohio and Indi-ana," in *Indians of Ohio and Indiana Prior to 1795* (New York: Garland, 1974), pp. 340–47; Downes, *Council Fires*, pp. 117–18.

22. Kenny, "Journal of James Kenny" p. 188.

23. Newcomb, "Culture and Acculturation of the Delaware Indians," pp. 64, 77. There are several reports of early elements of the Big House religion and ceremony that precede the 1763 national religion. See Harrington, "Religion and Ceremonies of the Lenap," pp. 41, 52, passim. Also see note 12.

At least until the reformation of the Munsee Prophetess in 1805, Delaware and Munsee towns each had a long house where the annual sacrificial festivals and dances were held. The long houses also served as council houses. The phratry chiefs addressed the people during the ceremonies and admonished them to live moral lives that would be pleasing to God. These moral teachings very closely resemble the teachings of the prophets of the early 1760s. Lawrence Henry Gipson, ed., *The Moravian Indian Mission on White River* (Indi-anapolis: Indiana Historical Bureau, 1938), pp. 613–14.

24. Groghan, "George Coghan's Journal," p. 7.

25. Groghan, "George Coghan's Journal," pp. 1–6; *Pennsylvania Colonial Records*, vol. 9, 1762–1771, pp. 226–29.

26. Croghan, "George Croghan's Journal," 6–7; David Zeisberger, *David Zeisberger's History of the North American Indians,* ed. A. Hulbert and William Schwarze (Columbus: Ohio State Archeological and Historical Society, 1910), pp. 92–97; Vernon Kinietz, "Delaware Culture Chronology," *Prehistory Research Series,* vol. 3 (Indianapolis: Indiana Historical Society, 1940), 130–32; Weslager, *Delaware Indians,* p. 288.

27. Anthony Wallace, *The Death and Rebirth of the Seneca* (New York: Vintage, 1972), pp. 117–20; Wallace, "New Religions among the Delaware Indians," passim; see also Barber, "Acculturation and Messianic Movements," pp. 177–82.

28. Heckwelder, *Indian Nations,* p. 291; Wallace, *Seneca,* pp. 117–20; Kinietz, "European Civilization as a Determinant of Native Indian Customs," p. 118; John M'Collough, "A Narrative of the Captivity of John M'Collough, Esq.," in *Incidents of Border Life,* ed. Joseph Pritts (Lancaster, PA: G. Hills, 1841), p. 98; Howard Peckham, *Pontiac and the Indian Uprising* (Princeton, NJ: Princeton University Press, 1947), pp. 99–101; Wallace, "New Religions among the Delaware Indians" p. 9; Loskiel, *History,* pp. 34–37.

29. Kenny, "Journal of James Kenny," pp. 171, 175.

30. Similar arguments have been made by Max Weber, *The Protestant Ethic and the Spirit of Capitalism* (New York: Scribner's, 1958); Michael Walzer, *The Revolution of the Saints: A Study in the Origins of Radical Politics* (Cambridge: Harvard University Press, 1965); S. N. Eisenstadt, "The Protestant Ethic Thesis in an Analytical and Comparative Framework," in *Modernization and the Protestant Ethic,* ed. S. N. Eisenstadt (New York: Basic, 1968), pp. 19–21; Loretta Fowler, *Arapahoe Politics, 1851–1978: Symbols in Crises of Authority* (Lincoln: University of Nebraska Press, 1982).

31. M'Collough, "A Narrative of the Captivity of John M'Collough," pp. 98–99; Loskiel, *History,* pp. 34–39.

32. See, for example, Gipson, *Moravian Indian Mission,* pp. 256, 262, 297, 333, 358, 450, 455, 553, 604, 616, 632.

# Colonial and Contemporary
# Religious Movements

**12**

S INCE EARLY CONTACT with European settlers and explorers, Native
Americans have defended their land, cultures, religions, and political
rights. Often Native efforts to preserve their communities and cultures
took the form of religious, military, political, and cultural movements. The
ways Native nations sought to preserve their cultures and territories varied
throughout colonial history and in the contemporary world. There were
many wars, battles, and strategic political alliances during the colonial period
before and after the establishment of the United States. Religious movements
(or revitalization movements) characterized Native North American responses
to colonialism as Native peoples sought cultural solutions to drastically changing economic, political, and cultural situations. Many Native traditions, religions, and revitalized cultures continue to the present as living communities.
During the last quarter of the twentieth century, Native peoples openly practiced, reclaimed, and maintained Native religious beliefs and understandings.
If there is one generalization about Native communities over the past five
hundred years of colonial contact, it might be that Native nations have sought
to preserve their cultures, communities, political rights, and territories. Social
and religious movements are some of the ways in which Native people sought
to preserve core aspects of their cultures while accommodating to changing
political, economic, and cultural relations in an increasingly globalized world.

## Military and Diplomatic Movements

Eastern North America was colonized by several rival colonial powers, including the English, French, Spanish, Dutch, and Swedes. The competitive
and warring nation-states of Europe were transferred to the colonies. Wars,

as well as diplomatic and economic rivalries, were played out in the colonies as part of policies from the mother countries. While the hunt for gold was an early endeavor by the colonists, they soon turned their attention to export of furs and skins. The Natives were willing to trade furs for European manufactured goods such as iron goods, rifles, traps, cloth, pots, and pans. Native trappers and hunters became sources of labor in long intercontinental markets extending back to European capitals. Native communities became dependent on trade with Europeans, since they could not produce iron goods, rifles, and other manufactured materials. Economic dependence required a European trading partner, and hence the eastern Native nations soon found themselves forced to ally with one or another European colony for trade and military protection. Trade allies became military allies during times of war, and the Native nations were soon swept into a series of conflicts initiated for European interests far away from North America. Warfare became more frequent, involved more combatants, marshaled greater firepower, and was deadly than Native warfare.

European traders demanded more and more furs from the Native hunters and trappers to satisfy demand in the European markets. Native trappers were induced into trapping more furs by reducing the value of furs relative to trade items, thus inducing more hunting for furs to gain necessities. Traders used alcohol as an inducement to encourage the Natives to bring in more furs or to trade badly and require additional hunting. Market demands for furs led to Native hunters overhunting local animal resources. Many tribes (e.g., the Delaware and Munsee) fell back into the interior to follow the disappearing hunting grounds. Movement into the interior, however, often led to conflict with Indian nations who claimed the hunting grounds from time immemorial. By the 1640s the Iroquois (Hodenosaunee) saw their local beaver and deer supplies shrink to levels that could not sustain trade with the Dutch colony of New Amsterdam. Consequently, the Iroquois sought trade agreements with the Native nations of the interior but were rebuffed, since the interior had their trade and diplomatic alliances with the French. With Dutch support, the Iroquois initiated a series of battles and wars in the middle 1640s that lasted until about 1700 and are called the Beaver Wars. From the 1640s until 1820 in eastern North America, there was nearly continuous warfare, as well as economic and diplomatic competition, that ended only with the emergence of the United States and the extension of its control over the region.

The trade and diplomatic ties of the Native nations to European colonies not only involved them in the European wars but intensified military and economic relations among the Native nations. As the Iroquois, supported by

Dutch and later English alliance and weapons, pushed or dispersed many of the Native nations of the lower Great Lakes and forced the Ojibway, Potawatomi, Odawa, Sac and Fox, Wyandot, and others farther west. The migrating Native nations in turn, often better supplied with weapons, pushed other Native nations like the Lakota, Dakota, Nakota, Gros Ventre, Cheyenne, and others farther west and onto the plains.

The intensification of diplomatic, military, and trade relations greatly affected the ability of many Native nations to maintain their land and economic integrity. Most Native in eastern North America were forced into a trade, military, or diplomatic alliance with one or another European colony. Many coastal nations were quickly subjugated by the English colonies. The Pamunkey Algonquins under Powhatan (1550?–1618) were early subjected to English land encroachments, taxes, and pressure to convert to Christianity, which resulted in several conflicts that ended with the social, political, and cultural marginalization of the Virginia Native nations by 1675. At about the same time, the Natives of New England were increasingly forced to cede land and political autonomy to the English, which resulted in King Philip's War (1675–1676). The Wampanoags did not believe they could live under English rule, since the economic and cultural changes were corrupting their way of life. The defeat of the Wampanoags and allied New England Native nations led to their relegation to small tracts of land and communities often called Indian praying towns. The New England Natives adopted town government democracy and Protestant religion, although maintaining a sense of Native identity to the present.

While most Native nations in the thirteen original U.S. colonies were eventually brought under colonial control, most Natives farther west continued to engaged in trade, diplomatic, and military relations with the rival European colonial powers. By 1700 some Natives began to realize that the expansion of English colonies included land and threatened the sovereignty and traditional territories of the Natives. The Iroquois and Creek Confederacies began to form alliances of Native nations in order to manage relations with the Europeans more effectively. The Iroquois during the early 1700s often boasted they had the military alliance of fifty Native nations, although most likely this claim was a bargaining ploy when negotiating with the European colonists. The Iroquois Confederacy held together an alliance of Native nations based on economic treaties that allowed the Iroquois access to western hunting grounds and in exchange gave the western Native nations access to British trade goods at Albany in New York Colony. While the Iroquois managed this alliance for their own and English trade and diplomatic interests, the Iroquois alliances unraveled after the 1750s as trade moved farther west and Pennsylvania traders moved into the Ohio region. The alliance of Native nations, formally led by the Iroquois was increasingly taken over by Shawnee and Delaware leadership. During the early 1760s, Pontiac collected many groups from the northern confederacy to attack British forts in the Great Lakes region. This same confederacy united to oppose U.S. settlement expansion during the 1790s during Little Turtle's War, and in 1812 Tecumseh was appointed warrior head of the confederacy, which fought with the British against the United States in the War of 1812. After the War of 1812 the northern alliance was depleted and in disarray.

The Creek nation also tried to strengthen its trade and diplomatic position by inviting coastal groups and other nations or villages to join the Creek Confederacy. The Creek leadership tried to manage relations among the English, French, and Spanish colonies of the south, and tried to gain diplomatic and trade advantages. The Creek were relatively successful with these methods during the second half of the 1700s. During the early 1760s the southern tribes including the Creeks rejected efforts by the Shawnee and Delaware to induce them to join with the northern confederacy against the British. And in 1811, the southern Indian nations generally declined to ally with the northern confederacy, by declining Tecumseh's offers to join together to oppose the expansion of the United States into Native lands.

Many Native nations during the late 1700s and 1800s engaged the United States in warfare. Most were defending territory and their way of life, or moving to preserve an economic resource like the buffalo. Native military alliances were usually loose coalitions of friendship and often seasonally deployed. In general, they were hard to sustain in the field, could not manufacture their own rifles and ammunition, and depended on the backing of a strong European colonial ally who was willing to provide military supplies and, hopefully, armed forces. After the War of 1812 and the sale of Florida and West Florida (present-day Alabama and Mississippi) from Spain the United States, the eastern Native nations were left without effective allies and were forced to recognize U.S. authority in the region.

# Movements of Religious Fundamentalism and Reform

As eastern North America became increasingly engaged in trade, diplomacy, and economic markets, the expansion of colonial power and land encroachments led to dispersion and social and economic degradation of Native life and culture. Native communities were forced to migrate farther west, game disappeared, colonists took over land and made farms, disease greatly reduced the numbers and life expectancy of Native peoples, and economic and political dependencies required interaction and compliance with colonial authorities and traders. European trade goods, access to alcohol, overspecialization into the fur trade economy, and new Christian religious ideas and concepts were changing and modifying Native everyday life. Native social and life conditions deteriorated noticeably, and the colonial expansion westward became readily apparent. Under these conditions many Native leaders and spiritual guides began to lament the declining conditions of the Native American Nations and sought answers. While military action was one form of action, many leaders looked to understand the spiritual and religious significance of changes that were occurring and sought remedies through spiritual means. As early as the 1720s there are reports of spiritual preaching among the Iroquois, but the movements did not fully develop. There may have been many spiritual leaders who discussed the issues of the day in spiritual terms, but many did not lead to recognizable movements or have been lost in history.

Among the Delaware in the 1740s there was distress because of migrations and declining conditions and some hints of spiritual unrest. Several prophets appeared among the Delaware in the late 1750s and early 1760s. The British had just won the French and Indian War, and many tribes in the northern alliance, including the Delaware and Odawa, who both had allied themselves to the French, were highly suspicious of British motivations. The British now controlled trade and gained control of the military forts in the Great Lakes region. The Natives in the region were expecting British retaliation and were unhappy under British administration. Under these conditions two religious movements emerged among the Delaware. One led to the unified national Delaware Big House religion, and the other to the militant teachings that the Odawa Pontiac endorsed and used to collect a military coalition to force the British out the Great Lakes region. The militant prophet's teachings combined elements of Christianity with selected Native teachings. The militant prophet had a near-death experience and dreamed he went to heaven and gained instruction directly from God. In general, the teachings suggested that the Natives had abandoned the religious teachings and lifeways of their forebears, and had adopted too many of the European ways such as clothing, trade, alcohol, and Christianity. These changes had corrupted Native life, and the solution was to return to the beliefs and lifestyle of their ancestors, which would help restore the Natives to their former health and prosperity. In addition, the Europeans would have to be pushed off the continent through warfare, and no Native warrior could reach the next world if he did not believe in the prophet's teachings and do his bidding.[1] Pontiac and the militant Delaware Prophet used these teachings to organize the northern confederacy against the British, but after they lost Pontiac's War, the teachings were lost or went underground. This movement, which emphasizes spiritual solutions to colonial situations and return to the culture and religion of the ancestors, we can call fundamentalist.

The second Delaware religious movement during the early 1760s led to the political, social, and religious reform of Delaware society. The prophet synthesized elements of traditional Delaware religious views, brought them together into a common ceremonial structure—the Big House, unified three phratries of a dozen clans each into a common religious-kinship structure, and established unified chief and leadership positions for all three phratries. The phratries are known to us as the wolf, turkey, and turtle divisions, or perhaps more generally as four-leggeds, two-leggeds, and those that walk on land and water. The newly established chief of the turtle division was the first leader of the newly reformed Delaware nation. The reformed Delaware religion society helped centralize and unify Delaware political and religious relations and helped the Delaware more effectively manage relations with other tribes and Europeans.[2] The Delaware Big House religion was practiced until at least the 1920s.[3] The Delaware national religious movement we can call a reform movement, since it led to long-term and durable institutional change in Delaware society. Its intention was religious and moral as well as social and political reform.

The Native religious landscape had numerous fundamentalist and reform movements. The often colorful fundamentalist movements gained considerable attention. The Pueblo Revolt (1680s), Shawnee Prophet (1805–1811), Cherokee Prophet (1811–1813), Red Stick War (Creeks in 1813–1814), White Path's Rebellion (1826), Winnebago Prophet (1830–1832), the first Ghost Dance (1869–1870) and the second Ghost Dance (1889–1890), and the Snake movements among the Cherokee, Choctaw, and Creeks during the 1890s were generally fundamentalist movements, favoring a return to traditional ways and rejecting the social, cultural, and economic changes of the colonies or the United States.[4] Many of these movements adopted elements of Christianity, like a second coming or a concept of heaven and a single anthropomorphic God, but their solution to economic, demographic, and political decline of the Native communities was to seek a solution through spiritual intervention and a restoration of the way of life before the Europeans arrived. The second Ghost Dance asked the faithful to dance at regular intervals in a circle to induce dreams and communication with ancestors to learn about their eminent return and restoration of the Native way of life. The Cherokee Prophet in 1811–1813 taught that the changes in Cherokee society were corrosive and that the community would be destroyed in a hailstorm of fiery rocks. Only those who went to Lookout Mountain were going to be saved. The first Ghost Dance taught that the Natives would be saved by train loads of manufactured goods that would arrive only for the Native people. This movement is reminiscent of the cargo cults in the Pacific. The Winnebago Prophet taught that by resisting the Americans militarily, the Winnebago and Sac and Fox would regain the traditional lands when a group of spiritual warriors would appear to defeat the U.S. army. The Creek Red Sticks opposed economic and political change introduced by American Indian agents and started a civil war for culture reasons that later developed into the Creek War (1812–1813). The Pueblo Revolt was strongly influenced by a rejection of Christianity and Spanish political domination and gained the right for the Pueblo to practice their own religion, although the most Pueblo people were returned to Spanish control in the 1690s. The Cherokee, Choctaw, and Creek Snake movements were carried on as ways to mobilize political organization to oppose the abolition of their tribal governments and force their inclusion into the state of Oklahoma. The members of the Snake movements were primarily the most culturally conservative members of the Cherokee, Choctaw, and Creek nations.

The fundamentalist movements strongly resisted cultural and political change and favored military or spiritual solutions to the degradation of life under colonial domination. Some of the movements relied on a cataclysmic spiritual event to intervene and restore the old order and tradition. If the significant spiritual event does not occur, most people lose faith in the movement, and the movement disintegrates. Small groups of adherents remain and carry on the beliefs, however, often in secret.

Reform religious movements are aimed at changing or supporting the community to accommodate changing political, cultural, and social conditions. Some reform movements include the Yaqui religion (1500s to present), the Handsome Lake movement (1797 to present), the Munsee Prophetess (1804 to 1805), the Kickapoo Prophet movement (1815 to present), the Cherokee Keetoowah Society (1858 to present), Washat Dreamers religion (1850 to present), the Indian Shakers (1881 to present), the Native American Church (1800s to present), Shoshoni Sun Dance (1890 to present), and perhaps the New Tidings religion of the Canadian Sioux (1900 to present) and Ojibway Drummer movement (contemporary).[5] Most of these religions adopt some concepts from Christianity but have a predominantly Native cultural and philosophical focus that would not be generally recognized as Christian.

The most characteristic of the religious reform movements is the Handsome Lake movement among the Seneca and Iroquois. Handsome Lake, after having a near-death experience, brings back a message of reform to the

Seneca from God. Elements of Catholicism and Quakerism are integrated with selected features of traditional religion and ceremony to create a reformed message. The Handsome Lake message emerges as the Iroquois are relegated to small reservations. He advocates no gambling and no drinking and legitimates the role of men in farming. Previously farming was women's work, but Handsome Lake urges males to take up horse and plow, while women focus on horticulture using hand implements. The prophet advocates social and culture reform as a means of community adaptation to small reservation life. Strong emphases are given to moral issues and individual responsibility; Christian concepts of heaven and hell are emphasized for those who would break the new moral code. Handsome Lake is given credit for introducing significant social reform into Iroquois society. His followers established a church about fifteen years after his death.[6]

The Kickapoo Prophet, Native American Church, and Indian Shakers follow analogous patterns of moral and community reform and continue as contemporary religious movements. The Yaqui religion is an example of the formation of a reformed religion, borrowing significantly from Catholic teachings but recreated and resituated within Yaqui tradition and history. Some movements are less influenced by teachings of social or cultural change and emphasize continuity of community and tradition. Such movements are the Munsee Prophetess, the New Tidings religion, and the Ojibway Drummer movement.

The Religious reform movements were a response to radically changing social, culture, political, and economic conditions experienced by Native communities over the past two centuries. Traditional religions may seem ill equipped to interpret and give guidance under radically changing colonial conditions, and some people look for new ways to understand the world and make accommodations to it. Some Natives adopted Christianity but continued to engage in Native community and beliefs. Native Christian churches were predicated on Native language and social and cultural organization (e.g., the Cherokee, Seminole, Choctaw, and Creek Native churches).[7] Native religious reform movements provided syncretic religious solutions to communities undergoing rapid change, as well as a new set of moral values, beliefs, ceremonies, and sometimes community organization to endure and live under the new conditions. The reform movements usually retained central Native concepts and philosophies.

## Contemporary Social Movements

Currently Native American social movements take many forms. Native peoples are actively engaged in many movement activities in the areas of land claims, education, Native rights, international rights, and many others. Here we will focus on the movements that are related to religious issues.

During the 1970s the Red Power movement spanned the occupation of Alcatraz Island to the second Long Walk in 1978. Contemporary Red Power activities have been less visible, but have taken the form of occasional protests, especially over nuclear waste and sites on or near reservation land, as well as sacred walks or runs. American Indian Movement (AIM) chapters are still active, meet in national meetings, and are engaged in community issues and cultural events. Native Students at colleges and universities are engaged in Native issues, recruitment, cultural events, and community activities.[8]

One major outgrowth of the Red Power movement was the open revival of Native tradition in many Native communities. Native activism in the 1970s started in urban areas and extended to the reservation communities where young Native people sought greater knowledge and understanding of traditional culture. These events emboldened many spiritual leaders and traditionals to bring Native ceremonies, dances, the Sun Dance, and stories out into public view, when they had been hidden away for many years.[9] Elders and traditionals gained more respect, and they became more active and visible in Native communities.[10] Tribal community colleges started teaching Native language and culture. Native religious freedom issues were defended in courts to preserve the right to smoke sacred peyote in ceremonies.[11] Twice congressional bills were written for preserving Native religious rights through the American Indian Religious Freedom Acts. Natives moved to protect sacred sites and places of worship, both on and off the reservations. Native religion and traditional knowledge became more highly regarded within Native communities.

Contemporary Native peoples are actively engaged in the world through a variety of social, political, and cultural movements aimed at preserving their communities, identities, religions, and political autonomy.

## Notes

An earlier version of this chapter appeared as Duane Champagne, "North American Religions: Modern Movements," in *The Encyclopedia of Religion,* 2nd ed. (Farmington Hills, MI: Macmillan Reference, 2005), 10: 6664–68.

1. William W. Newcomb Jr., *The Culture and Acculturation of the Delaware Indians* (Ann Arbor: University of Michigan Museum of Anthropology, 1956); Anthony F. C. Wallace, "New Religious Beliefs among the Delaware Indians, 1600–1900," *Southwest Journal of Anthropology* 12 (1956): 1–21.

2. Duane Champagne, "The Delaware Revitalization Movement of the Early 1760s: A Suggested Reinterpretation," *American Indian Quarterly* 12, no. 2 (1988): 107–26.

3. Frank Speck, *A Study of the Delaware Big House Religion* (Harrisburg: Pennsylvania Historical Commission, 1931).

4. James Mooney, *The Ghost Dance Religion and Wounded Knee* (Minoela, NY: Dover, 1973); Andrew L. Knaut, *The Pueblo Revolt of 1680: Conquest and Resistance in Seventeenth-Century New Mexico* (Norman: University of Oklahoma Press, 1995); R. David Edmunds, *The Shawnee Prophet* (Lincoln: University of Nebraska Press, 1983); William McLoughlin, *The Cherokee Ghost Dance* (Mercer, GA: Mercer University Press, 1984); Frank Stevens, *The Black Hawk War* (Chicago: Frank Stevens, 1903); Cecil Eby, *"That Disgraceful Affair," The Black Hawk War* (New York: Norton, 1973); Michael Hittman, *Wovoka and the Ghost Dance* (Yervington, NV: Yervington Paiute Tribe, 1990); Leslie Spier, *The Prophet Dance of the Northwest and Its Derivatives: The Source of the Ghost Dance* (Menasha, WI: George Banta, 1935).

5. Joseph G. Jorgensen, *The Sun Dance Religion: Power for the Powerless* (Chicago: University of Chicago Press, 1972); David F. Aberle, *The Peyote Religion Among the Navajo* (Norman: University of Oklahoma Press, 1991); Omer C. Stewart, *Peyote Religion: A History* (Norman: University Press of Oklahoma, 1987); Robert H. Ruby and John A. Brown, *John Slocum and the Indian Shaker Church* (Norman: University of Oklahoma Press, 1996), Cliff E. Trafzer and M. A. Beach, "Smohalla, the Washani, and Religion as a Factor in Northwestern Indian History," in *American Indian Prophets,* ed. Cliff E. Trafzer (Sacramento, CA: Sierra Oaks, 1986), pp. 71–86; Jane B. Hendrix, "Redbird Smith and the Nighthawk Keetoowahs," *Journal of Cherokee Studies* 8 (1983): 73–86; Joseph B. Herring, *Kenekuk: The Kickapoo Prophet* (Lawrence: University Press of Kansas, 1988).

6. Anthony C. Wallace, *The Death and Rebirth of the Seneca* (New York: Vintage, 1972); Arthur C. Parker, *Parker on the Iroquois* (Syracuse, NY: Syracuse University Press, 1968).

7. Jack M. Shultz, *The Seminole Baptist Churches of Oklahoma: Maintaining a Traditional Community* (Norman: University of Oklahoma Press, 1999).

8. Troy Johnson, Joane Nagel, and Duane Champagne, *American Indian Activism: Alcatraz to the Longest Walk* (Urbana: University of Illinois Press, 1997).

9. Luke E. Lassiter, "Southwestern Oklahoma, the Gourd Dance, and 'Charlie Brown,'" in *Contemporary Native American Cultural Issues,* ed. Duane Champagne (Walnut Creek, CA: AltaMira, 1999), pp. 145–66.

10. Joseph Epes Brown, *The Spiritual Legacy of the American Indian* (New York: Crossroad, 1995); Melissa Pflug, *Ritual and Myth in Odawa Revitalization: Reclaiming a Sovereign Place* (Norman: University of Oklahoma Press, 1998).

11. Huston Smith and Rueben Snake, eds., *One Nation under God: The Triumph of the Native American Church* (Santa Fe, NM: Clear Light, 1996).

# Culture, Differentiation, and Environment: Social Change in Tlingit Society

**13**

T HERE ARE PRESENTLY 16,000 NATIVES of southeast Alaska, primarily Tlingit, who have during the present century responded to world market incorporation and colonial domination with increased political and economic differentiation, while preserving core aspects of their traditional culture, values, and social organization. For over two centuries southeast Alaska natives have participated in world economic markets. During the present century the Tlingit have organized a political center and formed a separate political institution that manages their political relations with the U.S. government. Furthermore, since the early 1970s southeast Alaska natives have controlled a multimillion dollar corporation with sales that have in recent years placed it on the Fortune 1,000 list. Nevertheless, Tlingit social and ceremonial relations continue to be upheld by traditional kinship groups and contemporary potlatch ceremonies. How is it possible to account for the pattern of differentiation, dependency, and sociocultural continuity in Tlingit society?

To explain social change in the Tlingit case, a comprehensive argument involving internal cultural, political, economic, and social relations must be combined with an analysis of geopolitical and dependency relations. Several recent theories of social change, both Marxist and functionalist, have moved toward convergence on the issue of using both exogenous and endogenous variables in an explanation for social change. Neo-Marxists have criticized functionalist theory for its primary emphasis on internal variables. Wolf argues that anthropology and sociology analyze societies as autonomous entities that do not have important interrelations or dependencies. He emphasizes that societies are open systems and that because of the rise in the past several centuries of world economic trade and markets, societies, especially those outside the Western world, must not be considered as isolated, integrated, and bounded systems that have few relations with other equally bounded and integrated societies or social systems.[1] Furthermore, Giddens argues that Parsonian functionalism presents an "unfolding" model of social change, a model that "treats social change as the progressive emergence of traits that a particular society is presumed to have within itself from its inception."[2] Unfolding models of social change concentrate on endogenous factors as causes of social change. In many respects, Parsons's theory of societal evolution is an unfolding model, since it views social change as increasing specialization and the autonomy of primary subsystems' functions. Nisbet, rejecting the unfolding model, argues that significant social change derives only from external events.[3] Giddens argues, however, that an emphasis on exogenous sources of social change tends to treat societies as internally closed systems.

Neo-Marxist dependency and world-system theorists have taken an externally open system approach to the study of social change. The neo-Marxist arguments, however, have concentrated on analyzing the internal relations of dependent societies in terms of class structure or mode of production. While such an approach presents an interesting hypothesis, it leaves the analysis open to the functionalist criticism that a Marxist class or mode of production argument treats societies as internally closed systems. Eisenstadt and Curelaru argue that Marxist theory has the characteristics of a closed rather than an open system approach because it tends to assume a relatively invariant relation between modes of production and political power and other aspects of the societal superstructure.[4] An internally open system approach would allow norms, values, cultures, and political systems to have variable relations with the mode of production or the economic organization of a society.

An analytical framework that incorporated the open system aspects of dependency theory and the functionalist open system approach to the study of internal societal relations would have the potential to account for a greater amount of variation in social change than can either the neo-Marxist and functionalist theories, taken individually. Both the neo-Marxist and functionalist theories are currently exploring the possibilities of a more internally-externally open system of theory of social change.

## Neo-Marxist Theories

Much recent sociological theory has emphasized the primacy of economic dependency and location within the world market system as major determinants of economic and political organization in less developed or peripheral societies.[5] Recent criticism of the dependency approach within the Marxist tradition has emphasized that dependency theory, like earlier theories of imperialism, has failed to provide an adequate understanding of the impact of the world market on the internal sociopolitical order of non–European societies.[6] Major criticisms of the dependency argument have suggested that it is overly economistic and conceptualizes "the colonized-imperialized world [as] a mere object of external determination, and not as a variegated system of historically constituted and very real social formations."[7] Some recent theoretical trends have shifted their emphasis from external world market relations toward internal class and mode of production arguments.[8] Furthermore, these arguments more closely approximate an internally–externally open system approach by their analytical consideration of international economic processes that account for the formation of new local capitalist classes, proletarians, and semiproletarians.[9] Chinchilla approaches a more internally–externally open system argument: while she suggests that the overall determinant for a change is economic, she allows for the possibility that political and ideological structures may make independent contributions to change, and precapitalist cultural and collective institutions may persist and become associated with the new capitalist formations introduced by the interpenetration of international capital. She argues that the articulation of the mode of production approach, which focuses on how internal social structures (classes and states) are influenced by dependency relations, is more capable of explaining the variation of social formations in third world societies than are the evolutionary Marxist mode of production argument, the externally deterministic world-system argument, or the unilinear convergence arguments of modernization and Parsonian theory.[10]

Skocpol, following Hintze, argues that uneven development within the world division of labor is a secondary factor in determining the causes of social revolutions.[11] For Skocpol, situations in a society's geopolitical environment (defeat in war, imperial invasion, and subordination) are major causes of crisis that can lead to loss of legitimacy by groups critical to the state's capacity to cope with competition from other nation-states or with tasks thrust upon it by changing world political and economic conditions.[12] The specific outcome of a state crisis will depend on the organization of the state, the internal class structure, and state and society relations.

Thus some neo-Marxists have moved toward a systematic consideration of both internal and external forces within the same framework in order to more adequately understand the empirical variation in the economic and political formations in third world societies. The neo-Marxist arguments of Skocpol and the articulation of production argument emphasize dependency and geopolitics while attempting to utilize a more open system approach to state and class relations. Generally, however, there is little systematic analysis of culture, values, and norms as independent variables in the neo-Marxist theories; a comprehensive internally-externally open system argument must at least consider these as potential explanatory variables.

## Differentiation Theory

While neo-Marxist theories have emphasized world market and geopolitical perspectives, functionalists have continued to stress the primacy of social structure and culture in social change processes. Although Parsons does not provide a theory of societal change as a response to changing geopolitical and economic conditions, he does offer a relatively comprehensive theory of social action and an evolutionary theory of functional differentiation. Parsons argues that not only are more modern societies more differentiated or complex but, more specifically, that they differentiate according to system functions.[13] Thus societies will tend to develop by forming increasingly autonomous and specialized cultural, political, economic, and integrative institutions. More differentiated societies will have greater capacity to mobilize resources and effect collective goals and will develop increasing autonomy in relation to environmental contingencies.[14] The appealing aspect of Parsons's theory, from the point of view of the search for an open internal-external argument, is that his theory specifies a relatively comprehensive set of interrelated factors. Parsons's framework allows for the potential mutual differentiation of all four major functions of the social system: the polity, the economy, the societal community, and the pattern maintenance system, as well as the differentiation on the general action level between the social, cultural, and personality systems. Such an argument approaches the internally open system approach, since it conceptualizes more relations as potentially variable.

In several ways, however, Parsons's theory conceptualizes a limited view of the environment. Using a biological analogy, Parsons's paradigm assumes that more internally stable social systems react to their environments through interchanges and adjustments of internal functions in order to accommodate and adapt to changing conditions in the external environment.[15] Parsons tends to conceptualize a physico-organic environment as devoid of other social, political, or economic systems. Parsons's social system operates in a transsocietal vacuum, where its interchanges with the environment are primarily concerned with physical inputs. The personality system and the adaptive and goal attainment functions manage relations with the environment, but Parsons does not systematically analyze the possibility that more than one social system is active in the environment or that some societies may be politically, culturally, and/or economically subordinated or dependent on other societies.

While Parsons tends to ignore unequal development and geopolitical relations, he argues, following Weber, that cultural systems can gain relative autonomy from particular societies and have influence on societal
developments across history and territory. Parsons's main examples are the
influence of secular Greek philosophy, the Greek notion of citizen within
the city-state polis, rational Roman law, and the Hebrew concept of moral
religious community, all of which contributed to the formation of modern
secular culture, nationalism, and normative order.[16] Parsons's main contribution to understanding external influences of social change derive from the
cultural sphere. Not all functionalists have neglected the relations between
internal and external sources of change; Johnson argues that changes in the
environment (colonial domination, market incorporation, the introduction
of new value systems, demographic changes) will create demands that the
system be adjusted through political action.[17] Johnson's theory of disequilib-
rium and readjustment handles transsocietal "environmental" relations more
concretely than Parsons, but Johnson does not concern himself with
processes of differentiation.

Badie and Birnbaum argue that the concept of differentiation is not itself
an explanatory variable, but rather that specific modes of differentiation are
determined in precise historical contexts, which are related to the combined
impacts of market and economic transformations, the breakdown of traditional forms of authority, international market relations, and the resistance of
traditional elements of the society.[18] A proposed differentiation, however, may
not be accepted at all, and its introduction may lead to conflict between pro-
ponent and opposition groups.[19] For Eisenstadt, differentiation is carried out
by specific groups, who rely on cooperation from other groups that provide
resources and commitments to newly differentiated and institutionalized
structures. Since commitments to similar values and norms may not be
equally shared between rival groups, differentiation is beset with conflict,
since some groups may not be willing to contribute to the new structure. The
innovators must solve the problems of creating and maintaining new levels of
social integration through the creation and maintenance of cultural legitimation for their proposed change. Innovators may be countered by competing
groups or fundamentalists who resist change or propose alternative solutions,
or wish to accept a slower rate of change.[20] Thus the process of differentiation involves specific historical conditions and direct struggles between
groups, who carry alternative cultural models as solutions for change.

Thus some recent work on the theory of differentiation indicates that the
unfolding or evolutionary theory of societal differentiation must be extended
beyond conceptualization of the environment in terms of the physico-

organic environment; it must also include consideration of the impacts of transsocietal economic, political, and cultural relations as potential causes of differentiation. Furthermore, the process of differentiation and institutionalization must be explained by specific historical causal sequences that result from the interaction or struggles of groups within the society.

## Culture

Eisenstadt argues that world political competition, changing world capitalist economy, and internal pressures and conflicts can give rise to loss of legitimacy or conditions of relative deprivation that are associated with a variety of societal outcomes such as the collapse of regimes, revolutions, or relatively smooth transitions to modernity.[21] He argues, however, that in addition to analyzing the specific historical conditions of changing state and world market relations that can lead to a widespread loss of legitimacy in existing sociopolitical institutions, an analysis of major cultural orientations and worldviews, in addition to the structural organization of society, will lead to a theory that will be capable of explaining more variation in the empirical range of societal change responses. Eisenstadt argues that within a given level of structural differentiation there is considerable variation in cultural orientation and worldview. Accordingly, a predominantly structural argument (class, division of labor, level of structural differentiation) cannot support a general theory of social change. This view claims that there is a close connection between basic cultural orientations, the organizational basis of society, and the type of response a society will have to modernization problems or to incorporation into transsocietal economic or political systems.

Weber and Eisenstadt focus on how cultural orientations provide guidelines for the participation and organization of political and economic institutions.[22] For example, Weber argues that Calvinist doctrine created new orientations that gave religious legitimation to acceptance of a calling and the ascetic accumulation of wealth for economic reinvestment, both of which contributed to the breakdown of traditional capitalism and the development of rational capitalism. Weber indicates, however, that by the beginning of the nineteenth century Western economic behavior had been stripped of its religious foundations.[23] While the Protestant ethic thesis may be appropriate for understanding the initial breakthrough to rational capitalism or modern society, the features of non-Western cultural systems that support market participation, social solidarity, and political centralization may be more appropriate areas of focus in a world where capitalism already prevails and transsocietal political and economic relations have become increasingly dominant.

In summary, recent literature suggests the possibility of constructing an internally-externally open system framework for analyzing social change. Such a framework must include consideration of transsocietal geopolitical relations, incorporation of the world economy, and the interpenetration of transsocietal cultural systems. Furthermore, while not denying the Marxist mode of production hypothesis, an internally open system must consider the independent analytical contribution of culture, values, norms, and social integration. More specifically, I have tried to combine differentiation theory with an externally open system argument, which requires consideration of world economic market incorporation, geopolitical relations, and transsocietal cultural relations as conditions that may contribute to further societal differentiation. In the case study of social change in Tlingit society, I wish to show that the dependency, geopolitical, and unfolding differentiation theories cannot individually account for the economic and political differentiation of Tlingit institutions and, at the same time, account for the centrality and continuity of core aspects of Tlingit culture and social organization. It is suggested that an internally-externally open system model will be more appropriate for understanding social change in Tlingit society.

## The Tlingit Case Study

There are considerable ethnographic and historical materials on the Tlingit. Much of the analytical work on the Tlingit and other northwest Alaska societies has focused on explaining the economic behavior of the potlatch, or "giveaway." In exchange for social prestige, a host chief distributed blankets, copper plates, and slaves, often leaving himself and family with few worldly possessions.[24] The interpretation of potlatch behavior given here draws on Weber's and Parsons's focus on culture and values. The Tlingit potlatch is described as a cult that emphasizes honoring clan ancestors.

Kinship groups formed the societal community of early Tlingit society.[25] There were two matrilineal exogamous moieties—raven and eagle (some groups use wolf)—and both contained about twenty-five clans. The clans and moieties were distributed over villages and thirteen territorial groupings or "tribes." Both moieties were represented in every village, although a clan was often represented in only one or two villages. Moieties regulated marriage and ceremonial obligations. Clan members considered themselves descendants of a single maternal line that shared a common name and historical-mythological tradition.[26] The clans were further divided into one or more houses that included from two to eight families. The ties between villages and between houses even in the same clan were relatively weak.[27]

The house groups were the major political, economic, social, and ceremonial units in Tlingit society. Each house held territory and owned myths, crests, songs, dances, and other distinctive ensignia.

Tlingit social order was maintained by mutual reciprocities and obligations between moieties, clans, and houses. The moiety-clan organization and reciprocal relations were directly legitimated by Tlingit myths.[28] The mythical figure Raven is credited with creating the moiety system and for instituting the potlatch ceremonies, which, as will be seen, bind the houses, clans, and moieties into economic, social, and cultural reciprocities.

The shared culture, myths, and norms of moiety-clan relations did not necessarily ensure harmonious relations between the Tlingit clans and houses. Relations between the clans and territorial groups were often antagonistic and competitive. During potlatch ceremonies, if proper respect was not shown or one house humiliated the other by gifts that were too small, by incorrect dancing, or by knowing more songs than the other houses, potlatches could break into open conflict between antagonistic houses. On such occasions the host house would try to stop the fighting by intervening with a display of its moiety crest, either eagle or raven, while imploring the combatants to respect this common symbol of peace and solidarity.[29] Past incidents of humiliation, disrespect, and feud were incorporated into the traditions of each clan and caused friction whenever members of traditionally antagonistic clans came together. Similarly, villages were not necessarily harmonious social groupings but were composed of politically and economically autonomous houses that jealously protected their social, economic, and political prerogatives. House, clan, and territorial antagonism toward outside groups served to intensify within-group identity and clarify group boundaries.[30]

Clans, houses, and individuals were ranked in Tlingit society, and all ranks were validated through distributions of wealth in potlatch ceremonies.[31] Consequently, the accumulation of wealth—copper plates, blankets, slaves, and selected shells—were a necessary condition for a man and his house to properly legitimate social status and succession in rank. The distribution of wealth through the potlatch ceremony was a primary criterion for legitimating individual and house rank. Without enough wealth to properly legitimate succession to chieftainship, both the new chief and the house lost rank and prestige.[32] Many men could not give a potlatch during their lifetime, and for some men giving of one potlatch might be the high point of life. Men of wealthy or aristocratic lineages might give several potlatches, while a man who gave eight potlatches was considered a "prince."[33] The social standing of individuals and houses was open to change and depended on the individuals' and houses' ability to distribute wealth in fulfilling their potlatch obligations.

# Culture and the Social Community

Tlingit society was characterized by social and economic inequality at both the individual and house levels. Rank and hierarchy in Tlingit society were legitimated by the value of honoring clan ancestors with a potlatch and by the Tlingit worldview, which incorporated a belief in rebirth.

Weber and others argue that the belief in rebirth in Buddhist and Hindu religion serves to legitimate inequalities in political and social organization.[34] Although caste relations may be antagonistic, members of the lower caste groups perform their caste duties (dharma) in the belief that in their next rebirth or reincarnation they will be born into a caste of higher rank. To neglect caste obligations threatens the individual with a decline in caste rank or even nonhuman rebirth. Compared to Tlingit society, the Hindu belief system legitimizes a vastly more differentiated economic division of labor and much greater differentiation of political and cultural roles. In Tlingit society there were shamans, but there was no specialized priesthood who rationalized the meaning of the rebirth belief, and there were no centralized political structures or differentiated leadership that materially and politically benefited from the social stability that accompanied the rebirth belief, as did the upper warrior castes and patrimonial political structures of ancient India.[35] Nevertheless, the Tlingit belief in rebirth serves a similar role in legitimizing social and economic inequality.

The Tlingit believed that the soul of the deceased returned to earth and was reborn as a female of the same clan. There was the possibility of social mobility through rebirth, since one could be reborn into a house or lineage that had higher rank and wealth; "therefore some Tlingit who are dissatisfied with their lot are supposed to express the wish that they may die soon so that they can start over again under more favorable conditions by being born into the clan of some envied chief."[36] Individuals of wealthy and prestigious lineages needed to make sure, through properly performing clan obligations, that they were reborn within the same family and thus again under favorable social circumstances.[37] Men who sacrificed their lives in war could be assured of a higher rebirth and a relatively quick return to earthly existence. To be killed in battle or to allow oneself to be executed in fulfillment of clan obligations to the law of blood ensured that one had a happy situation in the next world and a speedy return to a socially favorable earthly existence.[38] According to the Tlingit law of blood, the victim's clan, in cases of murder, would demand not necessarily the life of the murderer but the life of a man of social rank equal to that of the victim. Any man who allowed himself to be executed in fulfillment of clan obligations to the offended clan was given a highly honorable funeral and was said to have entered "highest heaven." Thus, in the latter instance, the belief system directly legitimated the performance of clan roles and obligations with promises of both otherworldly and this-worldly rewards. The Tlingit belief in rebirth provided a theodicy, or rationalization and legitimation of rank, inequality, wealth, and misfortune. If a man faithfully performed his clan obligations and continued to suffer earthly misfortunes or low caste, he could expect a better social situation in his next rebirth.

Tlingit rebirth beliefs had a strong this-worldly orientation. The primary goal was not to achieve salvation in heaven, as in Christianity, or to escape the wheel of life, as in the Hindu religion, but rather to use the rebirth mechanism for social mobility within one's clan. One hoped to be quickly reborn within an aristocratic lineage in order to command social prestige, wealth, and honor. The Tlingit did not have a conception of salvation as a means to escape earthly life and imperfections, but rather affirmed enjoyment of this-worldly social position as a greater good than otherworldly existence.

In addition to the belief in rebirth, the potlatch validated individual, house, and clan rank. In Tlingit society potlatches served to honor the dead and provide payment for funeral services performed by members of the opposite moiety.[39] Whenever someone died, relatives from houses of the opposite moiety managed the funeral rites and the cremation of the body. The deceased's house and moiety were not allowed to handle the remains. The related houses of the opposite moiety provided food, clothes, and comfort to the bereaved house. The deceased was symbolically prepared for travel in the next world and had to be supplied with appropriate food, clothes, shoes, and weapons, all of which were cremated with him and were considered to aid him in his extraterrestrial travels.

After a period of mourning, during which the bereaved house gathered wealth, the houses that contributed to the funeral expenses were invited to a potlatch. If a house chief had died, his successor would hold a major potlatch. The potlatch ceremony itself lasted eight days, and the invited guests might remain for another two weeks if they found the hospitality congenial. Furthermore, if a new chief was raised to succession, the related house of the opposite moiety constructed a new house or refurbished the old house and raised a totem pole. The contributions of each individual were carefully noted. Those who contributed the most to the funeral expenses, totem raising, and house building were rewarded accordingly in honor and gifts in the potlatch. A man who wished to be publicly distinguished in a potlatch had to make substantial material and/or service contributions to the bereaved family. Men of rank were obliged to make large contributions in order to preserve their rank, while aspiring men might wish to make contributions that would enhance their social standing and honor during the potlatch giveaway.[40]

The Tlingit potlatch, however, was more than a repayment of services and gifts provided during the mourning period. The potlatch giveaway was the primary means by which the Tlingit honored the deceased members of their clan.

> The putting up of a house or pole, and the secret society performances, feasts, and distributions of property which accompanied it, were all undertaken for the sake of the dead members of a man's clan, and to them every blanket was given away and a great deal of food that was put into the fire was supposed to go.[41]

During the potlatch, the souls of the dead were believed to partake of the spirit of the goods, clothes, and food that were given away.[42] When a gift was given away, the giver might announce the name of a deceased ancestor in whose honor the gift was given and to whom the spirit of the gift was sent. While the houses of the opposite moiety received the material embodiments of the potlatch gifts for their funeral and other services, the souls of the deceased ancestors were honored by each giveaway.[43] In fact, "what is consumed is thought to be for the benefit of the deceased, indeed, for all the dead of the host sib."[44] The guests represented their own deceased ancestors, who came to "show respect" and comfort the mourning house.[45] The house chiefs were considered representatives of the clan ancestors and in this relation were invested with the management of the house economic estate and were the keepers of the house totems and emblems.[46] Consequently a Tlingit potlatch or feast was an occasion of communion between the dead and living members of related houses from both moieties.

The primary purpose of the potlatch was to honor and show respect for the dead members of one's clan. The means of honoring the dead were to give away gifts and food. Not to give a potlatch or to give away few gifts was to show disrespect for the clan ancestors and was accompanied by loss of individual and house standing in the community.[47] Individual and house rank was determined by how much was given away at potlatches. Rich men were in the best material circumstances to undertake elaborate potlatches and earn the higher-ranking potlatch titles. Wealth was easily translated into rank in Tlingit society, but material accumulation was a means to an end. A man did not consume his wealth, but accumulated it in order to honor clan ancestors in the potlatch and make his name and house honorable within the community.[48] The more wealth given away, the greater the extent to which reciprocal obligations to the related houses of the opposite moiety were fulfilled, and the greater the honor to the individual, house, and clan ancestors.

Individual and house rank in Tlingit society was linked to the moral obligation to honor clan ancestors with feasts and giveaways.[49] Men who were active in obtaining and managing wealth had the means to fulfill the morally necessary and community monitored potlatch obligations. Individual achievement, social mobility, and the accumulation of wealth were sanctioned by the Tlingit sociocultural system. Houses and individuals who showed the greatest respect and honor for the ancestors were accorded the highest moral and social prestige. In Tlingit society, moral and social standing was contingent on accumulated wealth, since only the wealthy could show proper respect for the clan ancestors. A person whose actions did not conform to the moral standards of the community was considered to be of low caste.[50] Since only through the accumulation of wealth could individuals or houses advance or maintain their social rank, the primary Tlingit value of honoring ancestors legitimated clan and individual rank based on differential capabilities to materially underwrite potlatch giveaways. The accumulation of wealth was not an end in itself but a means of fulfilling Tlingit values and moral obligations.

While some aspects of Tlingit society—the accumulation of wealth, competition, and social mobility—appear similar to those of Western societies, the Tlingit value of honoring the clan dead through the potlatch giveaway gave a very different orientation to Tlingit norms in comparison to Western culture. Tlingit material accumulation cannot be defined as rational capitalism in the Weberian sense or as capitalism in the Marxist mode of production sense. Economic production in Tlingit society was based primarily on the house-kinship group. There was no formally free labor force that was required to sell its labor power on the market in Tlingit society. There were slaves who were captured in warfare, and their labor was exploited to increase wealth, but such a labor form is not capitalism for Marx or rational capitalism for Weber. While the Tlingit traded luxury goods with interior tribes, most Tlingit economic activity was devoted to subsistence and the accumulation of luxury goods for exchange in the potlatch. The Tlingit did not accumulate wealth as a means to reinvest capital in economically productive enterprises that might result in more profits and more reinvestment in the means of production.[51] Although there was rational calculation, amassing of wealth, and exploitation of slave labor, Tlingit values and culture directed that wealth be expended for the purpose of honoring clan ancestors rather than for economic investment and further accumulation. Perhaps Tlingit material accumulation can be termed a form of "social capitalism," since the distribution of wealth in a potlatch was the means of gaining moral approbation, social prestige, and rank.[52]

## Polity and Economy

The Tlingit polity and economy were not differentiated from the Tlingit kin-ship system. The primary political and economic units in Tlingit society were the house matrilineal kinship groups. The house economic estate consisted of territory that gave the house access to fishing, hunting, and gathering grounds. The house chief was responsible for managing the house economy.[53] Similarly, there was no political center in traditional Tlingit society. The Tlin-git did not have an institutionalized national council or political hierarchy that made binding decisions on matters of national interest. There was no formal political organization beyond the authority of the house chiefs, except per-haps the village headman who was the chief of the highest rank in the vil-lage.[54] The village chief was chosen according to his rank within the kinship system or societal community, and consequently there was little indication of a political system that was differentiated from the rank and kinship relations of the Tlingit societal community. Primary political commitments and loyal-ties were reserved for the household kinship group.[55] The Tlingit polity con-sisted of segmentary house kinship groups that were organized into clans and moieties. The clans and moieties, however, never functioned as collective po-litical groupings.[56]

In summary, traditional Tlingit society was relatively nondifferentiated. The cultural system defined social rank and explicitly legitimated the kinship organization of the societal community, which dominated the organization of the Tlingit polity and economy. In the precolonization period, Tlingit cul-ture, values, and norms did not support political centralization or any signifi-cant forms of economic or political differentiation. Therefore the nondifferentiated Tlingit social structure and Tlingit culture and norms can-not, by themselves, provide an explanation for the political and economic dif-ferentiation in the postcolonial period. Nevertheless, the nonascriptive, achievement, and acquisitive norms of Tlingit society may help us understand the potential of further societal differentiation of the post-Western contact period. An explanation for Tlingit social change, however, cannot depend only on internal social and cultural variables, but must also look to the impact of world economic markets, colonization, and the interpenetration of West-ern values for an explanation for the political and economic differentiation of Tlingit society in the postcontact period.

## Differentiation before 1912

Early Tlingit contacts with Europeans centered around the fur trade. Euro-peans traded metal goods, tools, guns, and other articles of manufacture for otter and seal skins, which found a lucrative market in China. Through the fur trade the Tlingit and other northwest Alaska coast societies were drawn into the world economic system.[57] The Tlingit were active and shrewd traders, and some houses controlled monopolies on internal trade routes. By acting as middlemen between the Europeans and the interior tribes, some Tlingit houses gained significant profits. Houses that monopolized trade routes used the new economic opportunities afforded by the fur trade to increase their wealth and, through giveaways in the potlatch, to increase their social and political prestige in Tlingit society.[58] Houses that resided farther from the trade routes were less able to accumulate wealth and tended to be of lower caste rank.[59] The fur trade increased both the availability of wealth and competition for social rank. "The Tlingit were well adapted to compete with the Europeans at their level of interest. Europeans wanted furs and the Tlingit wanted prestige items, and both wanted to increase their own wealth and social standing."[60] Families with lower birthrights challenged wealthy leading lineages. Competition increased between houses and among individuals as the new wealth gathered from the fur trade was channeled into more elaborate potlatches.[61]

Between the early 1800s and 1867 the Russians maintained two settlements in southeast Alaska at Sitka and Wrangell. The Russians, however, were not able to politically dominate the Tlingit, although efforts were made to incorporate the house chiefs into a system of indirect rule and to curtail Tlingit clan feuds and the sacrifice of slaves at potlatches. At Sitka, the Tlingit traded foodstuffs at a daily local market on which the Russian settlement depended for survival.[62] The material life of the Tlingit, however, changed with the fur trade economy. There was increased economic effort to produce for a market, and new demand and dependency on externally produced manufactured goods, especially metal goods, guns, and, later, traps. By the 1820s, the Tlingit had overexploited the local supply of fur-bearing sea animals and were forced to hunt land animals in order to supply European traders. Some Tlingits converted to the Russian Orthodox religion, and the population declined owing to the introduction of new diseases associated with contact with Europeans. During the Russian period, the Tlingit did not institutionalize a political center or society-wide political organization. While the Tlingit were incorporated into the fur trade, they did not abandon their subsistence economy, which continued to rely on fishing, hunting, and gathering. Much greater change in Tlingit society came after the U.S. purchase of Alaska in 1867.

The U.S. government did not assume administration of Alaska until 1877, after which the forces of change in Tlingit society were greatly accelerated.

The Tlingit became politically subordinated to U.S. law and administration, incorporated into U.S. commercial and labor markets, and interpenetrated with U.S. values from missionaries and schools. By 1900, many Tlingit were absorbed into the U.S. economy. Tlingit men began working in the Alaskan gold mines, fished for the canneries, cut timber, hunted and trapped, worked on steamships, packed for mines, worked as guides and interpreters, and made traditional crafts for the tourist trade. Tlingit women worked in the canneries and salteries, did laundry, and made baskets and beadwork.[63] In the late 1870s two commercial fishing and canning companies moved into southeast Alaska, and by 1914 there were forty canneries. The canneries provided the Tlingit with opportunities for wage labor employment and also created a demand for a commercial fishing market. The canning industry, however, usurped control over the better salmon streams and monopolized most of the salmon harvest. Tlingit landownership was not recognized in the transfer of territory between Russia and the United States. Hence the Tlingit houses were denied legal rights to traditional salmon streams, which formed a large part of their subsistence economy. By 1910 the Tlingit had lost control over most of their traditional subsistence base resources.[64] Tlingits found it difficult initially to finance fishing boats, but increasingly fishing became the primary economic occupation of the men in the outlying villages. The canneries provided seasonal work from April to September for whole families, who migrated to the canneries when work was available and returned to their winter villages when the work season was over. Most Tlingit were unskilled laborers and few engaged in capitalistic entrepreneurial activities.[65] Commercial fishing with boats, besides providing a marketable product, also allowed the Tlingit to sustain a subsistence-level economy by fishing, which was also supplemented by hunting activities.[66] Consequently the Tlingit were not completely disassociated from the means of production. In Marxist terms, many Tlingit were semi-proletarianized, meaning that part of their livelihood was earned in the subsistence economy while they sold their labor power to the canning industry.

There are no statistics available on the extent to which the Tlingit were absorbed into the southeast Alaska labor and commercial economy; historical reports indicate that many Tlingit were active participants in the new commercial fishing and wage labor markets. Shortage of labor in Alaska made the Tlingit an attractive labor source. Efforts by the canneries to import Asian workers were opposed by the Tlingit on the grounds that the Tlingit were willing to supply the labor needs of the canneries. "Within a few years after United States acquisition of the territory, the Tlingit were busying themselves with every job they could get."[67] While the loss of traditional house salmon runs was a push factor for the Tlingit to enter the commercial fishing and wage labor markets, Tlingit sociocultural orientations provided additional impetus for the Tlingit to seek material gain in the newly available U.S. markets. The Tlingit, with their traditional emphasis on individual achievement and accumulation of wealth as a means to validate social rank, actively participated in the new markets.[68] House chiefs, who were the traditional economic managers in Tlingit society, were themselves early engaged in the fur trade and in trade with the Americans. House leaders did not significantly resist Tlingit participation in the new markets, but rather encouraged participation in commercial fishing and cannery labor. There was little dispute as to whether the Tlingit would participate in the commercial economy.[69]

As commercial fisheries took over their source of wealth, Tlingit could at least find employment utilizing their traditional skills of sailing and fishing. Because their attitude toward economic competition had much in common with that of their new masters, they had less difficulty in substituting the new system of wage earning and profits for the old system of subsistence and barter by which they had lived for many generations.[70] In general, the Pacific northwest cultures adapted to the discipline of wage labor and a market economy more easily than Native Americans of other cultures.[71]

Wyatt argues that there are several reasons within Tlingit society and culture that motivated the Tlingit to seek economic gain in U.S. commercial and labor markets.[72] While the Tlingit were eager to earn cash in order to purchase commodities and raise their material standard of life, they also sought to acquire wealth in order to uphold traditional institutions. Although U.S. authorities tried to curtail the blood revenge and settlement of civil infractions between the clans, these institutions continued informally in some villages into the 1920s. Settlements often required payment from the offending clan, and cash or goods purchased by cash were one way to settle accounts. The potlatch continued to attract Tlingit attention and wealth. The new economy presented new opportunities to acquire wealth that was necessary for potlatch distributions. For example, a Presbyterian lay worker at one village noted in 1904 that "a few years ago the only ambition of many a native seemed to be to earn a few hundred dollars that he might give a big feast to his friends, and so make his name 'high' among the tribes, even though he might have to live the remainder of his days in poverty."[73] Giving potlatches was one motivation to earn money among the Tlingit, and large potlatches continued into the first decade of the present century despite U.S. government and missionary opposition. The payment of shamans for medical services also constituted an additional need to earn cash income within the traditional society.

Incorporation in markets contributed to the increased differentiation of economic organization from Tlingit kinship structure. The primary economic unit, the traditional communal house, began to break up into nuclear family units. Younger Tlingit protested against the social constraints of the traditional communal houses, and during the 1890s many preferred to move into single-family U.S.-style houses, which were considered more comfortable and prestigious. Many Tlingit migrated in search of employment to nearby towns such as Sitka, Wrangell, Juneau, and Ketchikan, where they moved into single-family houses.[74] During the 1880s and 1890s the Tlingit, because of missionary influence and a declining population (a drop from 10,000 to under 5,000 by 1912), began to concentrate into year-round villages. Missionaries, with the intention of proselytizing and bringing education to the Tlingit, persuaded the Tlingit to gather near the missions and live in nuclear family houses. The missionaries encountered difficulties when they tried to locate a mission near a particular group of houses because the other houses in the territory refused to relocate or attend mission activities at the site of other house groups. Consequently missionaries were forced to seek neutral locations for their missions that were acceptable to all of the rival house groups in the area. By the early 1900s, the Tlingit were concentrated in thirteen villages and towns. They left their old communal houses and either migrated to nearby towns or formed permanent villages consisting of single-family houses that were congregated around Protestant missionary churches and schools.

Tlingit economic activity became more individualistic. Oswalt argues that the shift to a trapping trade economy led to increased economic individualism and the relative decline of the house as a primary economic unit.[75] Individual trappers moved onto house lands and staked out exclusive trapping territories. Similarly, Tollefson and Oberg agree that the fur trade trapping economy obligated individual men to occupy trapping territories within the house domain.[76] House economic activities became less important after the fur trade. The dissolution of the house economy was further accelerated during the 1880s and 1890s with the introduction of commercial fishing and wage labor forms of economic activity. Economic activity became an individual and nuclear family matter.[77]

U.S. political domination and administration led to increased differentiation of education and judicial functions from the Tlingit societal community. After 1880, the Alaska territorial government took over control of Tlingit judicial affairs and imposed U.S. laws over Tlingit society. Informally, however, Tlingits preferred to settle their own affairs within the clan-based retributive system of justice. As late as the 1920s, many Tlingit secretly continued traditional forms of justice, while at the same time outwardly conforming to U.S. law and procedures. It is doubtful during this early period that most Tlingit internalized U.S. law and procedures.[78] Furthermore, just as U.S. law and administration refused to recognize Tlingit kinship-house claims to territory, the U.S. government refused to recognize Tlingit clans and houses as political units. U.S. law recognized villages as political units, although villages were not well-defined groups in Tlingit society.[79]

Protestant missionaries lauded Tlingit willingness to work for pay but discouraged the potlatch as a waste of money. Nevertheless, some Tlingit maintained a belief in witchcraft and animism well into the 1920s, and a general belief in rebirth was held by most of the older generation into the 1960s.[80] The Tlingit, while not willing to surrender their own culture, were willing to adopt education and some Christian practices, which they believed facilitated absorption into the U.S. occupational structure. Missionary contact coincided with Tlingit dispossession and incorporation into commercial fishing and wage labor markets, and the Tlingit house leaders were generally willing to accept the aid and advice of the missionaries as a strategy of adapting to changing economic and political conditions.[81] Education offered by the missionaries provided linguistic and cultural skills such as reading and arithmetic that were necessary for obtaining jobs in the U.S. economy.[82] Schools were welcomed and students encouraged as a means to enhancing the prospects of future material gain.[83]

While traditional clan judicial functions were absorbed by U.S. courts and economic and education activities were increasingly differentiated from the moiety-clan system, the Tlingit societal community continued to operate. Missionaries and U.S. government agents attacked Tlingit beliefs and the potlatch but did not directly threaten the kinship system. Most Tlingit retained identifications to house, clan, and moiety groups.[84]

## Differentiation of a Political Center

In 1912, a group of twelve Tlingit and one Tsimshian formed the Alaska Native Brotherhood (ANB).[85] The organization had a constitution, bylaws and elected officers, and within a few years formed local camps, which sent three delegates to an annual grand camp meeting. Business was conducted according to rules of parliamentary procedure. An auxiliary, the Alaska Native Sisterhood, was organized on similar principles a few years later. By the mid-1920s, most native communities in southeast Alaska had ANB chapters.[86]

The ANB was formed in response to the declining social, economic, and political conditions of the indigenous societies in southeast Alaska. As indicated earlier, the Organic Act of 1884 gave Alaska territorial status but did not define the civil, legal, and land rights of the Alaska natives. Alaska natives were not granted U.S. citizenship, nor were their rights to traditional kinship fishing streams and territories recognized by U.S. courts. Consequently, by the 1890s the U.S. fishing industry had appropriated the most productive Tlingit salmon-fishing streams and relegated the Tlingit to smaller streams, commercial fishing, and wage labor as a means to gain a livelihood. Furthermore, the Tlingit were reduced to minority status as U.S. citizens began to outnumber the native population in southeast Alaska. The Tlingit also felt culturally oppressed, since U.S. officials and missionaries were attacking Tlingit beliefs and agitating for an end to potlatches.[87] By 1910, "the Indians regarded their economic problem as their major one, but the question of their civil rights was related."[88] The primary goals of the early ANB were to provide an organizational basis for Alaska natives to gain U.S. citizenship, equal civil rights, and a return of dispossessed territories.[89]

The initial formation of the ANB had few roots in traditional Tlingit culture.[90] The ANB was formed by a group of Christianized and acculturated men who strongly identified with the values of U.S. society and firmly rejected traditional culture and society. The ANB founders received education from Presbyterian missionaries at the Sitka Training School or were active in the Presbyterian or Russian Orthodox churches. "It is doubtful that the organizers could have done as effective a job or sacrificed so much without the religious commitment and personal dedication that they had to their cause."[91] Others who had been educated on the U.S. mainland joined the founders, and together they encouraged Christian morality, education, civil government, commercial participation, and preservation of Indian history; they also worked against social discrimination and moved to improve health and labor conditions.[92] "The Christian perspective of the Brotherhood, then as now, formed a common bond among the members."[93] Grand camp meetings were opened with the singing of "Onward Christian Soldiers," and in the early days the Bible was read and interpreted to the annual convention. All prayed together as a unified community, "which was reflected in a standard of selflessness that put aside all meanness."[94] "This period of time is fondly remembered by old time members as a time of action comparable to a religious revival."[95]

Between 1912 and 1920, the ANB leadership favored the abolition of traditional customs that were considered a bar to U.S. citizenship. The leadership of the ANB remained acculturationist throughout the history of the brotherhood. The executive committee vetoed traditional dancing at ANB meetings until the early 1950s, and then relented only after bitter opposition. The early assimilationist orientation of the brotherhood, however, encountered opposition from local house leaders, who were not eager to abandon Tlingit traditions but favored and encouraged participation within the ANB as a means to form a collective organization that could combat social discrimination and pursue native political and economic goals. After 1920 the ANB central leadership agreed to a policy of preserving traditional customs. Nevertheless, it was Christian values, organization, and procedures that dominated the ANB, while local house leaders upheld more traditional values.

Changes in Tlingit social solidarity were associated with the development and organization of the ANB. The concentration of the Tlingit into permanent villages led to changes in clan-moiety and potlatch relations. The disintegration of the communal house, relative Tlingit impoverishment, and population decline all contributed to the pooling of wealth among clans in order to maintain potlatch obligations. Moiety unity and moiety participation in the potlatches became more emphasized as opposed to traditional house participation.[96] Tlingit moieties came to play a central role in Tlingit potlatches. After 1912 every clan in the community participated in the potlatch. This more broadly based potlatch system served to create greater solidarity between the clans and ameliorate internal conflicts between rival clans and houses. The ANB stressed brotherhood and moiety unity. Now moiety groups were hosts in the potlatch, while the guests in the potlatch were the members of the opposite moiety.[97]

The ANB was differentiated from the Tlingit societal community in the sense that the Tlingit kinship system had no formal role in the organization and operation of the ANB. The Tlingit clan and moiety categories of social organization were not recognized by the ANB, which as a voluntary organization recruited its membership according to individual commitment. Clan and moiety rank did not carry over into rank and office in the ANB. Nevertheless, there are affinities between ANB and Tlingit norms. Tlingit norms of individual achievement, nonascriptive leadership criteria, rank, and competition favored the Tlingit in adopting the procedures and organization of representative government.[98] For example, the Tlingit do not necessarily vote for fellow clansmen or moiety members, and often fellow clansmen compete for the same office. Past service, education, ability to manage one's affairs in the U.S. economy, and willingness to assume non-self-interested leadership are criteria for gaining office in the grand camp or local camps of the ANB. At least one past president of the ANB credits the wisdom of the Tlingit ancestors and elders for the emphasis on achievement criteria in the selection of ANB leadership.[99]

The ANB became an influential force in Alaska politics; it lobbied for passage of the act that granted U.S. citizenship to Native Americans in 1924. In

1928, the ANB test case guaranteed Tlingit and native children access to public schools in Alaska. An ANB boycott in 1929 led to the gradual removal of discriminatory signs from public facilities. The ANB worked for passage of the Alaskan Antidiscriminatory Act of 1946, as well as for extended workmen's compensation legislation, aid to dependent children, and relief for aged Alaska natives. It represented Alaskan fishermen and cannery workers in labor negotiations until the union was consolidated with the CIO in the mid-1940s. Through ANB efforts the Indian Reorganization Act of 1936 was extended to Alaskan villages. The Alaskan villages were then enabled to organize legal claims against the United States for lands lost during early colonization. Between 1929 and 1971 the ANB supported legal cases and provided political support to a variety of land suits against the United States. In 1965, the Tlingit and Haida won a joint suit against the United States for lands taken to create the Tongass National Forest. Furthermore, the ANB provided scholarships to students, worked to preserve the Indian subsistence economy from U.S. intervention, assisted the elderly and destitute, and contributed other social benefits to southeastern Alaska natives.[100] In effect, the ANB became a powerful political force that provided the southeastern Alaska natives with a collective political organization that could effectively compete and protect their social, political, economic, and cultural interests within the framework of U.S. society.

In summary, the formation of the ANB, or Tlingit political center, was dependent on a variety of factors. U.S. political combination and associated legal, social, and political subordination of the southeast Alaska natives, as well as the dispossession of southeastern Alaska native land and economic resources, were all structural conditions that threatened economic, political, and social interests of the southeastern Alaska natives. However, such an argument by itself cannot account for the formation of the ANB. Why didn't the Tlingit fragment politically like so many other American Indian societies have done before the onslaught of U.S. political domination and market economy? An answer to this question lies in the continuity and strengthening of the solidarity of the Tlingit kinship moiety system. Given that the Tlingit solved the problem of integration, what traditional values legitimated collective political organization beyond the house group? There were none. Protestant missionaries and the U.S. school system externally introduced the cultural models, norms, and values that uphold the ANB. A highly acculturated Presbyterian Christian group of southeastern Alaska natives formed the ANB and they took their values, procedures, and models of collective organization from their missionary mentors. Thus the interpenetration of new values and models of political organization, increased solidarity within the societal community, the structural conditions of political and social subordination, and economic dispossession combine to explain the formation and institutionalization of a differentiated political center in Tlingit society.

## Further Economic and Political Differentiation

Since the formation of the ANB, two new organizations have been formed by southeastern Alaska natives—the Tlingit-Haida Central Council (THCC) and Sealaska Corporation, both of which represent further developments in political and economic differentiation.

In 1929, the ANB decided to pursue the right to sue the United States for loss of territory. After ANB lobbying efforts, the U.S. Congress passed the Jurisdictional Act of 1935, which granted the Tlingit and Haida the right to present a land claims case against the U.S. government. Between 1935 and 1939, a specially appointed ANB committee failed to develop a case. The ANB convention of 1939 decided to form a political organization, the THCC, to prepare the claim. Between 1941 and 1956, an experienced ANB leader headed the THCC, and a land claim case was presented in 1947. After twelve years the THCC won recognition of ownership of traditional lands under U.S. law. Since the ANB was an organization whose membership was not restricted to the Tlingit and Haida, the U.S. government ruled that the ANB could not represent the Tlingit and Haida in court, nor could the ANB manage the distribution of proceeds connected with the case. In 1959 the THCC was recognized by the U.S. as manager of the funds ($7.5 million) awarded in the land claims suit. In 1965 the U.S. government recognized the THCC as the governing body of the combined Tlingit and Haida tribes of southeast Alaska.[101] The following year a convention was held to reorganize the THCC. A movement emerged to demand a 100 percent per capita distribution of the land claim funds, but ultimately the money was kept as an endowment to finance the THCC. The THCC became a nonprofit organization dedicated to improve the social and economic welfare of the Tlingit and Haida. The THCC administers economic development, employment, housing, and education programs. Between 1966 and 1985 the THCC administered and contracted for numerous government aid and Bureau of Indian Affairs programs and built a small scale bureaucracy that was financed by the claim's endowment and Alaska state and federal sources. Currently the THCC has twenty-one local community councils, which elect one delegate for every hundred registered Tlingit and Haida voters. The delegates meet at an annual convention to elect officers and an executive committee, which governs when the convention is not in session. The THCC has the power to manage Tlingit and Haida affairs and property.[102]

Between 1966 and 1971 the THCC represented southeast Alaska natives in a movement that was aimed at regaining rights to traditional territory.[103] With the enactment of the Alaska Native Claims Settlement Act of 1971 (ANCSA), the U.S. Congress legislated a compromise solution between the state of Alaska, interested oil companies, and the united Alaska Native groups, who were called the Alaska Federation of Natives (AFN). ANCSA granted to the Alaska natives nearly $1 billion in compensation and the right to retain 44 million acres of land. In addition, it provided for the establishment of thirteen regional profit-making corporations and numerous village corporations. The regional corporations were to manage the land estates and administer the distribution of funds. The ANCSA plan allowed native leaders to control economic and financial resources free from administrative constraints of the U.S. government and the Bureau of Indian Affairs. According to the ANCSA, the regional corporations were not required to pay income tax for twenty years and the stock in the corporations was not transferable until 1991. After 1991, new transferable stocks were to be issued and the regional corporations would lose their tax-exempt status. The possibility of significant sales of stock by native shareholders enabling corporate takeovers presented new threats to the Alaska native control of regional corporations, land, and resources. Much of the action of the AFN is currently directed toward securing a method to ensure native control of the regional corporations, land, and resources after the expiration of the 1991 protection of the ANCSA.

The THCC was designated to form the regional corporation in southeast Alaska, and the Sealaska Corporation was incorporated in June 1972. According to the regulations of the ANCSA, Sealaska would eventually receive $200 million; about half of this would be redistributed to the village corporations or passed out as per capita distributions. Sealaska received $100 million as capital and was given control over the mineral rights of the native land in southeast Alaska. The Sealaska Corporation was initially owned by nearly 16,000 southeast Alaska natives, each of whom owned one hundred shares in the corporation.

By 1982 Sealaska operated much like a holding company, having either bought existing companies or organized new companies. Sealaska owned a large fish-packing subsidiary, a construction company, a sea transportation company, a timber subsidiary, and a business loan company. Furthermore, Sealaska owned small percentages of oil lease tracts off the North Slope of Alaska, as well as some real estate. In 1981 Sealaska had sales of $224 million and was ranked 745 on the Fortune 1,000 list.[104] In subsequent years, sales have advanced at a slower rate to nearly a quarter of a billion dollars, although profit margins have been meager owing to a sluggish U.S. economy and the strong U.S. dollar, which discourages the export of Sealaska's major products of fish and timber.

## Contemporary Tlingit Society

The four major institutions in current Tlingit society are the Sealaska Corporation, the THCC, the ANB, and the moiety-clan system. The ANB, the "grandfather" institution, is considered to have the most prestige and is viewed as the structure that laid the foundations for the creation of the THCC and Sealaska. While the ANB is considered the seminal institution, its actual political influence has declined in recent years as more specialized institutions have taken over some of its tasks. Sealaska, with its substantial concentration of economic resources, is now the most powerful Tlingit-Haida institution. Nevertheless, as a voluntary association the ANB is free to pursue political goals and engage in political activities that are not proper for both the THCC and Sealaska. The ANB endorses political candidates, campaigns on political issues that affect its membership, organizes and mobilizes voter participation, and presents arguments before state and federal commissions and committees. The ANB continues its role as guardian of the southeast native political, economic, and cultural interests. The THCC administers social programs designed to aid the Tlingit and Haida, while Sealaska has the task of managing and developing land and resources. A division of labor has emerged among the differentiated institutions; activities are consciously coordinated by the leadership in order to maximize the possibility of attaining Tlingit-Haida goals.[105]

The THCC, Sealaska, and the ANB are specialized institutions that manage Tlingit-Haida relations with the U.S. economic and political system, but the core of Tlingit society remains in the clan-moiety system and the potlatch complex. While the ANB, the THCC, and Sealaska are differentiated from the clan-moiety system in the sense that their operations are not organized or determined by kinship or ceremonial prerogatives, there is a complex and intimate relation between the kinship system and the differentiated institutions.

As noted earlier, at the turn of the twentieth century and in association with the new collective solidarity espoused by the ANB, Tlingit potlatches were transformed from events involving related lineages to events that included community members of both moieties. The clan-moiety system continues to operate in the organization and obligations of the potlatch. Clan and house groups, however, do not openly participate in political activities, do not own land (villages now control land as ANCSA corporations), are not economic units, and are functional primarily in the ceremonial activities of funerals and potlatches. Contemporary potlatches are one- or two-day affairs, often held on weekends. The northern villages of Hoona and Angoon and the city of Juneau hold the larger potlatches. The southern and Haida villages have less elaborate potlatch ceremonies. Death, funeral obligations, and honoring of the dead remain central features of Tlingit culture. The contemporary potlatch is focused on honoring dead clan relatives.[106] The Tlingit are still conscious of their obligations to give a potlatch and conscious of the value of the things that are given in a potlatch. Families that give small potlatches are not highly regarded. The total value of goods given away in a potlatch are compared, and more prestige is associated with the giving away of larger amounts of money and goods. Individual achievement is recognized by potlatch rank. Contributions to a funeral or potlatch are recorded and announced publicly, and outstanding material or service contributions are specially honored with potlatch gifts and attention.[107]

Nevertheless, potlatch rank is not exclusively given to men who participate actively in the ceremonies. Men who have shown leadership ability and gained private economic success are sometimes drafted into potlatch (clan) rank, despite their lack of knowledge of potlatch etiquette. A former president of the THCC and chairman of the board of Sealaska informed me that he was instated as a house chief although he had little traditional knowledge and had participated sparingly in potlatch ceremonies.

Traditionally the potlatch signified solidarity between related lineages. During the present century, however, the Tlingit have increasingly emphasized moiety participation in the potlatch, although related households continue to make up the core of a potlatch distribution and associated mutual obligations. The unity of the clans and moieties is tied directly to the potlatch ceremony in the mutual endeavor to fulfill the value of honoring the clan ancestors. In traditional society a show of disrespect might trigger open conflict and revenge on the part of the offended house, but in contemporary society a show of disrespect results in dissatisfaction with the potlatch and a tendency to grant the hosts less esteem for their potlatch efforts. If the potlatch is satisfactory for the guest moiety, the honor and reputation of the host clan is increased and good feelings prevail between the houses and clans. Rivalries and competition between clans and houses continue in Tlingit society, especially in the isolated village communities where clans and houses can influence the management of ANCSA village corporations and village government.[108]

While the solidarity of the clan-moiety system (or Tlingit societal community) is tenuous and culturally grounded, the combined moiety figures of the eagle and raven are used as symbols of collective identity. The logos for both the ANB and Sealaska are the joined figures of a raven and eagle, which symbolize the unity of the two Tlingit moieties or whole society. Furthermore, as both the Haida and Tsimshian have eagle and raven moiety systems and associated potlatch cultures, the joined eagle and raven is a symbol of unity for all three major southeastern Alaskan societies. The use of the joint symbol as the logo for the ANB and Sealaska is a means of symbolically integrating these differentiated institutions with the societal communities of the southeastern Alaska native societies. The leadership positions of the ANB, Sealaska, the THCC, and the moiety-clan system operate like interlocking corporate directorates. Many members of the Sealaska board of directors have held prominent positions within the ANB and THCC and are from large families of high caste within the traditional kinship system. For example, in 1982, thirteen of eighteen board members were leaders within the traditional tribal system or had strong family support for their election to the board. Four persons were considered contemporary leaders who were elected to the board based on their abilities as businessmen or political leaders. Six members of the board had played prominent roles in the ANB or Alaska Native Sisterhood, and at least four members served in prominent leadership positions in the THCC. One board member, who had been on the board since Sealaska's incorporation, was serving a second term as president of the THCC, was a past president of the ANB grand camp, and was serving on the ANB executive committee. He also participated with his clan in potlatch ceremonies.[109] Most members of the board participated to some extent in each of the major Tlingit institutions.

All leadership positions in the ANB and the THCC and on the board of Sealaska are elective. Several criteria play a role in gaining access to prominent positions of leadership in anyone of these organizations. Family support, caste, economic success, and visible leadership ability are all important criteria in the selection of Tlingit leadership. Members of upper-caste lineages still tend to dominate leadership in Tlingit institutions. A man who is born into a prominent lineage has access to power if he shows ability and leadership qualities. Being born into a commoner lineage is not, however, an ascriptive bar to leadership if the person shows visible leadership capabilities. A man (or woman) can gain visibility through willingness to work for Tlingit goals in the ANB, where people can see his or her commitment and leadership qualities. Service in the ANB is often considered a training ground for future leaders. Personal economic success in the U.S. economy is another criteria for leadership, since a man who cannot manage his own personal economic affairs will not be entrusted with managing Tlingit collective affairs. The Tlingit continue to equate leadership, wealth, and wisdom. The achievement criteria of proven leadership capabilities and personal economic success are more salient than knowledge and participation in traditional Tlingit social activities. For example, one board chairman of Sealaska had little knowledge of or willingness to participate in traditional Tlingit social institutions such as potlatches. This was a source of grumbling among people from his home village, but he was nevertheless generally considered to be the man most capable of managing Sealaska. Another board member, who was from the small Tsimshian group, did not have strong family support but had a past record of leadership in the AFN and in the movement that led to the ANCSA.

Support from one's clan and village does play an informal role in the selection of leadership for Tlingit institutions. Candidates for office do not openly rally for support from their clan or village. Informally, however, clan leaders and elders may endorse a candidate and inform their kinsmen of the choice. The clan elders, however, can only endorse a candidate; each person decides independently how to vote in any given election. For example, a THCC president informed me that his sister, who was an influential member of his matrilineal clan, rarely gave him her political support. If a clansman is running for an important office, clan membership may be one criteria for voting for him, if the man is capable and respected. The influence and relation of the traditional clan system to the differentiated institutions of the THCC, the ANB, and Sealaska play themselves out primarily through informal networks of votes. Clan elders and prominent clan matrons can have an impact on the selection of Tlingit leadership through use of their influence to support specific candidates and issues.[110]

In summary, contemporary Tlingit is composed of differentiated economic and political institutions, while at the same time the Tlingit societal community remains undifferentiated from the Tlingit cultural and value system. Tlingit culture and values continue to motivate participation in the potlatch ceremonies, provide a sense of common identity, and legitimate the moiety-clan organization of the Tlingit societal community. The Tlingit emphasis on individual achievement, competition, economic success, rank, and individual mobility continue to operate within the potlatch complex and are also operative within the frameworks of the differentiated economic and political institutions.

## Discussion

A dependency argument would emphasize that the Tlingit, starting with the earliest fur trade era, became increasingly incorporated into the world economic system. The Tlingit increasingly produced for markets and, especially in the present century, have come to rely primarily on commercial fishing and seasonal labor. Tlingit villagers have been semiproletarianized since they rely on fishing for part of their subsistence requirements. Tlingit village economics are subject to variations in fish markets, which affects both the price of fish sold to canneries and the demand for Tlingit wage labor.[111] The Sealaska Corporation depends on the production of primary goods such as timber and canned fish. Furthermore, the Tlingit were subject to colonial political and cultural domination by the United States. There can be no denying the economically dependent and politically subordinate nature of Tlingit society. Nevertheless, a dependency argument does not explain the formation of a Tlingit political center (ANB), the formation of the THCC and Sealaska, or the continuity and importance of Tlingit cultural and clan-moiety institutions.

On the other hand, the differentiation and institutionalization of Sealaska, the THCC, or the ANB did not derive from an unfolding of preexisting structures within the Tlingit societal community or from the generalization of Tlingit values. The Tlingit clan-moiety system did not provide the organizational base or collective solidarity for any of the differentiated institutions. The Tlingit values of honoring the clan ancestors did not legitimate the organization and goals of the ANB, the THCC, or Sealaska. The ANB was formed in 1912 to struggle against loss of Tlingit land, loss of civil rights, and changing economic conditions. These conditions, however, were not sufficient, since Tlingit kinship organization and tenuous social solidarity did not enable the Tlingit to form a concerted collective political organization. The founders of the ANB rejected traditional culture and tried to form an organization based on Protestant values, rules, and forms of organization. Protestant Presbyterian values were instrumental in the formation of the ANB, and it was these values, not traditional Tlingit values, that supported the collective instrumentality of the ANB and its derivative organizations, the THCC and Sealaska.

Nevertheless, many central aspects of traditional culture persisted. The increasing social solidarity of the Tlingit societal community and the support of the newly differentiated institutions by the clan and house leaders were critical to their institutionalization and continuity. The ANB leadership has been more acculturated than the rank-and-file membership. Early conflict between kinship leaders and the ANB leadership centered on the place of traditional culture in Tlingit affairs. Ultimately the ANB leadership was forced to tolerate and help preserve traditional culture. The more traditional clan leaders gave their consent to the new institutions because they were seen as instruments for preserving Tlingit culture and for regaining land and civil rights.

While Tlingit culture and values did not directly legitimate the differentiation of political and economic institutions, Tlingit belief in rebirth and a nonsalvation worldview legitimated this-worldly orientations and social inequality, while the Tlingit value of honoring the dead legitimated rank based on individual economic achievement. Tlingit acquisitiveness was a "pull" factor in the readiness of the Tlingit to accept wage labor employment and participate in the U.S. economy. Tlingit culture does not, however, legitimate capitalist accumulation in the sense of rationally organizing the means of production in response to market demands.[112] Tlingit accumulation was oriented toward honoring the deceased clan ancestors in potlatches, since this was the route to honor and high caste in Tlingit society. Furthermore, the principles of leadership selection in the three differentiated institutions continue to follow the traditional emphasis on economic success and proven leadership ability. These nonascriptive and achievement-oriented criteria for leadership supported the organizational and instrumental requirements of the THCC, Sealaska, and the ANB.

In conclusion, both dependency and functional differentiation arguments are not sufficient, by themselves, to account for Tlingit political and economic differentiation. Tlingit political and economic differentiation was not the result of a natural unfolding of the societal community, but rather was created in direct response to specific conditions of political, economic, and social subordination in combination with the acceptance of Protestant values by a leadership group, increasing social solidarity, and cultural orientations that legitimated individual achievement and material accumulation. Although Tlingit society represents a small-scale case, it illustrates the need for analyzing social change with a consideration for endogenous factors of culture, social solidarity, and processes of differentiation in conjunction with the exogenous factors of market incorporation, geopolitics, and the interpenetration of new values and belief systems. Because of the increasing importance of transsocietal political, economic, and cultural relations in recent world history, such a comprehensive internally-externally open framework will be necessary in order to more fully understand contemporary social change processes.

# Notes

I gratefully acknowledge research and writing support from the Rockefeller Foundation and National Science Foundation grant number RII 85-03914. An earlier version of the chapter appeared as Duane Champagne, "Culture, Differentiation, and Environment: Social Change in Tlingit Society," in *Differentiation and Social Change: Historical and Comparative Perspectives* ed. Jeffrey C. Alexander and Paul Colomy (New York: Columbia University Press, 1990), pp. 52–87.

1. Eric Wolf, *Europe and the People without History* (Berkeley: University of California Press, 1982).

2. Anthony Giddens, *Central Problems in Social Theory* (Berkeley: University of California Press, 1979), p. 223.

3. Robert Nisbet, *Social Change and History* (New York: Oxford University Press, 1969), p. 251.

4. S. N. Eisenstadt and M. Curelaru, *The Form of Sociology: Paradigms and Crises* (New York: Wiley, 1976), p. 95.

5. Kenneth Bollen, "World System Position, Dependency and Democracy," *American Sociological Review* 48 (1983): 468–79; Samir Amin, Giovanni Arrighi, Andre Gunder Frank, and Immanuel Wallerstein, *Dynamics of Global Crisis* (New York: Monthly Review Press, 1982).

6. Ronald Chilcote, "Introduction: Dependency or Mode of Production? Theoretical Issues," in *Theories of Development,* ed. Ronald Chilcote and Dale Johnson (Beverly Hills, CA: Sage, 1983), pp. 20, 25.

7. Aijaz Ahmad, "Imperialism and Progress," in *Theories of Development,* ed. Ronald Chilcote and Dale Johnson (Beverly Hills, CA: Sage, 1983), p. 40.

8. Wolf, *People without History*; Anibal Quijano, "Imperialism, Social Classes, and the State in Peru, 1890–1930," in *Theories of Development,* ed. Ronald Chilcote and Dale Johnson (Beverly Hills, CA: Sage, 1983), pp. 107–38; Ronald Chilcote and Dale Johnson, *Theories of Development* (Beverly Hills, CA: Sage, 1983).

9. Henry Veltmeyer, "Surplus Labor and Class Formation on the Latin American Periphery," in *Theories of Development,* ed. Ronald Chilcote and Dale Johnson (Beverly Hills, CA: Sage, 1983), p. 204.

10. Norma Chinchilla, "Interpreting Social Change in Guatemala: Modernization, Dependency, and Articulation of Mode of Production," in *Theories of Development,* ed. Ronald Chilcote and Dale Johnson (Beverly Hills, CA: Sage, 1983), p. 163.

11. Theda Skocpol, *States and Social Revolutions* (New York: Cambridge University Press, 1979); Otto Hintze, *The Historical Essays of Otto Hintze,* ed. Felix Gilbert (New York: Oxford University Press, 1976).

12. Skocpol, *States,* p. 32.

13. Talcott Parsons, *Social Systems and the Evolution of Action Theory* (New York: Free Press, 1977), pp. 285–86.

14. R. N. Bellah, "Religious Evolution," *American Sociological Review* 29 (1964): 358–74.

15. Parsons, *Social Systems,* p. 230.

16. Parsons, *Social Systems,* pp. 51–52; Parsons, *The Evolution of Societies* (Englewood Cliffs, NJ: Prentice-Hall, 1977), p. 114.

17. Chalmers Johnson, *Revolutionary Change* (Boston: Little, Brown, 1966), pp. 65–67, 92.

18. Bertrand Badie and Pierre Birnbaum, *The Sociology of the State* (Chicago: University of Chicago Press, 1983), pp. 58–59.

19. S. N. Eisenstadt, "Institutionalization and Change," *American Sociological Review* 29 (1964): 246–47.

20. S. N. Eisenstadt, "Institutionalization," pp. 246–47.

21. S. N. Eisenstadt, *Revolution and the Transformation of Societies* (New York: Free Press, 1978), pp. 196–204.

22. Eisenstadt, *Revolution,* p. 13.

23. Max Weber, *General Economic History* (New Brunswick, NJ: Transaction, 1981), p. 369.

24. For a review of the literature discussing potlatch behavior, see Margaret Sequin, *Interpretive Contexts for Traditional and Current Coast Tsimshian Feasts,* Canadian Ethnology Service Paper no. 98 (Ottawa, ON: National Museum of Man, 1985).

25. Frederica de Laguna, "Some Dynamic Forces in Tlingit Society," *Southwestern Journal of Anthropology* 8 (1952): 2–7.

26. Frederica de Laguna, *Under Mount St. Elias: The History and Culture of the Yakutat Tlingit* (Washington, D.C.: Smithsonian Institution Press, 1977), p. 451.

27. Kalevero Oberg, *The Social Economy of the Tlingit Indians* (Seattle: University of Washington Press, 1973), p. 40.

28. Catherine McClellan, "The Interrelations of Social Structure with Northern Tlingit Ceremonialism," *Southwest Journal of Anthropology* 10 (1954): 83–86, 96.

29. Esther Billman, ed., "A Potlatch Feast at Sitka, Alaska," *Anthropological Papers of the University of Alaska* 14 (1969): 55–64.

30. Lewis Coser, *The Functions of Social Conflict* (New York: Free Press, 1956), p. 33.

31. Abraham Rosman and Paula Rubel, "The Potlatch: A Structural Analysis," *American Anthropologist* 74 (1972): 658–71; Julia Averkieva, "The Tlingit Indians," in *North American Indians in Historical Perspectives,* ed. Eleanor Leacock and Nancy Lurie (New York: Random House, 1971), pp. 317–42.

32. R. L. Olsen, "Social Structure and Social Life of the Tlingit in Alaska," in *Anthropological Records* (Berkeley: University of California Press, 1967), 26:6.

33. Oliver Salisbury, *Quoth the Raven: A Little Journey into the Primitive* (Seattle: Superior, 1962).

34. Max Weber, *The Religion of India* (New York: Free Press, 1958), pp. 18–25; Coser, *Social Conflict,* p. 37.

35. Max Weber, *Max Weber on Capitalism, Bureaucracy, and Religion,* ed. Stanislov Andreski (Boston: George Allen & Unwin, 1983), p. 89.

36. Aurel Krause, *The Tlingit Indians* (Seattle: American Ethnology Society, 1956), p. 193; Ian Stevenson, "Seven Cases Suggestive of Reincarnation among the Tlingit Indians of Southeastern Alaska," *Proceedings of the American Society for Psychical Research* 26 (1966): 234.

37. Stevenson "Seven Cases," p. 231.

38. Stevenson, "Seven Cases," pp. 197, 234; Kalevero Oberg, "Kinship Sentiment and the Structure of Social Action," in *Exploring the Ways of Mankind,* ed. Walter R. Goldschmidt (New York: Holt, Rinehart & Winston, 1960), pp. 290–95.

39. Laguna, *Yakutat Tlingit,* p. 611.

40. Salisbury, *Quoth the Raven,* p. 43.

41. J. R. Swanton, "Social Condition, Beliefs, and Linguistic Relationship of the Tlingit Indians," *Twenty-Sixth Annual Report of the U.S. Bureau of American Ethnology, 1904–05* (Washington, D.C.: U.S. Government Printing Office, 1908), p. 343.

42. Swanton, "Social Condition," pp. 343, 462.

43. Swanton, "Social Condition," p. 463.

44. Frederica de Laguna, "Tlingit Ideas about the Individual," *Southwestern Journal of Anthropology* 10 (1954): 185–91.

45. McClellan, "Northern Tlingit Ceremonialism," p. 80.

46. Averkieva, "Tlingit Indians," p. 331.

47. Salisbury, *Quoth the Raven,* p. 210.

48. Oberg, *Social Economy,* p. 103.

49. Salisbury, *Quoth the Raven,* p. 215.

50. Swanton, "Social Condition," p. 427.

51. Robert Spencer and Jesse Jennings, *The Native Americans* (New York: Harper & Row, 1965), pp. 188–90.

52. Salisbury, *Quoth the Raven*, p. 40.

53. Kenneth Tollefson, "A Structural Change in Tlingit Potlatching," *Western Canadian Journal of Anthropology* 7 (1977): 17–20.

54. Wendell Oswalt, *This Land Was Theirs* (New York: Wiley, 1978), p. 335.

55. Oberg, *Social Economy*, pp. 24, 30.

56. Olsen, "Social Structure," p. 1; Oberg, *Social Economy*, p. 48.

57. Wolf, *People without History*, pp. 182–94.

58. Olsen, "Social Structure," p. 4; Laura Klein, "Contending with Colonization: Tlingit Men and Women in Change," in *Women and Colonization*, ed. Mona Etienne and Eleanor Leacock (New York: Praeger, 1980), pp. 94–96.

59. Swanton, "Social Condition," p. 427.

60. Klein, "Women in Change," p. 96.

61. Averkieva, "Tlingit Indians," p. 334.

62. Paul Golovin, *Civil and Savage Encounters* (Portland: Oregon Historical Society, 1983), pp. 82–85.

63. Victoria Wyatt, "History of Relations between Indians and Caucasians in Southeast Alaska" (Ph.D. diss., Yale University, 1984).

64. Tollefson "Tlingit Potlatching," p. 21.

65. David H. Looff, "Growing Up in a Dying Community," in *The Dying Community*, ed. Art Gallaher and Harland Podfield (Albuquerque: University of New Mexico Press, 1980), p. 209.

66. Federal Field Committee, *Alaska Natives and the Land* (Washington, D.C.: U.S. Government Printing Office, 1968), p. 283.

67. Philip Drucker, *The Native Brotherhoods: Modern Intertribal Organization on the Northwest Coast*, Bureau of American Ethnology Bulletin 168 (Washington, D.C.: U.S. Government Printing Office, 1958), p. 10.

68. Drucker, *Native Brotherhoods*, pp. 9–10.

69. Drucker, *Native Brotherhoods*, pp. 38–40.

70. George W. Rogers, *Alaska in Transition* (Baltimore, MD: Johns Hopkins University Press, 1960), p. 179.

71. Philip Drucker, *Cultures of the North Pacific Coast* (San Francisco: Chandler, 1965), pp. 211–14.

72. Wyatt, "Southeast Alaska."

73. Wyatt, "Southeast Alaska."

74. Olsen, "Social Structure," p. v; Kenneth Tollefson, "From Local Clans to Regional Corporation: The Acculturation of the Tlingit," *Western Canadian Journal of Anthropology* 8 (1978): 10.

75. Oswalt, *This Land*, p. 365.

76. Tollefson, "From Local Clans," p. 5; Oberg, *Social Economy*, pp. 60–61.

77. Samuel Stanley, "Changes in Tlingit Social Organization," (Xerox copy, 1965), pp. 19–21; Drucker, *Cultures of the North Pacific*, p. 221.

78. Salisbury, *Quoth the Raven*, p. 228.

79. Stanley, "Tlingit Social Organization," pp. 5–6.

80. Stevenson, "Seven Cases," p. 192; Olsen, "Social Structure," p. v.

81. Drucker, *Cultures of the North Pacific*, p. 218.

82. Wyatt, "Southeast Alaska."

83. Krause, *Tlingit Indians*, pp. 230–31.

84. Drucker, *Cultures of the North Pacific*, p. 218; Tollefson, "Tlingit Potlatching," pp. 16–24.

85. The Haida, Tlingit, and Tsimshian are similar societies of the northwest Alaska coast. They share the potlatch complex, belief in rebirth, and the dual kinship structure between the

Raven and Eagle moieties. While the man who originated the ANB was a Tsimshian, most of the members of the ANB have been Tlingit, mainly because the Tlingit are the largest group in the area. Today the three groups share and participate in the potlatch complex, the ANB, and several other organizations. There are subtle differences in the culture and social organization of each group, but a comparison of the three societies is beyond the scope of this discussion. The Tlingit dominate the ANB, but the two other groups are represented and integrated politically and socially. Nevertheless, clear distinctions remain and it is difficult for the Haidas and Tsimshian to gain the highest positions in the institutions shared by all three groups.

86. Drucker, *Native Brotherhoods*, p. 21.

87. *The Alaska Fisherman,* special ed. (Juneau, AK: Tlingit-Haida Central Council, 1980), p. 2.

88. Drucker, *Cultures of the North Pacific*, p. 222.

89. Tollefson, "From Local Clans," p. 1; Andrew Hope III, *Founders of the Alaska Native Brotherhood Sitka, Alaska,* special ed. (Xerox copy, 1975), p. 2.

90. David Case, *The Special Relationship of Alaska Natives to the Federal Government: An Historical and Legal Analysis* (Anchorage, AK: Alaska Native Foundation, 1978), p. 142.

91. Hope, *Alaska Native Brotherhood,* p. 2.

92. *Alaska Fisherman*, p. 1.

93. *Alaska Fisherman*, pp. 3–4.

94. *Alaska Fisherman,* p. 28.

95. Herbert Hope, "An Overview of ANB History," *Alaska Native News*, 1983, p. 14.

96. Tollefson, "Tlingit Potlatching," pp. 23–24.

97. Tollefson, "Tlingit Potlatching," pp. 23–24.

98. George W. Rogers, "Party Politics and Protest: Current Political Trends in Alaska," *Polar Record* 14 (1969): 453–54.

99. Duane Champagne, Field Notes: Interviews and Observations (unpublished data source, Department of Sociology, University of California, Los Angeles, 1982).

100. *Alaska Fisherman*, pp. 1–2; Tollefson, "Tlingit Potlatching," pp. 13–17.

101. Peter Metcalf, *The Central Council of the Tlingit and Haida Indian Tribes of Alaska: An Historical and Organizational Profile* (Juneau, AK: Central Council of the Tlingit and Haida Indian Tribes, 1981), pp. 1–10.

102. THCC [Tlingit-Haida Central Council], "The 'Tlingitization' of Social and Economic Programs." *Alaska Native News* 1, no. 2 (1982): 30–31.

103. A discussion of the social movement that led to the enactment of the Alaska Native Claims Settlement Act of 1971 (ANCSA) is beyond the scope of this discussion. The interested reader should consult Robert Arnold, *Alaska Native Claims* (Anchorage, AK: Alaska Native Foundation, 1978), and Gerald McBeath and Thomas Morehouse, *The Dynamics of Alaska Native Self-Government* (Lanham, MD: University Press of America, 1980).

104. *Sealaska Shareholder,* 1981–1982 (Juneau, AK: Sealaska Corporation, 1982).

105. *Sealaska Shareholder,* p. 8.

106. Laguna, *Yakutat Tlingit*, pp. 531, 611; Champagne, Field Notes.

107. Champagne, Field Notes.

108. Champagne, Field Notes.

109. Champagne, Field Notes.

110. Rogers, *Alaska in Transition*, p. 257; Stanley, "Tlingit Social Organization," pp. 40–53; Hope, *Alaska Native Brotherhood.*

111. Looff, "Growing Up"; Averkieva, "Tlingit Indians."

112. *Sealaska Shareholder.*

# Economic Incorporation, Political Change, and Cultural Preservation among the Northern Cheyenne

# 14

M
ANY NATIVE AMERICAN COMMUNITES are confronted with the dilemma of choosing between preserving tribal culture and asserting self-government based on participation in the increasingly globalized market economy. Most tribal communities are not averse to economic development and market participation; nevertheless, if they have a choice, they do not prefer economic change that may seriously change their culture and institutional relations. Native American governments and communities will prefer economic development that supports and upholds community culture and sovereignty. The patterns of economic development on the Northern Cheyenne reservation are conditioned by market relations and external bureaucratic control, but economic decision making and the capacity and willingness of the Northern Cheyenne community to institute capitalist economic enterprises are subject to and informed by Northern Cheyenne cultural orientations, economic values, and the form of differentiation of Northern Cheyenne institutions. Within the external economic and political constraints imposed by the world economy and the American bureaucracy, the Northern Cheyenne attempted to realize their own cultural ends and preserve their own social and political institutions.

For many American Indian communities, such as the Northern Cheyenne, the process of acceptable and enduring market-based economic development will require negotiation and consensus building over the effects of institutional change and economic values associated with market participation. Within a self-governing Native community, economic innovations that do not gain sustained Native community and institutional support will not endure and therefore will not provide enduring access to market opportunities. As global market forces and the U.S. market economy are extended over more aspects of reservation life, Native communities are increasingly tested to find culturally acceptable ways to participate in the market and not sacrifice cultural community and identity. The ways in which Native communities will address the challenges of the marketplace depends on their specific cultural orientations, institutional relations, and market exposure. The conservative Northern Cheyenne pattern of economic change is most likely found among many Native communities; nevertheless, each community has a holistic cultural and institutional order that will require specific forms of negotiation and processes of tribal government and community relations in order to make accommodations to market forces. In this chapter, I analyze the Northern Cheyenne community's strong resistance to economic market participation that does not support their primary cultural and historical values of community and cultural preservation.

## Theoretical Overview

In recent years theories of economic development for peripheral societies have had a decidedly materialistic bent, while the theories of modernization are generally considered in disfavor. Modernization theories are considered to be based too much on the historical conditions and experience of European economic development. In the post–World War II period, economists sought to industrialize the economies in third world nations, but after several decades economic progress in many peripheral societies did not come near the expectations of the early development strategists.[1]

As an alternative, dependency theories sought to explain the absence of autonomous domestic economic development in many non–European countries from a materialistic perspective of unequal market relations in the world economy.[2] More recently, however, the mode of production and articulation of mode of production theorists have challenged the primarily market-centered and transsocietal emphasis of the world-system theorists.[3] The latter theorists argue that internal class relations should theoretically predominate over world-system relations, although world-system relations interconnect extant and multiple (capitalist and precapitalist) modes of production. Chinchilla, for instance, argues that while the overall determinant of change is economic, there are degrees of freedom for autonomous conflict in the cultural and political spheres, which can make independent contributions to social and economic change.[4]

The trend toward analytical emphasis on internal political and economic factors is also seen in recent investigations into the autonomy of the state, where the world-system is relegated to a background condition rather than a primary determinate of intrasocietal political relations.[5] The latter researchers and the articulation of mode of production theorists argue that the interrelations between economic and geopolitical transsocietal contexts and intrasocietal must be investigated empirically and that no grand theory is yet able to explain the variation in state and society relations or the variation in economic and societal development in the periphery.

The dependency and autonomy of the state literature often assumes that social actors are rationally motivated. They speak in terms of rational economic decision making, competitive markets, and rationalized bureaucratic action. Applied to non-Western societies, however, such assumptions of instrumental/purposive rationality may not hold. Max Weber's investigations into the causes of the rise of capitalism in the West were premised, in part, on the unique form of cultural rationalization that characterized Western culture but was not characteristic of other major cultures in world history.[6] Weber proposed a multidimensional approach to explaining the development of capitalism, arguing that rational bookkeeping, calculable law and administration, and a free labor force are necessary but not sufficient conditions for the rise of capitalism.[7] According to Weber, rational capitalism was not possible until Protestant values legitimated individual accumulation of wealth and provided motivation and moral legitimation for sustained competitive market participation.[8] After the market system came into being, it developed a logic of its own that forced men to participate competitively or suffer impoverishment. Parsons disagrees with Weber's analytical atomism and with notion of a rationalized economy that is not regulated by societal norms and values.[9] Parsons proposes a systematic analytical framework for understanding the relations between values, culture, norms, polity, economy, and personality. Although Parsons advocated an evolutionary theory of social change, the paradigm of societal differentiation need not be wedded to evolutionary theorizing and can be useful for analyzing the internal relations of any social-cultural system. Nevertheless, since the theory of societal differentiation largely provides a set of categories for conceptualizing social order and social action, the specific relations of societal differentiation, and the content and imperatives of culture, norms, and values on political and economic action can be determined only after empirical investigation.[10]

Like the mode of production theorists and the advocates of the autonomy of the state perspective, some neofunctionalist theorists have placed their analysis within the context of transsocietal, especially world-system contexts. The neofunctionalist, while attempting to extend their analysis with the incorporation of conflict, relations of culture and power, and the negotiability of social system environments, also recognize the necessity of nesting their analysis with transsocietal geopolitical and world-system contexts.[11] The convergence of all three theoretical perspectives on incorporating geopolitical and world-system contexts within their modified theoretical or methodological frameworks is a recognition of the force that transsocietal relations have in contemporary social change patterns. Nevertheless, the three theories do not consider geopolitical or world-system contexts as determinant over internal political, class, or sociocultural relations.

Economic development on the Northern Cheyenne reservation occurred in the context of external bureaucratic domination and economic dependency, but such conditions, while powerful, do not exhaust all the possibilities of social and economic action on the part of the Northern Cheyenne. This approach is informed by studies of voluntarism or human agency under external coercive conditions such as were obtained among the English working class as given by Thompson, and American Black slaves as told by Genovese, and by the theoretical investigations of coercive and normative arguments by Alexander.[12] In an analogous way, Hall argues that American Indians have also played an active role in interpreting and responding to the process of incorporation into the world-economic system.[13] Consequently, in following the latter line argument, it is argued that while bureaucratic domination and economic dependency explain the limiting conditions for economic development among the Northern Cheyenne, external coercive conditions do not explain the Northern Cheyenne interpretation of bureaucratic and dependency conditions, nor do they explain the willingness or lack of willingness to participate in commercial economic enterprises nor do they totally explain Northern Cheyenne economic decision making. Northern Cheyenne culture, values, norms, and societal differentiation provide the basis for an explanation of Northern Cheyenne economic decision making and economic development patterns that complements and extends the dependency and bureaucratic domination arguments. Dependency and bureaucratic domination set material and political limits on Northern Cheyenne economic development, but within those limits Northern Cheyenne normative and cultural order further specifies Northern Cheyenne social action and decision making in the economic sphere. In the following analysis, I wish to describe and explain the pattern of economic development on the Northern Cheyenne reservation. I begin with some background on Northern Cheyenne culture and society.

# Northern Cheyenne Institutions

Traditional Northern Cheyenne political and social structure were integrated by the religious sphere and were subordinate to it. In the early European contact period, the Cheyenne, an Algonkian-speaking people, were probably located in Canada. They were forced by European expansion and intertribal warfare to migrate to present-day Minnesota and then onto the plains during the latter half of the 1700s. On the plains, ten bands formed the Cheyenne society. Associated with the transition to the plains culture based on buffalo hunting came a religious movement that reorganized Cheyenne ceremonial life and determined the superordination of the religious sphere over all other aspects of Cheyenne society. Perhaps around the year 1775, a prophet named Sweet Medicine gave the Cheyenne a sacred bundle of four arrows and established a code of sacred laws that were understood to have been handed down directly from the Cheyenne supreme being, Maheo, or the Creator. Acting as an intermediary between the Cheyenne people and the Creator, Sweet Medicine brought a covenant from the Creator to the Cheyenne people. If the Cheyenne would conform to the law transmitted by Sweet Medicine and perform the prescribed ceremonies, then the Creator would ensure the cultural and physical survival of the Cheyenne. The sacred arrow bundle symbolized the covenant relation with the Creator, and as long as the Cheyenne kept it in good condition and ceremonially renewed it every year, then the Cheyenne would prosper as a people. Two arrows symbolized control over animals to ensure good hunting, while the other two arrows symbolized control over man. The power of the sacred arrows inform all aspects of Northern Cheyenne society and are symbolic of unity and communication with the Creator.[14] The sacred arrow bundle was the Cheyennes' greatest resource for ensuring cultural and physical survival.[15] The prophet Erect Horns from the Suhtaio band brought the Cheyenne the Sacred Buffalo Hat and the Sun Dance. The Sun Dance was performed for world renewal, while the ceremonial care of the Sacred Buffalo Hat also ensured tribal survival and well-being.

Since the Cheyenne were a peripheral people forced across half a continent to avoid the onslaught of the European colonial expansion, physical and cultural survival was a central concern and was reflected in the cultural and religious orientations of the tribe.[16] For the Cheyenne, their survival was linked to their adherence to traditional laws and norms, religious beliefs, and the continuity of the ceremonial ways that maintain and renew the sacred tribal bundles. The Creator had a purpose for every Cheyenne, but enlightenment in regard to the Creator's purpose and meaning could be gained only through participation in the ceremonial and sacred life of the tribe.[17] Individual ends were religiously and ceremonially integrated into the tribal goal of cultural and physical survival. Northern Cheyenne cultural orientations are this-worldly, emphasizing tribal well-being and survival in the present world. There is no individual otherworldly salvation as in Christianity or as Weber emphasized in the Protestant ethic, but there was a belief in transformation or transmigration. Those who acted against the Cheyenne moral-religious order or died in a bad way, a death irrelevant to tribal ends, forfeited their right to reincarnation or spiritual participation in the tribal community.[18] Consequently the individuals who contributed to tribal preservation helped ensured that future generations of Cheyenne, and their own transmigrated or spiritual existence, would have a place in the tribal community. The spirits of the Cheyenne were believed to advise and participate in tribal society even after death. The Northern Cheyenne emphasis on cultural and physical survival was institutionalized in religious and ceremonial activities, and internalized by the individual through belief in reincarnation and spiritual participation in tribal life after death.[19]

## Economic Norms and Values

The Cheyenne valued wealth and the wealthy man only if the wealth was ceremonially redistributed within the tribe to nonkinsmen. Wealth was not accumulated merely for personal consumption or investment in further economic gain; rather, the distribution of wealth affirmed the good character of the giver and promoted interpersonal and kinship solidarity between the giver and the receiver.[20] Chiefs and all men aspiring to tribal leadership were required to provide material aid to anyone who was in need. A chief who did not or could not provide material aid to the needy lost esteem and respect within the community. He was called a "nothing chief." In the period when the Cheyenne lived on the Great Plains, men accumulated horses through raiding enemies and gained prestige by giving the horses away to the old, the poor, and relatives, while keeping only a few for themselves.[21] Sharing material goods was the means to establishing respectful relations with other tribesmen and keeping care of fellow kinsmen.[22] Ideally obligations for sharing wealth have precedence over individual material interests and accumulation.

Individual Cheyenne achievement orientations were focused on the acquisition of sacred knowledge, powers, and abilities, which were transferred through participation in Cheyenne ceremonies and religious life, as well as dreams and visions.[23] Young men were actively encouraged to seek the personal sacred knowledge, and with religious instruction, they obtained higher symbolic ranks. Without sacred knowledge, man could not become a full adult or survive in a world that the Cheyenne considered potentially threatening to tribal and individual survival.

While Cheyenne were encouraged to develop their individuality, ultimately the abilities and powers of the individual were oriented toward serving the tribal group.[24] Tribal ceremonies promoted tribal religious integration, which discouraged familialism, competition, and factionalism.[25]

For the Cheyenne, the land and sacred bundles were gifts from the Creator and were considered public property, while private goods were to be generously shared with other tribal members.[26]

## Polity

In traditional Cheyenne society, the religious sphere predominates, legitimates, and defines the political structure. When the prophet Sweet Medicine handed down the Creator's laws, they included the organization of chiefs from the ten bands into a council of forty-four members. Every ten years, the bands would select four leaders, usually the headmen of the dominant lineages within the bands. Four men from the group of retiring chiefs were selected by the new council to serve as "old man chiefs." One man from the new group of chiefs was selected to be the Sweet Medicine chief. A primary purpose of the Council of Forty-Four was to organize the annual ceremonies and buffalo hunt. On the plains the Cheyenne gathered communally only during the summer to carry out the ceremonies and hunt buffalo. During most of the year, they were divided into the ten bands at different camping and hunting locations. The Council of Forty-Four made political decisions, but only after consulting with the warrior societies and gaining their assent to the decisions of the council. The four soldier societies implemented council decisions.

The Creator himself bestowed the Council of Forty-Four directly to the Cheyenne. When in council, the chiefs were believed to be in direct communication with the Creator through his prophet, the Sweet Medicine chief. The Creator directly and explicitly legitimated negotiated and unanimous decisions of the council. A religious figure headed the council, and many council functions concerned ceremonial matters. The Creator guided and directed the Cheyenne through the Council of Forty-Four. The religious or spiritual sphere was an integral part of the Cheyenne political organization; the political structure itself was a sacred gift.[27]

A chief to the Council of Forty-Four was not delegated political authority; his influence depended on the will of the kinsmen and band members who had selected him as chief. Council decisions were discussed until the entire council came to unanimous agreement. Even the Sweet Medicine chief could not speak for the council without unanimous consent and agreement. Ideally, a chief served the people and expressed their views in the council.[28] Thus the Cheyenne polity was not differentiated from community consensus and negotiated decision making.

The Cheyenne had a religiously integrated political structure; kinship ties were not formally recognized as an organizing principle of the Council of

Forty-Four. The ten traditional bands were composed of lineage groups, but membership in a particular band was made by choice, not determined by kinship affiliation or inheritance. Within the band groupings, the dominant lineages controlled the bands and selected their own kinsmen for chieftainship in the Council of Forty-Four. Kinship ties were nevertheless important politically within the bands. When a man addressed the council, he was assumed to be speaking on behalf of his extended kinship group. The tribal religious ceremonies focused on tribal-wide commitments, while kinship allegiances were considered secondary to religious-political integration. The Council of Forty-Four did not manage the tribal economy, although the symbolism of the sacred arrows ceremony was thought to ensure the availability of hunting animals. At the annual buffalo hunt, the council designated one of the soldier societies to police and organize the hunt. Throughout the year, bands and kinship groups managed the gathering of their own economic subsistence, while Cheyenne values and norms regulated the redistribution of wealth from the more successful hunters and war leaders to the orphans, elderly, and the poor.

Traditional Cheyenne society was dominated by the tribal religious system.[29] The political structure was integrated and organized by religious myth, while tribal social solidarity was premised on the tribal ceremonial activities, the symbolic unity of the sacred bundles, and the shared norms and laws that were handed down from the Cheyenne supreme being. The Cheyenne normative order and political structure were regulated and informed by Cheyenne religion, while kinship affiliation was a secondary principle of political organization. Strong normative emphasis was placed on the redistribution of wealth rather than private consumption.

## Economic Dependency

The Northern Cheyenne are now located in eastern Montana on a half-million-acre reservation. During the early nineteenth century, the Northern Cheyenne were buffalo hunters who also traded buffalo skins with American traders. The decline of the buffalo on the plains and the final settlement of the Northern Cheyenne on the Tongue River reservation in 1884 left them without any means of economic support. They were reduced to taking government rations for subsistence, while reluctantly adopting subsistence farming and cattle raising as advised by U.S. Indian agents.[30] Tongue River reservation economic conditions were unfavorable. Most land was not tillable and most tillable land was already farmed by U.S. citizens who had claims preceding 1884. Furthermore, the reservation was one hundred miles from the nearest railroad station, which discouraged marketing of agricultural crops.[31] Between 1900 and 1914, most Americans were removed from the reservation and the Indians agents tried to establish a reservation economy by distributing cattle to individual families. After 1914, a new Indian agent introduced a program of subsistence farming that lasted until the early 1930s.[32] Even during this period, farming and raising cattle were not enough to maintain economic subsistence. Indian Affairs officials provided government rations on a monthly basis.[33] By 1932, owing to drought, depression, and marginal land resources, the Northern Cheyenne became disillusioned with dry farming, while the Tongue River reservation cattle range was not sufficient to support the Northern Cheyenne population as a whole.[34] Between 1932 and 1940, about 90 percent of the Northern Cheyenne obtained their living on relief funds or employment as wage laborers in New Deal programs. The reservation economy based on New Deal programs collapsed, however, in 1942. In the 1950s, the Northern Cheyenne had few consistent sources of income, and regular reservation unemployment was perhaps as high as 80 to 90 percent and median family income was $936.[35] During the 1960s, there were few economic opportunities and most employment came from antipoverty programs, missions, tribal government bureaucracy, and jobs with the local offices of the Bureau of Indian Affairs.[36]

Today, 87 percent of Northern Cheyenne are wage laborers, while about 10 percent (50 to 70 families) are engaged in ranching. In 1975 the median reservation income was $5,402, less than half of the national median income of $13,720. Per capita income was about one-fourth the per capita national income. The Tongue River reservation unemployment rate is at least 40 percent. Many Northern Cheyenne do not migrate for employment because most have not fared much better off the reservation.[37] The tribal government was the largest employer on the reservation with four hundred employees in 1980, most of whom were employed by federally funded programs. The three reservation schools and one mission school were the next largest employers (300), while the BIA employed 70 and total private sector employment in timber, ranching, retail business, mining, and construction was 230.[38] In the market economy, ranching is the primary productive enterprise, while farming and timber are of little significance.[39] Most of the local retail business is owned and operated by non-Cheyennes, and the prospects for local retail expansion are limited.[40] The Northern Cheyenne economy is hindered by the lack of access to private capital, the outflow of local capital, high unemployment, and an underdeveloped economic base.

Northern Cheyenne cattle and timber production are oriented to metropole markets. The Northern Cheyenne reservation was estimated to have 25 billion tons of coal deposits, of which about 5 billion tons are available to strip mining. During the energy crisis of the 1970s, coal and oil deposits in eastern Montana gained the attention of large energy corporations. By 1973, six energy companies held BIA-approved coal leases totaling 56 percent of the Northern Cheyenne reservation surface. In many respects, the Northern Cheyenne reservation economy is subject to the same economic constraints and opportunities as the rest of the rural and peripheral economy of eastern Montana. In general, the southeastern Montana economy is oriented toward producing primary goods such as coal, wheat, and cattle for market in large metropole centers.[41]

## Bureaucratic Domination

Between 1880 and 1934, the Office of Indian Affairs implemented a policy of assimilation. The traditional Northern Cheyenne chief and warrior societies were ignored while the American bureaucratic officials and managed local governmental functions, and tried turn the Northern Cheyenne into farmers and husbandmen while missionaries tried to educate and Christianize them. Cheyenne ceremonial and religious life were suppressed and forced to go underground.[42] The chief and warrior societies were excluded from political authority, but retained traditional forms of political influence on the reservation and helped organize the preservation of the Cheyenne sacred bundles.[43] In 1937, the Northern Cheyenne voted to accept a constitutional government under the provisions of the Indian Reorganization Act of 1934 (IRA), although many traditional Northern Cheyenne opposed the new government as an American attempt to destroy the old sacred form of Cheyenne government based on sacred laws given by the Creator to the prophet Sweet Medicine.[44] After establishment of the IRA government, the political influence of the traditional warrior and chiefs societies steadily declined, and both societies became more concerned with organizing ceremonial functions, while being largely excluded from political decision making.

The Northern Cheyenne IRA tribal government is subject to BIA regulation. The BIA monitors tribal government action in order to see that it observes its owns laws and constitutional articles. The BIA and the secretary of the Interior have the right to review all decisions of the tribal council and to veto or modify them if they do not conform to regulations or policy. The tribal council cannot pass laws or ordinances without approval of the BIA and secretary of the Interior. In effect the BIA, because of its assimilation mission, controls schools and training programs, economic infrastructure and regulates tribal government economic decision making. Because of treaty obligations, the BIA is responsible to see that Northern Cheyenne land and natural resources are used in the best interests of the tribe. In the capacity of their trust obligation, BIA officials are to guard against and stop any transaction that would result in the permanent loss of land or would unfairly encumber the economic resources of the Northern Cheyenne. The tribal governments do not have expertise to make contracts and, owing to the BIA's trust responsibility, the Northern Cheyenne must depend on the BIA to monitor and approve its contracts. Consequently the BIA controls and regulates the major productive resources and often makes them available through contracts to exploitation by American cattlemen and businessmen.[45]

BIA bureaucratic regulation of Northern Cheyenne economic resources and decision making creates a major obstacle to economic development, since economic development programs are oriented toward BIA interests rather than those of the tribe.[46] Current efforts to centralize and rationalize the tribal government organizations, including the Northern Cheyenne tribal government, have been interpreted as a mechanism by which the federal bureaucracy can subordinate the cultures and social structures of the energy-rich American Indian tribes and thereby gain access to natural resources (e.g., coal) that are needed for the national energy program.[47] The BIA is actively oriented toward exploiting the available reservation resources as a means of creating jobs and developing a self-sustaining reservation economy. On the Northern Cheyenne reservation, the BIA has managed the leasing of grazing lands to non–Cheyenne ranchers, monitored the harvesting and shipping of timber, and, before 1973, sold leasing agreements to coal companies for the mining of Northern Cheyenne coal deposits. As on many reservations, the BIA regulates most Northern Cheyenne reservation social and economic institutions. Tribal government leaders are subject to BIA budgets and authority, and hence are often reluctant to directly oppose bureaucratic policies and interests.

## Contemporary Northern Cheyenne Society

Many of the cultural, religious, and nondifferentiated aspects of traditional Cheyenne society have survived to the present and inform contemporary Northern Cheyenne social and economic action. Northern Cheyenne culture, values, and kinship affiliations have maintained themselves relatively intact and independent of the conditions of economic marginalization and dependency and the adoption of a formally secular and differentiated IRA tribal government organization.[48] Cheyenne norms and values are still transmitted from generation to generation, while the teachings of the prophets, the sacred bundles, and the ceremonies are still an integral part of contemporary life for most Northern Cheyenne.[49] The theme of cultural and physical survival through the preservation of traditional ways of life and through ceremonial participation continues to inform contemporary Northern Cheyenne social action.[50] "The center of social values is the tribe, the community living of Northern Cheyennes, and the concern for the continuity of this community into the past and into the future."[51]

Northern Cheyenne norms and values still do not legitimate self-interested accumulation of wealth. The giveaway continues as a primary means of redistributing wealth to fellow tribesmen. Instead of giving away horses, as was done during the traditional period, since the 1930s, food, kitchen, and household items are given away. Families pool their resources and give away tables loaded with gifts at powwows and funerals. The ideal way is to give to the poor, from whom no reciprocal gifts of comparable value can be expected.[52] The community continues value sharing and egalitarianism, which tend to inhibit self-interested profit seeking.[53] Cheyenne values emphasize cooperation, sharing, generosity, religious spirituality, and tribal welfare, in contrast to Western notions of economic rationality that emphasize competition, materialism, self-interest, and individual achievement.[54] Cheyenne values do not motivate individual economic entrepreneurship in the marketplace. The Northern Cheyenne feel that the entire community should benefit from economic development and not just individuals.[55] "Efficiency and profit orientation characterize outside development interests. . . . Cheyennes think first about the present and past welfare of their people, Tribe, culture, natural resources, and homeland."[56] Furthermore, obligations to kinship and social relations are valued more highly than making money or working regularly.[57] Saving or accumulating wealth is not congruent with Northern Cheyenne kinship obligations to materially aid relatives and friends who are in need.[58] Most Northern Cheyenne continue to evince a subsistence labor ethic; they will work to secure a local standard of material comfort or subsistence, after which they will not strive to acquire additional wealth or to maximize their income.[59]

The relation between Northern Cheyenne economic norms and values is illustrated by Morningstar Enterprises, a construction firm that was majority owned by a Cheyenne but managed by a non–Cheyenne. During the 1970s, most reservation construction was federally funded and allocated toward low-cost housing and administrative buildings. The tribe could have awarded the federal construction contracts to Morningstar Enterprises, but a faction within the tribal council opposed awarding contracts to Morningstar Enterprises, arguing that tribal members should not take advantage of their tribal membership to gain individual economic advantage or profit. Furthermore, it was argued that the owner and manager of Morningstar Enterprises would be making too much money, and that the money would not be redistributed to benefit the tribe. For these reasons, Morningstar Enterprises was not awarded a federal construction contract on the Northern Cheyenne reservation. The normative injunction that tribal members should be economically altruistic and that economic wealth should be redistributed to the needy were used to legitimate the decision to block award of construction contracts to the local Cheyenne firm.[60]

## Tribal Government and Economy

After the IRA government was adopted in the middle 1930s, the traditional religious-political structure of the chief and soldier societies was progressively excluded from political decision making, and they busied themselves with Northern Cheyenne ceremonies and religion.[61] The IRA government was an electoral system with formal delegation of decision making to a tribal chairman and tribal councilmen. The IRA government was formally differentiated from kinship and religion, and it had formally delegated power to act on behalf of the entire Northern Cheyenne people. In practice, however, many of the nondifferentiated institutional forms of the traditional Northern Cheyenne polity persist to the present day and inform Northern Cheyenne social and political action. Kinship ties, locality, religion, and community consensus decision making continue to inform Northern Cheyenne political decision making.

The IRA government is formally secular, meaning that religious institutions and beliefs do not have a direct role in the organization of the tribal government or in the political decision making process. While the Cheyenne religion and ceremonies do not directly inform the political action of the IRA government, as they informed the decision-making of the traditional Council of Forty-Four, the contemporary IRA government maintains links to the Northern Cheyenne religious and ceremonial sphere. The IRA tribal government funds tribal representatives to attend the annual sacred arrows ceremony held by the Southern Cheyenne of Oklahoma, a salary is allocated for the keeper of the Sacred Buffalo Hat, which is located on the Northern Cheyenne reservation, the chiefs and warrior societies are given a small amount of financial assistance, and the tribal government contributes to giveaways, as well as the organizing and financing of the annual Sun Dance.[62] More acculturated Northern Cheyenne view the tribal government as a secular instrumental organization, but the traditional members of the tribe still believe that Northern Cheyenne religion, prayer, and ceremonies should give guidance, purpose, and meaning to the tribal government.[63] John Woodenlegs was tribal chairman for over twenty years, and he was president of the local chapter of the Native American Church and a firm believer that Northern Cheyenne religion was the means to political and social integration of the Northern Cheyenne people.[64] Since Woodenlegs's death, recent tribal chairmen have not used traditional forms of spiritual guidance to inform their political actions. Some of the traditionalists believe that current tribal government needs religious guidance, without which the Northern Cheyenne have lost direction and political unity. The traditionalists hope that religion will be reestablished over the tribal government to the place it had before American law and political organization were established on the reservation. Solving of the social and political problems of the Northern Cheyenne requires the continued spiritual guidance of the tribal ceremonies and the sacred bundles.[65]

Kinship and locality or old band alliances continue to command the social and political allegiances of Northern Cheyenne tribal members.[66] The basic sociopolitical unit in Northern Cheyenne society is still the extended family.[67] The bureaucratic rules and regulations that the BIA enforces on the tribal government often contradict the traditional normative injunctions to give priority to the kinship ties and those in need.[68] In the economically depressed Northern Cheyenne economy, individual and family ties are often stronger than tribal collective loyalties, which creates internal competition and conflict.[69] Tribal councilmen often choose their own kinsmen to receive tribal government jobs and program benefits.[70]

In addition to the religious, kinship, and locality influences on the tribal government, the Northern Cheyenne community demands that it participate in any major decisions that are made by the tribal government. The IRA government formally delegates political authority to the tribal council, but the Northern Cheyenne community is reluctant to delegate decision-making power to a small group of men. The tribal government is considered the protector and caretaker for the culture and social organization of the tribe.[71] They do not think it is desirable to have a small group of men make their decisions . . . they feel very strongly that all segments of the Cheyenne population must be involved in the decision making process."[72] The IRA constitution allows a referendum vote on all tribal ordinances and resolutions. If the members of the community are dissatisfied with a decision, they can petition the tribal council, which then must hold a referendum vote. Consequently major economic decisions such as whether to allow coal strip mining or oil drilling on the reservation were decided by community discussion and vote, rather than by the tribal council. Routine political decision making is delegated to the tribal government, but decisions that are perceived to have a major impact on Northern Cheyenne society and culture are decided by negotiation and consensus within the community at large.

From the standpoint of external differentiation, religion, kinship, and locality as well as community norms and consensus and interaction inform
Northern Cheyenne political and economic decision making. The Northern
Cheyenne IRA tribal government also evinces an internally nondifferentiated
governmental organization. The relations between the judicial, executive, and
legislative branches are overlapping and dominated by the tribal council or
legislative branch. Most of the decision making within the tribal government
resides with the elected tribal council, while the tribal chairman generally
makes proposals and chairs the council meetings. The administration of the
tribal government is conducted by an executive committee and subcommit-
tees of the tribal council. The separation of powers between the tribal council and the tribal administration is diffusely defined. Attempts to create rules
and regulations that would define relations of authority between the legislative and administrative branches must be first passed by the tribal council and
have been voted down in recent years (1980–1983).[73] Furthermore, the IRA
constitution gives plenary power over judicial affairs to the tribal council. The
tribal courts do not have any power other than that the tribal council explicitly delegates to the courts.[74] Consequently, lawmaking, law enforcement, and
legal interpretation tend to originate in and are subject to the decisions of the
tribal council. The councilmen, however, are embedded in a web of kinship,
political, and local community demands that are consequently not insulated
from tribal bureaucratic and judicial administration. The nondifferentiated
Northern Cheyenne polity allows the politicization of the judicial and administrative spheres of government, thereby contributing to inefficient administration and particularistic administration of justice.[75]

Both the internally and externally nondifferentiated aspects of the Northern
Cheyenne tribal government directly influence economic decision making. By
tribal constitution and BIA regulation, the tribal government has decision-
making power over tribal resources and federally assisted tribal economic enterprises. Consequently, tribal government economic decision making is not based
solely on economic criteria, but is informed by the values, norms, political interests, and kinship obligations of the Northern Cheyenne community. The
nondifferentiated Northern Cheyenne polity with its control over economic decision making inhibits what in the Western world is considered economically rational decision making and efficient economic administration.

Tribal government management has difficulties supporting competitive
economic ventures and is more likely to inhibit an economic development
project than assist it. Because the tribal council is burdened with community,
kinship, judicial, political, and administrative concerns, it does not have sufficient time to give to economic management and decision making. Furthermore, the elected members of the tribal council are usually not businessmen

and most do not have expertise in economic affairs. Tribal councilmen have two-year terms, and the composition of the tribal council tends to change significantly with each election. New tribal administrations tend to abandon the projects of the previous council and initiate their own programs. Economic enterprises administered by the tribal government suffer from political interference, nonaccountability of goods and funds, internal factionalism, and an absence of technical expertise. The Northern Cheyenne have a directly interactive, politically and economically egalitarian community that recognizes age and charismatic leadership abilities more than bureaucratic authority, procedural rules, and regulations. Consequently tribal administration lacks a sound management structure for the day-to-day administration of a business enterprise.[76] Factional cleavages exist between more acculturated members of the Northern Cheyenne community who are willing to support policies of economic development and traditionalists who oppose entrepreneurship because it is contrary to tribal norms of economic egalitarianism. This leads to political delays in approving and organizing economic projects. Conflict between acculturated and traditionalist tribal members inhibits economic development because it causes disunity and transforms political discussion into controversy over fundamental concepts of culture and the purpose and meaning of economic development.[77]

Tribal political goals take precedence over economic development goals, and contract negotiations are often shunted aside owing to pressing political controversies within the tribe and tribal council.[78] The tribal government is primarily concerned with preserving tribal sovereignty and will support economic projects that facilitate tribal control over reservation resources. Any project that threatens tribal government control over reservation resources or threatens long-term Cheyenne political control will not be supported. To do otherwise would instigate hostile reactions from the reservation community, for the tribal leaders will be accused of making decisions that jeopardize the cultural and physical survival of the Northern Cheyenne people.[79] Tribal government conflict, instability, and abrupt policy changes lead to failure in the economy and in business development.[80]

# Northern Cheyenne Economic Development

According to Robert Pringle, three major attempts before the 1950s to create a self-sufficient economy on the Tongue River reservation ended in failure.[81] Attempts to build a self-sufficient economy by subsistence farming, cattle raising, and participating in New Deal programs did not succeed, and by the 1950s the Northern Cheyenne were largely unemployed and depended on government aid. While limited resources in tillable land and suitable grazing land helps account for the limited success of cattle raising and the decline of local agriculture, Pringle argues that Northern Cheyenne cultural conservatism and institutions also inhibited Northern Cheyenne willingness and ability to accept economic change.[82] While Northern Cheyenne were willing to work, they, with their religiously informed consensus and egalitarian forms of leadership, were not able to lead and manage economic or bureaucratic organizations. Northern Cheyenne workmen, while accepting bureaucratic and management authority from a non-Indian, would not accept such authority from a Northern Cheyenne, while at the same time Northern Cheyenne individuals were reluctant to exert bureaucratic authority. Consequently there was a "chronic lack of leadership, which still plagues every phase of Cheyenne life."[83] In analytical terms, Northern Cheyenne decision making and authority relations were informed by societal norms, and values and decisions were arrived at through a process of direct negotiation and consensus. Consequently the absence of bureaucratic procedures in Northern Cheyenne society inhibited the acceptance of impersonal, rational-legal, delegated, and procedural forms of bureaucratic authority from members of their own community.

Between 1937 and 1956, the Northern Cheyenne Steer Enterprise operated with an initial $2 million from an IRA loan. Pringle argues that this major attempt at Northern Cheyenne economic development experienced difficulties because of the absence of effective leadership, and the subordination of economic rationality to community political goals and values. The Steer Enterprise, as an economic organization, was not sufficiently insulated or differentiated from the direct demands of the Northern Cheyenne community. Hence the enterprise was seen as a tribal asset, and since the Northern Cheyenne were economically destitute during the late 1940s and 1950s, there was considerable community pressure on the tribal government to divide the assets of the Enterprise among the people and divide the profits evenly rather than reinvest them, as well as buy local cattle stock at higher prices than could be obtained elsewhere.[84]

Pringle argues that despite Northern Cheyenne poverty, even existing reservation resources were not used effectively. He attributes the unwillingness to maximize exploitation of reservation economic resources to the influence of Northern Cheyenne culture and values. By the 1950s, the old chief and warrior societies were still influential over most Cheyenne, Cheyenne religion was flourishing, and Cheyenne values and norms regarding material gain still were contrary to Western norms of economic rationality and accumulation of wealth.[85]

During the 1960s, the major economic strategy of the tribal government was to buy back all reservation lands that had been sold to non-Cheyenne. John Woodenlegs, then the tribal chairman, tried to buy back land that was no longer owned by enrolled tribal members. By the early 1980s, 61 percent of reservation land was controlled by the tribal council, 37 percent of the land was controlled by individuals who inherited land from the reservation allot- ment in the 1920s, and about 2 percent of the land was held in fee simple.[86] Since the establishment of the IRA tribal government in the middle 1930s, a major goal has been to buy all the allotted land and bring it back under the collective control of the tribal government.[87] The tribal government has been successful in regaining grazing rights to 88 percent of the reservation surface, which can support between 12,000 and 13,000 head of cattle. Before the 1960s, the BIA leased much of the Tongue River reservation grazing land to non-Cheyennes. The long-term strategy of regaining tribal government con- trol over all the reservation land is congruent, not necessarily with the tribal government's desire to bring it under economic production but rather with the tribal government's concern for controlling the land base in order to ensure tribal sovereignty and tribal continuity. The strategy of bringing the reserva- tion lands under collective tribal control is informed partly by economic mo- tives, but also by political and cultural motives of ensuring tribal survival.

As a rule the Northern Cheyenne tribal government has met with little success in promoting Cheyenne-operated private sector economic enter- prises. Most local reservation small businesses are owned and operated by non-Indians. Economic development projects that were at least partially funded by the federal government during the 1960s and 1970s also have met with limited success.[88]

Perhaps the two major economic events in recent Northern Cheyenne history have been the controversy over coal development in the 1970s and the ARCO deal for drilling oil in the early 1980s. Both of these events illustrate how the Northern Cheyenne made decisions that were based on ecological, economic, political, community, and cultural considerations. Although mul- tiple political, ecological, and economic considerations entered into the Northern Cheyenne decision to reject strip mining and accept oil explo- ration, these economic decisions were evaluated against and informed by Northern Cheyenne values, cultural orientations, and community consensus decision-making mechanisms.

By 1973, the BIA had signed coal mining leases with six energy compa- nies encompassing 56 percent of the Tongue River reservation surface. The leases contained relatively low royalty rates of 17.5 percent per ton and pro- posed electrical generating plants to be located on the reservation.[89] There were an estimated 5 billion tons of coal deposits for strip mining on the reservation, and U.S. energy policy was aimed at exploiting American reserves and reducing American dependency on foreign energy sources. In 1973 the tribal council was approached by an energy company that wanted to make coal leases directly with the tribe rather than pass through the BIA intermediary. The BIA normally made and monitored all Northern Cheyenne coal leasing arrangements. The energy company proposed to strip mine coal and build coal gasification facilities. Such a project would at least temporarily attract about 30,000 non-Cheyenne onto the reservation for construction, while the reservation population was no more than 3,500. The tribal council quickly realized the threat that the BIA leases held for the Northern Cheyenne community. In 1974, the tribal council submitted a legal petition to the secretary of the Interior for cancellation of the coal leases on the Tongue River reservation. The secretary was compelled to suspend the leases as the Northern Cheyenne petition cited over thirty violations of Department of the Interior rules and regulations concerning leasing contracts. Some of the gross violations were failure to undertake environmental impact statements, and many of the tracts were leased in excess of the 2,500-acre limit that was the maximum lease tract for coal leases within the Department of Interior. The secretary ruled that the lease contracts would have to be renegotiated between the Northern Cheyenne tribe and the energy companies. The Northern Cheyenne have refused to renegotiate any commercial coal leasing contracts with any of the companies, effectively nullifying the earlier BIA-negotiated leasing contracts.

The impoverished Northern Cheyenne stood to make millions from the coal leasing agreements.[90] But community opposition was so strong against commercial coal development that the tribal council would not consider renegotiation of the contracts. A survey showed that 80 percent (N = 342) of the Northern Cheyenne did not want to see the land disturbed by coal mining.[91] During the 1970s the Northern Cheyenne tribal council went into debt by employing attorneys to oppose nearby off-reservation coal mining and electrical generating plants that could adversely affect the reservation ecology.[92] Some members of the newly elected council in 1978 favored coal development, and in the summer of 1979, two coal companies approached the Northern Cheyenne with an offer for a partnership with the tribe to develop strip mining. The two coal companies offered $3 million for signing the contract and promises of over $1 billion in Northern Cheyenne profits through the next twenty years. The plan to mine commercial coal, however, failed to get widespread community support and no contract was signed, although some members of the tribal council strongly favored coal development.[93] The same group of tribal government leaders turned their attention to oil development and signed an agreement with ARCO. Traditionalist opposition groups eventually forced the tribal government to allow a referendum vote, as stated in the tribal constitution, to affirm the decision of the tribal council's contract. In summer of 1980, the referendum vote favored acceptance of the oil drilling contract, which promised an upfront per capita distribution of $1,500. Consequently the Northern Cheyenne rejected coal development by widespread community consensus, but a majority were willing to accept oil exploration on the Tongue River reservation.[94]

As already noted, an estimated 80 percent of the Northern Cheyenne opposed commercial coal development. The reasons for the widespread opposition to coal development included considerations of culture, values, ecology, politics, and economy. A survey revealed that 66.8 percent of the Northern Cheyenne thought that commercial coal development would improve reservation economic conditions. They expected more numerous and better-paying jobs, more local businesses, improved financial conditions for the tribe as a whole, and a better standard of living. Thus the Northern Cheyenne clearly had an appreciation for the economic and material benefits that would derive from coal development. The negative aspects of coal development were indicated by the Northern Cheyenne as damage to the environment, threat to the Cheyenne way of life by allowing too many outsiders onto the reservation, an expectation that most of the jobs would go to non-Cheyennes, fear of increased alcoholism and drugs, and threat of total destruction of Cheyenne culture.[95] The Northern Cheyenne favored economic development for themselves, the tribe, and for future generations only if the economic development reduced existing problems and did not create new problems.[96]

One of the greatest Northern Cheyenne fears was that the influx of outsiders associated with coal development would reduce their chances of passing their culture to succeeding generations or even surviving as a people.[97] Coal strip mining threatened the ecological destruction of the land, which their ancestors won through great sacrifice and which has symbolic and religious value. Land symbolizes Northern Cheyenne physical and cultural survival.[98] Some traditionalists don't believe that the land, because of its symbolic and sacred role in Cheyenne religion and history, should be used for commercial purposes.[99] Most Northern Cheyenne did not want economic development that would aggravate existing social problems within the community or would endanger Northern Cheyenne culture and bring a majority of non-Cheyenne onto the reservation.[100] The Northern Cheyenne elders warned that if outsiders came onto the reservation to mine coal, they would eventually control and own the reservation and subordinate the Northern Cheyenne people.[101] The traditionalist Northern Cheyenne were willing to pass up immediate and substantial economic gain if it meant that economic development would threaten their homeland, institutions, political autonomy, and culture.[102] For most Northern Cheyenne, the potential economic gain from coal strip mining was subordinated to the imperatives of political and cultural continuity. The more acculturated ranchers on the Tongue River reservation joined the traditionalists in opposing strip mining because the ecological effects of strip mining threatened to destroy the rancher's economic livelihood.

The acceptance of the agreement to allow ARCO to drill for oil on the reservation cannot be attributed to the offer of $1,500 per capita by the oil company. Similar material inducements were made in the coal contract of 1979 and could have been had even with the relatively unfavorable BIA contracts of the early 1970s. The traditionalist opposition to the oil contract was unwilling to pursue any resource development, but this position was overwhelmingly defeated in the 1980 referendum. The defeat of traditionalist opposition to the ARCO contract indicates that the traditionalists, who are not willing to subject Northern Cheyenne natural resources to commercialization, were a vocal and significant force on the reservation, but in the minority. The majority of Northern Cheyenne were willing to accept oil extraction because the economic benefits were clear and oil exploration did not threaten the land base, reservation political autonomy, and Northern Cheyenne culture in the dramatic way that a large influx of non-Cheyenne onto the reservation and massive strip mining would have threatened the reservation ecology, land base, institutions, and culture.[103]

During my fieldwork on the Northern Cheyenne reservation in the winter of 1982–1983, most of the tribal councilmen who had negotiated the ARCO contract had been removed from office, and the majority of the council was ambivalent toward the agreement, often citing examples of how the oil drilling upset the reservation water tables and ecology. When the price of oil then plummeted, external pressures on the Northern Cheyenne to sell their natural energy resources abated. There is little interest currently in Northern Cheyenne coal, and ARCO has a long-term contract to drill Northern Cheyenne oil, although preliminary drilling did not indicate commercial-size oil reserves under the Tongue River reservation. Perhaps one day, when the price of oil rises again, so too will the search for domestic oil reserves and alternative energy sources like coal. Large energy companies, with the blessing and assistance of the U. S. government and BIA, will most likely seek an accommodation with the Northern Cheyenne for extracting coal, oil, and gas. Based on the Northern Cheyenne cultural, religious, and institutional orientation toward tribal survival, it seems likely that the Northern Cheyenne will again seek to protect their tribal homeland and reject any economic initiatives that threaten tribal physical and cultural survival. Since the Northern Cheyenne are an almost infinitesimal political grouping in U S. society, their chances of successfully resisting unwanted exploitation of their natural resources is ultimately dependent on the use or restraint of force by external bureaucratic, state, and economic institutions. For the time being, American laws and bureaucracy have not infringed on the Northern Cheyenne's right to refuse commercial exploitation of their coal reserves. If, however, the world economy becomes energy poor, then changing economic conditions may force the United States to place national energy requirements above Northern Cheyenne religious and cultural imperatives to retain tribal integrity.

## Discussion

While the world-system and bureaucratic domination arguments are essential to understanding the conditions of Northern Cheyenne economic development, their rational assumptions about social action preclude them from giving a complete explanation of the economic decisions and institutional conditions of economic change among the Northern Cheyenne. If the Northern Cheyenne were motivated primarily by economic calculations, then they would be expected to sell their natural resources in order to alleviate their poverty and then move to more desirable economic locations. Such is not the case. Certainly the conditions imposed by external bureaucratic controls and by the economic marginalization caused by location and relations with metropole centers inhibit and perhaps are sufficient to prevent the formation of economic self-sufficiency among the Northern Cheyenne. Bureaucratic domination and economic dependency and marginalization interpenetrate every aspect of life on most Indian reservations. Nevertheless, the conditions of bureaucratic domination and economic dependency do not exhaust all the possibilities of social action on the part of reservation populations like the Northern Cheyenne. The Northern Cheyenne sought to express their cultural, normative, and institutional ends within the conditions imposed by economic dependency and bureaucratic domination.

From the point of view of fostering economic development on the Tongue River reservation, Northern Cheyenne culture, values, norms, and institutional order served to inhibit formation of competitive economic enterprises and reoriented Northern Cheyenne social action away from economically rational exploitation of existing economic resources and opportunities. Northern Cheyenne cultural and religious institutions orient social action toward ceremonial activities and concern for preserving culture and for tribal survival. Northern Cheyenne values do not legitimate accumulation of wealth or individual entrepreneurship. Important political and economic decisions are made by negotiation and consensus formation within the community at large. The tribal government, subject to BIA bureaucratic constraints, controls economic decision making on the reservation. The nondifferentiation between the tribal government and the economy inhibits formation of a differentiated or autonomous economic sector. Furthermore, the Northern Cheyenne polity is only partially differentiated or insulated from the cultural, kinship, normative, and value orientations of the Northern Cheyenne community. Since the tribal government is responsible for reservation economic affairs, tribal government economic decision making is also not differentiated or insulated from traditional prerogatives of kinship, culture, values, and community consensus and negotiation. Thus economic decisions are not made solely on consideration of economic criteria, but are informed by and subordinated to Northern Cheyenne societal norms, values, and political considerations. Finally, even when economic projects are approved, the internally nondifferentiated tribal government organization constrains bureaucratic rationality, implementation, and management. The domination of administration and the court system by the tribal council injects instability and arbitrariness into tribal administration and legal decision making, which inhibits conditions for the formation and institutionalization of private sector capitalistic enterprises and constrains management of economic projects by the tribal government. In general, the relations of societal differentiation in Northern Cheyenne society, which is informed by cultural and value orientations that direct social action toward noneconomic ends, all contribute toward understanding Northern Cheyenne reluctance to maximize economic exploitation of reservation economic opportunities that inhibit community control and the modest track record in tribally managed economic development projects.

# Notes

I gratefully acknowledge research support from the Rockefeller Foundation, National Science Foundation Grant SES 8503914, Ford Fellowship, Cultural Survival, Inc., and the American Indian Studies Center at UCLA.

1. S. N. Eisenstadt, *Tradition, Change, and Modernity* (New York: Wiley, 1973).

2. Andre Gunder Frank, "The Development of Underdevelopment," *Monthly Review,* September 1966, 17–31; Immanuel Wallerstein, *The Politics of the World System* (New York: Cambridge University Press, 1984).

3. Eric R. Wolf, *Europe and the People without History* (Berkeley: University of California Press, 1982); Ronald H. Chilcote, "Introduction: Dependency or Mode of Production?

Theoretical Issues," in *Theories of Economic Development,* ed. Ronald R. Chilcote and Dale L. Johnson (Beverly Hills, CA: Sage, 1983), pp. 26–27.

4. Norma Stoltz Chinchilla, "Interpreting Social Change in Guatemala," in *Theories of Economic Development,* ed. Ronald H. Chilcote and Dale L. Johnson (Beverly Hills, CA: Sage, 1983), pp. 161–62.

5. Theda Skocpol, *States and Social Revolutions* (New York: Cambridge University Press, 1979); Skocpol, "Bringing the State Back In: Strategies of Analysis in Current Research," in *Bringing the State Back In,* ed. Peter B. Evans, Dietrich Rueschemeyer, and Theda Skocpol (New York: Cambridge University Press, 1985), p. 28; Peter B. Evans, Dietrich Rueschemeyer, and Theda Skocpol, "On the Road toward a More Adequate Understanding of the State," in *Bringing the State Back In,* ed. Peter B. Evans, Dietrich Rueschemeyer, and Theda Skocpol (New York: Cambridge University Press, 1985), pp. 350, 356.

6. Max Weber, *The Sociology of Religion* (Boston: Beacon, 1964).

7. Max Weber, *General Economic History* (New Brunswick, NJ: Transaction, 1981), pp. 275–369.

8. Max Weber, *The Protestant Ethic and the Spirit of Capitalism* (New York: Scribner's, 1958).

9. Talcott Parsons, *The Evolution of Societies* (Englewood Cliffs, NJ: Prentice-Hall, 1977).

10. Parsons. *Evolution,* 1977; Niklas Luhmann, *The Differentiation of Society* (New York: Columbia University Press, 1982).

11. S. N. Eisenstadt, "Macro-Societal Analysis: Background, Development, and Indications," in *Macro Sociological Theory: Perspectives on Sociological Theory* ed. S. N. Eisenstadt and H. J. Helle (Beverly Hills, CA: Sage, 1985), 1:14, 16; Frank J. Lechner, "Modernity and Its Discontents," in *Neofunctionalism,* ed. Jeffrey Alexander (Beverly Hills, CA: Sage, 1985), 172.

12. E. P. Thompson, *The Making of the English Working Class* (New York: Vintage, 1966); Eugene D. Genovese, *Roll Jordan Roll: The World the Slaves Made* (New York: Vintage, 1976); Jeffrey Alexander, *Theoretical Logic in Sociology,* 4 vols. (Berkeley: University of California Press, 1982).

13. Thomas Hall, "Incorporation in the World-System: Toward a Critique,"*American Sociological Review* 51 (1986): 390–402.

14. Peter J. Powell, *Sweet Medicine: The Continuing Role of the Sacred Arrows, the Sun Dance, and the Sacred Buffalo Hat in Northern Cheyenne History* (Norman: University of Oklahoma Press, 1969), 1:580.

15. Henri V. Whiteman, paper read to the American Studies Convention, October 20, 1973 (Lame Deer, MT: Northern Cheyenne Planning Office, 1973), p. 1.

16. E. Adamson Hoebel, *The Cheyennes: Indians of the Great Plains* (New York: Holt, Rinehart & Winston, 1978), pp. 1–13.

17. John Woodenlegs, "The Cheyenne Way of Life," *Occasional Papers of the Museum of the Rockies* 1 (1979): 57–61.

18. Anne Straus, "The Meaning of Death in Northern Cheyenne Culture," *Plains Anthropologist* 23 (1978): 1.

19. Straus, "Meaning of Death," pp. 3–4.

20. Hoebel, *Cheyennes,* p. 99; E. Hoebel Adamson, "Personality and Culture," *Anthropology Full Circle,* ed. Ino Rossi, John Janusch, and Dorian Coppenhover (New York: Praeger, 1977), p. 231.

21. K. Weist, "Give Away: The Ceremonial Distribution of Goods Among the Northern Cheyenne of Southeastern Montana," *Plains Anthropologist* 18 (1973): 97.

22. Interviews.

23. Straus, "Meaning of Death," p. 340; John H. Moore, "The Utility of Cheyenne Cosmology," *Papers in Anthropology* 20 (1979): 9.

24. Straus "Meaning of Death," p. 5.

25. Moore, "Cosmology," p. 10; Hoebel, *Cheyennes*, p. 103.

26. Hoebel, *Cheyennes*, p. 104.

27. Whiteman, "American Studies," p. 2; Peter J. Powell, *The Cheyennes: Maheo's People: A Critical Bibliography* (Bloomington: Indiana University Press, 1980), pp. 54–60; Hoebel, *Cheyennes*, pp. 18, 48–49.

28. Peter J. Powell, *People of the Sacred Mountain: A History of the Northern Cheyenne Chiefs and Warrior Societies, 1830–1879, with an Epilogue, 1969–1974* (San Francisco: Harper & Row, 1981), p. 105; Hoebel, *Cheyennes*, p. 97.

29. Hoebel, *Cheyennes*, p. 104.

30. Robert Maxwell Pringle, "The Northern Cheyenne Indians in the Reservation Period" (BA thesis, Harvard University, 1958), p. 2.

31. Pringle, *Northern Cheyenne*, pp. 16–17.

32. Pringle, *Northern Cheyenne*, p. 30.

33. Nancy Owens and James P. Boggs, *The Reservation in the Regional Economy* (Lame Deer, MT: Northern Cheyenne Research Project, 1977), p. 14.

34. Pringle, *Northern Cheyenne*, pp. 82–83.

35. Weist, "Give Away," pp. 194–97.

36. Weist "Give Away," pp. 197–201.

37. Owens, "Regional Economy," pp. 14–17.

38. Nancy Owens and Ken Peres, *Overcoming Institutional Barriers to Economic Development on the Northern Cheyenne Reservation* (Lame Deer, MT: Northern Cheyenne Research Project, 1980), pp. 14–15.

39. Steve Chestnut, "Coal Development on the Cheyenne Reservation," *Proceedings of the U.S. Civil Rights Commission. Development in the Intermountain West: Its Impact on Women and Minorities* (Washington, D.C.: U.S. Government Printing Office, 1978), p. 161.

40. Duane Champagne and Jennie LaFranier, *The Potential for Small Business Development in Lame Deer, Montana* (Lame Deer, MT: Northern Cheyenne Planning Office, 1983).

41. Owens, "Regional Economy," pp. 2–3, 17.

42. Powell, *Sweet Medicine*, pp. 339–41.

43. Powell, *Sweet Medicine*, p. 394; Powell, *Sacred Mountain*, p. 1276.

44. Powell, *Sacred Mountain*, p. 1276.

45. James P. Boggs, "The Challenge of Reservation Resource Development: A Northern Cheyenne Instance," in *Native American and Energy Development II*, ed. Joseph G. Jorgensen (Boston: Anthropology Resource Center & Seventh Generation Fund, 1984), 205–36; Stephan Cornell, "Crisis and Response in Indian–White Relations: 1960–1984," *Social Problems* 32, no. 1 (1984): 44.

46. Boggs, "Challenge"; Owens, *Institutional Barriers*, pp. 32–42.

47. Boggs, "Challenge"; Cornell, "Crisis," pp. 44–59.

48. Jean Nordstrom, James Boggs, Nancy J. Owen, and Jo Ann Sooktis, *The Northern Cheyenne Tribe and Energy Development in South Eastern Montana*, vol. 1, *Social, Cultural, and Economic Investigations* (Billings, MT: Old West Regional Commission, 1977), pp. 25, 134, 208–10; Weist "Give Away," p. 211.

49. Whiteman, "American Studies," p. 3.

50. Owens, "Regional Economy," p. 13; Nordstrom, *Energy Development*, pp. 3, 112–43.

51. Nordstrom, *Energy Development*, p. 125.

52. Weist, "Give Away," p. 101.

53. Owens, "Regional Economy," p. 21; Owens, *Institutional Barriers*, p. 78; Duane Champagne, fieldwork, 1983.

54. Owens, "Regional Economy," p. 27.

55. Owens, "Regional Economy," p. 30; Nordstrom, *Energy Development*, p. 180.

56. Nordstrom, *Energy Development*, p. 146.

57. Nordstrom, *Energy Development*, p. 182; Interviews, Northern Cheyenne Reservation, 1983.

58. Owens, *Institutional Barriers*, p. 48; Interviews, Northern Cheyenne Reservation, 1983.

59. Interviews, Northern Cheyenne Reservation, 1983.

60. Owens, *Institutional Barriers*, pp. 21–22.

61. Nordstrom, *Energy Development*, p. 209.

62. Margot Liberty, "Suppression and Survival of the Northern Cheyenne Sun Dance," *Minnesota Archeologist* 27 (1965): 133–43.

63. Interviews, Northern Cheyenne Reservation, 1983.

64. Interviews; *Northern Cheyenne Tribal Records* (Lame Deer, MT: Northern Cheyenne Planning Office, 1983).

65. Interviews; Powell, *Sacred Mountain*, pp. 1273–75.

66. Nordstrom, *Energy Development*, pp. 110, 121.

67. Weist, "Give Away," p. 201.

68. Owens, *Institutional Barriers*, p. 49.

69. Liberty, "Suppression," p. 129.

70. Tribal Council Meeting, April 18, 1983.

71. Owens, *Institutional Barriers*, pp. 9–10.

72. Interview; *Northern Cheyenne Tribal Records*.

73. Tribal Council Meeting, February 28, 1983.

74. Tribal Council Meetings, February 28, 1983; April 18, 1983.

75. Tribal Council Meeting, February 28, 1983; PCIRE (Presidential Commission on Indian Reservation Economies) Report and Recommendations to the President of the United States (Washington, D.C.: U.S. Government Printing Office, 1984), p. 29.

76. Fletcher and Associates, "Feasibility Study for the Northern Cheyenne Tool Manufacturing Company," presented to the Northern Cheyenne Tribal Council February 28, 1983 (Lame Deer, MT, 1983), pp. 18, 28.

77. Owens, *Institutional Barriers*, pp. 98ff.

78. Fieldwork; Northern Cheyenne Tribal Records; Owens *Institutional Barriers*, pp. 49, 66–70, 98.

79. *Northern Cheyenne Tribal Records.*

80. Boggs, "Challenge."

81. Pringle, *Northern Cheyenne*, pp. 67, 77.

82. Pringle, *Northern Cheyenne*, pp. 77, 88–93.

83. Pringle, *Northern Cheyenne*, pp. 77-78.

84. Pringle, *Northern Cheyenne*, pp. 88-89.

85. Pringle, *Northern Cheyenne*, pp. 86–88, 92.

86. *Northern Cheyenne Tribal Records.*

87. Hoebel, *Cheyennes,* p. 130.

88. Owens, *Institutional Barriers*, pp. 16–18, 27.

89. Boggs, "Challenge," p. 211.

90. Hoebel, *Cheyennes*, p. 132; Boggs, "Challenge," pp. 221–22.

91. Nordstrom, *Energy Development*, p. 171.

92. Boggs, "Challenge," p. 223.

93. "The New Indian Elite: Bureaucratic Entrepreneurship," *Akwesasne Notes*, Spring 1980, pp. 18–19, 35.

94. Boggs, "Challenge."

95. Nordstrom, *Energy Development*, pp. 160–63.

96. Nordstrom, *Energy Development*, p. 163.

97. Interviews, Northern Cheyenne Reservation, 1983; *Northern Cheyenne Tribal Records*; "New Indian Elite," p. 18; Nordstrom, *Energy Development*, pp. 164–65.

98. Interviews; *Northern Cheyenne Tribal Records*; Nordstrom, *Energy Development,* pp. 174–75.

99. Boggs, "Challenge," p. 235.

100. Nordstrom, *Energy Development*, p. 178.

101. Interviews; *Northern Cheyenne Tribal Records*.

102. Chestnut, "Coal Development," p. 167; Majel Bird, *The Effects of Reaganomics on the Northern Cheyenne Reservation: Preliminary Report* (Lame Deer, MT: Northern Cheyenne Planning Office, 1983).

103. Boggs "Challenge," p. 228.

# Indigenous Strategies for
# Engaging Globalism

**15**

⊞

THANK YOU FOR INVITING ME to Israel and the Ben Gurion University. I am very honored to be a guest here at the Center for Bedouin Studies. Let me lay out some observations and issues about indigenous peoples and issues that I hope will contribute to the discussion among the panels offered at the conference today and tomorrow. Most of my observations and comments will be framed by my own scholarship and experience with indigenous peoples of North America, particularly the United States. Let me say by way of identification that I am a member of the Turtle Mountain Band of Chippewa Indians. The Turtle Mountain Reservation is located in the state of North Dakota, about ten miles from the Canadian border. The Chippewa, or Ojibwa, people straddle both sides of the U.S.-Canadian border from North Dakota to Ontario and from Michigan to the Hudson Bay. At conferences like the one we have here, it is often the custom among Native Americans for speakers to identify their tribal and often clan affiliations. I am not claiming that my background gives any particular foresight into the issues that will be taken up in the present conference, but I have come to realize that my life experiences have influenced my scholarly thinking, perspectives, and interests.

I am glad to see many representatives from various parts of the world. I believe that more conferences of this character will emerge in future years. Many of us who work as scholars of indigenous groups increasingly realize that indigenous studies form a natural avenue of scholarship, if not an emergent discipline. Native peoples around the globe face analogous colonial experiences and face nation-states that are strongly bent on forming their own strong nationalities, and therefore are predisposed through legal, educational, or other means to assimilate Native communities. Native communities represent many different cultures, political orders, forms of land tenure, and religions. The diversity of state and colonial relations to the wide variety of cultural and political indigenous communities forms a natural set of issues for comparative policy scholarship and provides many possible alliances for indigenous peoples themselves.

Theories of race, ethnicity, multiculturalism, and identity have useful aspects, but I do not believe these theories are broad enough to encompass the critical issues confronting indigenous peoples. While theories of race, ethnicity, and identity are popular among current scholars, Native peoples and their perspectives are not well conceptualized in these theories and are often marginalized to residual theoretical categories. The study of indigenous peoples requires a different conceptual language and understanding of history. The concepts of owning land or practicing self-government from time immemorial are not well understood by current theories of the minority, by the general publics of nation-states, and by policymakers. The study of indigenous peoples needs to focus on land rights, self-government, and community preservation as well as collective relations to nation-states. Indigenous philosophies and political and social perspectives should inform our work and analysis. Such views will respect and preserve the understandings and interests of Native peoples and will contribute to the diversity and richness of scholarly and policy debate.

While much work has been done on the colonial relations of indigenous nations, I always insist that the study of indigenous peoples must be about the groups themselves, not the relations of domination, since that is a story about the actions of the colonizers and leaves the indigenous peoples victims of history. Thus I believe that the focus of any indigenous studies must be the history, community, and culture of the indigenous, while the conditions of colonialism must be considered as contextual and important, but not the center of attention. The focus of indigenous studies must be the story of the people themselves, their history, culture, religion, music, and dance, as well as their colonial experience and their efforts to survive and live within the nation-states that surround them.

Furthermore, the past is useful and interesting in order to understand how indigenous peoples came to their present conditions. Ethnic studies and Native American studies have focused on reclaiming history and reinterpreting cultural and community change among Native nations. Such research activities are important and assist in cultural preservation of Native communities. In my view one of the fundamental tasks of any indigenous studies paradigm must include active participation in Native issues, as well as bringing Native wisdom and concepts to the university while assisting Native communities with scholarship, technical advice, and the training of students and indigenous community members who are dedicated to the tasks of community, cultural, and political preservation. Such a task, I believe, is often alien to contemporary university disciplines that work through bureaucratic organization and with theories and policies of minority and ethnic assimilation.

One of the great contributions of an indigenous perspective and discipline is the preservation of the philosophies, governments, arts, and knowledge of thousands of indigenous peoples who deserve to be understood on their own terms and from their own perspectives. These views, communities, ways of doing, and ways of knowing will enrich and contribute to world culture and to human knowledge and understanding. One can already argue that indigenous peoples have contributed significantly to world culture through information about medicine, ecology, environmental philosophies, government, and democracy, as well as with spiritual understanding.

The way is open for the emergence of national, regional, and world indigenous studies disciplines. In order to do this right, the indigenous studies should center the philosophies and issues of the people and communities who are the focus of study. Furthermore, I do not believe that indigenous studies should follow the contemporary given path of disciplinary organization and scholarship. Scholars of indigenous studies should be actively involved in the social, political, religious, and educational issues that confront indigenous peoples. Furthermore, the rules of organization and social relations should reflect the organization of indigenous communities more than the university, although few contemporary universities are willing to go so far. Nevertheless, much can be done in these directions with dedicated faculty, staff, and students in joint efforts with communities and community leaders, as well as community support.

The formation of a world indigenous studies discipline may be one of the significant university and scholarly events of the twenty-first century. Again I want to commend Ben Gurion University and the Center for Bedouin Studies for their foresight in organizing the present multination and multicontinent conference. I believe that the challenges of the twenty-first century will be a central focus of a new indigenous scholarship. We must also look to the future, which promises even greater challenges in terms of technology and accumulations of power and wealth, all of which will continue to contexualize the political and cultural ways of indigenous peoples. How will indigenous peoples face the challenges of the twenty-first century? Some of these issues are discussed and presented at the present conference. I wish to make some observations about several of the topics under discussion. These comments mostly come from my understanding and work with Native peoples in the

United States. I hope that these observations of patterns and trends among Native Americans will be informative and helpful in understanding policy, scholarly research, and community relations in other countries and with other indigenous communities. Comparisons across nations and indigenous communities will enable greater understanding of the effects of policy on indigenous peoples and will contribute to more sensitive and culturally informed policy and scholarship. Several topics in education, social development, and political relations are covered in the conference agenda, and so let me comment on some of those issues here.

# Education

The major trend in Native North American education over the twentieth century, especially the past thirty years, is local community control of education institutions, if not curriculums. The experiences of boarding schools in the United States, Canada, and Australia have been harsh and disruptive to many indigenous communities and individuals. Native communities have increasingly sought to gain local control of schools in K–12 grades. Students are not moved away from their communities and can have the support of family and kin, and local responsibility for education subject matter can be more easily introduced into school courses. In the United States most schools are funded by the Bureau of Indian Affairs (or the BIA), and consequently BIA organization and rules exercise great influence over school management in many Native communities. In the early 1970s, Ramah Community School on the Navajo reservation contracted its school from direct BIA management. Soon other reservation communities followed suit and organized school boards and made contracts with BIA officials to assume control over schools. Most American Indian communities have sought greater community control over schools and many have made significant progress.

One education issue recently taken up by a few California Native tribes is the education of the general public about the legal status and government-to-government relation that U.S. Natives have under treaty and federal law. California Natives find that the general public, as well as congressional and state officials, do not have a clear understanding of Native political self-government, and Native lobbyists much reeducate each new class of legislators. Hence the plan to introduce concepts of Native rights and self-government into the K–12 curriculum and to introduce materials to the textbook industry so that such concepts can be introduced to students and the general public.

A highly significant educational development is the founding of tribally controlled community colleges. The first was Navajo Community College, established in 1970, and in the next few years it was followed other community colleges on other reservations. Currently there are thirty-three tribal colleges, including several allied colleges in Canada. The tribal community colleges provide access to higher education for many students who for cultural, community, or financial reasons prefer to pursue an education in their local community. Research suggests that many traditional students prefer to stay home and attend the tribal community college. Less traditional students are more willing to leave the reservation community and attend four-year institutions. Many tribal community college students are older, have children, and are often female. The students at tribal colleges are often less willing to leave the community and are more willing to participate in tribal social and political life. Those students who attend four-year or outside institutions are often less likely to return to reservation life and more likely to find employment in urban, government, or pan-Indian settings, or to take positions that are not related to Native issues.

The tribally controlled community colleges have been established outside of direct BIA controls, although financial support from Congress is passed through BIA organization. Dedicated individuals who created opportunities for community control over tribal education materials helped form the tribally controlled community colleges. The capability to provide education to a reservation population and give a second educational chance to high school dropouts and those who prefer not to leave the Native community has greatly strengthened the skills and availability of cultural capital to reservation communities and governments.

About the same time that the community colleges were formed, in the late 1960s and early 1970s, many American Indian studies centers were formed. There are over 125 Indian studies programs and departments in the United States and Canada. The great majority of Native studies programs are small interdepartmental degree programs that use faculty from mainstream disciplines. Consequently many do not provide Native perspectives directly as a disciplinary approach. There are about a dozen majors and a handful of M.A. programs and several Ph.D. programs, most notably at the University of Arizona, which is by far the largest program in the United States with about twenty departmental and affiliated faculty. At best, Indian studies programs and departments provide communities and scholarly homes for faculty and students. The program at UCLA consists of a research center and a interdisciplinary program of teaching, which has few direct resources. Both the research center and IDP are mutually supporting and provide support for faculty and students who are interested in Native research and education. At UCLA we have been working directly with Native communities on a variety of issues such as health, community theater, tribal court development, social welfare concerns, and student recruitment, as well as with political issues such as campaigns concerned with Native rights to engage in casino-style gaming. Our strategy has been to develop a community of students, staff, tribal community members, and faculty, all of whom are directed toward Native cultural and contemporary issues. We believe this method has resulted in considerable student retention, and many of our undergraduates go on to professional school or graduate school. We believe that the model of creating a community of indigenous studies faculty, community members, students, and staff is a way of assisting Native students while they are at university, and also a way of introducing Native concepts and understandings to students and the rest of the university. In a sense, we suggest a process of "reverse colonialism," where Native and other students establish small colonies of intellectual and social community to facilitate education and accommodation of university and mainstream life for Native students, but also provide an on-campus community of social and intellectual support and commitment.

Native studies should be about Native people, their communities, interests, worldviews, and values. Those views should be taught to students and ethics of community participation and support should be promoted. Native worldviews of holism, harmony, and interconnectedness should be made available to students and to the university community. Such views should be respected and communities allowed to make their own social and political decisions according to their own ways. Students should respect the indigenous communities and learn to work within them, and avoid introducing Western techniques and knowledge directly into communities that are culturally alien and often overtly resistant. Students can learn technique at university, but indigenous wisdom and cultural knowledge are needed to complement Western knowledge in order to promote patterns of change acceptable to indigenous communities and their traditions. There is no worse university product than a Native student returning to his home community to rebuild the community according to Western models learned at university. As well meaning as such students may be, they need the cultural and policy work of an indigenous studies department in order to learn respect and understanding of how indigenous communities work and change.

Indigenous education should facilitate community building or nation building, if you will. If there is a possible unifying theme for indigenous studies, I believe, it is the study and preservation of indigenous nations or communities, or simply nation building. Indigenous studies should take on the projects of study, policymaking, and education in ways that facilitate social,

economic, and cultural preservation, as well as consensual change within indigenous communities.

## Nation–State and Indigenous Relations

Relations between indigenous communities and nation-states will become an
increasingly explicit issue during the twenty-first century. Many nations in the
world refuse to acknowledge that they have indigenous communities within
their borders. Most indigenous groups have traditions of self-government according to their own rules, traditions, and religion. Many have creation stories that outline social, political, and cultural relations, as well as ties to land.
Indigenous communities were self-governing before colonial and state
regimes were established. Although the mythologies of colonialism and
nation-states generally overlook the history of nonconsensual or forced participation, this is the situation that most indigenous peoples find themselves
in. The indigenous histories and traditions uphold claims to land, self-
government, and cultural autonomy that are no longer recognized by the
colonial or nation-state regimes. But they are remembered and often maintained covertly by suppressed or ignored indigenous communities. Native
views of self-government are often based on religious and sacred conceptions.
There are many such examples from North America such as the Iroquois,
Pueblos, and Navajo, where religious belief, mode of political government,
and claims to territory create religious ties to land, particular forms of government, and community organization. Religious or sacred underpinnings
enforce strong motivations to preserve community, land, and political order in
many indigenous communities. Self-governance and territory are sacred
blessings given from time immemorial. This inherent counterclaim to political action, territory, precedence, and cultural autonomy brands the indigenous communities as antagonists to nation-states. Indigenous communities are
often feared by nation-states because they assert claims to self-government and
cultural autonomy that threaten the territorial and political stability of nation-
states. Unstable and impoverished nation-states or authoritarian nation-states
with little capability to manage dissent or democratic debate and practice will
prove barren ground for the open assertion and practice of Native rights and
claims.

Many indigenous communities are willing to work within the framework
of their local nation-state. However, while many indigenous communities do
not argue the nationalist position of secession from state governments, since
that is often politically impractical, a pragmatic position of negotiating for
more democratized political relations is often sought. Furthermore, many in-

digenous communities wish to manage the delivery of social welfare, health programs, and other services to their own communities. They believe they can do it better and in a more culturally acceptable way. Some indigenist activists argue that nation-states will not be forthcoming on many indigenous issues, and they have appealed to the United Nations and have worked to present Native issues within the Human Rights Declarations. The granting of NGO (nongovernmental organization) status provides indigenous peoples with a presence within international organizations and provides a rallying point for discussion of indigenous issues from groups around the world.

In the United States, nation-state and indigenous relations revolve around treaties, certain clauses in the U.S. constitution, and resultant legal history of many cases continuing to the present. Such a body of treaties, law, and limited recognition of self-government is found nowhere else, except in Canada. But for historical reasons, no comparable complex body of law and legislation has arisen in other colonizing situations, such as in Latin and South America, New Zealand, and Australia. The extensive treaty-making period in North America created the recognition of Native communities as independent nations with rights to territory, self-government, and powers to make war and peace. With the increasing power of the U.S. government and nation, Native nations were subordinated. Their standing as independent nations was diminished and policies of limited rights to self-government under U.S. law emerged. Reservation tribal governments have powers of self-government as long as such powers or rights are not explicitly taken away by congressional act. Today Native American reservation governments operate under a pattern of limited and shared self-government with local city-county, state, and federal governments. Most Native communities and people accept these arrangements as an everyday matter, but arguments for greater autonomy and greater assertions of national powers are often heard in political debates as well as in the classroom.

In recent decades Native claims to self-government and claims to recognition of territory have been strong in the United States, Canada, Australia, and New Zealand. One might argue that since the early 1970s land claims and assertions of self-government have been more successful in Canada than in the United States. The Canadian First Nations have actively participated in debates over constitutional powers and have demanded, although unsuccessfully, that rights to self-government be guaranteed in the Canadian constitutional propositions. While none of the constitutional agreements passed, this opportunity is similar to the somewhat oblique references to Native Americans as foreign powers in the U.S. constitution and provides a means for preserving Native rights and powers of self-government within the organic document of the nation-state. The widely publicized Nunuvut recognition, however, granted self-government along the lines of a province within the Canadian Confederation, not in accordance with First Nation rights, and cannot be necessarily seen as upholding Native self-government. Similarly in Australia, where for many years Aborigines were deprived of land and governmental recognition, their continuous lobbying for their rights yielded limited recognition and access to land but few powers of self-government. Comparisons of nation-state policies and indigenous efforts to retain control over land, sustain self-government, and maintain their cultural communities are fruitful ways for indigenous communities and scholars to gain greater understanding of processes for the greater democratization of indigenous and nation-state relations.

Around the world many indigenous communities wish to retain local control and management over local political problems and issues. Some questions that will need further attention are: How do indigenous individuals and communities join nation-states, enjoy rights and privileges of nation-states, and at the same time maintain community self-determination, land, community, and culture? Are such relations between nation-state and indigenous relations compatible or even possible? Will nation-states seek to assimilate indigenous communities, or will they move to create new political and cultural means of gaining their loyalty and participation in the nation-state, but at the same time preserving indigenous rights to territory and self-government? New issues such as these will require creative solutions if consensual and democratic relations are to prevail in the end.

## Social and Economic Development

The twenty-first century will bring increased demands and political competition from nation-states and more indigenous participation in the international arena. It will also bring a highly intensive and global market system that will test the economic and social autonomy of all indigenous communities. Many indigenous communities are tied into markets as consumers and producers, but the challenge to indigenous communities is to gain access to markets as significant organizers of capital and avoid victimization and economic marginalization in the marketplace. These are extremely difficult issues since indigenous social, political, and economic relations are not traditionally well suited to open market capitalism. Nevertheless, without some accommodation to the marketplace, Native communities may suffer increased social fragmentation and economic marginalization. Undoubtedly some communities will not meet the challenge for cultural or political reasons, but many may try to find creative ways to preserve their social, political, and cultural ways and at the same time become producers and managers of indigenous capitalism. Such a prospect, of at least partially market-based indigenous communities, holds out the promise of additional resources for the support of indigenous cultural forms; preservation of language, history, and investment in religious forms and practices; as well as strengthening of indigenous political forms and organization.

Some examples, again from the United States, may be helpful, since the U.S. economy is highly competitive and Native and government officials have tried to promote economic development. As is probably the case for indigenous communities around the world, Native American communities are culturally, socially, politically, and philosophically not predisposed to individual or corporate capitalist enterprise. Sharing and redistribution is generally preferred to as accumulation for reinvestment in the marketplace. Native religious philosophies emphasize respectful relations with plants, animals, rocks, and other powers of the universe. One seeks to accommodate and understand the flow of the universe rather than try to remake the raw material of the earth as in the Western view.

Native peoples in North America, while adept and familiar with trade and gift exchange, did not take to capitalist enterprise in the sense of accumulating wealth for the primary purpose of reinvestment according to the demands of the market. Hence while Natives participated in markets, they usually were engaged as part-time labor and had little control over the capitalist means of production. U.S. government efforts to promote economic development on reservations through much of the nineteenth century had little general success, with few exceptions. Some tribes lucky enough to have minerals or oil did well, and by the 1970s some resource-rich tribes banded together to gain greater capability to market their resources. Resource-rich tribes like the Navajo, however, generally sold their resources through government contracts to outside corporations, in some cases gaining labor concessions. The resource tribes were seldom engaged in direct business management or production but instead received royalties, often at reduced government rates. The Mississippi Choctaw, a prime example of a reservation economy built primarily on diversified manufacturing plants, is an exception. Other interesting examples are the Alaska Native corporations that were initiated by congressional act in 1971 and imposed alien economic forms that Alaska Native peoples adapted to protect their cultural and land interests. The Alaska Native corporations were invested with considerable capital and land from the loss of the major portion of Alaska land and resources. Nevertheless, while the Alaska corporation and land claims settlement have aroused considerable interest from indigenous groups around the world, no other indigenous group or nation-state has been willing to take the risks of for-profit corporations given in the Alaska Native Claims Settlement Act.

Perhaps the new emphasis on casino-style gaming provides some insight into the possibilities of indigenous capitalism. Unlike most economic development efforts among Indians in the United States, gaming was initiated largely by tribal communities, often desperate for some form of income while occupying marginal land bases. This was certainly the case among the Cabazon people of California, who fought and won, in the late 1980s, an important legal precedent enabling Native gaming rights as a power of self-government. For many Native communities, gaming enterprises were controversial, and some such as the Navajo have voted against engaging in the gaming business. Others, as among the Seneca, have engaged in heated political debate over the issue. In order to ensure the right to establish gaming enterprises, the tribes had to fight many and continuing legal and political issues, most of which were based on Native rights to self-government under U.S. law, and often difficult negotiations with state governments over the scope of gaming and the redistribution of gaming proceeds. One of the outcomes of the negotiations was the congressional passage of the Indian Gaming Regulation Act of 1988. Many tribes agreed to support this act because they believed that it would reduce lawsuits by states that wanted to shut down their gaming enterprises.

A further stipulation of the Indian Gaming Regulation Act is that 70 percent of the gaming profits be redistributed for purposes of community improvement. This precluded private gaming enterprises and was compatible with tribal government management of tribal economic assets and resources. Efforts by groups among the Mohawk reservations to establish private gaming enterprises failed because of community opposition and the legal empowerment of tribal government within the gaming act's provisions. The collective reallocation of gaming assets is compatible with Native concepts of exchange and redistribution. The purpose of the gaming enterprise was not individual enrichment but community wealth, and redistribution of the wealth for community goals. Many tribes have done well with gaming and have accumulated significant amounts of capital. In many cases, gaming income is redistributed to community members as a regular per capita share. Many gaming tribes have made provisions for elders, provided housing and support for poorer members, and granted scholarships and introduced community college courses. Other tribes have invested in real estate, hotels, and other industries in an effort to diversify their economic holdings and reduce their dependence on gaming income. Large amounts of money have also brought political influence and political access to state and local government officials in ways that were not imaginable even five years ago.

Relatively few tribal communities, certainly fewer than thirty, have made significant incomes through gaming (while about 220 Native communities are engaged in gaming). Most communities are too isolated to earn the large amounts of cash that are made by the tribal communities located near major metropolitan centers. Nevertheless, the gaming enterprise provides some insight into how indigenous capitalism might emerge. For cultural and institutional reasons, the path the indigenous capitalism is probably not by way of the Western mode of individualism and private property. Native worldviews, social ethics, and governments feel threatened by significant property and wealth; but consensual and collective control of economic enterprises, capitalist enterprise for the collective benefit of the community, and reinvestment in community and cultural resources are acceptable and motivating factors for some indigenous communities to engage market enterprise. Indigenous capitalism must subordinate the individual accumulation of wealth to the collective accumulation of wealth. Individual capitalism in some circumstances may well work at the individual level, but it threatens to disrupt community organization, values, and power relations, and may transform indigenous community relations beyond recognition in ways that are not acceptable to the communities themselves. The Mississippi Choctaw manufacturing success works along similar principles of tribal government managing economic resources for collective community benefit. Individual tribal members willingly work for tribal enterprises, and the tribal government manages and invests in multiple enterprises like a parent holding company. One advantage of the gaming and Mississippi Choctaw economic development models is that these solutions were worked out by the communities themselves without (and often in spite of) government regulation. Most likely the collective enterprise model is not for every culture or indigenous community, but some indigenous communities may be able to creatively reconcile their cultural and institutional inhibitions about capitalist enterprise and function competitively in the marketplace while retaining their values and preserving their cultural orientations and communities intact. This should give us hope for more creative solutions from indigenous communities in the future. Ability to work in the marketplace may help ensure the survival of many indigenous communities.

## Cultural and Community Preservation

Most indigenous communities put high value on cultural and community preservation, and these values can often prevail over external pressures for political, economic, and cultural change. Many indigenous communities strongly resist change that is not to their own liking, and this conservatism carries over to recognition of land, cultural autonomy, and rights to self-government.

This strong attachment to maintenance of the cultural community is closely related to the religious foundations of many indigenous social, cultural, and political communities. Indigenous rights are not merely rational political claims, but are deeply embedded in the religion and institutions of indigenous communities. Consequently indigenous communities will be highly motivated to preserve their core institutions and values and will resist change that threatens to materially disturb those institutions without an acceptable rationale within the community cultural understandings. Indigenous people strongly want to preserve their community and way of life, and I believe they will do so into the twenty-first century and beyond. Despite intensive and global pressures for change, many communities will not accept political, economic, and cultural change without some appropriate reinterpretation from within their own culture. Indigenous cultures will ultimately accept change, but on their own terms.

For indigenous peoples throughout the world, cultural and political survival at all costs is a strong motive. For example, Latin and South America have significant populations that often resist speaking Spanish and secretly maintain non-Western language, community, kinship, cultural, and political relations. Native peoples will survive into the future centuries, and they will do so through both change and selective retention of Native views of religion, community, and political rights. Nation-states will increasingly have to recognize and accommodate these issues as they have to a limited extent in the United States, Canada, New Zealand, and Australia. Nation-states that do not apprehend and begin to negotiate with Native peoples will have difficulties creating stable and homogeneous nationalities. Even a country like Japan, which claims to have a homogeneous culture, has been challenged by the Aino people of Hokkaido Island and the indigenous peoples of Okinawa Island. While in most countries, the indigenous populations are a small percentage of the total national population, indigenous peoples have strong senses of community and territory and are not easily assimilated into the nation-state. New methods of respect and recognition of indigenous rights, of cultural differences, and autonomy will go a long way toward democratizing and consensualizing relations between Native peoples and nation-states. Native nations cannot survive easily in an era of global political and economic competition, but they will strive retain their identities, memories of territory, and community organizations. Nation-states need to start negotiating more consensual and culturally respectful means of understanding loyalty, citizenship, and national identity that includes the possibility of cultural, racial, and subnational or indigenous identity, as well as cultural and local self-determination. Such consensually constructed and pluralistic nation-states would more easily accommodate the demands and values of indigenous peoples and make for creation of more democratic, freer, and culturally dynamic cultures and nations.

## Note

This chapter previously appeared as Duane Champagne, "Indigenous Strategies for Engaging Globalism: Keynote Address," in *The Future of Indigenous Studies: Strategies for Survival and Development,* ed. Duane Champagne and Ismael Abu-Saad (Los Angeles: UCLA American Indian Studies Center, 2003), pp. xix–xxxii.

# Native Issues in the Twenty-first Century

## 16

**M**ANY ISSUES CONFRONTED NATIVE PEOPLE during the colonial period such as loss of land, loss of political autonomy, population losses, challenges to culture and identity, and strong pressures for social and cultural assimilation. Nevertheless, Native peoples have struggled to retain their identity, land, government, and cultural way of life. The strength of Native commitments to their own communities and ways over the past five centuries suggests that Native nations will strive to preserve themselves in future centuries. Natives will try to restore and retain their culture, language, art, music, stories, values, and religion. This effort is not necessarily a rejection of Western or world cultures, but rather an affirmation of Native or tribal cultures. Each of the cultures provides a philosophy for living, a worldview, and a religious interpretation of the world that differs from the Christian religion and other world religions. In many Native cultures, the Creator placed the Indian people on the earth for a specific purpose within the grand plan for the cosmos. Many Native cultures say that the Native people have certain gifts from the Creator, such as consensual-democratic relations, a philosophy about humans and the rest of the beings in the universe, a philosophy about the nature of the universe and the role that humans have in it, and special tasks for Native communities and individuals. The rituals and ceremonies of Native communities honor the Creator for the gifts of life, the beneficence of the earth, and the tasks and missions that Native people have for their communities and themselves. The preservation of the community and culture are tightly related to religious and philosophical requirements to preserve the earth, land, and nature resources, and for maintaining harmonious relations with other humans and other beings of the universe.

If the covenants with the Creator are broken or abandoned and people of the earth fail to honor and give thanks for the gifts of life, the earth, and the universe, the Creator will not provide guidance and the universe will experience disharmonies that might be dangerous to human survival and well-being. Native people must perform the ceremonies and uphold and maintain harmony within the community, as a means for preserving harmonious relations with the powers and beings of the universe. One of the strongest imperatives for Native nationalism is the central role that Native communities and peoples play in the order of the universe. If Native people do not uphold their end of the bargain through ceremonies and respectful social relations among themselves and with other peoples and with the beings of the universe, then harmony is disrupted and fearsome consequences will beset the Native people and their communities. Death, disease, disorganization, natural disasters, ecological disasters, wars, conflict, and other maladies will visit the people. The foundations of Native nationalism, their commitment to community and common religious and moral order, are ultimately religious and philosophical.

Although all Natives do not hold the same religious and philosophical beliefs, the justifications for Native sovereignty and rights to land, from the Native perspective, derive from the views that Native lands, governments, and community relations were granted as gifts from the Creator. These notions give a deep sacred and philosophical character to Native interests in preserving culture, land, government, and community relations. While many Natives in the twenty-first century have been exposed to globalized culture and media, are well educated, have adopted Christian religious beliefs, and are very familiar with U.S. and Canadian society, the foundations of Native nationalism lies in the religious and philosophical realm as they are maintained and retold by the elders and spiritual leaders.

Attempts over the past five centuries to assimilate Native people into U.S. and Canadian social and political life have not been wholly successful because of the strong commitments that Native people have to their own communities and philosophical beliefs. Native beliefs and understandings of the universe have been attacked and subordinated by missionaries and government officials. While many Natives have adopted Western lifestyles and religion, those who remain attached to their communities often continue to understand and adhere to many of the beliefs and norms of their own communities. A few communities are torn by religious and philosophical differences between Western views, religions, and philosophies, and Native views. In these communities there is controversy over the propriety of economic development, whether personal accumulation of wealth is permitted, and often about the form of government, whether traditional or Western democratic. Such conflicts have emerged among many of the upstate New York Iroquois communities over the past several centuries. Open cultural conflict within Native communities is relatively rare, as many communities have methods of handling multiple beliefs and permit multiple ceremonies and paths to the sacred. Nevertheless, the presence of multiple and often philosophically conflicting understandings of the role of communities and humans to each other and to the powers of the universe can lead to difficulties and misunderstandings. When Europeans introduced Christian and Western ways to the Native peoples, they expected the Natives to abandon their own beliefs and communities. To a certain extent this has happened; some individuals have withdrawn from Native communities and have made a life for themselves in U.S. or Canadian society. American and Canadian policymakers, as well as the general public, believed that Native peoples would not survive physically or culturally as communities. Reservations and reserves were considered temporary waiting stations as the Natives were prepared for entry into American or Canadian society. Natives were taught to abandon their cultures and languages and prepared to live in American or Canadian society in Western communities and living under Western religious and moral codes.

Many Natives submitted to the strong pressure to assimilate, and others accommodated but did not abandon their communities and commitments to Native values and life. Most Native communities are now multicultural with elements of both tribal and Western worldviews. The situation of multiple beliefs both complicates and creates possibilities for the future preservation of Native communities. Western worldviews can provide models for government, economic development, and religious organization that many tribal communities selectively adopt and incorporate within their cultures, plans, and values. Nevertheless, justification for preservation of Native communities, culture, land, and self-government derives from Native philosophies and their understanding of the place of Natives within the universe. Western law and philosophies relegate Native communities to marginal reservations as conquered peoples with legal rights based on treaties, legislation, and court decisions. These contemporary legal developments are based largely on American and Canadian legal and legislative philosophies. They provide a justification for Native sovereignty, land, and self-government within U.S. and Canadian legal and political history. Native interpretations of self-government from time immemorial are not generally heard in these mainstream interpretations.

Over the past thirty years U.S. Indian policy has allowed greater self-determination for Native peoples. Similarly, since the early 1970s, the Native peoples of Canada have argued for constitutional clauses affirming Native rights to land and self-government. They have won court cases and public support for modern treaty negotiations and politically negotiated land settlements. The past thirty years affirm that the United States and Canada are willing to recognize many Native rights. Natives have struggled hard to have their views and interests understood and recognized. Native rights are better understood and respected today than through most of the twentieth century. Much of this recognition and respect is still within Western views and philosophical frameworks, and certainly within the constitutional and political constraints of U.S. and Canadian government. Native views and philosophies are often ignored or subordinated to American and Canadian views.

There are many challenges confronting Native peoples in the twenty-first century. Primary among them is reclaiming their own philosophical view of the universe and the place of Native communities within the changing world of the twenty-first century. Native communities continue both explicitly and informally to advocate their worldview. The basis of Native sovereignty is ultimately the preexistence of Native self-government for thousands of years before the formation of the U.S. and Canadian governments. Natives have religious and philosophical justifications within their traditions and beliefs for preserving themselves as nations and communities and retaining rights to self-government and to territory. The challenge for Native communities is not just to survive as legal and political entities, but to do so within the religious and philosophical understandings of their forebears. Secular and Westernized Native governments do not justify self-government for Native peoples within their own beliefs and understandings. It may well happen that secular Native governments and communities emerge and operate. Such a culmination would be one logical outcome of the strong programs of education and assimilation that still permeate much of U.S. and Canadian Indian policies. Such secular Native governments can be justified within U.S. and Canadian legal and legislative frameworks, since they are both devoid of Native religious and philosophical thought. The secularization of some Native governments may well be a trend, but such secularization and rejection of Native worldviews would delegitimize claims to Native self-government and would move justifications out of the realm of culture, religion, and self-government toward racial and ethnic interpretations that would be devoid of Native philosophical understandings and views.

The challenge for Native peoples in the twenty-first century is not necessarily physical survival or affluent survival, but rather surviving as Natives communities that continue to be informed by Native worldviews, values, and philosophies. This does not mean that Native intellectual life will not change, but Native philosophies of the nature of human beings and of the universe are what justify the continuity and constitution of Native communities and their right to self-government, territory, and cultural heritage. After the strong assimilationist onslaught of the twentieth century, Native communities need to take stock of their community, government, religious, and cultural assets. Girding to take on the challenges of the twenty-first century will require religious and philosophical support, even more so than meeting the challenges of direct assimilation carried on by the U.S. and Canadian governments. Native governments and communities also need to preserve the core aspects of religion, community, and philosophy that justify Native nationality and a Native way of life. The powerful forces of global markets, politics, and culture bring new challenges to Native views and community. Regaining and retaining Native perspectives and bringing them to bear creatively to meet the challenges of the twenty-first century is a priority for Native communities. Native peoples have been meeting the challenges of a changing environment for thousands of years, and Native peoples will meet the challenges of the next century in their own ways and on their own terms.

## Reuniting with All Our Relations

Reclaiming a Native worldview or philosophy does not necessarily mean reconstructing a timeless traditional way of thought and belief. Group beliefs are not static and are socially constructed according to changing circumstances in the world or immediate environment. There are many reasons for such changes. Change can be caused by generational differences. Each new generation grows up in somewhat different circumstances than do their parents and grandparents, and so experiences and knowledge can vary. Any community includes shared aspects of culture and religion, but there is usually contention about religious, cultural, and moral issues. Elders and spiritual leaders may have different training and teachings than others, and so there may not be any complete consensus on many cultural and religious understandings. This does not preclude the practice of religion in many Native communities, since such differences are often recognized and respected by community members.

Spiritual leaders have their own training and their own experiences. They have knowledge about certain aspects of religions and philosophical thought. Spiritual leaders do not dispute in Native communities nor do they seek disciples or converts. Generally each Native person has a direct relation to the sacred, and they keep their experiences and knowledge to themselves. Ceremonies are group and community experiences, but even then vows and sacrifices are made based on personal relations to the sacred but intended for the benefit of others and the community at large. Only certain individuals who have special relations to spiritual leaders or special callings take up religious and philosophical thought, although beliefs and life ways are upheld by most community members. Religious beliefs in most Native communities were shared all members of the community. A small number of priests or spiritual leaders possessed knowledge based on the spiritual leaders' personal relations to the sacred. Religious knowledge and understandings were imbued throughout much of Native life and did not necessarily form a set of rules or dogma maintained by a priesthood or religious hierarchy.

Reclaiming Native religious belief and philosophy will help restore the cultural and religious foundations of contemporary Native communities. Many aspects of Native religion and culture are still practiced by contemporary communities. The pattern that some people engaged in religious life more than others reflects the diversity of older Native communities, where religious knowledge and practice varied among community members. Consequently reclaiming Native philosophy does not resemble the formation of Western churches but does imply that Native beliefs and understandings will become more openly discussed and inform the community-based construction of contemporary institutions and life in ways that were inhibited or even prevented during most of the twentieth century. Most contemporary economic and political institutions on Native reservations have their origins in U.S. or Canadian society and are foreign institutions with foreign cultural and normative justifications. Natives do not generally share the values of the institutions, and therefore the imposed institutions do not work well on reservations. One of the challenges of the future is to reconcile Native worldviews and philosophies with contemporary bureaucratic, technological, and market institutions.

While Native philosophies have developed over thousands of years, even before colonial contact, the philosophies have changed over time. Contemporary assertions of Native self-determination based on Native viewpoints require Native people and leaders to examine Native forms of ethics, social arrangements, and philosophies to use them in ways that facilitate community survival and development within the contemporary world. Elders, scholars, spiritual leaders, and community people need not only to reclaim the wisdom and ethics of Native worldviews, but also to agree upon ways in which Native philosophies can be used to solve the social, economic, and cultural issues that confront Native nations. Contemporary Native communities emphasize preserving ceremonies, religious teachings, language, dance, music, and other aspects of culture. Preserving past knowledge is important, but using that knowledge to maintain and support contemporary living Native communities, governments, and nations is the means to preserving Native life well into the future. Native cultures are living cultures, but the experience of colonialism has influenced Native communities to give up their perspectives in favor of U.S. and Canadian ones. Many Native nations survived the colonial experience with their values and perspectives intact. Many Native communities continue to negotiate cultural relations with the United States and Canada and seek to preserve their culture and philosophies while accommodating U.S. or Canadian policies and administration. Many Native communities have taken Western institutions and have attempted to introduce their own philosophies into them. Since government agents directly managed most reservation and reserve communities, Native views and expressions were underscored. As Natives gain more control over reservation institutions, they can reclaim and recreate colonial reservation institutions, such as courts and constitutional governments, in their own cultural image. As tribal communities in Native North America manage their own institutions, they will reclaim and modify their own cultural views and reinterpret reservation institutions to fit with their views of government and social relations.

Native communities were not in a position to make cultural, economic, or political decisions while they were living in a politically subordinated colonial relation. Through great persistence and allegiance to Native values, perspectives, and beliefs, Native peoples in the United States and Canada demanded respect for their rights and views. At the beginning of the twenty-first century Native North Americans find themselves in a position to assert their culture and nationality in new ways. Reclaiming Native culture will reaffirm the survival of Native communities as culturally and philosophically Native peoples, but the challenge of the twenty-first century is to continue adapting Native culture and philosophies to support Native sovereignty, culture, and tribal government and economic institutions in ways that will assure continuity of Native perspectives as living cultures and will support Native communities and institutions in ways that will meet looming economic, political, and technological challenges.

## Tribal Government

Native governments face many challenges. U.S. and Canadian tribal governments are largely funded and administratively guided by the BIA or Indian and Northern Affairs, Canada (INAC). The strong administrative hand of the Canadian and U.S. governments limits the power and action of tribal governments. Native North American tribal governments work within the laws and constitutional arrangements of U.S. or Canadian governments. Most Native North American people have accepted this situation based on history and legal precedents, not to mention power relations between the governments of the United States and Canada. Some Native political leaders argue for Native nationality in international fora, but these voices are largely the minority. At the international level, most Native people want respect for their culture, land, and rights to self-government, but they are willing to work within the U.S. and Canadian governments and are not asking for international status, but rather fairer, more respectful acknowledgment of Native cultural perspectives, land, and political rights.

Over the past thirty years the U.S. self-determination policy led to recognition of Native governments with limited jurisdiction over reservations within the U.S. government system. Government jurisdiction in the United States is divided among federal, state, and local county and city governments. This authority is divided among the different governments that have different powers and responsibilities. Native nations are gradually incorporated into the U.S. federal system. Based on history, treaties, congressional acts, and executive orders, Native tribal governments have retained jurisdictions and limited powers over reservations lands. While the U.S. government wanted to terminate Indian reservations as late as the 1950s, since the 1960s and 1970s Native activism has moved Congress to enact legislation and administrative procedures that support greater resources and decision-making powers for tribal governments. Canadian reserve governments have also over the past fifty years argued for more recognition of decision making and control over resources, but perhaps with more varied success than in the United States.

Native communities during the last half of the twentieth century affirmed and gained limited recognition of their rights, governments, and cultures from the U.S. and Canadian governments. Many Native communities aim to maintain and expand the rights to self-government within the American or Canadian government and legal systems. Many Native leaders argue that tribal governments must be more assertive of their rights, engage in real decision making, depend less on government oversight, and make tribal governments reflect the cultures and interests of Native reservation or reserve communities.

Tribal governments and communities are confronted with difficult obstacles to greater decision making over their communities and institutions. Most contemporary tribal governments in North America were created by government policies and instituted by government officials. The colonial forms of constitutional governments, or band and reserve governments in Canada, were tied directly to U.S. or Canadian government administrative control and were probably not designed for considerable decision making or use of political power. Consequently most Native communities are saddled with government organizations that were designed to be appendages to the

Indian service bureaucracy. Most contemporary tribal governments need considerable modification and strengthening. Most of the colonially imposed tribal governments do not serve Native communities well, and so Native people must develop ways to make the governments more responsive to the economic and political interests of their communities and reduce the load of U.S. or Canadian government administrative constraints and controls. This situation requires considerable discussion and agreement among Native communities, leaders, elders, and government officials.

A few Native communities retain largely traditional forms of government. While some argue for a return to traditional political forms, they will have to be modified to meet the globalized market, political, and cultural demands of the twenty-first century. Native political patterns were not designed to manage competitive markets, hierarchical bureaucracies, or competitive federal, state, or local governments. Native political organization and leadership patterns from the past several centuries most likely will not meet the demands of the contemporary world and will not protect Native cultural, national, political, or economic interests. Nevertheless, most Native communities will accept and abide by Native forms of political action and organization. Most Natives reservation and reserve communities will not accept Western forms of political organization, but informally include their own political processes even within Western constitutional and political forms. Native communities will want to retain significant aspects of Native leadership patterns, political norms, political symbolism, ceremony, and organization, but these patterns will need change and renegotiation within the community so as to meet the challenges of an increasingly competitive and globalized world.

Since neither Native traditional governments nor imposed colonial forms will strengthen Native government institutions to allow for effective Native government action, then will wholesale adoption of Canadian or U.S. government models help? Most likely Native communities will reject U.S. and Canadian government philosophies and forms. Native culture is too far removed from Western emphasis on self-interest and individualism and its radical separation of the human world from the plant, animal, and natural world. The great gap in cultural interpretation of the cosmos and the role of humans within the cosmic order inhibits most Native communities from accepting Western political rules and organization. Even when imposed through colonial regimes, Natives often try to reinterpret colonial tribal governments to fit their own worldviews and generally only comply to the imposed political order. Native people do not have strong commitments to Western political institutions that require Western values and understandings of human nature. Wholesale adoption of U.S. or Canadian political forms is incompatible with fundamental cultural understandings among Native North Americans.

A major dilemma confronts Native nations. If the colonial tribal governments, traditional Native governments, and U.S. or Canadian government models will not work to develop Native national self-government, then what alternatives are available? How can Native tribal governments preserve culture and community and at the same time effectively manage relations with local and central governments? Can tribal governments effectively protect the cultural and political interests of Native communities? Is it possible to construct tribal government institutions based on and informed by Native culture, philosophies, and political processes? Native political arrangements are decentralized, egalitarian, and negotiated, while colonial tribal governments and Western political forms are hierarchical, centralize power and decision making, and are geared for greater political competitiveness. Will Native tribal governments need to centralize political authority and institutional relations in order to more effectively manage relations with non-Indian governments and bureaucracies? Will Native political and cultural patterns allow more centralized authority? Will tribal communities need to find new ways to balance the need for decisive action versus the tradition of decentralized and consensual decision making? How will Native governments manage market relations, personal property rights, and possible economic inequality of wealth associated with market entrepreneurship?

Native communities are working toward greater assertion and autonomy of their cultural and political rights. This means they will need different forms of government than they had in past centuries and during the recent colonial period. The new market, competition with local and central governments, new technologies, and globalized cultural elements are new challenges to Native communities that wish to preserve their cultural and communities and maintain a degree of autonomy and political decision-making power over their futures and lives. Many communities are now confronting these issues in ways that are generally coherent with their own histories, cultures, and institutional relations. This movement toward more effective and culturally informed Native governments most likely will be incremental. Many tribes will not immediately change their current forms of government, but will begin discussions about reforming and revising their constitutions and government forms. This process has already started for many Native nations and will most likely proceed through the rest of the twenty-first century. Since there are many different Native cultures and histories, there will be many different solutions to meet the needs of Native governments in the future. This diversity in Native government forms and organization will continue to reflect the cultural and institutional diversity of the Native peoples themselves. The path will be hard for many communities, but the future promises much experimentation and hopefully some interesting and culturally innovative ways for Native communities to realize self-determination and preserve their cultural and philosophical identities.

## Markets and Native Communities

Native cultures and communities have managed exchange and trade for thousands of years. With colonialism came capitalist markets. Native cultures, however, did not emphasize individual accumulation of wealth, and Natives did not meet European expectations in the marketplace. Natives did not respond to incentives of greater income or more favorable exchange of goods with greater production. They often brought fewer trade goods, skins, and furs when offered more goods for exchange. Native ethics of not overexploiting the environment, even when incrementally incorporated into trade markets, were retained among many communities well into the twentieth century. Many Natives believed they must respect the environment and especially the plants and animals they depended on for food and sustenance. Yet Natives do not refrain from killing animals or harvesting plants, since they depend on them to live. One must take food and energy from the plants, animals, and forces of the cosmos. Exploitation of the environment is necessary for human life, but according to Native philosophies one must not overexploit the environment in destructive or disrespectful ways. If plants and animals are disrespected, then imbalances will occur and humans will suffer negative consequences. The plants, animals, and other forces of the cosmos will not negotiate relations with humans and will not provide food and other living necessities.

Native philosophies of the human role in the cosmos have not been compatible with the capitalist or market organization of production. Well into the twentieth century, few Native people were market entrepreneurs, while most retained their cultural views about production and distribution. Natives often accumulate wealth but are usually obligated to give wealth away in potlatches or other ceremonies. Giving to others is highly valued among most Native communities, while anyone who accumulates wealth and does not redistribute it is considered miserly and often despised.

Native economic values persist in most Native communities. In many parts of North America, Natives continue to struggle to protect their rights to hunting, fishing, and gathering wild plants. In Wisconsin and Michigan there were court cases over whether Ojibway Indians retained treaty rights that ensured them access to traditional hunting, fishing, and gathering territories that were now in state or federal hands. Natives wanted to retain fishing, hunting, and wild rice harvesting in the places where they had traditionally engaged in these economic activities. The Ojibway were not interested in commercial sale or production of their treaty subsistence rights but in supplementing their food supply in the way they had done for thousands of years. Similarly in Alaska, the Alaska Native Claims Settlement Act of 1971 (ANSCA) has not resolved the issues of subsistence hunting and fishing among the Alaska Natives. After the Alaska Natives agreed to retain only 44 million acres of Alaska, they found out that they were restricted from hunting, fishing, and gathering in many places where accustomed. Natives demanded the right to fish, hunt, and gather without the State of Alaska's interference. For the past thirty years, this controversy has raged in Alaska without a solution. Similarly in the more isolated and northern parts of Canada, many Natives continue to rely on hunting, fishing, and gathering for part of their livelihood. At least 80,000 trappers, mostly Natives, in Canada supply food for themselves and furs for the market. Many Native communities continue to respect traditional nonmarket ways of gathering subsistence and the associated values of respect for the harvested beings.

Many Native communities, especially isolated ones, will continue to rely on subsistence economic production and limited trade. Most Native communities will continue to supplement their food supply through hunting, gathering, and fishing. The effects of political and economic marginalization of most Native communities have left few viable subsistence or market economies. Especially in the lower forty-eight states, few reservation communities have the natural or economic resources to sustain their community's needs.

Many Native communities are confronted with choices between long-term dependency on limited federal funds or attempting to work in the U.S. economy, which most tribal communities have found to be a difficult proposition. The reservations are isolated, have few resources, have little access to capital, and have communities that are reluctant to engage in capitalist accumulation or support individual entrepreneurship. At the end of the twentieth century, many Natives were taking up small business. The number of Native-owned businesses increased 93 percent from 1987 to 1992, from 52,980 to 102,271. The rate of increase in business ownership for the same period for all U.S. firms was 26 percent. From 1987 to 1992 receipts from Native owned businesses increased 115 percent, while the rate of increase for all U.S.-owned businesses was 67 percent. Native business ownership and business activity rose at significantly higher rates than all other business during early 1990s. There is a very strong trend toward Native entrepreneurship, but most of these Native owned and operated business are not on reservations but in urban areas and serve non–Native people and markets. The experience gained by Native entrepreneurs and business will benefit Native reservation and reserve communities.

Native reservation and reserve communities are generally not interested in fostering broad individual entrepreneurship. Most reservation governments have shied away from creating economic development corporations with independent boards of directors and Native community members as shareholders. This corporate plan was offered with the Indian Reorganization Act (IRA) in 1934 and only one tribe accepted the corporate organization for its business plan. The twelve Native regional corporations of the ANCSA are created under U.S. law and are modeled after U.S. corporations, but this design was given by the U.S. Congress and was the invention of the Alaska Natives. Since 1971, many Alaska Native corporations have gained experience managing for-profit corporations, and the arrangement separates business and tribal government and social services delivery. Nevertheless, few tribal governments have voluntarily separated business enterprises from community–Native government organization or are willing to foster an entrepreneurial group in their communities. While many Native people manage market-oriented businesses in non–Indian business environments, most Native communities will not accept individualistic and autonomous capitalist business enterprise within their communities. Such market forms of economic production do not fit well with most Native community institutions and cultural orientations.

Nevertheless, many Native leaders realized that self-determination will always be limited and restricted if Native communities do not have access and control over economic enterprises and capital. Native communities need to work within the global market system that emerged in the late twentieth century, since it has all indications of intensifying and penetrating to most communities on earth. Realizing cultural integrity and at least limited self-determination requires the capability not only to use subsistence resources but, for most Native North American communities, the capability to generate wealth, capital, and economic well-being within the global market system. Native people usually are willing to participate in economic enterprises, but on their own terms and in ways that do not compromise their values, culture, and community institutions. Most Native communities have rejected individual entrepreneurship, because they do not like individual accumulation of wealth and the resulting economic inequalities. In most Native communities, the tribal government manages the economic enterprises. Tribal employees work for the community and profits go to the tribal government. Business, government, community, and culture are not separated, as they generally are in U.S. and Canadian societies. Even the recent and often lucrative investment in gaming casinos is accomplished through tribal government organization and management. Most gaming profits are redistributed through the tribal governments to individual by means of payments, or are redistributed through support of government, social, and education programs. Employees can be motivated to work for the collective community, but are less inclined to work for a Native individual entrepreneur who will keep the value of production as private property. The Mississippi Choctaw have managed tribal community manufacturing and tribal member employment with great success. Other Native communities may adopt similar economic, governmental, and cultural models that work with their own history and institutions.

Natives are confronted with the task of gaining profitable access to competitive markets to generate sustainable economies, but most tribal communities will not sacrifice their culture, community organization, or values for the accumulation of market-based wealth. Natives need to participate in the market system, but need also to maintain their communities, cultures, and values. When confronted with choices between wealth and serious disruption of Native community, most reservation communities have opted for preserving Native culture and institutions. As with constructing viable and culturally appropriates governments, Natives are confronted with developing ways of accommodating to contemporary global markets while retaining their preferred values. To the extent possible, each Native community, having its own unique history and culture, will meet the challenges of the marketplace on its own terms.

## Native Communities and Global Culture

Contemporary Native communities are subject to many cultural influences from the non-Indian world. Television, the English language, movies, education, and the Internet have influenced Native people. Many Native elders fear that the new media technologies have gained influence among young Native people. Inuit elders complain that their children know more about the Los Angeles Lakers than about their own cultural teachings. Hopi and Navajo elders fear that their languages are disappearing among their children and blame television. Native communities are part of a globalized and technologically interconnected world. Even physically isolated Native communities do not escape the spreading influence of contemporary media. Most likely the spread of global media will continue into the twenty-first century. Native communities will be more exposed to ideas, values, and imagery from the non-Indian world. Resisting the influences of a globalized world may leave Native peoples culturally marginalized, although this may be an option that some Native communities will adopt.

Many Native communities have for the past several centuries incorporated ideas and innovations from American and Canadian societies. No single group can control new media technologies. New ideas and worldviews may create differences within the community. Multicultural views will most likely become part of Native communities, and not all Native members will share traditional philosophies and worldviews. Many communities who define themselves as Native will have to reconcile the multiple views and values that have arisen in Native communities over the past century and will continue to arise and inform some members, sometimes the majority of members, in Native communities. Most Native communities tolerate tribal members with different perspectives, whether scientific, Christian, or foreign. With different values and worldviews represented in Native communities, how can they build Native governments, nationalities, identities, and economies that reflect Native perspectives and understandings? Reconciling the multiplicity of values and worldviews and maintaining coherent cultural and social relations will be a major challenge for many Native communities.

Since new technologies and media are not easily excluded from Native communities, most communities will have to use them in ways that facilitate Native goals of cultural and community preservation and nation-building. Many Native people, mostly those living in cities, have made creative use of new technologies to express their views to Indian and non-Indian publics. Natives are exploring music and art that is informed by Native views and perspectives, but use abstract art techniques and contemporary forms of music such as rock and roll and rap. Native drum groups who play at powwows are cutting CDs and writing original songs, as well as preserving traditional music. Native writers were highly prolific during the last decade of the twentieth century, and there is every indication that more Native writers will tell stories from a Native point of view. Natives writers are educated in English departments and participate in contemporary intellectual trends in English literature. Native writers have become part of the American and Canadian writing scene, and many have gained wide recognition for their work. Many Native artists work in contemporary abstract and modern techniques, while their art still carries Native themes and viewpoints. Contemporary Native artists express the Native condition in more techniques and perspectives than were allowed in traditional art forms. Native theater and cinema is active in Canada, supported by generous Canadian government funding. Natives write plays and television and movie scripts. Native producers, actors, and directors are seeking to produce films that provide more Native voice and explore Native perspectives. Native dancers perform to primarily non-Indian audiences and create new dances and movements never seen in traditional dance sequences. Dancing as performance on stage and theatrical telling of Native stories does not mean that older forms of Native dance and public performances will fade away, but both forms may well live side by side, and enrich cultural and educational life of the Native community.

Globalized media and culture may open greater possibilities for Native people and communities to realize their artistic expression, and build and enhance Native culture on a new technological base. While Native community theater is not a traditional art form, Native theater is a means to tell stories, and for the retelling of traditional stories and creation of new stories that explore the community and individual dilemmas of the contemporary and future Native world. New technologies and arts can be used to enhance and strengthen Native cultural life and community organization.

The struggle for cultural homogeneity and holism continues among Native communities. The forces of global cultural change based on non-Indian values and worldviews may potentially divide and inhibit Native community, political, and cultural survival. Natives must face the potentially corrosive effects of non-Indian values and culture that might challenge their fundamental beliefs and institutions. On the other hand, access to the cultures of the world provides new possibilities for cultural expression and change. Some Native communities may accept cultural innovations and incorporate them into their own worldview and use cultural innovations and change to enhance and extend their own cultural forms and institutions. How Native communities meet global media and multicultural expression will determine the patterns of Native nation-building in the twenty-first century.

## Holistic Native Health

Throughout the twentieth century, Native communities experienced relatively poorer health than other North Americans. When compared to general U.S. and Canadian populations, Native people have shorter average life spans; higher rates of diabetes; higher rates of depression, alcohol, drug, and tobacco abuse; higher suicide rates; and higher accident rates. To a considerable degree the poor health conditions found on Native reserves and reservations is caused by poor socioeconomic conditions, the oppressive character of colonial administration, and the loss of culture, land, and autonomy.

Native communities remain very poor. Most have lost access to traditional ways of gathering food and receive food from government agencies. The food programs, however, are heavy in carbohydrates (sugars) and fats. Natives have become dependent on American foods. Food distribution programs ensure that Natives are not eating as healthily as before European contact, when they were free to exploit their environment for fresh foods.

Food was highly valued in Native communities. Many tribes had special ceremonies of thanksgiving and honoring of salmon, deer, buffalo, and corn. Many eastern nations grew corn for hundreds of years before the Europeans came, and the Natives celebrated the ripening of the harvest with the Green Corn Ceremony. Corn is also a central power spirit among the Pueblos and Navajo. On the plains, many nations, like the Blackfeet and Mandan, had ceremonies honoring the buffalo. Plants, water, and animals were part of the cosmic order, and people needed their powers for sustenance. In many creation stories, Native people have a covenant with the plants and animals, who give themselves up voluntarily so that the people can live. In return, the people honored, respected, and performed thanksgiving ceremonies, which in many Native cultures preserved the spirit of the consumed plant or animal. Native people took from the environment, but the acts of respect and thanksgiving preserved the spirits of the plants and animals, who continued to sacrifice themselves for the benefit of the humans. The humans were sustained and the spirits of the plants and animals were preserved, and reborn, and balance and harmony was established. In this worldview, the animals, plants, and humans were sustained in ritual and spiritual relations. Natives honored animals and plants, partly because they provided food and medicine, and sustained human life.

Most Native communities lost much of their territory and hence their ability to live on the land. After the buffalo were destroyed, the plains Indians were reduced to dependency on food from the U.S. government. Being relegated to small reservations prevented many northern Native nations from hunting and fishing in their usual and accustomed places. Natives were forced to turn to government dependency and wage labor, and sometimes farming, to sustain themselves. In other situations, as among the various pueblo communities in the U.S. southwest, the tradition of growing corn fell victim to new food markets and the cash economy. The pueblos grew most of their own food, depending on corn, beans, and squash as their staple vegetables, supplemented by game, wild nuts, and berries. When railroads were built near pueblo communities, food from around the country and later the world became available. Many pueblos were drawn into the wage labor market and began purchasing many of their foods at stores and grew their own traditional crops less and less.

With the loss of traditional territories and food supplies and the introduction of cheap and abundant food from non-Indian suppliers, Native food and diet has become less healthy. Since most Natives are poor and depend on government food programs or local food markets, their diets have deteriorated. In the early reservation days, government officials gave new foods to the Natives that they did not recognize. On most reservations, lard and flour were the primary foods given to Natives. The Natives made the flour into a batter and fried it in the lard. The "fry bread" became a common food on most reservations. Beans, lettuce, and tomatoes were added to the fry bread to make what is commonly known today as Indian tacos, which for many communities has become a "traditional" food. The deep-frying of the bread, however, makes the tacos very high in fat. A fatty, starchy diet combined with a lack of exercise results in obesity and diabetes. Poverty and poor diet are also associated with depression, substance abuse, suicides, and other health and social issues.

Native communities are beginning to understand the causes of poor health and psychological well-being. Many Native communities are starting to emphasize a return to Native values and philosophies for individuals who are depressed, have problems with substance abuse, are not well physically, or have contemplated or attempted suicide. Many Native people are only partially assimilated into Western worldviews, and combined with other issues such as poverty, little education, and discrimination, many Natives are not culturally or psychologically prepared to live their lives in the norm of either Western or Native societies. Hence many Natives have no strong commitments to a coherent worldview or associated values that will help them over the obstacles of poverty, discrimination, and the hard parts of life.

Increasingly, many Native leaders and elders are advocating reconsideration of Native religion and philosophies for those who have not found strong guiding values within U.S. or Canadian societies. Presenting distressed Native people with the history, culture, and values of their traditions has had positive effects for many. It has given new understandings of life and ways to live, where non-Indian ways have not been always helpful to many Native people. Native service providers increasingly believe that Native people benefit more from their help when the services are provided in a Native cultural context. Native organizations and service providers believe that Natives prefer to work in their own communities. Some of this view is already inherent in the self-determination policy and the Indian Health Services plan to subcontract local health clinics to tribal governments.

Reclaiming and further developing the moral and ethical implications of Native philosophies will help provide a foundation of Native nation-building and help restore physical, spiritual, and psychological health to many Native individuals and communities. For Natives good health requires good relations within the community, within the nation, and with the power beings of the cosmos. Individual health is not only a biological issue but a social and spiritual issue. For the past several centuries of colonialism, from a Native perspective, the cosmos has been out of balance for Native communities, and it is very difficult for individuals and communities to stay healthy when social, political, and cosmic relations are not in harmony and balance. The creation of healthy individuals, spiritually and physically, will depend on restoring social and cosmic relations back to harmony by respectful and sincere ceremonies and intentions. Where possible, this may mean a return to growing and gathering Native foods. Greater use and production of Native foods will create less dependence on market and government food sources. Native individual health and well-being will not be fully restored until Native nations are capable of restoring balanced relations with the rest of the earth and cosmic order. Native community and individual health requires the restoration of capable and culturally aware Native nations that can look after Native interests in a globalized world and carry out Native philosophies and values in their actions. Native nation-building, Native community and individual health, relations with the environment, and relations with U.S. and Canadian governments are all related to one another. Native communities and individuals will not be healthy until Native nations uphold Native worldviews in their policies and actions and work to restore balance and order with non-Indian governments, competitive markets, multiculturalism, environmental concerns, and other powers and forces in the cosmos.

## Toward a World Indigenous Paradigm

Indigenous peoples are stateless communities that have come under the colonial domination of more powerful colonial or modern governments. Native people claim territory, religion, and self-government from time immemorial and are not parties to the formation of modern states or colonial governments. Most Native communities want to preserve their land, religion, culture, and powers of self-rule. In the United States and Canada, Native peoples have asserted their claims and right through treaties, courts, and, often, protest. The debate between indigenous communities and central governments is ongoing and often changing. Native peoples have obtained limited recognition of their rights in North America because they have been active in asserting those rights over the past several centuries. In North America, the tradition of British colonialism and law has recognized treaties and agreements with Native nations as binding, and has developed legal arguments and justifications for the rights of Native peoples. Nowhere else in the world are the legal arguments and justifications of government-to-government relations between Native nations and the Canadian and U.S. governments so complicatedly developed as they are in English-speaking North America.

The view of Natives that their communities and cultures have persisted from time immemorial and precede formation of the U.S. and Canadian governments creates a justification, from a Native perspective, that Native nations should have the right to continue their own rule within their own institutional and community arrangements, and with their own governments. The indigenous view is very different from racial and ethnic interpretations of social relations in North America. Most ethnic groups have an immigration experience from a homeland. Most Native communities have creation stories that place them in North America for thousands of years, if not since the beginning of time. Ethnic and racial studies are about adapting to U.S. or American society. Much of the race and ethnicity literature is about adjustment to and incorporation and assimilation into U.S. or Canadian society. The experiences, values, worldviews, and goals of incorporation and inclusion into U.S. or Canadian society are very different from Native communities, who try to retain coherent worldviews, territory, and rights to self-government within their own institutions. Ethnic and racial groups do not necessarily have common worldviews, or territory, or rights to self-government from time immemorial. The Native experience in North America is very different from the ethnic and racial experience, and often Native perspective carried values and goals that clash with the assimilationist and participatory goals of racial and ethnic perspectives and groups. Many Native people have left their reserves or reservations and have attended college or moved cities to find work, and in many ways this migration is analogous to the experiences of other ethnic and racial groups. Many Native people, or people of Native descent, have taken on Western lifestyles and values, and for them, the analysis of ethnic or racial studies might be more appropriate than the nationalist views of most indigenous communities. However, for the Native people who retain ties to tribal communities, the arguments of land, preservation of culture, and self-government define their historical experiences and future values and goals.

The view that Native nations have rights to self-government from time immemorial is applicable to most indigenous peoples of the world. Most indigenous peoples around the world have their own creation stories, religion, community organization, and form of government. These communities were self-sustaining for hundreds and thousands of years before colonial and governments imposed their rule and culture, and absorbed Native lands. Bedouins in Israel, Australian Aborigines, Laplanders in Sweden, New Zealand Maoris, and many of the Native peoples of Central and South America have analogous relations to colonial communities and settler governments. While the cultures of all these Native peoples are diverse, they appeal to the United Nations for recognition of their rights. Even in the United States and Canada, the Native communities represent many cultural and religious traditions. Common or shared culture, or even the construction of a unified ethnic cultural perspective, does not bind indigenous peoples together. Most Native peoples want to preserve their own cultures and rights from other Native communities. Native nations want to preserve their land, rights, and cultural institutions and want others to respect their views. Native communities will exchange ideas and trade views with other indigenous nations, but they want to retain their own distinct national, cultural, and institutional ways, since they are often given in the creation stories and are defining characteristics of the community. Native communities accept change and new ideas, but they want to accept change from within their own views and selectively adopt and modify innovations so that they can be incorporated into their own culture, worldview, and community institutions. In this way, the Native nations can change, but at the same time they preserve their own cultures, while reinterpreting and redefining innovations to fit within their cultural and institutional relations. Native peoples do not want other Native peoples to impose their views or force change on them any more than they want central or colonial governments to impose change upon them.

At the beginning of the twenty-first century there are increasing trends toward the development of world indigenous studies. Most likely there will be a movement among scholars who will feel compelled to make comparative policy, culture, social change, government, health, economic, and other studies about Native peoples in many parts of the world. The study of the history, cultures, governments, and government policies may well form a coherent set of comparisons, analysis, and theories that will form a scholarly discipline. There are emerging university study programs that focus on international indigenous studies, and even scholarly journals that complement and extend the work of Native studies journals that continue to focus on the indigenous peoples of one nation or region within the world. Most Native studies continue to concentrate on one nation, such as the United States or Canada. Tribal communities concentrate on the study of their own local histories and cultures within the tribally controlled community colleges. Native American studies departments in the United States and Canada have taken Native people as a field of study. Most Native studies programs have concentrated on the Native people living in the area as primary groups of study, because it is easier to maintain relations with people who live nearby. The Cornell Indian studies program has many Mohawk students and is located near the Mohawk reservation; therefore it tends to work on Mohawk and Iroquois issues.

Most Native studies programs will concentrate on the indigenous peoples in their nation and local area. Nevertheless, increasing interest and more contacts and relations among Native peoples on the international level has generated more interest for cross-national studies of policy and more interest in the international indigenous rights issues such as the Draft Declaration on the Rights of Indigenous Peoples. The similarity of relations between indigenous peoples around the world and the analogous views of holistic culture, the sacredness of land, and the tradition of self-government from time immemorial invites comparative analysis of policy, culture, legal studies, government, social change, and social movements. Scholars are beginning to emerge, conferences are occurring in many places in the world, and indigenous scholars are traveling to other parts of the world to see how Native peoples there are managing their social, political, and cultural issues. World indigenous studies may emerge as a discipline building on the work and intellectual development already carried on by scholars and indigenous people at the national and local level.

Indigenous studies will develop perspectives, theories, arguments, and course curriculums. Native studies should represent the cultural views and social and political interests of the Native people. To a large extent, the intellectual views and theories represented in most Western universities represent the accumulated cultural issues and social and political interests of Western societies. Science and humanities in Western universities represent the interests and problems that are of most concern for Western societies. There is no fault in this, since knowledge must be something that is useful or practical or informs one about values and goals. The highly compartmentalized departments and disciplines of contemporary scholarship reflect the specialization of knowledge, information, and work in modern large-scale Western societies. Universities serve the interests of the societies they work in and provide analysis, findings, education, and training.

In a similar way, Natives studies should serve the cultural, social, and political interests of Native communities. This means that the values, worldview, and social and political organization of Native communities should inform the organization, values, activities, and goals that inform indigenous studies. Indigenous studies should reflect the views of Native people and should be free to pursue the study of Native philosophies and support Native nation-building and efforts to preserve language, religion, and community organization. Native worldviews contrast sharply with those in the Western world, but scholars of indigenous peoples and Native peoples should be free to articulate, express, and teach Native views.

Native views and community organization differ greatly from university and Western traditions. In contrast to Christian views, Natives see spirits in all forces of the universe, not just humans. Consequently humans are not the center of the universe but part of interconnected relations with the forces and powers of the cosmos. Native worldviews are not quaint artifacts of Stone Age life carried forward by Native peoples to present times. Native philosophies have informed Native life for hundreds and thousands of years, and they will continue to inform Native communities as they struggle with the challenges of the twenty-first century. Native worldviews are a valid interpretation of the forces and direction of the cosmos and provide a set of community and individual ethics that can guide individuals through life. When brought to university or scholarly context, they challenge Western tradition, but the university is a place to discuss and investigate alternative views and positions. Native studies can articulate the Native worldview and positions in ways that could help Native nations reconstruct their communities to meet the demands of the twenty-first century, and at the same time introduce greater intellectual diversity and understanding into the university context, where students, scholars, and community residents could benefit from the wisdom and struggles of Native peoples.

## Conclusion

Native peoples will survive in the twenty-first century, just as they have the past five centuries of colonial relations. The world changes in ways that no nation or individual controls, and Native nations will be not exceptions to this general rule. The trend toward technological innovation and competitive world market relations will not bypass most Native communities. Such massive change creates issues and processes that no one community can anticipate. The conservative tendencies of Native communities resist change, but fundamental changes in globalized technology, market, political, and cultural relations will produce deep and not necessarily desirable change in Native communities. Most Native communities will try to manage change and provide justifications for change in terms of their own interests and cultural worldview. If they cannot do so, they may resist change, or change will be slower.

As Native peoples have done for the past five centuries, they will seek to preserve land, community, self-government, religion, language, and culture. There is some indication that Native peoples will have greater understanding from the general public and the central government. Small but important opportunities for self-government may allow Native peoples to preserve and restore their communities in ways that represent their cultural views and traditions. So there may be some optimism at the beginning of the twenty-first century that Native nations will have fewer constraints from central governments and better economic and political conditions to construct more effective and more culturally informed nation-building. Ever since the beginning of colonial relations, the Native peoples have had a singular goal of community and cultural survival on their own terms to the extent that it has been politically, economically, and culturally possible. After such a long and hard trail over the past five centuries, Native communities will likely continue with their quest to retain Native identities, land, sovereignty, communities, and cultural traditions. The powerful forces of change in the twenty-first century will certainly weigh heavy on the Native nations and often push them in directions unanticipated and often undesired, but Native peoples will hold steady to their religion, philosophies, and nationalities, which will guide them through the rough waters of history and the unknown future. Some Native communities have a saying that all decisions should be made with the good of the next seven generations at heart. If the Natives stay true to their worldviews and philosophies, they will do well enough in the twenty-first century and beyond.

## Note

An earlier version of this chapter appeared as Duane Champagne, "Native Issues in the Twenty-first Century," in *Indigenous Peoples, Racism, and the United Nations,* ed. Martin Nakata, pp. 61–88. Altona, Australia: Common Ground, 2001. This chapter is printed with permission from W. W. Norton and Company.

## Suggested Reading

Alfred, Gerald. *Heeding the Voices of Our Ancestors: Kahnawake Mohawk Politics and the Rise of Native Nationalism.* New York: Oxford University Press, 1995.

Brown, Lester, ed. *Two Spirit People: American Indian Lesbian Women and Gay Men.* Binghamton, NY: Haworth, 1997.

Cajete, Gregory, ed. *A People's Ecology: Explorations in Sustainable Living.* Santa Fe, NM: Clear Light, 1999.

Champagne, Duane, and Joseph Stauss, eds. *Native American Studies from the Ground Up: History and Prospects.* Walnut Creek, CA: AltaMira, 2001.

Cook-Lynn, Elizabeth. *Why I Can't Read Wallace Stegner and Other Essays: A Tribal Voice.* Madison: University of Wisconsin Press, 1996.

Deloria, Barbara, Kristen Foeher, and Sam Scinta, eds. *Spirit and Reason: The Vine Deloria Jr. Reader.* Golden, CO: Fulcrum, 1999.

Ferrera, Peter. *The Choctaw Revolution: Lessons for Federal Indian Policy.* Washington, D.C.: Americans for Tax Reform Foundation, 1998.

Jacobs, Sue-Ellen, Wesley Thomas, and Sabine Long, eds. *Two Spirit People: Native American Gender Identity, Sexuality, and Spirituality.* Champaign: University of Illinois Press, 1997.

Mihesuah, Devon A. *Natives and Academics: Researching and Writing about American Indians.* Lincoln: University of Nebraska Press, 1998.

Pommersheim, Frank. *Braid of Feathers: American Indian Law and Contemporary Life.* Berkeley: University of California Press, 1995.

Smith, Dean Howard. *Modern Tribal Development: Paths to Self-Sufficiency and Cultural Integrity in Indian Country.* Walnut Creek, CA: AltaMira, 2000.

Smith, Tuiwai. *Decolonizing Methodologies: Research and Indigenous Peoples.* New York: Zed, 1999.

Snake, Reuben. *Reuben Snake: Your Humble Serpent.* Santa Fe, NM: Clear Light, 1996.

# Index

# About the Author

**Duane Champagne** is a member of the Turtle Mountain Band of Chippewa from North Dakota. He is professor of sociology and American Indian Studies, a member of the Faculty Advisory Committee for the UCLA Native Nations Law and Policy Center, and a member of the TLCEE (Tribal Learning Community and Educational Exchange) Working Group. Professor Champagne was director of the UCLA American Indian Studies Center from 1991–2002 and editor of the *American Indian Culture and Research Journal* from 1986–2003. He has authored or edited over one hundred publications including *Native America: Portrait of the Peoples*; *The Native North American Almanac*; and *Social Order and Political Change: Constitutional Governments Among the Cherokee, the Choctaw, the Chickasaw, and the Creek*. Champagne's research focuses primarily on issues of social and cultural change in both historical and contemporary Native American communities. He has written about social change in a variety of Indian communities including: Cherokee, Tlingit, Iroquois, Delaware, Choctaw, Northern Cheyenne, Creek, California Indians, and others.